BLOOD on the WATTLE

BLOOD on the WATTLE

Massacres and maltreatment of ABORIGINAL AUSTRALIANS since 1788

Third Edition

BRUCE ELDER

Published in Australia by
New Holland Publishers (Australia) Pty Ltd
Sydney • Auckland • London • Cape Town

14 Aquatic Drive Frenchs Forest NSW 2086 Australia
218 Lake Road Northcote Auckland New Zealand
81 Edgware Road London W2 2EA United Kingdom
80 McKenzie Street Cape Town 8001 South Africa

First edition 1988
Reprinted 1992, 1994, 1996
Revised edition 1998
Reprinted 1999, 2000, 2002
Third edition 2003

Publishing Manager: Anouska Good
Editor: Monica Ban
Designer: Tricia McCallum
Typesetter: Midlands Typesetters
Printer: Griffin Press, Adelaide

10 9 8 7 6 5 4 3 2 1

National Library of Australia Cataloguing-in-Publication Data:

Elder, Bruce.
Blood on the wattle: massacres and maltreatment of Australian Aborigines since 1788.

3rd ed.
Bibliography.
Includes index.
ISBN 1 74110 008 9.

1. Massacres - Australia - History. 2. Aborigines, Australian - Treatment. 3. Aborigines, Australian - Wars. 4. Aborigines, Australian - Government relations. I. Title.

994.0049915

The National Library of Australia, Canberra, supplied all photographs except for the following: National Library of Australia/Rex Nan Kivell Collection: p 1, p 6, p 11, p 32, p 39, p 55, p 62, p 72, p 81, p 93, p 253; Mitchell Library, NSW State Library, Sydney: p 4, p 5, p 66, p 86, p 103, p 136, p 153, p 173, p 186, p 188, p 226; John Oxley Library, Brisbane: p 138, p 142; National Trust of Australia Northern Territory), Alice Springs: p 181.

Contents

PREFACE

All they seem'd to want was for us to be gone.

Captain James Cook, 29 April 1770

There is a body of opinion within the Aboriginal community which believes that books such as this should be written by Aboriginal historians. The problem with such an argument is that the events described here are, to my shame, as much a part of my history, as a white Australian, as they are a part of the history of any black Australian. To argue that the massacres of Aboriginal people are exclusively chapters in Aboriginal history is to ignore the fact that Europeans perpetrated these atrocities. It is like the Jews claiming Buchenwald as their own.

The inspiration for this book was *Bury My Heart at Wounded Knee*, Dee Brown's account of the decimation of the American Indians. The emotional power of that book came from Brown's ability to tell the story of the various massacres from the point of view of the Indians. It is a sad comment on Australian historians, and particularly upon the way Europeans regarded Aboriginal people in the nineteenth century, that there are few contemporary Aboriginal accounts of the massacres available. It seems that our European forefathers didn't consider the Aboriginal version of events worth reporting.

It has been popular mythology in liberal white Australia to be vaguely aware of these massacres and to complain that no book has been written chronicling the scale of the atrocities. This book is an attempt to dispel that criticism. However, it would be unfair and unjust to my sources not to claim that most of this information has been available, at least for the last decade, to those who cared enough to make the effort.

This book has no thesis. It tries, probably unsuccessfully, to grind no polemical axes and to cast no judgements. It seeks to achieve only two things: (a) to draw together, in a single volume, most of the information about the massacres of Aboriginal people which has been recorded in books and journals and (b) to create a broad-based level of awareness of the scale of the massacres of Aboriginal people so that this dimension of Australian history can become part of the Australian consciousness. The massacres of Aboriginal people, painful and shameful as they are, should be as much a part of Australian history as the First Fleet, the explorers, the gold rushes and the bushrangers.

Ignorance can no longer be a defence against the criticism that the white history of Australia is little more than over two hundred years of shame.

Bruce Elder

Introduction

Consider the following scenario. Tomorrow, totally unexpectedly, a spaceship arrives from another galaxy. It is filled with males of human shape but of a previously unimaginable, and decidedly unpleasant, skin colour.

These strange beings have developed technology which is all but incomprehensible to us. Communication is achieved by extrasensory perception. People can travel at the speed of light. Law and order is based on a value system which we find bizarre, irrational and basically evil. Food production is achieved by reprocessing soil and rocks in huge factories. They can neutralise nuclear weapons and their own weaponry is so powerful that, as they inform us, if we don't obey their every instruction, they will use their selective ray gun which can destroy humans and leave all other species intact.

At first they don't interfere in human affairs. They have brought their own labour force and, within weeks, they are building factories and installing scoopers and earthmoving equipment.

Their consumption of land is voracious. In weeks they have entirely demolished and consumed the Great Barrier Reef. Uluru is blasted and removed. The botanical gardens in Sydney are wiped. A series of huge, eroding holes, filled with polluted water, are left.

Before long they are forcibly moving people out of areas. Residents of Vaucluse and Toorak are moved to hastily constructed inner city, high-rise blocks where the lifts don't work and electricity and water are available only one day a week. The beach-side suburbs in all the capital cities are evacuated because the invaders want sand.

People, no matter how skilled or wealthy or talented, have become redundant. Who needs a journalist or a talk show host or a radio disc jockey when extrasensory perception is universal? Who needs motor mechanics or pilots or used car salesmen when transport is instantaneous?

Suddenly everyone is redundant. Guerrilla movements form. They start by stealing food supplies. Soon they are shooting factory guards and lobbing Molotov cocktails, which bounce ineffectually off the walls of the factories.

The aliens make little attempt to locate the culprits; it is easier to blame all citizens. One Saturday night everyone in the centre of Melbourne is exterminated by a peculiar ray gun. The aliens make it clear that this massacre is in retribution for stealing some of their food. They don't care who actually did the stealing.

Entrepreneurs and high-flying executives apply for jobs but their masters put them to work on sewage disposal and demolish their self-esteem by describing their attempts as 'inept', 'lazy' and 'useless'. Psychologically destroyed, the men start drinking heavily. The overlords start raping the women. Strange half-castes are born. They belong in neither society.

This image can be elaborated almost indefinitely. It may be laboured but it makes a point. Put yourself into that scenario and you'll have little trouble railing against the inequities of a system driven by greed and indifferent to the culture which it has plundered and destroyed.

Think of Sydney in 1787. There were about 3000 people living in the Sydney basin. They woke up each morning to views unsullied by concrete, asphalt, brick and steel, and enjoyed a lifestyle made easy by an abundance of natural delicacies.

Aboriginal Australians had what we all now want. We, the European invaders, took it all away. We destroyed it. We took the land as if it was our own. We destroyed the native fruit-bearing trees to create pastures for cattle and sheep. We killed off native wildlife if it tried to compete with sheep and cattle for the pastures. We replaced ecology with aggressive nineteenth-century exploitative capitalism. We built roads over sacred sites. We denied the land its spirituality. We killed off Aboriginal people with guns and poison and disease. We refused, through ignorance and arrogance, to see any tribal differentiation in those Aboriginal people who survived our insidious, long-term holocaust. Those Aboriginal people who did survive were herded into reserves or 'allowed' to live in humpies on the fringes of towns.

We took away their reason to exist and when, in their despair, they took to the bottle or simply threw up their hands in hopelessness and gave up on life, we had the arrogance to accuse them of drunkenness and laziness.

The blood of tens of thousands of Aboriginal Australians killed since 1788, and the sense of despair and hopelessness which informs so much modern-day Aboriginal society, is a moral responsibility all white Australians share. Our wealth and lifestyle, the much touted 'Aussie way of life', have all been achieved as a direct consequence of Aboriginal dispossession. We should bow our heads in shame.

Introduction to Third Edition

Will anyone ever accurately understand the true scale of the massacres and maltreatment of Australian Aborigines? When I wrote the first edition of this book I scoured the libraries for books and journals recording any and every massacre. Some, like the Myall Creek massacre and the Coniston station massacre, were well reported. They had found their way into the courtrooms of white Australia and consequently the records were detailed and accurate. But, over the past twelve years, the stories have just kept coming. There are literally dozens of massacres recorded in Geoffrey Blomfield's *Baal Belbora: The End of the Dancing* and, as I continue to read local histories from around the country, I keep finding reports of killings ranging from minor skirmishes involving one or two people through to massacres of unknown but substantial numbers. Consequently this book, if it is to remain accurate and reasonably comprehensive, needs to grow and grow.

This third edition contains all the original material as well as the material that was added in the second edition. The main new elements here are a chapter devoted to the massacres in the New England area of New South Wales and around the Three Rivers — the Hastings, the Macleay and the Manning — on the mid-north coast of the state. This information, which should have been included in this book many years ago, comes from Geoffrey Blomfield's excellent *Baal Belbora*. I have added information about the Mowla Bluff massacre in Western Australia to the long chapter entitled Massacres, Massacres, Massacres. This information has come from some excellent work done by my colleague at the *Sydney Morning Herald*, Tony Stephens, and Michelle Torres, who has made a documentary called *Uncovering the Mowla Bluff Massacre*.

The final addition is a response to a particularly unattractive moment in recent Australian historic research when a number of people, spearheaded by Keith Windschuttle and P.P. McGuinness and encouraged by the federal government's inflexible line on reconciliation, decided to attack the accuracy of many of the massacres. Three articles by Windschuttle appeared in the McGuinness-edited *Quadrant* — a respected journal of right wing opinion. Although this book has always been about massacres and maltreatment it seemed important that people reading this book should realise that there is an argument about the accuracy of many of the massacres. I have reported Windschuttle's arguments and tried to show exactly why they are wrong.

Information about the massacres and maltreatment of Australian Aborigines keeps being discovered and written about. My duty is to record the major findings so that people can pick up *Blood on the Wattle* and read an accurate, and hopefully comprehensive, overview of what has happened to Australian Aborigines since the arrival of the first fleet in 1788.

Bruce Elder

Kiama, NSW March 2003

CHAPTER 1

TWO HUNDRED YEARS AGO

They were nothing better than dogs, and . . . it was no more harm to shoot them than it would be to shoot a dog when he barked at you.

Reverend William Yate, 1835

'They thought they was the devil when they landed first, they did not know what to make of them. When they saw them going up the masts they thought they was opossums,' observed Mahroot, one of the last survivors of the Botany Bay tribe. He was recalling the stories which had been told around the camp fire. Born in about 1795, he was able, in 1845, to recall vividly the impression Governor Arthur Phillip and his 'First Fleeters' had made as they sailed into Botany Bay in mid-January 1788.

Joseph Lycett's 'Distant view of Sydney from the lighthouse at South Head' shows the paradise Sydney Harbour must have been prior to the arrival of the First Fleet.

Mahroot's tribe had numbered about four hundred in 1788. By 1845 they had been reduced to four. His people, who had lived in a semi-paradise, had been decimated by disease, alcohol and random killings. In such a short time white 'civilisation' had destroyed a lifestyle which was so simple, so uncomplicated and so bountiful.

Life had been good before the arrival of the whites. Botany Bay, the wide, deep-water estuaries of the Hawkesbury and Georges rivers, and the filigree of beaches and points which was Port Jackson, all had abundant supplies of fish, mussels and crustaceans. A hunter, with little effort, could kill twenty or thirty possums in a week. This was enough to offer an excess of food and to make a large, warm, possum-skin rug.

The trees, the bushes, the grasses and the fauna all provided more than adequately for the people of the Sydney basin. Life was easy. There was a time to hunt, gather and fish, and there was a time for relaxation — for lying in the shade, for talking around the camp fire, for sleeping in the hot, sub-tropical summer afternoons.

There was a balance and a rightness to the world. The cycle of the seasons brought times when fish teemed in the harbours and the bays, brought months when the trees were weighed down with succulent bush fruits and nuts, and brought a knowledge of the environment which appreciated the role of renewal and regrowth.

People understand an environment when childhood and work are integrated into it. Aboriginal people knew, loved and respected their land. It was their total raison d'être. It was their source of spirituality and strength.

The British who arrived in Botany Bay and Port Jackson had no such sentimental or emotional attachment to the land. They were, for the most part, city folk. They were the detritus of the Industrial Revolution. The scraps, the junk, the waste from a new age. They had been born and raised in 'the great city pent'. The 'dark satanic mills' had belched and glowed above the mean, rubbish-filled streets in which they lived.

These were people driven by profit and loss. For them the land was nothing more than a commodity to be bought, exploited and sold. Land was the basis of wealth. Wealth was measured in terms of property. And property was sacrosanct.

The fatal moment when Phillip stepped ashore was the moment when the conflict began. There was no spear thrown; no musket fired. But the course of events was set upon its inexorable path. The two cultures were so different. The value systems were so polarised. There was no possibility of compromise.

One side respected the land; one side exploited the land. One side was basically peaceful and benign; the other was essentially sadistic and autocratic. One sought harmony; the other was driven by aggression and competitiveness.

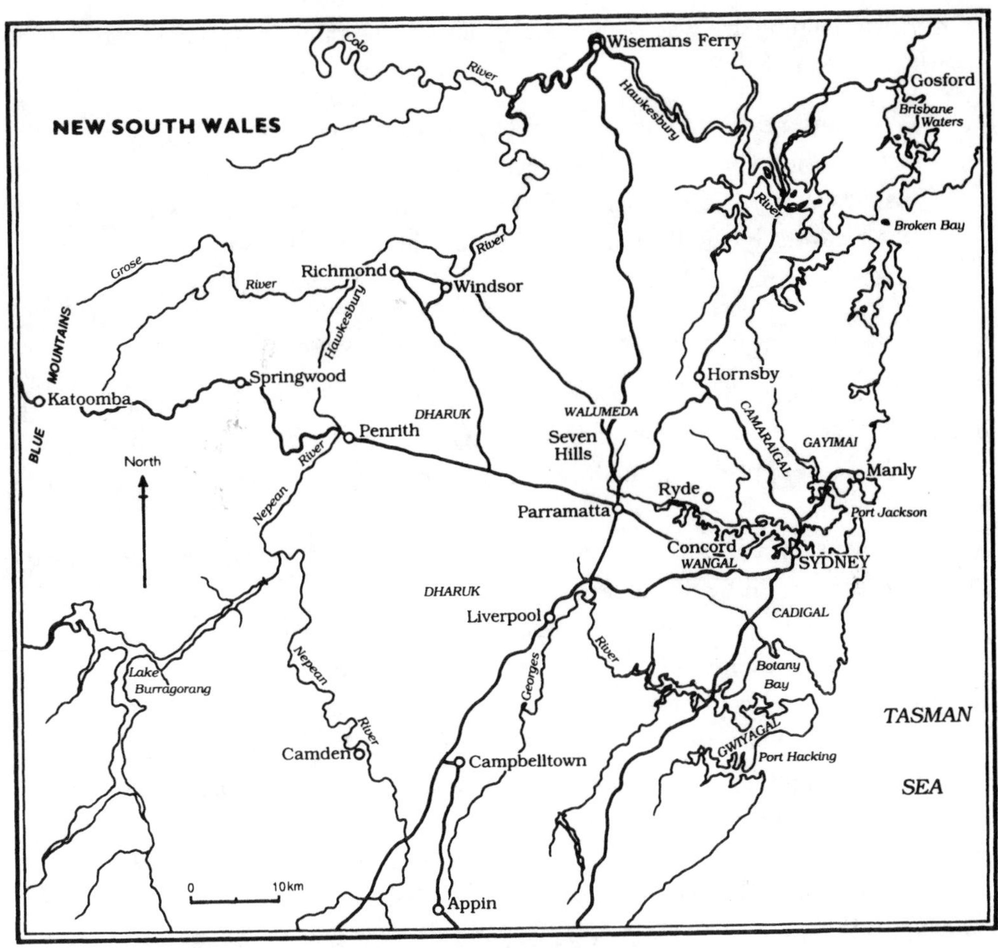

The Sydney basin, New South Wales.

The result was inevitable. As the ships of the First Fleet straggled into Botany Bay on 18, 19 and 20 January 1788, the Aboriginal people of the Sydney basin looked on with awe and amazement. Who were these strange creatures? Were they devils? Or ghosts? Or possums? What did they want? Why had they come?

Sitting in their cabins, sweating from the hot, close Sydney summer nights, and contending irritably with mosquitoes and moths, the officers of the First Fleet recorded their first impressions of the local Aboriginal people. 'We saw eight of them sitting on the rocks as we came into the Bay,' wrote Lieutenant William Bradley. He dipped his quill in the inkwell and added, 'They called to us, some of them walked along the shore and others kept sitting on the rocks.'

Little did he realise that the Aboriginal people, who almost certainly regarded the crew of the HMS *Sirius* as either demons or possums or both, were trying to ascertain what these strange creatures were.

Certainly when Lieutenant Philip Gidley King sat down to write his account of the first landing he was in no doubt of the basically antagonistic attitude of Aboriginal Australians:

> We went a little way up the bay to look for water, but finding none we returned abreast of the *Supply*, where we observed a group of natives. We put the boats on shore near where we observed two of their canoes lying. They immediately got up and called to us in a menacing tone, and at the same time brandishing their spears or lances.

In spite of assiduous efforts on the part of Phillip and the more humanitarian of his officers, it was quite clear that, if the Aboriginal people of the Sydney basin had a choice, they would prefer all the invaders to turn around and set sail for where they had come from.

The process of corruption, antagonism, brutality and viciousness had already started. There was to be no turning back.

At first curiosity prevailed. King describes an encounter on 20 January which is comic in its mutual curiosity. King offered a group of Aboriginal people some wine. They spat it out with distaste. They inquired whether the trousered and beardless King was male or female. King made one of his sailors pull down his trousers. Presumably curious to witness sexual intercourse between black and white, and to determine what kind of being these strange new creatures were, the Aboriginal men offered King one of the Aboriginal women. King declined and offered one of the women a handkerchief. The woman, to King's wide-eyed amazement, did 'apply the handkerchief where Eve did ye figleaf'.

Aboriginal people appeared to act with no consistency of purpose towards the whites. They were both curious and antagonistic, friendly and aggressive. On 21 January a group of men from the supply ship HMS *Sirius* went ashore. The task that faced them was simple. They had found fresh water and access to it was required. This involved the

The changing European attitude to Aboriginal people was obvious in the earliest paintings and drawings. This early French etching is a perfect depiction of Rousseau's notion of the 'noble savage' — tall, elegant and handsome.

clearing of land. It was the first act of agriculture and the first of 'land ownership' performed by whites in the Sydney basin. Lieutenant William Bradley recorded that, 'The Natives were well pleased with our people until they began clearing the ground at which they were displeased and wanted them to be gone.'

The whites were commandeering food and property which was not theirs and in return they were offering nothing. Aboriginal people soon learnt that the whites did not understand the morals of barter. They replied by asserting their right to recompense: they stole items they wanted. Eventually they killed whites to re-establish the unequal balance produced by dispossession.

Mahroot, when asked by the members of an unofficial inquiry, 'Did the black fellows all agree together to kill the white fellows, or did they do it without agreeing, every man killing as he liked?', offered a rare insight into one of the motives for black killings. He said, 'They did not agree exactly, some wild fellow maybe wanted that jacket off him, or the blanket, that is what it was done for.'

Relationships between the local Aboriginal communities and the whites deteriorated rapidly. The arrival of more than a thousand whites in a prison without walls inevitably strained relations between whites and blacks to breaking point.

The convicts were, for the most part, hardened recidivists. They had spent most of their lives in crowded, unsanitary houses, in gaols or brigs, and to them lashings

Thirty years later, Aboriginal people were regarded as a 'rural pest' and artists were depicting them as short, ugly and heavy-featured.

and hangings were part of the brutish, British world. They were simple, uneducated people for whom Aboriginal people held little interest.

As early as May 1788 a convict working beyond the narrow bounds of Sydney Cove killed an Aboriginal person. They replied by killing two convicts, William Okey and Samuel Davis, who were cutting rushes at the cove now known as Rushcutters Bay. Phillip, determined not to aggravate the situation, decided that no reprisal should occur and actually demanded a more cautious attitude from all people working beyond the settlement.

Aboriginal people adopted a different approach. They took every opportunity to harass the invaders. Although they knew their weapons were inferior, they adopted a guerrilla approach. In July a party of convicts were chased across the sand dunes between Sydney Cove and Botany Bay by a large number of Aboriginal people. Later that month a convict was speared in the head and another was caught and ordered to strip.

By winter it was clear that a food shortage problem existed for those groups who had lived around the Tank Stream and fished in Sydney Cove. The large white population were depleting the fish in the harbour by netting huge catches, they were reducing the kangaroo population and they were polluting the water. Near-starvation forced desperate measures. On 9 July a party of Aboriginal people attacked the crew of the *Sirius* and escaped with a recently caught haul of fresh fish.

This 1834 lithograph by Charles Rodius is titled 'Scene in a Sydney street'. Its depiction of brawling, drunken Aboriginal men reflects the influence white society was having on the local community.

Convicts who got lost in the bush began reporting that some small groups of Aboriginal people seemed to be dying of hunger. The near-paradise had been so delicately balanced. In six months the British had destroyed a lifestyle which had outlasted British history by tens of thousands of years. And the British dared to claim that they were civilised?

If starvation killed large numbers of the Aboriginal community in the winter of 1788, then disease struck a more deadly and far-reaching blow in the early months of 1789.

Aboriginal people, isolated for thousands of years from the diseases which had raged through Europe and Asia, had no resistance. They had no immune system; no defence. And the diseases carried by the sailors and convicts — smallpox, syphilis and influenza — were deadly.

In less than a year over half the Aboriginal population living in the Sydney basin had died from smallpox. No-one knew exactly how it started and the British, in their guilt, were eager to blame everyone except themselves. They blamed La Pérouse; they blamed Malays landing on the northern coasts. They protested that there were no cases of smallpox on the First Fleet, that the epidemic had broken out a year after the arrival of the First Fleet and that such a long gestation period meant that the disease couldn't possibly have been introduced by the British.

Whatever the reason, the results of the smallpox epidemic were devastating. Aboriginal people, with instinctive good sense, abandoned members of their family groups who contracted the disease, and fled into the bush in an attempt to escape the pestilence. Wherever the whites explored they came across Aboriginal people covered with pustules and slowly wasting away. 'I have seen myself,' wrote Captain John Hunter, 'a woman sitting on the ground, with her knees drawn up to her shoulders, and her face resting on the sand between her feet.'

Over and over again explorers in the Sydney basin came across small groups of corpses putrefying and decaying, unburied and forgotten, in the hot sun. There were times when explorers would come upon caves with human bones in them. The whole region, which had once been alive with Aboriginal communities, now fell silent. There were no canoes on the harbour, no hunting parties along the shoreline. No fishermen. No smoke from camp fires rising lazily through the smudgy blue above the dense eucalypts. David Collins later recalled:

> The number that it swept off, by their own accounts, was incredible. At that time a native was living with us; and on our taking him down to the harbour to look for his former companions, those who witnessed his expression and agony can never forget either. He looked anxiously around him in the different coves we visited; not a vestige on the sand was to be found of human foot; the excavations

> in the rocks were filled with the putrid bones of those who had fallen victims to the disorder; not a living person was anywhere to be met with.
>
> It seemed as if, flying the contagion, they had left the dead to bury the dead. He lifted up his hands and eyes in silent agony for some time; at last he exclaimed, 'All dead! All dead!' and then hung his head in mournful silence.

There was no need for massacres; no need for reprisals. Disease had done its deadly work. The resilience and will of the Aboriginal people had been broken without a single shot.

It did not take long for Aboriginal people to recognise that the invaders were committed to nothing less than total occupation of the land. They responded in the only way they could: they picked off convicts and soldiers who happened to wander too far from white settlement. They set fire to buildings and any combustible material; and they stole food, clothing and tools at every opportunity. It was hardly an organised attack on the invaders but it did harass and unsettle the new colony.

At first Phillip was determined to tolerate this harassment. If a convict was killed by an Aboriginal person, Phillip always blamed the convict. He also brought the British concept of 'innocent until proven guilty' to bear when he argued that reprisals were pointless because, 'it is not possible to punish them without punishing the innocent with the guilty, and our own people have been the aggressors'.

Such attitudes show that Phillip was determined to maintain a sense of fairness and reasonableness. They also highlight the frontier barbarism which emerged once the 'glory boy' landholders began grabbing vast tracts of land beyond the Blue Mountains.

In the first two years of the colony Phillip's military determination managed to keep potential conflict between whites and Aboriginal people in check. Then, in late 1790, Phillip's gamekeeper, John MacEntire, was speared while out on a hunting expedition. It was widely understood that MacEntire had been out shooting Aboriginal people and that the spearing was an act of reprisal. On his deathbed MacEntire protested his innocence. Few people accepted the protestation. Most people predicted that the attack on MacEntire would be ignored.

Who knows what strange set of circumstances changed Phillip's mind? What considerations shifted the pacifier into the prosecutor? What led to the abandonment of the 'innocent until proven guilty' principle?

Phillip set the pattern for frontier reprisal. There was no half-measure. The concept of law was to be abandoned. He created a punitive expedition of over fifty men. It was led by Captain Watkin Tench of the Marines and Captain Hill of the

New South Wales Corps. Below them were two subalterns, three sergeants, two corporals, a drummer, two surgeons and forty privates.

Phillip briefed Tench and Hill in unambiguous terms. He had reason to believe, on the advice of Bennelong, that the warrior responsible for the spearing of MacEntire was a tall, athletic man with a caste in one eye named Pemulwuy. He saw Pemulwuy in British terms. He was a leader; a commander. He was held responsible for seventeen recent deaths. He had to be caught before this spark of rebellion grew into a fire of resistance. If he could not be located, then it was imperative that he be stopped by a reprisal, a massacre of such magnitude that he'd realise what his rebellion would do to his people. Six men from Pemulwuy's tribe had to be captured. If they could not be captured, then they must be killed, decapitated and their heads brought back to Sydney. The one-time pacifier was establishing a murderous precedent which would be repeated over and over again along every frontier in Australia. He wanted to make 'a severe example of that tribe'. Massacre was the method.

The plan may have been aggressively authoritarian, but the execution was farcical. Two expeditions scoured the countryside around Botany Bay. Not a single Aboriginal person was captured. Tench wrote of the excursions in a dry, laconic manner. He reported tales of the troops being 'denied repose by swarms of mosquitoes and sandflies'; of Aboriginal people running away and of 'a contest between heavy armed Europeans . . . and naked unencumbered' Aboriginal people being 'too unequal to last long'; of the expedition losing their way; and of them nearly drowning in mud:

> We were immersed, nearly to the waist in mud, so thick and tenacious, that it was not without the most vigorous exertion of every muscle of the body, that the legs could be disengaged. When we had reached the middle, our distress became not only more pressing, but serious, and each succeeding step, buried us deeper. At length a serjeant of grenadiers stuck fast, and declared himself incapable of moving either forward or backward; and just after, ensign Prentice, and I, felt ourselves in a similar predicament, close together. 'I find it impossible to move; I am sinking;' resounding on every side. What to do I knew not . . . Our distress would have terminated fatally, had not a soldier cried out to those on shore to cut boughs of trees, and throw them to us; a lucky thought, which certainly saved many of us from perishing miserably; and even with this assistance, had we been burdened by our knapsacks, we could not have emerged; for it employed us near half an hour to disentangle some of our number. The serjeant of grenadiers in particular, was sunk to his breast-bone, and so firmly fixed in, that the efforts of many men were required to extricate him, which was

> effected in the moment after I had ordered one of the ropes, destined to bind the captive Indians, to be fastened under his arms . . .

Although the expedition was a failure, Phillip was not dissuaded from his broader purpose. By 1791 the policy of the governor was that Aboriginal people attacking whites had to be made an example of.

Around this time, Phillip created another unfortunate precedent when his protégé, Bennelong, became the first true Aboriginal fringe dweller. He existed from 1795 until his death in 1813 as a sad, pathetic figure, comfortable neither with his own people nor with the white settlers.

In December 1792 Phillip had taken two young Aboriginal men — Bennelong and a teenager named Yemmerrawanie — to Britain with him. Yemmerrawanie died there. Bennelong acquired the veneer of British civilisation. When Bennelong returned to Australia in 1795 he became lost in a sad half-world. He developed an eighteenth-century fastidiousness for dress, cleanliness and table manners. He chastised his relatives for their lack of 'graciousness' and 'decorum'. He found that his wife Gooroobarrooboollo had left him for a young lover named Caruely. He challenged Caruely to a fist fight, beat him, claimed Gooroobarrooboollo, but she refused him and returned to her family group. He tried to re-enter tribal society but was shunned. Women rejected him. He became frustrated at his lack of sexual success. This led him to become increasingly depressed and aggressive. He frequently became involved in brawls over women and started to drink heavily. His decline into despair became emblematic. Bennelong became a sad symbol of what white society was to do to so many Aboriginal people.

In 1799 the reality of British justice was tested in the colony's courts when five settlers from the Hawkesbury River district — Simon Freebody, William Butler, Ed Powell, James Metcalfe and William Timms — were brought to trial for the murder of two Aboriginal boys.

The trial was remarkably simple. In court Sarah Hodgkinson explained that about three weeks before the murders her husband had been killed by some Aboriginal people. She told the court how her grief had turned to revenge and how she had asked the men to kill the boys. It was irrational frontier revenge. There was no evidence that the boys had been involved in the Hodgkinson killing. The prosecution then brought Lieutenant Hobby of the New South Wales Corps to the dock. He told of how he had found the bodies of the two boys. Both boys had their hands tied. One had been nearly decapitated; the other had been killed by a series of sword stabs. The court had no alternative. The five defendants were found guilty. But instead of sentencing them, they were all set free and the case and the sentence were referred to His Majesty's Ministers in England.

Governor Hunter was not amused by the breach of protocol. He wrote to England

Bennelong became a sad symbol of what white society was to do to Aboriginal people. On his return from England, he became involved in brawls over women and began to drink heavily.

protesting, 'Those men found guilty of murder are now at large and living upon these farms, as much at their ease as ever . . .' Three years later the men were pardoned. It was hardly an example of British justice working at its best. It was certainly not the sort of case that inspired Aboriginal people to put their trust in the fairness of the invader's legal system.

The final act of destruction of the Aboriginal tribes in the Sydney basin came with a series of skirmishes which started in 1797 and finished by 1805. The focus of these skirmishes was the remarkable Pemulwuy. He is a rare example in nineteenth-century Aboriginal–white relations of a leader who managed to organise a quasi-military Aboriginal force. In a society where the normal size of a group was about thirty, he managed to form fighting forces in excess of one hundred. He does not appear to have been a tribal elder; his success seems to have been based on his extreme hatred of the white invaders. He gained his authority from this hatred, and gained his charisma and power from his determination to rid the country of all whites.

Pemulwuy was known around Sydney Town; his reputation had been established by Phillip's abortive attempts to catch him. He was considered an elusive rebel.

Prior to 1797 Pemulwuy's attacks on white settlements were intermittent. In that year things changed. A guerrilla force of over one hundred Aboriginal people started raiding farms in the Parramatta district. They used the classic lightning raid technique.

The settlers called upon the military to defend them. A party was sent out. They scoured the area around the Parramatta township and found nothing. It was not until the exhausted and bedraggled troops had given up the search that Pemulwuy appeared. He challenged the troopers and hurled his spear at one of the soldiers. The soldiers fired upon Pemulwuy and his followers, killing five and seriously wounding the leader. Pemulwuy, with seven pieces of buckshot in his head, was taken to hospital in chains. That night, still with an iron around his leg, he escaped.

Two years later a group led by Pemulwuy speared a settler on the Georges River. Then in 1801 he led a series of successful raids which resulted in Governor King posting a reward for his capture. In 1802 he was killed by two settlers, decapitated, and his head sent to Sir Joseph Banks in England.

In his own way Pemulwuy's resistance and his murder were the beginning of a series of frontier conflicts which echoed out across the Sydney basin like ripples in a pool. As the settlers began to convert the bush into pastureland, they met with resistance from the local Aboriginal communities. This resistance was inevitably met with firearms.

Although the governors continued to assert that the wanton destruction of Aboriginal communities would be prosecuted with the full force of the law, farmers turned a blind eye to such instructions. By the early 1790s settlers in the Hawkesbury River area were taking the law into their own hands. Reports of vicious maltreatment were common. In October 1794 some settlers, seeking to frighten Aboriginal people by example, caught a boy, bound him hand and foot, dragged his naked body a number of times across the red hot embers of a fire, before throwing the half-dead youth in a river and then shooting him.

An Aboriginal man tending his garden on the Hawkesbury River. By the early 1790s, reports of vicious maltreatment of Aboriginal people in the area were common.

In 1795 troops were sent from Parramatta 'with instructions to destroy as many as they could meet with the wood tribe'. It was the first legally sanctioned massacre. They were also ordered to curb Aboriginal attacks. The method suggested was 'in the hope of striking terror, to erect gibbets in different places, whereon the bodies of all they might kill were to be hung'.

It was never recorded how many of the 'wood tribe' the troops killed. The Aboriginal people of the Sydney basin were becoming intelligent in their resistance. The troops were unable to construct a single gibbet. They returned to Parramatta with about ten prisoners — five women, some children and one crippled man.

By the early 1800s the Aboriginal guerrillas were in retreat but they were fighting for every hectare of their land. The battle might have been unequal but Aboriginal people were unwilling to give up land which was vital to their existence.

When Governor King asked some Aboriginal people why there was virtual warfare between blacks and whites the answer he received was simple and unambiguous:

> They very ingenuously answered that they did not like to be driven from the few places they were left on the banks of the river, where alone they could procure food; that they had gone down the river as the white men took possession of the banks; if they went across the white men's grounds the settlers fired upon them and were angry; that if they could retain some places on the lower river they should be satisfied and would not trouble the white men. The observation and request appear to be so just and equitable that I assured them no more settlements should be made lower down the river. With that assurance they appeared well satisfied and promised to be quiet.

Of course, King could make no such promise. Skirmishes between whites and blacks continued along the river for years. Aboriginal people would attack a hut and kill a few whites. The settlers would retaliate by calling in the troops and killing a number of blacks.

Sometimes the reprisals became virtual battles. In May 1805, for example, the settlers living around Richmond Hill decided to organise major raids against the local Aboriginal communities. They claimed that a number of whites had been murdered and there had been serious raids on the flocks at Seven Hills and Concord. A local Aboriginal man, Yaragowhy, warned the tribes of the farmers' plans and this resulted in a number of groups joining together to repel the white enemy. The whites won with the aid of the guns. Some dozens of Aboriginal people were killed. The battle would have been more 'even' if the whites had not been warned of an ambush the Aboriginal people had planned.

By 1810 the Aboriginal resistance had been destroyed. The final process of destruction was based on ethnocentric 'good works'. The Church, which for a long time had ignored Aboriginal people, attempted to Christianise the remnants. This ill-conceived experiment had a peculiarly Victorian prudishness about it. Most of the experiments were based on such superficial things as regular washings, wearing clothes, being able to recite the Scriptures and, most importantly, acknowledging the superiority of the British way of life. It is a mark of the power and strength of Aboriginal belief systems that few converts were made and, in many instances, after years of instruction, the hapless 'civilised and Christianised' black was only too eager to return to a life of naked, 'uncivilised' freedom.

Such an experiment was conducted by the Reverend Samuel Marsden. He adopted two young Aboriginal children but, in spite of the religious environment, his efforts were singularly unsuccessful. In 1801 Marsden was visited by two British missionaries who reported:

> Today Samuel Christian, a Native Boy, came to see us, he lives with Revd. Mr. Marsden, who took him by the consent of his parents, when he was very young, he has been brought up in Mr. Marsden's family, has learned to speak English fluently, sometimes he runs to the Bush, for the purpose of seeing his parents, as he says, but he cannot converse with them, being ignorant of his Mother tongue, he can read well and now begins to write. Mr. Marsden's example here is worthy of imitation, this Boy is a proof of what may be done in respect to the Natives, the Generality of them would give their children to be educated by the English . . .

Four years later Marsden's view of the experiment was less optimistic. He complained that Samuel Christian (who sounds like a character out of *Pilgrim's Progress*) still preferred native food and, horror of horrors, 'he wanted that attachment to me and my family that we had just reason to look for; and always seemed deficient in those feelings of affection which are the very bonds of social life'. Samuel Christian was taken to England in 1810 but by this time he had put up with too much. He fled from Marsden at Rio de Janeiro and eventually returned to Sydney with Captain Piper.

After the failure of religion, the do-gooders turned to education. In 1814 Governor Lachlan Macquarie gave his approval to the establishment of a school. It was, even by the standards of the time, an idea of remarkable craziness.

Macquarie dreamed of a strange Anglo-utopia where Aboriginal people would find employment either 'as Labourers in Agricultural Employ or among the lower class of Mechanics'. With the aid of William Shelley, one of those shadowy Victorian educational entrepreneurs so frequently satirised by Charles Dickens, Macquarie established an Aboriginal school in Parramatta. It was to be 'an Experiment towards the Civilization of these Natives' and its aim was to inculcate 'Habits of Industry

One of the most famous images of Aboriginal life around Sydney in the early 1830s, this painting by Augustus Earle perfectly captures the profound effect of dispossession.

and Decency'. On a broader level it hoped to create a Europeanised class of Aboriginal workers. In all these aims it was totally unsuccessful.

On 10 December 1814, Macquarie organised a huge party at Parramatta for all the Aboriginal communities in the Sydney basin. The fatted calf was killed and spitted. Ten gallons of rum were consumed. Macquarie called upon Aboriginal people to sign up for a 'British education'. The school started in early 1815 with six boys and six girls. It lasted until 1823. It failed because it was never anything more than a rather strange appendage to Aboriginal life. As soon as the students reached puberty, even if their results had been brilliant (and one girl after three years of schooling actually beat all her white competitors in the public Anniversary School Examination), they returned to their tribe to marry. Years later Mrs Shelley dolefully recorded: 'Most of the girls have turned out very bad . . . I have frequently conversed with them since, on religious subjects, but they turned them into laughter, and said they had forgotten all about it.'

Macquarie's vision of an Aboriginal peasantry had even less success. An area beside Botany Bay was set aside, huts were built and a convict was installed to instruct a hand-picked group on the niceties of British agriculture. Aboriginal people once again showed the strength of their own culture; they rejected British agriculture.

They destroyed the houses, sold the bark, and within months the project was abandoned.

When these strategies failed, Macquarie turned to violence. He was not a violent man by nature but the ethos of the frontier was becoming the legal rationalisation and rationale of New South Wales' Aboriginal policy.

In March-April 1816 Macquarie decided to settle the question of ownership of the river in the Sydney basin once and for all. A military expedition was sent to the Grose, Nepean and Hawkesbury river areas. Their instructions were to capture every Aboriginal person they came in contact with and to shoot all resisters and hang their bodies in the trees. The aim, as Macquarie recorded it, was to 'eventually strike Terror amongst the Surviving Tribes'.

No-one knows how many massacres occurred. Aboriginal people, realising the intention of the whites, retreated into the hills. At Appin the soldiers came upon a large group. The troops did not care for the rule of law. They opened fire indiscriminately, killing at least fourteen men, women and children. Five Aboriginal people were captured. A number fled from the advance of the soldiers and preferred to jump off nearby cliffs rather than face the bullets and brutality. Macquarie seemed nonplussed by the massacre. The deaths of women and children were dismissed as an 'unavoidable result'.

The massacre was followed by a proclamation which declared that no Aboriginal person could carry 'Offensive Weapons' within 'a mile' of white settlement. Aboriginal people could not gather in groups of six or more near white settlement, peaceful Aboriginal persons should be issued with passports, and all Aboriginal brawling in Sydney was prohibited. It was a nineteenth-century version of apartheid. The lines had been drawn. The violence of the frontier had been legitimised.

So it was that the Aboriginal people of the Sydney basin, people who had lived peacefully in the area for forty thousand years, were all but wiped out.

The killing had been simple. First there had been the smallpox which had wiped out over half the population. Then there had been syphilis and alcohol, which had so lowered self-esteem that fighting and brawling had become normal. The removal of Aboriginal people from their traditional pursuits had created a sad dependency on white food and clothing. Then, for one brief moment, Pemulwuy seemed to hold the line. After his death Aboriginal people had continued to fight but their task was hopeless. The musket and the gun killed all those who tried to resist.

The pattern had been set. The process was inexorable. The decimation of the Sydney Aboriginal communities was followed by killings in the Bathurst region, on the north coast, in the New England Ranges, along the Darling, in Queensland and in Victoria. It was a ripple in a pool. Spreading wider and wider, further and further, until the will of the Europeans was imposed upon the whole of the land. So much that was beautiful and noble was destroyed. So much that was mean and greedy and ugly replaced it.

Mahroot, the last man of the Botany Bay tribe, summed up the situation when he poignantly observed:

> Well Mister . . . all black-fellow gone! all this my country! pretty place Botany! Little pickaninny, I run about here. Plenty black-fellow then; corrobory; great fight; all canoe about. Only me left now, Mister. Poor gin of mine tumble down and die. All gone! Bury her like a lady, Mister; all put in coffin, English fashion. I feel lump in throat when I talk about her; but — I buried her all very genteel, Mister . . .

CHAPTER 2

The Massacres to the South of Sydney

Seeking vengeance they murdered Bitugally's wife and two children while they slept — the woman's arm was cut off and her head scalped, the skull of one child was smashed with the butt of a musket, and their bodies were left unburied for the families to find

Carol Liston, A Bicentennial History of Campbelltown, *1988*

It is easy to romanticise the lifestyle of coastal Aboriginal people before the arrival of Europeans. Consider the simple routine of those groups who lived on the narrow coastal plains which stretch south of Sydney. They spent most of their time by the sea where they lived on a diet of crustaceans — the waters are rich with abalone, prawns, lobsters, mussels — and fish. If the tides were right, and the hunters were lucky, they probably had enough to feed the entire group after a couple of hours effort. When they needed to supplement their ocean diet the rainforest behind the coast had substantial colonies of opossums and small marsupials, and the coastal plain and escarpment were home to numerous varieties of kangaroo and wallaby. Even today, on the beaches which lie to the south of the Shoalhaven River, it is possible to see herds of kangaroos grazing peacefully along the shoreline at Durras and Pebbly Beach.

It never really gets cold beside the sea. You have to travel inland if you want to experience a winter frost. So most of the families lived in the open. They settled in rock shelters and caves with views across the Pacific Ocean or they built gunyahs near the freshwater creeks which meandered across the coastal plain to the sea. During the summer months the groups wandered the shores and the hinterland completely naked. In the winter, when the cold winds blew from the south they would wrap themselves in opossum rugs and move a little closer to their fires.

Life on the coast was easy and uncomplicated. The men hunted. The women cooked and raised the children. There were strong familial and social ties between the groups. They shared food supplies, gathered regularly for ceremonial occasions, and were happy with the complex ties produced by intermarriage and agreed land ownership. They were not tribal by any conventional meaning of the term. They operated in small, extended family social units which were deeply connected to streams, lakes, and stretches of the coastline, the foothills and the escarpment.

The people of the coast had lived this idyllic existence for thousands of years. The cycle of life was good. At certain times of the year the people from the high country made their way to the coast and the coastal people reciprocated by climbing up the narrow tracks to visit friends as far away as Appin and the grassy plains of the southern tablelands. The connections between the groups were so sophisticated and efficient that when Captain James Cook sailed up the coast news of the ship would have spread quickly. There is no doubt that his progress would have been watched cautiously from the forests which edged the coast. Inevitably Cook and his crew, those strange white men, would have been the subject of much discussion around the fires at night-time. What was that strange white-sailed object moving up the coast? Who were these strange creatures? Where did they come from? What did they want?

Joseph Banks, always the meticulous recorder of events, noted on Friday 20 April 1770 when the *Endeavour* was off the coast south of Batemans Bay that 'the countrey this morn rose in gentle sloping hills which had the appearance of the highest fertility, every hill seemed to be cloth'd in trees of no mean size; at noon a smoak was seen a little way inland and in the Evening several more'.

Around the area south of modern-day Ulladulla, Cook, on Sunday 22 April 1770, recorded in his log 'After this we steer'd along shore N.N.E. having a gentle breeze at S.W. and were so near the shore as to distinguish several people upon the Sea beach. They appeared to be of a very dark or black Colour; but whether this was the real Colour of their skins or the Cloathes they might have on I know not'.

The crew of the *Endeavour* continued to monitor the fires. By Wednesday 25 April, Cook was reporting smoke from several fires around Jervis Bay and the following day, as they reached the Illawarra coastal plain between Shellharbour and Port Kembla, Cook recorded that he 'Saw several smokes along the shore before dark, and 2 or 3 times a fire'.

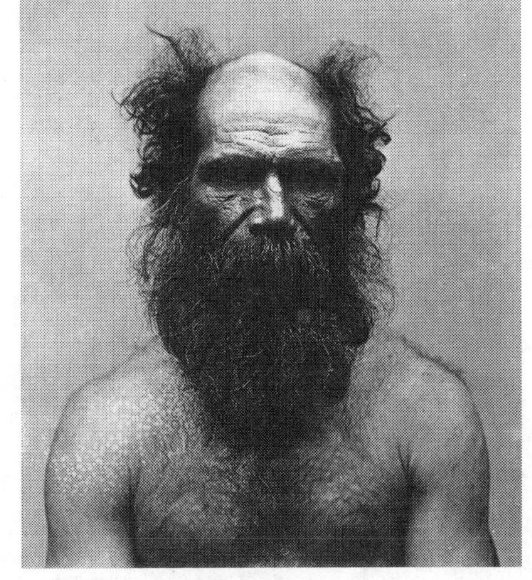

This old man from the Shoalhaven district, photographed in 1851, would certainly have heard the stories of Cook's journey up the coast in 1770 and may have been old enough to remember the arrival of the First Fleet.

A young woman from the Moruya tribe, just north of Murramurang, where, in 1832, another young woman was 'killed with Musket balls' for apparently no reason.

Eventually, emboldened by curiosity and eager to make contact, Cook attempted to land near the modern-day coastal suburb of Woonona. Banks reported:

> At noon we were very near [the shoreline]: one fire only was in sight . . . After dinner the Captn. proposed to hoist out boats and attempt to land, which gave me no small satisfaction . . . Four men were at this time observed walking briskly along the shore, two of which carried on their shoulders a small canoe; they did not however attempt to put her in the water so we soon lost all hopes of their intending to come off to us, a thought with which we once had flattered ourselves.
>
> To see something of them however we resolved and the Yawl, a boat still capable of carrying the Captn, Dr Solander, myself and 4 rowers was accordingly prepared. They sat on the rocks expecting us but when we came within about a quarter of a mile they ran away hastily into the countrey; they appeared to us as well as we could judge at that distance exceedingly black.

So what went wrong? When Captain Arthur Phillip sailed up the coast in 1788 with the First Fleet he brought with him the seeds of destruction of this Eden. Disease, greed, a blind belief in British and European superiority, an obsessive love of property and a legal system driven by the acquisition and protection of land, an inability to recognise that the simplicity of Aboriginal life was far more delicate and subtle than it appeared on the surface. And, perhaps most importantly, the wholesale exporting of the detritus of the world's largest city and the world's most industrialised country (with all the dehumanising effects that such an environment produces) conspired to pit 'modern man' against idyllic innocence. It is a judgement on this 'modern world' that, when confronted with near-paradise, there was no respect and a desire to destroy it.

By 1804 the Aboriginal people of the South Coast had changed from Cook's 'they are far more happier than we Europeans' to 'they were of a hideous Aspect, wore frightful beards, & hitherto were estranged to every race but their own & if the report of their civilized countrymen be true, they still adhere to their primitive cannibal habits' according to a report in the *Sydney Gazette*.

In the space of less than two decades the noble savage had been demonised. It is interesting that the *Sydney Gazette*'s description is of the Aboriginal people around Jervis Bay, presumably members of the same group Cook had seen in April 1770.

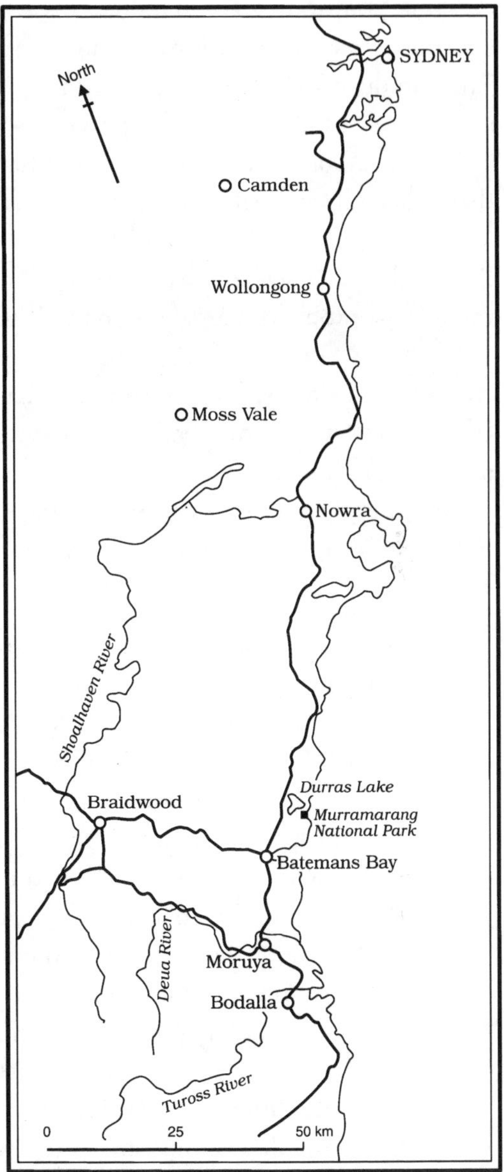

The New South Wales South Coast.

The demonising made the killing easier. After all, these people weren't human. They were 'estranged to every race but their own' and therefore killing them was an entirely reasonable thing to do. Thus, in July 1804, when the sloop *Contest* pulled into Twofold Bay near the present site of Eden, they had no qualms about shooting and killing an Aboriginal person who had carried 'off a knapsack with its whole contents'. The nature of settlement, and the nature of the Aboriginal groups living along the South Coast, was such that there were never any major massacres as there would later be in central and western Queensland. There were constant skirmishes and misunderstandings as the Europeans tried to assert their rights over the land and the Aboriginal people resisted this incursion.

In theory there was food for everyone and it should have been possible for everyone to live in peace. The farmers who settled the South Coast were, with few exceptions, dairy and cattle men who were primarily interested in the rich pasturelands. They produced milk, cheese and meat which they sent to Sydney on the many small vessels which plied the coastal ports.

But the Aboriginal people were not happy with the arrival of the Europeans and they fought against what they perceived as an invasion. If the experience of Tasmania is any guide the likely cause of the initial aggravation were the sailors, particularly the whalers and sealers. These men were hard, amoral and unforgiving. Certainly the earliest problems along the coast all seem to be connected to sailors.

In late 1805 a fight broke out between Aboriginal people at Jervis Bay and the crew of a whale boat. The result was that two of the Aboriginal people were shot and 'several' were wounded. A year late, on 6 April 1806, the *Sydney Gazette* reported the first 'massacre' when it revealed that the crew of the *George*, a sealing vessel, had killed nine Aboriginal people at Twofold Bay.

Referring to the 'inimical disposition of the natives of Two-fold Bay' the *Gazette* wrote:

> The sealers employed there were for many weeks past obliged to act with the greatest caution, two men with muskets being obliged to accompany the water bearers to and fro' for fear of assassination, and centinels being set at night, who were frequently compelled to alarm their companions, from the appearance of the natives near their huts.
>
> About five weeks ago a whole body shewed themselves, with a determined resolution to attack the gang enmasse. They advanced with shouts and menaces until within reach of a spear, several of which were thrown; and then the gang, eleven in number, in self defence commenced a fire, by which nine of their assailants were lain prostrate; whereupon all the rest made off.
>
> To intimidate them it was thought advisable to suspend those that fell, on the limbs of trees; but before daylight the next morning they were taken down, and carried off.

Why did this battle take place? Were the Aboriginal people fighting for the protection of their land or, more plausibly, had the sealers, as they had done in Tasmania, taken womenfolk for their sexual pleasures and to work as slaves? It is implausible that such a full-scale battle was not the result of some major provocation.

By 1814 the limits of the colony of New South Wales were reaching beyond the Sydney basin. A year earlier Blaxland, Wentworth and Lawson had crossed the Blue Mountains and already there was settlement to the south-west of Sydney around Appin (beyond the escarpment behind Wollongong) and the current dormitory suburbs of Camden and Campbelltown.

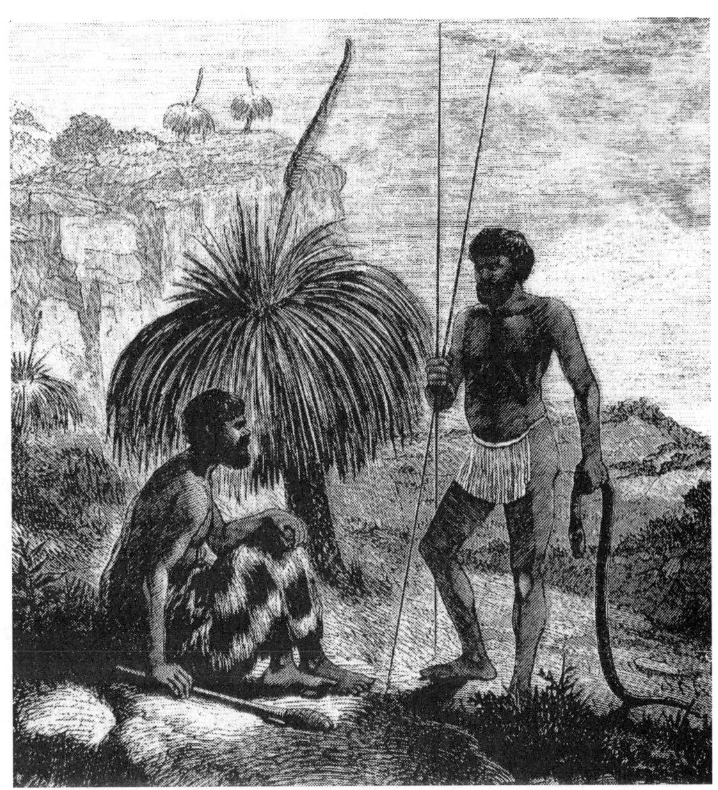

This engraving, depicting Aboriginal men near Camden, was taken from the Compte de Beauvoir's Voyage Around the World, *published in 1878.*

The pattern was clear. Aboriginal people lived off the land and they took from the land what the land offered them. When European farmers started growing vegetables and maize and grazing cattle and sheep, the Aboriginal people saw this as food for everyone. The Europeans retaliated with indiscriminate shooting and rape. They demonised the local 'blacks' as 'pests'.

The problem was always tit-for-tat killings. If one side transgressed, the other side immediately retaliated. And, as always, the spear and nulla nulla were no match for the musket and organised posses of troops. The story of the killing of four Aboriginal people at Appin is typical of the problem. A large group of local Aboriginal people were helping themselves to the corn in a farmer's paddock near Appin when three privates from the Veterans Corps arrived. They fired at the Aboriginal people to try and disperse them. Instead of firing over their heads they fired directly at the group. A young Aboriginal boy was killed. The Aboriginal people, determined to revenge the killing, turned on the troopers and one of them, Isaac Eustace, was speared and killed. That was enough to ensure the beginning of a cycle of bloody revenge. In her history of Campbelltown, Carol Liston wrote that 'Seeking vengeance they murdered Bitugally's wife and two children while they slept — the woman's arm was cut off and her head scalped, the skull of one child was smashed with the butt of a musket, and their bodies were left unburied for the families to find'.

Not surprisingly the Aboriginal people retaliated, by killing a storekeeper, William Baker, and a woman named Mary Sullivan. Shortly afterwards two convicts, John Price and Dennis Newingham, were surprised at an Appin farm by a party of Aboriginal people who speared and killed them.

This exercise in reprisal and counter-reprisal reached such a point that on 18 June 1814 Governor Macquarie issued a General Order in which he laid the blame squarely with the settlers noting:

> The Number of Lives sacrificed, as well by the Settlers as by the natives, in Retaliation for real or supposed injuries, but without due Regard either to previous Agression on the part of the unfortunate Settlers, or to the Dictates of Humanity, have already given rise to a Legal Investigation before the Bench of Magistrates; and although it was not sufficiently clear and satisfactory to warrant the Institution of Criminal Prosecution, it was enough so to convince any unprejudiced Man that the first personal attacks were made on the Part of the Settlers, and of their Servants . . .
>
> It will be highly becoming and praiseworthy in the British Settlers to exercise their Patience and Forebearance, and therein to shew the Superiority they possess over these unenlightened Natives.

The sentiment may sound appallingly pompous but the aim was to remind the settlers that they were not exempt from the rule of law and that murdering Aboriginal people, because they were 'stealing' some maize, was not something the governor and the authorities in Sydney would ignore. Of course, the challenge was how to monitor the behaviour of the settlers who Macquarie described, in a letter to Earl Bathurst in London, as 'idle and ill disposed Europeans'.

Sadly this conciliatory, legalistic tone gave way to undeclared warfare. By 1816 Macquarie, trying to grapple with continued killings in the Appin-Cow Pastures-Bringelly district, sent three detachments of the 46th Regiment to the district with the specific instructions to take the Aboriginal people as 'prisoners of war' or to shoot them. The result was that, with great loss of life, the Aboriginal people in the area were dispersed so that their threat to the inexorable movement of European settlement was removed forever.

The killing was ugly and indiscriminate. In spite of the 'humanitarian' protestations of the officers, there was little real attempt to solve the problem. Thus when Captain Wallis of the 46th Regiment, who was in charge of operations in the Airds and Appin districts, reported the events in his journal his description was a bizarre mixture of killing, sorrow and apologies:

> 17 April 1816: A little after one o'clock a.m. we marched. Noble joined us, and led us where he had seen the natives encamped. The fires were burning but deserted. We feared they had heard us and were fled.
>
> A few of my men who wandered on heard a child cry. I formed line ranks, entered and pushed on through a thick brush towards the precipitous banks a deep rocky creek. The dogs gave the alarm and the natives fled over the cliffs. A smart firing now ensued. It was moonlight. The grey dawn of the moon appearing so dark as to be able early to discover their figures bounding from rock to rock.
>
> Before marching from Quarters I had ordered my men to take as many prisoners as possible, and to be careful in sparing and saving the women and children. My principal efforts were now directed to this purpose. I regret to say some had been shot and others met their fate by rushing in despair over the precipice. I was however partly successful — I led up two women and three children. They were all that remained, to whom death would not be a blessing.
>
> Twas a melancholy but necessary duty I was employed upon. Fourteen dead bodies were counted in different directions. The bodies of Dunell and Kincabygal I had considerable difficulty in getting up the precipice — I regretted the death of an old native Balyin and the unfortunate women and children — from the rocky place they fell in. I found it would be almost impossible to bury these.

The problem was always the contradiction. Here were the governor's troops engaged in legalised massacre. Yet, at the same time, the governor was insisting on the rule of law. How was anyone on the frontier to interpret these contradictory messages? Inevitably the legalised killing by the troops spilled over into private murders.

Thus when Charles Throsby, who was largely responsible for the opening up and development of the South Coast, wrote to Governor Macquarie in 1818 complaining about vigilante action against Aboriginal people at Yallah, south of Wollongong, the governor gave him full support.

In essence Throsby was complaining about the actions of Lieutenant Weston, the owner of a property at Dapto, south-west of Wollongong, and Cornelius O'Brien, the overseer on William Browne's property at Yallah. According to depositions presented to the Sydney Bench of Magistrates on 24 October 1818 O'Brien and Weston, armed with muskets, cutlasses and bayonets attached to long sticks, and accompanied by a posse made up of seven labourers and convict workers including a man variously known as McLease/McAlese/Macaleise, headed south supposedly to recover two muskets which had been lent to a group of Aboriginal people who were living around the Minnamurra River, north of Kiama.

A report submitted from Joseph Wild, a district constable at Illawarra, reveals:

> Bundle a Native came and told me that the Natives (Men and Women) at the river were all killed, he said a Black Woman had told him so. It was about 5 o'clock in the afternoon. Next day I went over to Mr O'Brien's and asked him why they had shot the Natives who were doing no harm.
>
> McAlese said he had shot one who had howled like a Native Dog, and that he would shoot all before him even if the Governor stood by, if they ship'd a spear at him.

The magistrates, presided over by D'Arcy Wentworth, decided that the case had not been proved and that McAlese 'fired his musket in consequence of the apprehensions excited by a Native having shipped his Spear at him'.

Governor Macquarie was furious. He wrote to D'Arcy Wentworth from Government House in Parramatta on 1 November 1818:

> . . . it appears most clearly proved that a Party of White Men headed by Mr O'Brien, armed for the purpose, proceeded, in hostile array, to attack most wantonly and unprovokedly, the poor unoffending Black Natives of Illawarra, and actually fired on them, it being also in proof that one Native Boy was wounded.
>
> After much clear proof of those circumstances, I cannot help expressing, and thus conveying to you, Sir, for their information, my surprise, regret, and displeasure, at the Bench of the Magistrate treating this wanton attack on the Natives with so much levity and indifference.

Macquarie then ordered Wentworth to issue a warrant for Macaleise's arrest and to have him 'lodged in Sydney Jail'.

This was always the problem. Evidence was hard to get, people on the frontier told different versions of the event, the lives of local Aboriginal people were disposable, and no-one ever had the intelligence to try and determine the root causes of the antagonism.

Four years later a convict named Seth Hawker, working as an overseer on Captain Richard Brooks' farm in the Illawarra, surprised an Aboriginal woman who, with the cover of darkness, was helping herself to some corn in his master's fields. He shot at her and set his dogs onto her. The result was the woman was shot in the stomach, mauled savagely by the dogs, and died shortly after. The murder was duly reported to the nearest constable who resided in Appin and on 9 June 1822 Seth Hawker

A posed and self-conscious photograph of an Aboriginal family living on the banks of the Minnamurra River, north of Kiama.

was tried in the Sydney Criminal Court. Although the evidence was overwhelming he was acquitted. While the Judge Advocate 'wished it to be properly and lastingly pressed upon the minds of all, that the aboriginal natives have as much right to expect justice at the hands of the British law' it was clear that such a trial was a farce. The rule of property was sacrosanct. An Aboriginal person who stole corn was breaking one of British law's most sacred codes and therefore someone like Seth Hawker, in the eyes of the court, had every right to defend his master's property, even to the point of killing someone.

These kinds of confrontations were to continue until the Aboriginal people on the South Coast finally gave up all hope of defending the land which they had lived on for thousands of years. The final massacre of major proportions (at least the last one which was brought to court in Sydney) was at Murramarang (now a National Parks and Wildlife protected coastal area between Durras and Batemans Bay) where, just before Christmas 1832, Joseph Berryman, accompanied by a posse of convicts and freemen, killed an undisclosed number of Aboriginal people.

According to an eyewitness report from local contractor Hugh Thompson, Berryman, an overseer on one of the nearby properties, accompanied by about seven ticket-of-leave men, assigned servants and convicts, fired on two Aboriginal men.

The men were hit but managed to flee to a nearby beach where they swam out to sea while Berryman and his posse kept shooting at them. The group then moved to a nearby Aboriginal camp and, as Thompson explained in the deposition, '[I saw] Three Blacks — two men, one being very old, and one woman being old — all lying dead from Musket ball wounds and the bodies not cold' and later the local Aboriginal people brought him 'to the body of a Black woman lying at some distance from the Camp, and appeared to be dead from Musket ball wounds. The Blacks drew off a Blanket which had covered her, and Examinant saw that she had been killed with Musket balls. She was a young woman, and appeared to be large with Child.'

In spite of Thompson's clear distress at the murders, and his willingness to report them (he travelled up the coast to Wollongong to present his deposition to the resident magistrate), the government were incapable of decisive action. Berryman was arrested and removed to Wollongong but, as far as can be determined, he was never brought to trial. The contradiction between the half-hearted law in Sydney and the bloody law on the frontier was becoming absurd. There was a need to take firm action. A need for the authorities to telegraph the official line. However, the murderers, knowing the reality and knowing that they would not be punished, felt at liberty to take the law into their own hands and to kill Aboriginal people in the certain knowledge they would never be convicted.

CHAPTER 3

NEAR GENOCIDE IN VAN DIEMEN'S LAND

For every man they murder, hunt them down and drop ten of them. This is our specific — try it!

A Tasmanian settler, 1827

In 1835, in Hobart Town, a book titled *The History of the Island of Van Diemen's Land from the Year 1824 to 1835, Inclusive* was published. At one point in his description of the new colony the author, Henry Melville, summed up the history and plight of the Tasmanian Aboriginal people in a few succinct sentences:

> These poor bewildered creatures had been treated worse than were any of the American tribes by the Spaniards. Easy, quiet, good-natured and well-disposed toward the white population they could no longer brook the treatment they received from the invaders of their country. Their hunting grounds were taken from them, and they themselves were driven like trespassers from the favourite spots for which their ancestors had bled and had claimed by conquest . . . The stock-keepers may be considered as the destroyers of nearly the whole of the Aborigines — the proper, legitimate owners of the soil: these miscreants so imposed upon their docility, that at length they thought little or nothing of destroying the men for the sake of carrying to their huts the females of the tribes; and if it were possible . . . to record but a little of the murders committed on these poor harmless creatures it would make the reader's blood run cold at the bare recital.

Tasmania is one of the loveliest places on earth. On the west coast the barren, icy headlands and the seemingly endless flat white beaches are awe-inspiring. Its mountain ranges are rugged and forbidding. Its gloomy, dank forests include the remarkably beautiful Huon pine which, in many cases, has been growing on the island for over two thousand years.

At the outset contact between white explorers and the local Aboriginal communities was openly hostile. Abel Tasman saw no Aboriginal people when he landed near Blackman's Bay on 2 December 1642. Marion du Fresne, the second white 'visitor',

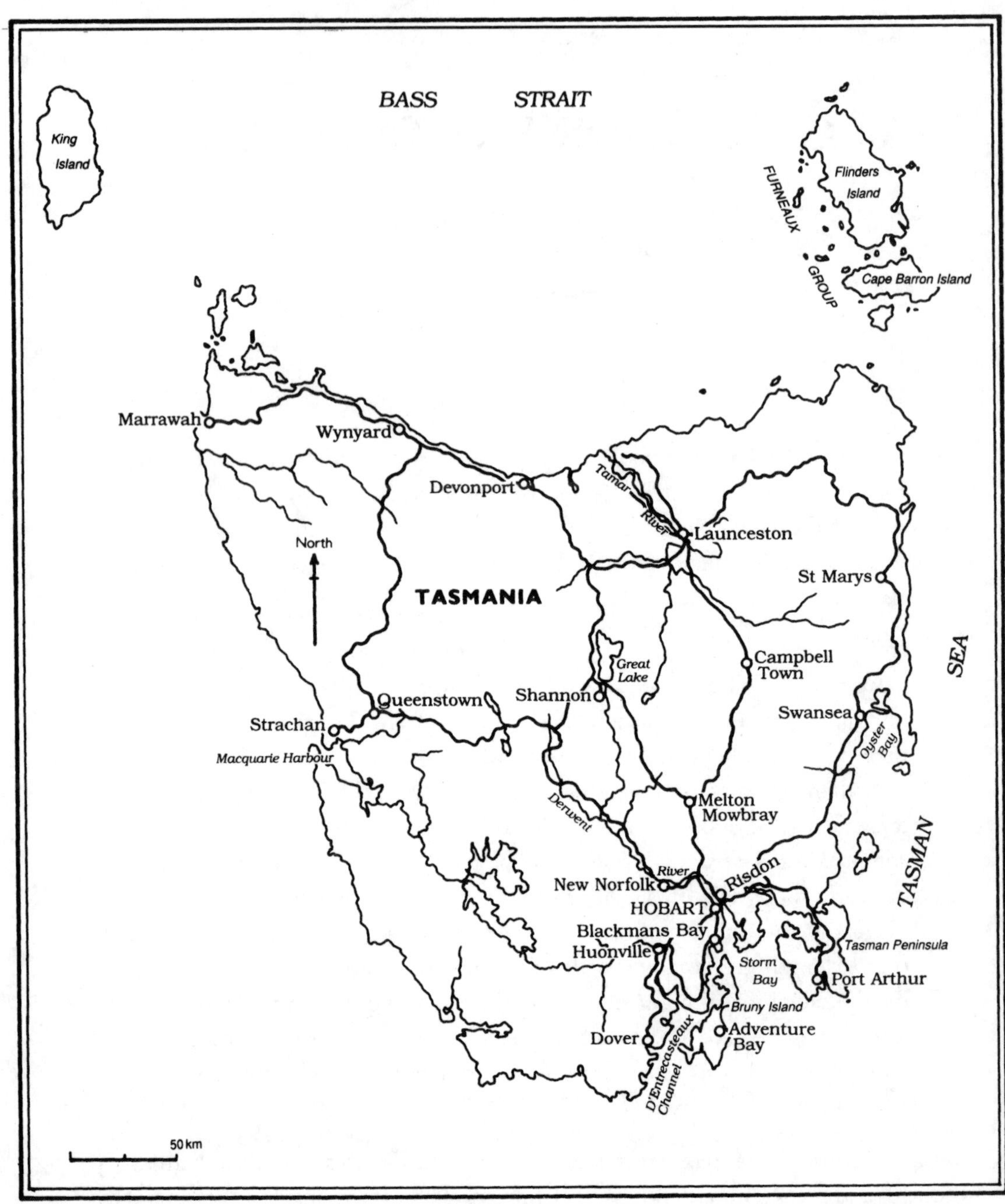

landed on 5 March 1772 and was greeted by a group of Aboriginal people who unambiguously demanded immediate departure by hurling stones at the invaders. Such was the accuracy of the group that du Fresne was hit and injured. Instead of retreating, the French replied to the 'attack' with rifle fire. A number of the Aboriginal people were wounded and one was killed.

The explorers who followed — Furneaux, Cook, Bligh, D'Entrecasteaux, Bass and Flinders, Baudin and Freycinet — all agreed that the Aboriginal people they encountered were friendly and hospitable.

The French saw Aboriginal Australians in terms of Rousseau's 'noble savage'. They eagerly talked and wrote of the purity, nay the perfection, of the race. In 1802 one French explorer wrote in his journal that:

> This gentle confidence of the people in us, these affectionate evidences of benevolence which they never ceased to manifest towards us, the sincerity of their demonstrations, the frankness of their manners, the touching ingenuousness of their caresses, all concurred to excite within us sentiments of the tenderest interest.

Within two years these sentiments were to be turned on their heads as, once again, the British, with a malicious and arrogant sense of their own superiority, proceeded on a path which would culminate some seventy-five years later in the virtual extinction of the Tasmanian Aboriginal people.

The original motive for the white settlement of Van Diemen's Land was political rather than economic. The British wanted to prevent the French from establishing a colony. They achieved this in September 1803 when a colony of forty-nine people was established at Risdon Cove. In February 1804, they were joined by the remnants of David Collins's abortive Port Phillip settlement.

Within three months the first massacre had occurred. On 3 May a large group of Aboriginal people, probably up to three hundred in number, descended the foothills towards Risdon Cove. The whites saw them approaching and were clearly disturbed. It seems that no-one stopped long enough to ask what the group were doing. In the paranoid minds of the whites three hundred Aboriginal people could only be interested in causing trouble.

In fact, the group was almost certainly on a kangaroo hunt. Edward White, a servant, was to report years later that he 'saw 300 Natives come down in a circular form, and a flock of kangaroos hemmed in between them'. It was a regular, probably an annual, collective food gathering exercise. The kangaroo was vital to the life of the local groups. It provided the warm coats which protected them against the coldness of the island's icy, and often snowy, winter and it provided a rich supply of food. Men, women and children from different groups gathered and, forming a huge arc across the valley, herded the kangaroos towards the cove. They had no spears; spears in such an enclosed space were dangerous. They carried large pieces of wood with which to beat the cornered animals when they tried to escape by rushing between the hunters. As the people moved closer to Risdon Cove the

Hobart Town, Van Diemen's Land. In May 1804 the first major massacre took place when an Aboriginal hunting party was mistaken for a war party.

soldiers, fearing the worst, grew edgy. Aboriginal people were not to be trusted. Large groups of Aboriginal people could only be out to harass the whites.

William Moore, a lieutenant in that most notoriously drunken military force, the New South Wales Rum Corps, had been drinking heavily the night before. Hung over, depressed and antagonistic, he saw the approaching group through blurry, bloodshot eyes and decided that it would be good sport to 'see the Niggers run'. He called his troops to arms. The Aboriginal people were oblivious to the danger. At around eleven o'clock in the morning, as they came within range, the troops started firing. Some of the Aboriginal people fell. The group suddenly became aware of what was happening. They started yelling and shouting and running for their lives. The troops fired again. Four or six Aboriginal people fell forward with bullets in their backs. Children, lost in the melee, were crying. The wounded were moaning. Those who could run were racing towards the nearest undergrowth.

No-one kept a record of how many people were killed that day. Moore would claim that only three had been shot but other evidence, more reliable than his attempts at an official cover-up, would suggest that the figure was somewhere between thirty and sixty.

Lieutenant Moore, trying to justify his actions, claimed that 'from the numbers of them and the spears etc. with which they were armed, that their design was to attack us'. Dr Mountgarrett had 'every reason to think it was premeditated' and also claimed Moore had 'informed me of the Natives being very numerous and that they had wounded one of the settlers, Burke, and was going to burn his house down and ill-treat his wife'.

It was bureaucratic nonsense. A glib rationale for a massacre. A justification without logic. Moore never explained why the local Aboriginal people, who had been friendly and non-confrontational up to that time, suddenly formed themselves into a gigantic, and very European, 'war party', and started attacking the tiny settlement. He didn't explain because there was no explanation.

As for Dr Mountgarrett he used the massacre to further his quasi-Christian and quasi-scientific interests. At six o'clock that night he wrote to the Reverend Robert Knopwood:

> Dear Sir,
>
> I beg to refer you to Mr. Moore for the particulars of an attack the Natives made on the Camp today and I have every reason to think it was premeditated, as their number far exceeded any that we have ever heard of. As you express a wish to be acquainted with some of the Natives, if you will dine with me tomorrow, you will oblige me by Christening a fine Native Boy who I have. Unfortunately, poor boy, his Father and Mother were both killed, he is about two years old. I have likewise the body of a man who was killed, if Mr Bowden wishes to see him dissected, I will be happy to see him with you tomorrow. I would have wrote to him but Mr. Moore waits.
>
> Your friend.
>
> J. Mountgarrett, Hobart

Van Diemen's Land, in spite of its rugged beauty, was, from the vantage point of Britain, at the very end of the world. In the minds of the authorities it became a penal colony whose very name was synonymous with terror in the minds of even the most hardened of criminals. Macquarie Harbour became a by-word for penal oppression. Port Arthur became an experiment in white slavery. There was little that was gracious or ennobling about the island.

Such a hard and inhospitable place inevitably attracted a certain kind of person. By the 1820s the flotsam and jetsam of the world, men seeking refuge from the law or seeking isolation from other human beings, had been drawn to the shores of the island. Some of the men came as convicts and were emancipated; some came as convicts and fled into the bush; and some walked off boats and ships in Hobart Town or Launceston and became sealers, whalers, farm hands or drifters. They were rough frontiersmen. Not frontiersmen in the sense of opening up new land; frontiersmen in the sense that they despoiled and exploited everything and everyone they saw. It was against these men's natures to form a 'posse' or to join forces with the military. They had laws of their own and those laws had nothing to do with the statutes and regulations which were being formulated in London.

Confronted with such a vicious and lawless ethic, the Aboriginal people of Van

Diemen's Land were helpless. They were not killed by large-scale or systematic massacres. They were simply disposed of in ones and twos and threes and dozens by occasional shootings.

The list of atrocities is almost endless. Contemporary writing is full of the most gruesome descriptions of the way in which the whites casually disposed of every Aboriginal person they could get their cruel hands on:

> A man named Harrington procured ten or fifteen women, placed them on different islands, and left them to procure Kangaroo skins for him, and if, on his return they had not procured enough, he used to punish them by tying them up to trees for 24 to 36 hours together, flogging them at intervals.
>
> If the women do not comply with their desires or orders in hunting etc., they, by way of punishment, half hang them, cut their heads with Clubs in a shocking manner or flog them most unmercifully with Cats made of Kangaroo Sinews.
>
> A shepherd kept an Aboriginal women chained up like a wild beast; and whenever he wanted her to do anything, applied a burning stick, a firebrand snatched from the hearth, to her skin.
>
> Stockmen used to shoot and hunt the natives; Captain Ritchie's men to the westward of Norfolk Plains used to hunt them on horseback and shoot them from their horses; one of these men told Mr. O'Conner that he had thrown a woman upon a fire and burned her to death.
>
> I have been credibly informed that the stock-keepers were in the habit of emasculating the men that they might obtain undisputed possession of their wives.
>
> Great ravages were committed by a party of constables and some of the 40th Regiment sent from Campbell Town; the party consisted of five or six; they got the Natives between two perpendicular rocks . . . has heard and does believe that 70 of them were killed by that party . . . the party killed them by firing all their ammunition upon them, and then dragging the women and children from the crevices in the rocks and dashing out their brains.

There were stories of using Aboriginal people as target practice. One old bushranger is reported to have said that he would 'as lief shoot them as so many sparrows'. Child stealing became a popular pastime. One particularly sadistic episode involved a man named Carrotts who chased a native man and woman. Having shot the man, he cut off his head, hung it around the woman's neck, and rode back into the nearby settlement proud of his success. It was said that the bushranger Michael Howe, who was known for his cunning and his callousness, liked to kill Aboriginal people 'better than smoking his pipe' and that one of his favourite pastimes was to lie his gun down, wait until the Aboriginal people approached, and then shoot them by pulling the trigger with his toe.

Another particularly ugly account involves two men who were chasing a very pregnant Aboriginal woman through the bush. Unable to escape them, the woman climbed up a tree and tried to hide in the branches. 'But she had been observed by the sportsmen. One of these proposed to shoot her but the other objected. The first, however, dropped behind and fired at the unfortunate creature. A fearful scream was heard and then a new-born infant fell out of the tree.'

It has been claimed that some settlers shot Aboriginal people so they could feed them to their dogs. 'It was common for the parties of the civilised portion of society to scour the bush and falling in with the tracks of the natives during the night to follow them to their place of encampment where they were slaughtered in cold blood.'

The accounts of brutality just go on and on. It is a great irony that Britain, a country which at the time was claiming to be the apotheosis of civilisation, was the home of these barbarians who set standards of inhumanity scarcely matched by the Spanish conquistadors or the slave traders and owners of the southern states of the United States of America.

Truganini, that much-abused tiny woman who has so frequently been incorrectly dubbed the last of her tribe, led a life which is symptomatic of the way in which the British wiped out Aboriginal people in Tasmania. By the time she was seventeen she'd been raped (and probably contracted syphilis), her mother had been stabbed to death, her uncle had been shot, her stepmother had been kidnapped by mutinous convicts who took her to China, her sisters had been enslaved by sealers, and her betrothed had been murdered. All over Van Diemen's Land this process was being

Truganini at the age of sixty-five. By the age of seventeen, she had been raped, seen her mother stabbed, her uncle shot, her stepmother kidnapped, her sisters captured and kidnapped, and her betrothed murdered.

repeated. In seventy-five years most family groups had been totally wiped out.

In Truganini's case each assault upon her family was violent and unprovoked. Her mother was stabbed to death by a shore party from a boat. As Truganini told it, the family group were sitting around a camp fire one night when suddenly a group of sailors burst upon them. Everyone ran for their lives. Her mother wasn't fast enough. The sailors caught her and stabbed her to death. Her tribal sisters, Lowhenunhe, Maggerleede and Murrerninghe, were kidnapped by a man named John Baker. Baker took the three girls to Kangaroo Island and sold them to sealers.

Tasmanian Aboriginal women were much prized by the sealers because they were highly skilled hunters who could earn a sealer substantial amounts of money. Murrerninghe was shot by a sealer named Robert Gamble. Lowhenunhe and Maggerleede spent the rest of their lives in slavery to a sealer named Hepthernet who slept with them and made them hunt and cook for him.

The treatment of Aboriginal women by sealers often verged on the indescribable. They seemed to delight in dreaming up sadistic punishments to ensure that their slaves did not slacken and did not attempt to escape. One popular torture for the women who were not working hard enough was 'for these white devils to fasten their women to the ground face downwards and put coals of fire and hot ashes upon their naked backs'. In one grotesque case some sealers caught a woman who had attempted to escape, tied her up, and proceeded to cut flesh from her ears and her thighs which they then forced her to eat.

Perhaps the most devastating event in Truganini's life occurred shortly after she agreed to marry a man called Paraweena. At the time Truganini was wont to visit the convict camps around Bruny Island. Paraweena, accompanied by a friend, came to call her back from the camp. The convicts protested; they wanted Truganini to stay. Eventually two convicts, Paddy Newell and Watkin Lowe, both of whom had reputations for their viciousness, agreed that Truganini could leave. They even offered to row the three across the narrow stretch of water to North Bruny Island. Halfway across the channel Newell and Lowe overpowered Paraweena and his friend and threw them overboard. As the two men attempted to clamber back into the boat one of the white men grabbed a hatchet which had been lying in the bottom of the boat and lashed out at Paraweena. He cut his hand off at the wrist. Then he turned and did the same to Paraweena's friend. Newell and Lowe rowed away, leaving the two injured men to drown.

Gratuitous violence such as this inevitably wreaked havoc on the local Aboriginal communities. It did much to engender the feelings of despair and hopelessness. The implicit support of the government and the military, who never convicted a single white for the murder of an Aboriginal person, did much to compound the problem. In fact, the sheer hypocrisy of the situation was evident when, after an orgy of killings, Lieutenant Governor Collins issued a proclamation declaring that:

> Any person whomsoever who shall offer violence to a native, or who shall, in cold blood, murder, or cause any of them to be murdered, shall, on proof being made of the same, be dealt with and proceeded against as if such violence had been offered or murder committed on a civilised person.

It was a case of a bureaucrat paying dull lip-service to a law he knew was not being kept and he knew was not going to be kept. The best Collins could do was have two convicts flogged. One of them had cut off an Aboriginal boy's ear; the other had cut off another's finger and was using it as a pipe stopper.

The brief moment of the noble savage was over. The Aboriginal population quickly learnt that their only defence was to attack. As always in any conflict the victims were those people least able to defend themselves — the shepherds, the small-time farmers, the travellers on the lonely bush roads. The killings were random. The government, in an attempt to curb Aboriginal aggression, placed pictographs depicting an Aboriginal man killing a white man and an Aboriginal man being hung for the crime at strategic locations around Hobart Town. It is unlikely that Aboriginal people understood the message. Certainly there is no evidence that they took heed of it.

Relations between black and white were now strained. The crimes committed against Aboriginal people had ensured that the trust and friendliness which had characterised early contact was now replaced by undisguised fear, suspicion and hatred. All the evidence pointed to errors on the part of the whites being the main provocation in conflicts between black and white.

By 1824 Aboriginal people had reached breaking point and by 1826 their attacks on settlers in outlying areas were becoming a regular hazard of Tasmanian rural life. The settlers, not accepting that white invasion had been the sole catalyst for Aboriginal attacks, started to lobby for a military solution. They argued that Aboriginal people needed to be controlled or wiped out.

The editor of the *Colonial Times* put the argument most succinctly when he argued:

> We deeply deplore the situation of the Settlers. With no remunerating price for their produce, they have just immerged from the perils of the bushrangers, which affected their property, and they are now exposed to the attack of these natives, who aim at their lives. We make no pompous display of Philanthropy — we say unequivocally — SELF DEFENCE IS THE FIRST LAW OF NATURE. THE GOVERNMENT MUST REMOVE THE NATIVES — IF NOT, THEY WILL BE HUNTED DOWN LIKE WILD BEASTS AND DESTROYED!
>
> In the first place, they must be removed, either to the coast of

> New Holland or King's Island. The latter is one of our Dependencies, fertile, well supplied with water, and no possibility of escape. There are two parties who have committed outrages — the Oyster Bay, and the Shannon parties. We would recommend them being taken, which could easily be effected — placed at King's Island, with a small guard of soldiers to protect them, and let them be compelled to grow potatoes, wheat, etc., catch seals and fish, and by degrees, they will lose their roving disposition, and acquire some slight habits of industry, which is the first step of civilisation.

The racism of such a solution never seems to have occurred to the editor. His suggestion to 'civilise' the indigenous inhabitants by rounding them up and shipping them to King Island was as inept as it was impractical. The massacres continued throughout 1827. The lawless world beyond the towns was now driven by reprisal and counter-reprisal. It was reported that near the Western Tiers a settler who had shot some Aboriginal men and abducted their women had himself been killed in reprisal. The settlers nearby went out on a raid. A brief official report claimed that about sixty Aboriginal people had been killed or wounded. In spite of Governor Arthur's feeble insistence on 'the common law of mankind' and British law, no-one was ever charged or brought to court to stand trial.

By 1828 the massacres had virtually become official government policy. Arthur, harassed and confused, appealed to the Colonial Office for a large reserve of land on the north-east corner of the island where all Aboriginal people could be removed to. He argued that access by sea would allow for the shipping in of food and clothing. He wrote to London describing how military posts could be established and how the Aboriginal people would be allowed to move out of the reserve once a year and for this they would be 'provided with a general passport under my hand and seal'. It was an early nineteenth-century attempt at apartheid. The Colonial Secretary, Sir George Murray, wrote a reply which is a classic statement of the invader position:

> I am aware of the extremely difficult task of inducing ignorant beings, of the description of those alluded to, to acknowledge any authority short of absolute force particularly when possessed with the idea which they appear to entertain in regard to their own rights over the country in comparison with those of the colonists.

Arthur continued to push for his 'apartheid' reserve but it was generally ridiculed because of the impossibility of the task. On 1 November 1828, with Aboriginal communities now engaged in a series of running, sniping raids in a last ditch attempt

The government, in an attempt to curb Aboriginal aggression, placed pictographs depicting an Aboriginal man killing a white man and the Aboriginal man being hung for the crime at strategic locations around Hobart Town. There is no evidence that Aboriginal people understood what the drawings were supposed to represent. A decade later the government reneged on this policy and massacres were virtually officially sanctioned.

to save their land, the government declared martial law. The rationale was unambiguous — 'To inspire them with terror . . . will be the only effectual means of security for the future.' It was a licence to kill. Arthur mouthed the liberal attitudes of his time when he stated:

> But I do, nevertheless, hereby strictly order, enjoin, and command, that the actual use of arms be in no case resorted to if the Natives can by other means be induced or compelled to retire into the places and portions of this island hereinbefore expected from the operation of martial law; that bloodshed be checked as much as possible; that any tribes which may surrender themselves up shall be treated with every degree of humanity; and that defenceless women and children be invariably spared.
>
> And all officers, civil and military, and other persons whatsoever, are hereby required to take notice of this my proclamation and order, and to render obedience and assistance herein accordingly.

But in his heart of hearts Arthur knew that his plea for a reserve had failed and that 'if you can't round them up you might as well exterminate them' had become the prevailing philosophy.

Melville had no doubts about Governor Arthur's intentions. His assessment of both the reserve and martial law shows that within the vicious insanity of Van Diemen's Land there was at least one voice of reason and rationality:

> Under the apparent pretext of charitable feelings towards these poor, deluded and perhaps misguided creatures, were the utmost cruelties permitted. At first the tribes were robbed of their land and their food — their females taken from them, and violated; then, in return, they became desperate from treatment they could no longer bear, when they resisted the violation of their wives and daughters, they were destroyed; and, when resenting these outrages committed upon them, they suffered death on the gallows! Nor did the shameful conduct of the Colonists stop there; for a proclamation divided their country, and prescribed imaginary bounds, over which these ignorant creatures were not allowed to step without a passport from the Chief Authority on pain of forcible expulsion. In the proclamation of martial law, the boundaries fixed were of a most extraordinary nature, and embraced a vast portion of the Island, over which the natives were prohibited from trespassing. When it is recollected that, within ten or fifteen miles of Hobart Town, the country is yet unexplored, the cruelty of this sweeping proclamation, by which these poor creatures were expelled from their own soil, may be more readily imagined by the stranger.

The next four years saw killing of Aboriginal people which was little more than legalised slaughter. It can be thought of, by modern analogy, as equivalent to a grazier attempting to clear his land of kangaroos.

It has been estimated that over sixty per cent of the total Aboriginal population of Tasmania was killed in the twelve months after martial law was declared. The British 'rule of law', which supposedly determined behaviour on the island, was waived. Settlers, policemen, the military, any white who could ride a horse and shoot a rifle, was given every opportunity to shoot Aboriginal people. The only issue which caused any discussion amongst the hunters was how the Aboriginal population was to be disposed of. The strategies for capture and slaughter were as complex as the minds of the killers. Some simply headed into the bush indiscriminately shooting and killing Aboriginal people. Others captured one or two and, after torturing them, forced them to lead the hunters to where other Aboriginal people were hiding. Once they located the groups it was merely a question of whether bullets were used on the men, women and children or whether bullets were saved and the men, women and children were bludgeoned to death with rifle butts and poles. In rare cases the hunters actually brought the captured Aboriginal people into Hobart Town where they were gaoled.

In 1830 these massacres were legitimised when the government began offering money for Aboriginal captives. The rate of five pounds per adult and two pounds per child meant that dozens of bounty hunters headed into the bush determined to make their fortune. It also meant that hundreds of Aboriginal people were shot by overzealous hunters whose warped logic argued that ten dead and three captured was a profitable day's work.

The profits from Aboriginal hunting were vast. A number of men, most notably John Batman, made fortunes by rounding up Aboriginal people. Although the details were never recorded, it was known that on one of his hunting expeditions Batman killed fifteen Aboriginal men while capturing one Aboriginal woman and a child. He had made seven pounds and killed fifteen people. On that scale an Aboriginal life was worth somewhat less than ten shillings. Few people seem to have questioned the dubious morality of the activity.

The financial rewards for capturing Aboriginal people ended in June 1832.

It was now obvious, even to the half-hearted government, that some systematic approach had to be developed. The *Colonial Times* noted:

> . . . the custom that has been almost universal among certain Settlers, and their servants whenever the Natives have visited their neighbourhood, to consider the men as wild beasts whom it was praiseworthy to hunt down and destroy, and the women as only fit to be used for the worst of purposes. The shooting of blacks is spoken of as a matter of levity.

It was out of such public observations that the concept known as the Black Line emerged. Like all of Arthur's other schemes designed to solve the 'Aboriginal problem', it was at once hilarious and monumentally naive. The plan was to drive, in a manner somewhat akin to herding cattle or catching rabbits, the entire Aboriginal population of Tasmania into the Tasman Peninsula. If Arthur had stopped and seriously thought about what he was trying to do, he would have realised the craziness of his plan. The very idea of getting all the white settlers on the island — farmers, policemen, sealers, government officers, military personnel, convicts who could be trusted, farm workers, businessmen, clerks and anyone else who was fit and able — to traipse through the bush in a vast line shooing the Aboriginal population in front of them like chickens or sheep was truly surreal.

In the first week of the operation three thousand bewildered whites wandered through the country believing that Aboriginal people were fleeing as they advanced. Arthur, like some confused antipodean Don Quixote, started sending dispatches and proclamations to his troops. Cynics laughed at the operation. Civilians clambered over mountain ranges, officers forded fast-flowing rivers, convicts scoured the undergrowth. All the time they believed that hundreds, perhaps even thousands, of Aboriginal people were being trapped. Those Aboriginal people who found themselves on the wrong side of the Black Line slipped back to the safe side, quietly chuckling at the inept stupidity of the whites. Still the line pushed on. At one point they fired upon a blackened tree stump believing it to be the enemy. The whites advanced and did battle with bush windmills. Their imagination fuelled the lacklustre reality.

In the end the statistics were more far-fetched than Cervantes's mind could have conceived. The total cost was about 35 000 pounds. One Aboriginal person had been captured. About five troops had been killed in accidents. The army returned defeated and humiliated:

> . . . their shoes worn out, their garments tattered, their hair long and shaggy, with beards unshaven, their arms tarnished; but neither bloodstained nor disgraced. They had seen much and dreaded more; but in general they met no other enemies than scrub and thorns, and they sat down on their own hearths, happy in having escaped the ramrods of their friends.

Although humiliated, Arthur would not give in. His next plan was to move the Aboriginal population to islands in Bass Strait. The first settlement of sixty Aboriginal people on Gun Carriage Island was a failure. There was little food on the island and the Aboriginal people spent their time either pining for home or dying of starvation.

In late 1831 it was decided to move the remaining Aboriginal people to Flinders Island where, according to one of Arthur's endless reports, 'every endeavour should be made to wean them from their barbarous habits, and progressively to introduce civilised customs amongst them'.

They were shipped there from Gun Carriage Island on 25 January 1832. In spite of a government report which spoke glowingly of 'an abundance of game on the island, consisting of kangaroo, wallaby, native porcupine, badger and a few ringtailed possums', the island was a scrubby, marshy wasteland. The Aboriginal people gazed from the decks of the *Charlotte* and moaned sadly at the starkly inhospitable island which was to be their new home.

The first group was forty strong. A second group of forty arrived some weeks later. Groups of ten, fifteen, sometimes over twenty, were progressively shipped across to the island. Like all of Arthur's other quixotic ideas, Flinders Island was a disaster. The land was inadequate and food supplies kept running out. Groups of Aboriginal people who had never had to live together before started quarrelling amongst themselves. The military, under the near-senile control of the sixty-six-year-old Sergeant Wight, started to treat the Aboriginal population as they had when they were living on the mainland. With breathtaking insensitivity sealers were invited on to the island to help guard the increasingly restless 'captives'.

There had been some possibility that Flinders Island might become a refuge from the brutality of the mainland. This was not to be. Aboriginal women were still raped; Aboriginal men were still murdered. Wight, his soldiers and the sealers, far from the eyes of the governor, began to maltreat their subjects. The sealers picked out fifteen of the strongest Aboriginal men, chained them up and took them off-shore to a large granite rock outcrop where they left them for five days without fresh water, food or firewood. With the men out of the way, the soldiers and sealers turned their attentions to the women whom they raped without fear of reprisal. On the fifth day the *Tamar*, while bringing more people to the island, noticed the hapless men on the rock and rescued them. The captain of the *Tamar* was appalled

In 1847 the settlement on Flinders Island was closed and the remnants of the original community were taken to Oyster Bay. By 1860 there were only nine left.

at the brutality. The fifteen men were dying from exposure, lack of food and lack of water.

Still Arthur was loath to admit his error. In his rose-tinted world Sergeant Wight was an excellent officer. In 1832 the ageing, incompetent Arthur was replaced by the officious, and very British, Lieutenant Darling. It was Darling's intent that civilisation and Christianity would be brought to Flinders Island. In his narrow view there was only one set of worthwhile values. Soldiers' wives attempted to teach Aboriginal women the 'rudiments of domestic economy and management'. Christianity was compulsory. Hats rather than red ochre were to be worn. Agriculture was to be established. Hard labour was prized.

By late 1832 there was an Aboriginal population of about one hundred on the island and maybe another one hundred on the main island. The population of Van Diemen's Land had been reduced to a mere two hundred in less than thirty years. Even then, of the one hundred on Flinders Island, twenty-three died of disease within months of their arrival.

Darling, for all his good intentions and undoubted philanthropy, was killing Aboriginal people by his refusal to respect the rightness of their culture. His main, though well-intentioned, crime was to insist that they wear clothes. Clothes, according to Darling, were symbolic of both civilisation and Christianity. To Aboriginal people they were associated with catching pneumonia. James Backhouse Walker, a Quaker, noted after his visit in September 1832 that:

> . . . to savages accustomed to sleep naked in the open air beneath the rudest shelter, the change to close and heated dwellings tended to make them susceptible, as they had never been in their wild state, to chills from atmospheric changes, and was only too well calculated to induce those severe pulmonary diseases which were destined to prove so fatal to them. The same may be said of the use of clothes. In their wild state the blacks had gone entirely naked in all weathers, protecting their bodies against the elements by rubbing them with grease. At the settlement they were compelled to wear clothes, which they threw off when they became heated or found them troublesome, and when wetted by rain allowed them to dry on their bodies. In the case of the Tasmanians, as with other wild tribes accustomed to go naked, the use of clothes had a most mischievous effect on their health. In their native bush the constant and strenuous exertion which they were compelled to make in hunting wild animals for necessary food kept them hardy and healthy. Cooped up in the settlement and regularly fed, they lost the motive for exertion, and sank into a life

> of listless inaction, in which they lost their natural vigour, and became an easy prey to any disease that attacked them.

This assessment was supported by Surgeon Allen who reported that:

> The great mortality amongst the aborigines has been caused, in most instances, by the application of cold, either in exposed situations or by an irregular use of improper clothing. The catarrhal and pneumonic attacks to which they are so subject and which are the only fatal diseases among them, are caused by the injudicious system of suddenly changing their habits, food and manner of life. The water at this settlement is not wholesome. It contains in addition to the impurities which it imbibes from the peculiar soil through which it percolates a considerable quantity of muriate of soda. The aborigines have a particular dislike to the use of this water, evidenced more strongly when they are sick or convalescing, as they often go to a considerable distance for a drink of good water. It is highly necessary for the natives to be located in a sheltered situation. The huts which the natives at present occupy are placed on the most exposed part of the settlement, the ground being high, bare and open to the cold bleak prevailing winds from the southward and west. They are decidedly improper for the natives to be kept in, being neither warm nor dry. Pea Jacket Point is not the most eligible place for locating the natives on Flinders.

The Aboriginal population on the island were dying as fast as the authorities could ship them over. In 1832, sixty-three were shipped from Van Diemen's Land; forty people died on the island. In 1833, forty-seven were shipped and fourteen died. The following year none was shipped and fourteen died. In 1836 the island was home to 123 Aboriginal people. Only seven more were shipped from Van Diemen's Land.

The final demise of Aboriginal people on Flinders Island was slow but inexorable. In 1838 there were ninety left; in 1841, fifty; in 1847 there were forty-seven; and by 1863 there were only seven remaining.

The final act was played out by George Robinson, that self-styled Protector of Aborigines and Conciliator, who took over control of Flinders Island in late 1835. Robinson was one of those bizarre Victorian eccentrics who are all but incomprehensible to people living in the late twentieth century. A short, plump Englishman of working-class origins, he saw his opportunity for immortality and, although ill-equipped, grabbed it. He was pompous, self-righteous, moralistic and hypocritical. He had spent the previous decade 'conciliating' the Aboriginal population. This was

This portrait titled 'The last of their race' features Mary Ann, William Lanney, Bessy Clark and Truganini, circa 1866.

a fancy euphemism for his attempts to Christianise them, which eventually, after Arthur's establishment of the Black Line, became a humane rounding-up of isolated groups.

If Darling's regime on Flinders Island had been inept, Robinson's was little more than murder in the name of Christianity. His policies were informed by that mean-spirited, life-denying Christianity which is narrow in its precepts and bigoted in its execution. He demanded strict observance of the Sabbath (all Aboriginal people were taught hymns and were not permitted to enjoy themselves or work on Sunday); a compulsory religious service was held every Tuesday; school was held for four hours every day of the week and was conducted along religious lines; and the Aboriginal people's names were changed. The name changes, symptomatic of Robinson's obsession with outward appearance, were hilarious. Truganini was renamed Princess Lalla Rookh, Little Jacky became Bonaparte, Big Jemmy became Alphonso and Wongeneep was renamed Queen Evelene.

While these cosmetic changes were going on, the bodily needs of the people were being ignored. Their clothes became dirty and tattered repositories of disease; their houses became dilapidated; and their diet was restricted to dirty water, flour and, occasionally, a small piece of inedible salted mutton.

Robinson was unconsciously distancing these Aboriginal people from the attitudes, values and way of life which had sustained them for over twenty thousand years. He was turning highly efficient hunters and collectors into shopkeepers and gardeners who wore dirty clothes and who could recite the Lord's Prayer by rote. In reality his British arrogance was slowly killing them. He simply could not conceive of a situation where any civilisation could exist other than his own.

Robinson's conception of civilisation and Christianity can be measured by the 'learning' which occurred in his classes. Visitors to the island would be dragged into a classroom where some miserable, maligned Aboriginal person, with a name like Leonidas or Peter Pindar or Neptune, would be stood up and Robinson would start questioning:

'What will God do to this world by and by?'
'Burn it.'
'What did God make us for?'
'His own purpose.'
'Who are in Heaven?'
'God, angels, good men, and Jesus Christ.'
'What sort of country is Heaven?'
'A fine place.'
'What sort of place is Hell?'
'A place of torment.'

The other Aboriginal pupils, disconsolate and defeated, would gaze out the windows of the schoolroom. On a clear day they could see the mountains of their homeland on the horizon. They pined for home. If ever a group died of broken hearts it was the Aboriginal people who spent their last days on Flinders Island.

To the end Robinson remained a deluded, pompous man. Towards the end of his stay on Flinders Island, and with barely one hundred survivors around him, he had the blind arrogance to write, 'History does not furnish an instance where a whole nation has been removed by so human and mild a policy'. In truth history does not furnish an instance of a man who was so blind to the genocidal reality that was going on around him.

In 1847 the settlement on Flinders Island was closed down and the sad remnants of the original community, now numbering only forty-four, were taken back to Van Diemen's Land to a reserve at Oyster Bay. Life at Oyster Bay was depressing. The meaning and purpose of their existence gone, they resorted to alcohol to kill the pain. By 1855 only sixteen were left. To the end the remnants of the group were exploited and abused. Sailors and sawyers raided the camp to rape the women and steal what they could. The two thousand pounds provided by the government to maintain the colony was pocketed by officials long before it reached the Aboriginal population. The end of the Aboriginal people who had once lived on Flinders Island was both ugly and immeasurably sad. Some died from disease; at least two fell into the Derwent River while drunk and drowned; and others pined away in despair.

It became popular in the late 1860s to see Truganini and William Lanney as the last of their tribe. This was not true. In fact some three thousand people who assert their Aboriginality still live in Tasmania today. When William Lanney, touted as the last Tasmanian Aboriginal male, died on 3 March 1869 his grave was plundered and his skeleton removed.

Fearful that she would meet the same fate, Truganini pleaded with the colonists on her death bed, 'Don't let them cut me up. Bury me behind the mountains'. Her pleas were ignored. For years her skeleton hung on public display in the Tasmanian

Museum. She died on 8 May 1876. She had lived too long and seen too much.

The following quote from Clive Turnbull's *Black Wars* aptly sums up the plight of the Tasmanian Aboriginal people:

> One by one they had all gone, some shot, some brained with musket-butts, others rotted with drink and disease or victims of strange and horrible clothing. They had been raped, emasculated, flogged, roasted and starved. They had been badgered from place to place, taken from their country to an unfamiliar island and brought back to die in the pestiferous ruins of a gaol. The colonists' lusts had been succeeded by their hatred, and their hatred by their contempt. The 'black crows' had become the 'savages' and the savages, the dirty, drunken, flea-ridden blacks.

On 1 May 1976 Truganini's bones were cremated and her ashes thrown to the winds in the D'Entrecasteaux Channel near her birthplace in Adventure Bay.

CHAPTER 4

THE MASSACRE OF THE WIRADJURI — 1824

The best thing that can be done is to shoot all the blacks and manure the ground with their carcasses.

William Cox, landowner, 1824

For a quarter of a century whites had been battering their heads against sheer walls. Everybody in the Sydney colony, from the lowliest convict who longed to put as much distance as possible between himself and the overseer's lash to the quixotic adventurers who had drifted into the tiny outpost of European civilisation, looked west.

On a clear winter's day it was easy to see the mountains touched with that distinctive smoky blue which rises, shimmering, from the dense monotony of the eucalypts. They called them the Blue Mountains although they were really a monocline and a series of box canyons. They thought the old exploration techniques would work. Follow a river to its source, climb the valley, cross over the mountains. Each time they followed a river upstream they came not to an ever-steepening valley or gorge but to a waterfall which fell hundreds of feet over a sheer, unclimbable cliff. They'd clamber up the scree slopes, gaze hopelessly at the wall above them, and mooch on back to Parramatta and Sydney Town chastened by the folly of their expedition and cursing nature's indifference to their ambitions.

It wasn't until 1813 that Blaxland, Lawson and Wentworth, with help from the local Aboriginal people who had been wandering backwards and forwards across the mountains for thousands of years, finally managed to traverse a ridge and gaze across the rich, undulating slopes which tumbled away to the west. They liked what they saw — good rivers, rich soil, quality grazing land.

The Wiradjuri saw the white men but decided to keep their distance. There seemed to be no threat. A few white men with a few horses wandering around the countryside was no cause for alarm. The Wiradjuri had lived on these slopes and plains for tens of thousands of years. Their culture, their lifestyle, the very reason for their existence, was rooted in the area. The region was rich. Life was good. They were, of tradition, shy and peaceful.

A few weeks after news of the first white men had flashed across the plains, another small party was sighted. Assistant Surveyor George Evans was moving out

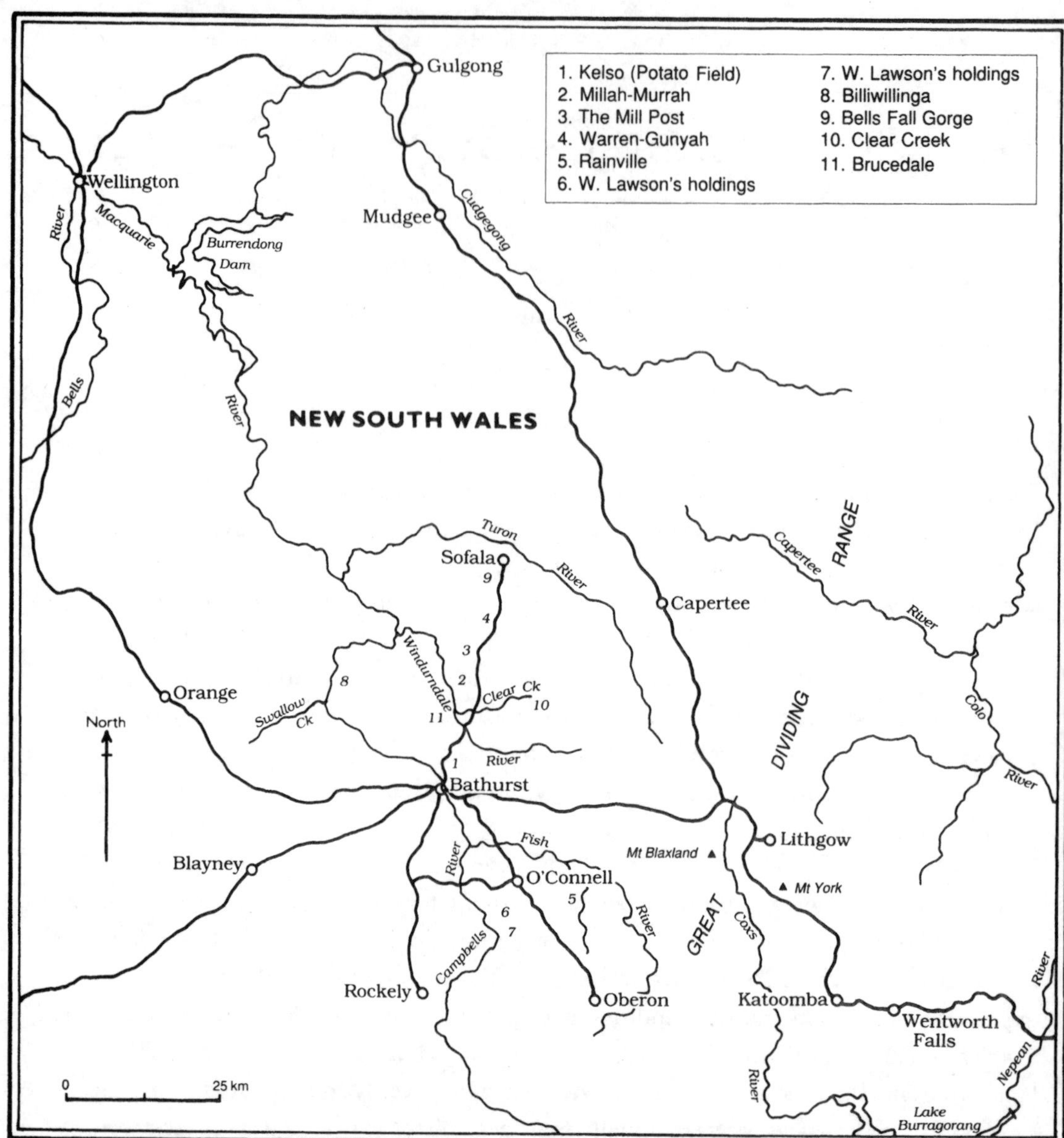

The Bathurst region in the central west of New South Wales.

across the plains, following the rivers, assessing the soils, evaluating the grazing potential. His progress was observed. The word which spread through the Wiradjuri camps was to keep well clear of the whites. Somehow one family didn't hear the news. A couple of women with their four young children had come down from the mountains to fish in the river when, to their horror, in front of them was Evans, his horses, and his colleagues and assistants.

That night, only four days before Christmas, in his tent, straining his eyes as the candles flickered on either side of the crude camp table and swiping irritably at the moths and mosquitoes, Evans wrote of the meeting in his journal:

> Returning we saw smoke on the north side of the river. At sunset as we were fishing I saw some Natives coming down the Plain. They did not see us till we surprised them ... There were only two women and four children. The poor creatures trembled and fell down with fright ... I think they were coming for Water ... I gave them what Fish we had, some fishhooks, twine and a tomahawk. They appeared glad to get them. Two boys ran away; the other small children cried much at first. A little while after I played with them and they began to be good humoured and laugh ...

The accidental meeting had been friendly. What little concern the Wiradjuri had voiced about the white man seemed to be unjustified. There was no need for antagonism.

Over the next eighteen months the Wiradjuri heard little of the white man. Occasionally news would flicker from one camp to another that a road was being built over the mountains. Such activity made little sense and therefore caused little concern. As winter came to the plains the Wiradjuri huddled closer to their camp fires. They gazed into the sharp night skies, wondering at the misty mystery of the Milky Way and the glorious arcs and parabolas of the stars. Word spread from camp to camp that a large party was slowly moving across the plains. There were thirty-seven whites, lots of horses and dogs, carriages and drays, and a sense of importance and occasion about the group. Governor Lachlan Macquarie, the liberal Scot, the friend of emancipated convicts like the forger-cum-architect Francis Greenway and mutineer-surgeon Dr William Redfern, was inspecting the road across the mountains. He was curious about the pasturelands which his assistant surveyor had spoken of with such enthusiasm.

Macquarie was a product of the Age of Enlightenment. He was a moral and reasonable man who shunned the narrow, pinched and exploitative aggressiveness of the local conservative lobby, preferring to embrace the liberal values of his age. He did not see Aboriginal people as 'vermin' and 'pests'. That night, after an enthusiastic greeting from the local people, he recorded in his journal that 'three male natives and four boys' had been at the Bathurst camp to greet him. In his careful hand, and dipping his pen frequently into his finely crafted inkwell, he wrote:

> They were all clothed with Mantles made of the skins of o'possums which were very neatly sewn together and the outside of the skins were carved in a remarkably neat manner. They appear to be very inoffensive and cleanly in their persons.

A week later he again wrote of the Wiradjuri. As he sat reflectively over his journal he realised that Aboriginal Australians were the kind of people that philosophers like Rousseau had written about. He saw the Wiradjuri as 'handsome' people who fulfilled the notions of a world unsullied by cities and industry. They were true 'noble savages' with all the meritorious innocence which that description implies. They were peace-loving, contented, shy, gracious and noble. In his journal he wrote:

> After breakfasting this morning we were visited by three male natives of the country, all very handsome good looking young men, and whom we had not seen before. I gave them presents of slops and tomahawks and to the best looking and stoutest of them I gave a piece of yellow cloth in exchange for his mantle, which he presented me with.

The party, impressed by both the land and the local Aboriginal population, departed a few days later.

Macquarie, curious to know more about the area, requested his assistant surveyor to explore further inland. So, as the governor and his party made their way back to Sydney Town, George Evans pushed on beyond the Lachlan River. Evans, like Macquarie, did not see the Wiradjuri as a threat. Although he was to travel hundreds of kilometres through their territory, he rarely saw them and when he did he was surprised at their shyness and apparent fear. On the night of 31 May he wrote in his journal:

> We see the natives two or three times a day: I believe we are a great terror to them; a Woman with a young Child fell in our way this afternoon, to whom I gave a Tomahawk and other trifles: she was glad to depart; soon after we suddenly came upon a Man who was much frightened; he ran up a Tree in a moment, carrying with him his Spear and Crooked throwing Stick; he hallowed and cryed out so much and loud, that he might have been heard half a Mile; it was useless entreating him to come down, therefore stuck a tomahawk in the Tree and left him; the more I spoke, the more he cryed out.

Macquarie was aware of the problems which could have resulted from rapid settlement of the area. He knew that the aggressive local landowners, local glory boys like John Oxley and John Macarthur who were devouring land with the obsessiveness of obese gluttons, were eager to expand into the area.

He held them at bay. The Wiradjuri, oblivious to the greedy politicking that was going on over their land, looked on as a small number of settlers trickled over the mountains. By 1820 there were only 114 whites living in the Bathurst region. A year later the number had not increased significantly. Relations between the Aboriginal population and the white invaders were amicable. Neither side perceived the other as a threat. A harmony, an unspoken truce, was achieved. Each side kept its distance.

Over the next three years this was all to change. Encouraged by a newly aggressive policy emanating from London, settlers began to pour over the mountains. By 1824 the white population of the area had increased tenfold to 1267 people. The 2520 acres (1020 hectares) of land which had been cleared and fenced in 1821 had increased to 91 636 acres (37 085 hectares) by 1825. The combined sheep and cattle population of the area leapt from 33 733 in 1821 to 113 973 in 1825. A new sense of *laissez-faire* aggressiveness transformed the previously peaceful life on the plains. By August 1824 whites were occupying an area approximately 100 kilometres wide by 200 kilometres long. Kangaroos and wallabies were being shot on sight. Prime riverbank locations were being settled. Sacred burial sights were being turned into stockyards and cattle runs.

The Wiradjuri saw what was going on. Their traditional hunting grounds were being destroyed. The paradise which had sustained them for thousands of years had been overrun. They were being dispossessed without discussion or debate. Like most wars, the conflict between the Wiradjuri and the settlers started as a series of minor skirmishes. If the Wiradjuri were by nature a peaceful people, they managed to acquire the skills of guerrilla warfare remarkably quickly. They seemed to have a flair for the short, sharp lightning raid. But then, when your very livelihood is being threatened, the survival instinct is a wonderful means of sharpening strategies.

The Aboriginal people rushed herds, speared cattle and occasionally killed shepherds who were foolhardy enough to try to protect their animals against attack.

The first attack was a minor affair. One morning, early in 1822, a small group of Wiradjuri attacked a station on the Cudgegong River. The terrorised station hands ran for their lives. The Wiradjuri set the cattle free, killed a couple of sheep and, as silently as they had arrived, melted back into the anonymous bush. The local settlers demanded military reinforcements and formed their own posse but no Aboriginal people were found.

Eighteen months later, a shepherd living in an isolated wooden hut 20 kilometres north-east of the Bathurst camp was killed by Aboriginal people in suspicious circumstances.

It was a sad irony that a settlement which had started so successfully was slowly and inexorably drifting into an anarchy which was to become total war. Between October 1823 and January 1824 the pressures along the new frontier exploded. The Wiradjuri, frustrated by the wholesale destruction of the kangaroos and possums which formed the basis of their meat diet, began to attack the settlers' livestock. They rushed the herds, speared cattle and occasionally killed shepherds who were foolhardy enough to try to protect their animals against attack. Although the more liberal and humane of the settlers conceded that 'the white persons in the first instances have been the aggressors', the bulk of the new landowners demanded that military forces be brought in to control the increasing violence.

This was no ordinary frontier confrontation. The Wiradjuri in the Bathurst area began to consolidate into a significant fighting force. The groups, which were normally no larger than thirty or forty, including women and children, began to form into all-male fighting forces numbering up to one hundred. A leader, a young and fearfully strong Aboriginal man named Windradyne (crudely nicknamed Saturday by the whites), emerged as a focus for black discontent.

Windradyne was masterful in his strategies. Within weeks his reputation, fuelled by tales of almost mythic proportions, had travelled across the mountains. In early January 1824 the *Sydney Gazette* reported that it had taken six men to capture him and 'they had actually to break a musket over his body before he yielded, which he did at length with broken ribs'. It also claimed that the Wiradjuri were killing cattle with such precision that:

> To avoid the imputation, too, of guilt upon these occasions, they manage to perforate a hole in the front of the skull with a spear, about the size of a musket ball, and when the carcass is found, they say, that the beast has been killed by white man, and point to the spot where the ball has entered!

The capture and incarceration of Windradyne was an error of judgement on the part of the area's new commandant, Major Morisset. Morisset believed he was 'teaching the natives a lesson'. In reality, by placing Windradyne in leg irons for a month, he

This lithograph titled 'A Native Chief of Bathurst' is thought to be Windradyne, a young, fearfully strong leader who emerged as a focus for black discontent.

was creating a martyr. Windradyne was released and returned to his people determined to continue the fight against the invaders. But by now the internecine war had acquired a deadly life of its own. The settlers were committed to the elimination of all Aboriginal people from the area. Aboriginal people, regardless of whether they were friendly or aggressive, male or female, adult or child, were seen as the enemy. Any method of extermination was justified; the cattle had to be protected. If that meant killing people whose ancestors had lived in the area for thousands of years then, according to brutal frontier logic, the slaughter was justified.

Aboriginal people were indiscriminately shot at. Shepherds were issued with guns. Then a new method was developed. The sheep in the area were prone to a disease called scab. The cure at the time was an arsenic dip. The shepherds, realising the poisonous qualities of arsenic and knowing that Aboriginal people would want to steal food left in isolated huts, began to mix up a deadly brew which would be used all over Australia for the next century to exterminate troublesome blacks. A pinch of salt, some flour, some water, a couple of spoonfuls of arsenic, mix together, knead into a dough, throw it on the hot embers of the fire — hey presto! — an arsenic damper, complete with its own death warrant, was ready to be eaten.

Feelings on the frontier were running high. Only the slightest spark was needed to inflame hostilities. That spark was thrown by accident.

On the banks of the Macquarie River, on the outskirts of the tiny Bathurst township, were a number of market gardens. The rich, alluvial river flats were ideal for the growing of vegetables and a number of small farmers worked the area and, apart from supplying the local community, managed to sell some of their produce in Parramatta and Sydney. One day in early March Windradyne and members of his family group were walking along the riverbank when one of the gardeners offered them some potatoes. The gardener showed them how to cook the vegetables and the group departed to experiment with the new foodstuff.

The next day the group, obviously impressed by the new taste sensation, returned to get some more. The potatoes were growing on their tribal land and they felt they had a right to the produce. Realising what was happening and totally misunderstanding the situation, the gardener called to his neighbours to help get the 'thieving blacks' off his land. Seeing angry whites running towards them, the group scattered. Some of the men stood their ground with their spears and boomerangs at the ready. A white settler opened fire. An Aboriginal person pitched forward, dead. Spears were thrown; rifles shot. In minutes the battle was over. No-one bothered to record the number of Aboriginal people who had been killed or wounded. The cynicism of the frontier had created a new ethic: Aboriginal people could be shot with impunity; murder would have no legal repercussions.

Windradyne would change that ethic. He was a survivor of the massacre. He had seen members of his family group shot down for no apparent reason. If the whites around Bathurst had consciously tried to create an Aboriginal revolutionary, they couldn't have done it better. They had placed Windradyne in irons for a month and only weeks after his release they had cold-bloodedly killed members of his family.

Within days Windradyne had drawn together a kind of war party. The group, armed with spears and bent on reasserting Aboriginal domination, operated like a highly efficient guerrilla corps. They were selective in their targets and powerful in their assertion of their rights.

On 24 May, on a narrow stream called the Windurndale Rivulet, to the north of Bathurst, at a hut called Millah-Murrah, they attacked and killed three white shepherds. The hut, owned by a rather unsavoury grazier called Samuel Terry, had been built on a sacred site which for aeons had been used by the local Wiradjuri for the initiation of young men. Terry had built stockyards and huts on the land in spite of Aboriginal protests. Now was the time to avenge the desecration of the site. The war party moved in with specific instructions to destroy the buildings. In the process three station hands, David Brown, John Donnelly and Joseph Ross, were killed. The hut was ransacked and twelve sheep were killed.

The party then moved about ten kilometres to the north to a property called the Mill Post which was owned by Richard Lewis. Here, they attacked and killed a hutkeeper and destroyed his hut, taking everything apart from the dead man's hammock. The next morning the party, now armed with a musket and two bayonets, raided a third property — Warren Gunyah. Here they cornered three shepherds and killed them all. Two of the victims were incinerated as one of the huts was set alight. The third victim was left lying in the yard with five spears protruding from his lifeless body.

Reprisals were quick and not directed at the warriors. The settlers called upon military support. Parties of soldiers roamed the plains and valleys to the north of Bathurst killing any Aboriginal people they made contact with. Somewhere to the north of Millah-Murrah soldiers came across three Aboriginal women and a boy. The group tried to escape but were shot and dumped in a nearby waterhole. It was hoped that their decomposing bodies would pollute the water.

The entire countryside was now at war. Aboriginal people walked the land at their peril. Shepherds and hutkeepers were armed for any attack. The killings became sporadic and irrational. By the end of May no-one, black or white, was prepared to venture out alone. Reprisals and counter-reprisals were occurring almost daily.

Aboriginal people, inspired by Windradyne, were confronting white settlers and disrupting white grazing at every opportunity. On the O'Connell Plains, which lay between the confluence of the Fish and Campbell rivers to the south-east of Bathurst, a party of fifty to sixty warriors killed stock. They then moved west, burning stockmen's huts as they went. Arriving at Rockley, some kilometres up the Campbell River, they rushed five hundred sheep, which were not recovered for some weeks.

On 31 May the party, having moved back to the O'Connell Plains, attacked a stockman, John Hollingshead. Although he was speared through the left arm, he managed to escape and report the attack to a neighbouring station. The overseer, a man named William Lane, formed a posse of six stockhands — John Johnston, William Clarke, John Nicholson, Alexander Grant, Henry Castles and John Crear. They headed off in search of the warriors. Near Raineville they came across a group of about thirty Aboriginal people. They opened fire on the group and killed two girls and a woman. In their eyes all Aboriginal people were guilty.

The frontier around Bathurst may have been fuelled by lawlessness but the calm British rule of law prevailed in Sydney. For all the society's brutality, for all its landgrabbing and hangings and lashings, for all its obsessively neurotic protection of property, it was adamant in the belief that it was a society ruled by humane and Christian values. When the *Sydney Gazette* heard of the killing of 'the poor inoffending creatures', its moral indignation was unambiguous. 'Heaven,' the editor declared, 'will not readily absterge so foul a stain — how then is it to be expected that man should justify such blood-stained guilt?'

Opinion in the local community was sharply divided. The workers and overseers felt that 'the blacks had had it coming to them'. The government officers, whatever their private feelings may have been, proceeded to treat the incident as a case of murder. Under British law the Aboriginal victims had been British subjects and, as British subjects, they were entitled to all the protection the law could offer. Major Morisset demanded an inquiry. Five of the six people in Lane's party were charged with manslaughter and sent to Sydney to stand trial. The trial was a farce. All five men were acquitted. British justice had not been done but it had been seen to be done.

The trial and acquittal of the five men was a salutary lesson to both the settlers and the soldiers in the area. If anyone was going out to kill Aboriginal people, they had to make sure that no records were kept and no reports were submitted. The 'liberals', the 'Christians' and the 'moral guardians' were seen as people who did not understand the real problems of the frontier. Frontier pragmatism had no moral sense. It was driven by simplistic and brutal solutions to very complex problems. William Cox stood up at a public meeting in Bathurst and gave expression to the new frontier pragmatism when he said:

> The best thing that can be done is to shoot all the blacks and manure
> the ground with their carcasses. That is all the good they are fit for!
> It is also recommended that all the women and children be shot.
> That is the most certain way of getting rid of this pestilent race.

These sentiments were echoed by young William Lawson who, writing to a friend, declared, 'We have now commenced hostilities against them in consequence of their killing a great number of shepherds and stockmen, but afraid we shall never exterminate them, they have such an extensive mountainous country for them to flee from their pursuers'.

The war that was being waged around Bathurst became a silent war. The only line of Aboriginal defence, given their lack of rifle power, was to attack the weaknesses of the white landowners — they killed unarmed hutkeepers and shepherds, they rushed the cattle and sheep, and they killed the occasional animal. By July 1824 somewhere between fifteen and twenty white stockmen, all of them living and working in isolated circumstances, had been killed by Aboriginal raiding parties. The number of blacks killed, most of them women and children, was in excess of one hundred. Rumours were filtering down to Sydney of massacres, some of them involving up to twenty or thirty people. There were now thirty-two troops in the area. No records of any of the massacres were kept.

It was the logic of the frontier, intermingled with the quasi-Christian homilies of the age, which prevailed. In August an anonymous letter to the *Sydney Gazette* summed up the predominant viewpoint:

> . . . would not the wisest of men say . . . this also is vanity and vexation of spirit? He that spareth the rod hateth the child. Every true friend to the Aborigines must desire that they should be made to learn by terror those lessons which they have refused to acquire under a milder discipline.

The solution the government took was the declaration of martial law. On 14 August 1824 Sir Thomas Brisbane proclaimed martial law west of Mount York. The wording of the proclamation proved to be a *carte blanche* for Major Morisset and was a virtual declaration of an 'open season' on all members of the Wiradjuri who came within the sights of any gun-happy settler or soldier. The proclamation had an even-handedness, even a humanity, about it but it was never really justified. It was an extreme over-reaction largely encouraged by absentee landowners living in Sydney who were having trouble keeping hired hands on their lands. It was really nothing more than a legitimising of Cox's cry to 'shoot all the blacks'.

Governor Brisbane immediately sent a detachment of the 40th Regiment to Bathurst. The total British armed presence in the area rose to seventy-five soldiers. To this could be added another fifty to one hundred gun-happy settlers. The phoney war was over; the systematic extermination of the once-peaceful Wiradjuri had begun.

Between 14 August and 11 December 1824, when Governor Brisbane repealed the Proclamation of Martial Law, the Wiradjuri were the unhappy recipients of a law which was as incomprehensible as it was brutal. The massacres were bloody. The sole rationale was total extermination. At Billiwillinga, about 20 kilometres north-west of Bathurst, a group of Wiradjuri, unaware of the dangers of martial law, settled themselves on the banks of the Macquarie River. A party of soldiers, hearing about the camp, rode to the area. Their presence did not alarm the camp. Cautious, friendly communication was established. The soldiers prepared some food — dampers, bully beef and the like — for themselves. Some of the food was placed on the ground near the Billiwillinga homestead. The Wiradjuri, believing the food to be a gesture of friendliness, approached. The women and children came first, with the men following at a suitable distance. As the women collected up the food, the soldiers raised their rifles: in minutes some thirty innocent Wiradjuri lay dead or dying.

At Bells Falls Gorge the soldiers found another group of Aboriginal people camped on the escarpment above the falls. The soldiers circled around the camp, firing shots in the air. The Wiradjuri, fearful for their lives, fled into the bush but all the time the soldiers advanced in a broad, deadly arc pushing them closer and closer to the falls. Some of the men, realising what the soldiers were trying to do, attempted to break through the advancing military line. Some succeeded; some were shot as they zigzagged through the undergrowth. Finally the group were forced into the creek bed above the falls. Their lines of escape were cut off. The choice was simple. In front of them was the possibility of jumping to their deaths over the falls. Behind them were the soldiers whose pincer movement was clamping them in a deadly vice. They had no option. Those who did not die from gunfire, grabbed their children and leapt. Their broken bodies piled up on the rocks below. Some twenty or thirty people, none of whom could be directly implicated with the killing of the white stockmen and hutkeepers, had been wiped out.

The Wiradjuri were now fleeing for their lives. They headed for the hills, hoping to lose themselves in the lush and rugged valleys. Some groups headed up Clear Creek; others moved into the deep, silent dells of the Capertee country. This time

This nineteenth century newspaper supplement takes a wry look at Aboriginal life before and after the arrival of Europeans.

the mountains offered little escape. The soldiers fanned out across the valleys and moved slowly towards the headwaters of the rivers and creeks. They caught the Wiradjuri at camp sites, they shot men, women and children as they clambered up the exposed rock faces trying to escape. The once-silent valleys echoed with gunfire and the moaning of the wounded. The creeks ran with blood.

No records were kept. If official explanations were sought they were couched in suitably ambiguous terms. 'Some of them have been killed whilst in the act of driving

The idyllic lifestyle was destroyed as European culture overwhelmed traditions which had existed for thousands of years.

off a considerable number of cattle belonging to Mr Cox near Mudjee,' read one report. It was always the same. The white perspective was that they were more sinned against than sinning; any Aboriginal people who were shot were clearly breaking the law.

Martial law was used to justify every atrocity and every massacre. Towards the end of September a number of stockmen came across some Wiradjuri warriors on the plains to the north of Bathurst. They presumed the Wiradjuri were attempting to steal cattle. Shots were fired; spears and boomerangs thrown. The stockmen rode away victorious. Three Wiradjuri had been killed and a number lay wounded. Next day the stockmen returned to the place of the 'battle' where they found the Wiradjuri burying their dead. Not content with the previous day's killings, the stockmen opened fire on the mourners. Another sixteen people were killed. The stockmen then gathered up the sticks, spears and boomerangs and burnt them. There was no justification for the killing. The murderers were never brought to justice; the massacre was never officially reported.

After two months of massacres the Wiradjuri were a broken people. They had fought for their lands against the invaders and they had lost. The rifle and musket, and the ruthless determination of the settlers, had overwhelmed the spear and the boomerang. It had been a condition of the martial law that Windradyne, who the whites in their strange way saw as the architect of the Bathurst uprising, be apprehended. In the end Windradyne was a broken man.

On 28 December he led his family and a large number of survivors of the massacres over the mountains and down to Parramatta where, according to white reports, he paid humble respect to Governor Brisbane. He was but a shadow of the angry young warrior who had led his people into a hopeless and unwinnable war. Some whites, in a hideously patronising gesture, had written 'peace' on a piece of

On 28 December 1824 Windradyne led his family and survivors of the massacres to Parramatta for the annual meeting of the tribes. He was a broken and defeated leader.

cardboard and attached it to a straw hat which had been plonked on Windradyne's head. The reporter from the *Sydney Gazette* looked at Windradyne and was awestruck:

> He is one of the finest looking natives we have seen in this part of the country. He is not particularly tall but much shorter and more proportionable limbed than the majority of his countrymen; which combined with a noble looking countenance and piercing eye, are calculated to impress the beholder with other than disagreeable feelings towards a character who has been so much dreaded by the Bathurst settler. Saturday is, without doubt, the most manly black native we have ever beheld — a fact pretty generally acknowledged by the numbers that saw him.

Windradyne lived for another decade during which he saw his fellow Wiradjuri slowly decline. Their land, their kin and their lifestyle had been destroyed. Their very reason for existence had been leached away by greed. Into the vacuum of their despair came European diseases, alcoholism, and a lifestyle which was without hope. Occasionally, and more and more infrequently, the Wiradjuri would kill cattle or rush sheep. The vengeance of the white settlers was fast and deadly. Windradyne died in 1835. By 1850 the Wiradjuri around Bathurst had all but been destroyed.

CHAPTER 5

Massacres Along the Darling River — 1835 to 1865

We must starve them off to get rid of them — they are a squalid dirty lot, with the exception of one or two.

A squatter in 1847

The push to the west was unceasing. If it wasn't the landowning glory boys seeking larger and larger stretches of land on which to graze their growing herds of cattle, it was the explorers looking forlornly across the flat semi-desert hoping to find new lands to conquer.

The great fascination was the possibility of an inland sea and a chance to write themselves into the history books, get a knighthood and become an instant member of the Royal Geographical Society. Find an antipodean Black Sea, or maybe even an inland Mediterranean, and history students till the end of time would be forced to pore over the details of their lives. So off they all traipsed, surrounded by supplies, lackeys, surveyors, cartographers, and Aboriginal guides who knew all the answers but weren't letting on. There was Sturt, McDouall Stuart, Hume, and a gaggle of lesser luminaries. They were all bound for immortality. They all found nothing more than a few soaks, the Murray and Darling rivers.

At first the Aboriginal communities along the Darling viewed the whites with mild bemusement. The network of communication had worked in such a way that, even though Aboriginal people had never actually seen a white, they had a very good idea of what to expect. The word which had passed along the Aboriginal communication lines told of the invasion, the encroachment on traditional lands, the skirmishes and the massacres.

It was something of a surprise when Sturt travelled through the area avoiding all confrontation and convincing Aboriginal people that it was possible to be both white and decent. The same was not said when Major Thomas Mitchell, Surveyor-General of New South Wales, set out to find the mouth of the Darling. He dreamed of an inland sea. Reality told him that the Darling almost certainly flowed into the Murray but he ignored the reality. Sturt had been cautious with Aboriginal people; Mitchell was full of braggadocio and self-righteousness. He saw the Darling River like some antipodean Mississippi and developed a strategy more reminiscent of Daniel Boone and the United States Cavalry than of an explorer trying to understand the unique circumstances of Australia.

In 1835 he arrived on the banks of the Darling with boats, horses, covered wagons, sheep, bullocks, trinkets, tools, tomahawks, bags of wheat and tea — a walking food supply surrounded by a movable town. He found a suitable site and started building Fort Bourke. He was re-creating the Wild West on the edge of the Australian desert.

The Aboriginal population looked on with amusement. The building made no sense. Still, they took the whole enterprise in their stride. The relationship between Aboriginal people and Mitchell's party was amicable. Mitchell gave the them tomahawks and trinkets; they reciprocated with gifts of fish. Inevitably Mitchell's men started sleeping with the Aboriginal women.

Mitchell had little humour and the arrogance of his rank did not allow for the possibility that the Aboriginal people might have a different value system to his own. So, when Aboriginal people started taking things from the 'fort', Mitchell perceived this as 'theft' and 'skullduggery' and, in his boorish military way, demanded 'proper' behaviour. About one such incident he was later to write that he had reprimanded the offending Aboriginal man:

> . . . demanding what more he wanted; whereupon he only laughed, and soon after pulled my handkerchief from my pocket. I restored it to its place in a manner that shewed I disliked the freedom taken with it. I then sent a ball into a tree a good way off, which seemed to surprise them; and having made them understand that such a ball would easily pierce through six blackfellows. I snapped my fingers at one of their spears, and hastened to the camp. I considered these hints the more necessary, as the natives seemed to think us very simple fools, who were ready to part with every thing. Thus enlightened as to the effect of our fire-arms, these thankless beggars disappeared; although several gins and some men still sat on the opposite bank, observing our boats.

Mitchell became irritated with Aboriginal people but he became even more irritated with the Darling River. The river was, at this time, little more than a collection of interconnected waterholes. He was unable to navigate the channel. This forced the whole expedition to travel along the riverbanks. Confrontation was inevitable. Aboriginal people saw both the land and the water as their property. They regarded Mitchell and his men as trespassers who travelled through the land at the behest of the local tribes. When Mitchell's dogs killed an emu, when Mitchell casually took water from the river, and when Mitchell's men started sleeping with the Aboriginal women, the Aboriginal communities demanded proper recompense.

At first the Aboriginal people along the Darling River viewed whites with mild bemusement. The network of communication was such that, even though the Aboriginal people had never seen a white person, they had a good idea of what to expect.

It seems that the whites, in spite of their obsessive interest in property and prices, felt that they had no obligation to pay Aboriginal people for anything. This assumption reached an ugly and bloody conclusion when a bullock driver, Joseph Jones, struck a deal with an Aboriginal woman whereby he exchanged an iron kettle for sexual intercourse. Jones slept with the woman but then refused to give her the kettle. The woman, with her baby on her back, came to demand the kettle. Jones, furious at the woman's demands, struck her violently across the face sending her sprawling in the sandy mud of the riverbank. The woman, sensing Jones's uncontrollable fury, picked up her baby and ran to the river. Jones reached for his gun and shot her as she fled. The woman pitched forward into the sand. Jones then rushed forward and grabbed the baby from the dying woman's arms. He picked the infant up by its feet, swung it around his head like a bullock whip, and hurled it head first against a nearby tree. The Aboriginal men who had accompanied the woman fled to the river hoping to swim to safety. Jones and his companions fired at them. No-one knows how many died.

In 1836 Mitchell returned to the region. The expedition, which was to last seven months, journeyed from Sydney to western Victoria. Instead of approaching the

Darling from the north and becoming bogged in the sandy, marshy areas which had halted the previous journey, Mitchell decided to explore the Lachlan, Murrumbidgee and Murray rivers with a view to connecting up with the Darling.

Once again he made contact with the local Aboriginal communities. It is certain that within the Aboriginal community Mitchell's reputation as a brutal man was now well established. The Aboriginal people regarded him with suspicion. They behaved courteously but experience had taught them that he was not to be trusted.

According to Mitchell nearly two hundred Aboriginal people met his party on 24 May 1836. Mitchell's party was on the north bank of the Murray. Most of the Aboriginal people stayed on the south bank. A number of canoes were paddled out into the centre of the river. On 25 May the two parties made contact. Mitchell claimed that the meeting was amicable, although he was later to insist that many of the ringleaders from his previous brush with the local Aboriginal community were present in the large party. On the night of 26 May the Aboriginal community performed a corroboree. Mitchell was convinced that this was the prelude to an attack. So, when they set some of the nearby scrub alight, he attacked.

Mitchell had quite specific orders from the New South Wales Government that he should use neither force nor firearms against the Aboriginal population. He wanted to disperse them, so he simply ignored instructions. His men were armed. The expedition party was divided into two. Had not one over-anxious ambusher fired before the instructions were given, the scale of the massacre would have been greater. As it was, the expedition party cornered the Aboriginal people and started firing on them. They fled to the river where Mitchell's men continued to fire on them even when they started swimming to the safety of the southern bank.

In his report on the expedition Major Mitchell reported the attack and the killings bluntly:

> The Aborigines betook themselves to the river, my men pursuing them and shooting as many as they could. Numbers were shot swimming across the Murray, and some even after they had reached the opposite shore.

There was no question that the shooting was indiscriminate. Eighteen years later Ludwig Becker met an Aboriginal man named Tilki who, as a baby slung on his mother's back, had lost most of his left thumb during the shooting. His mother had been collecting mussels on the riverbank when she had been caught in the firing. Tilki had been a casualty.

Mitchell's men fired about eighty shots at the Aboriginal people. When they returned they reported that they had killed seven and many more had been wounded. The figure was almost certainly conservative.

Years later Mitchell was to write: 'I still look back upon that eventful day with

entire satisfaction.' At the time, he expressed his 'satisfaction' by naming a nearby hill, Mount Dispersion.

Mitchell was rebuked by Governor Bourke for his unnecessary aggression. History was quietly rewritten. Mitchell is remembered for his discoveries; the massacre is conveniently forgotten. He is remembered as an explorer, not a killer.

The explorers opened up a route from New South Wales to South Australia. Within a year this path was being used by a new breed of frontiersmen known as overlanders. The life of the overlander was harsh and lonely. They often went for weeks without seeing another human being. They lived on the crudest food, slept under the stars, and prided themselves on their bushcraft and their skill at mustering cattle and sheep. Over the years the early overlanders have been romanticised. They were knights of the bush, courageous loners. The truth was less glamorous. They were, in the 1830s, most commonly social misfits and ex-convicts. People who, for one reason or another, turned their back on society. They treated Aboriginal people in the same brutish way they had been treated by British law.

Problems between the overlanders and Aboriginal people were constantly at breaking point. It was always the same story — non-payment for women, use of the land and the water supply, and the killing of native fauna. The overlanders, far

The Aboriginal people on the Murray River saw both the land and the water as their property. They regarded Major Mitchell and his men as trespassers.

removed from any organised justice, made laws that suited themselves. They shot Aboriginal people to 'teach them a lesson', they took women when they felt like it and they shot anyone who argued with them. If they were confronted by groups of Aboriginal people, they simply dug their spurs in and charged the group, shooting indiscriminately as they approached.

By 1839 the overlanders were being met by strong opposition from Aboriginal communities along the Darling and the Murray. As no white person was interested in the Aboriginal version of events, and as most of the overlanders had little ability or inclination when it came to recording their journeys, there is little evidence of the scale of massacres which occurred. One overlander who bothered to record his experiences spent much of his time complaining about Aboriginal people killing his cattle. He recorded that he often shot Aboriginal people to protect his cattle from attack but while he kept a meticulous record of the cattle killed, he did not bring the same fastidiousness to bear when reporting the number of Aboriginal people he shot.

A large party of overlanders came to the Darling River in mid-1839 with a herd of nine thousand sheep. They settled at the junction of the Murray and the Darling and began building simple punts to ferry the sheep across the river. Local Aboriginal people regarded the overlanders' movements as an invasion and decided that the whites should be taught a lesson. They stood by and watched as punt load after punt load of sheep were moved across the river. When the job was nearly completed, and when the overlanders were split with half on one side of the river and half on the other, the Aboriginal group attacked.

The attack was short-lived. The overlanders grabbed their rifles and started firing. The Aboriginal attackers dived into the river to escape. One of the overlanders was later to report proudly that 'There were five or six killed and a good many wounded. We then broke up their canoes and took all their nets and burnt them.' Frontier firepower was once again victorious.

A couple of days later one of the overlanders killed an Aboriginal man for no better reason than that he was too close to the camp. 'As we were putting the sheep in camp for the night,' he recorded, 'a black was seen in some reeds and the carter fired upon him and killed him. He had come there with no other intention but to spear sheep.' It was never questioned. Death, to the overlanders, was an appropriate punishment for an Aboriginal person intending 'to spear sheep'.

Most of the overlanders seemed to come into conflict with the local Aboriginal communities. It is difficult to measure the scale or the violence of the attacks. One contemporary newspaper reports a massacre in which an estimated forty Aboriginal people were killed. If this was in any way typical, then it is possible that many hundreds of Aboriginal people from the Darling River area were murdered by these overzealous and bloodthirsty shepherds.

The Aboriginal communities along the Darling River fought back. They harassed every overlander who attempted to cross the river. They killed any sheep that happened to stray from the flock. They happily refused to co-operate with the whites. In one famous conflict some five hundred Aboriginal people attacked a large overlanding contingent, killing some two thousand sheep and four overlanders. Aboriginal Australians were making it clear that there was no automatic right-of-way through land which they regarded as their own.

The whites reacted by bringing troops in. Two subsequent conflicts resulted in heavy Aboriginal casualties. The troops travelled from Adelaide to the Rufus River near the South Australian border with instructions to curb the conflict, to conciliate and to avoid any major loss of life. They arrived one day after a battle between twenty-six overlanders and an estimated three hundred Aboriginal people. There had been no casualties on the part of the overlanders but at least fifteen Aboriginal people had been killed.

The next day the Aboriginal people attacked again. This time the combined forces of troops and overlanders killed thirty Aboriginal people and wounded at least ten. This figure was probably a serious underestimation of the deaths. The figure was probably closer to sixty. Realising they could not defeat white rifle power, the Aboriginal guerrillas had fled into the reed beds at the side of the river, believing that the reeds would offer protection and cover. The troops and overlanders had fired into the reeds continuously for over half an hour. The result was a massacre and the killers made only a perfunctory attempt to count the bodies. A visitor to the area some years later was told that the Aboriginal bodies lay in heaps on the land and at the water's edge.

The troops took four prisoners — two women, a boy and a man. On the way back to Adelaide the troops and the overlanders repeatedly raped the women until the leader of the expedition was forced to assign an armed guard to protect them. The man, although wounded five times, was tied to a rope behind one of the drays, placed in irons and made to walk to Adelaide.

The whites saw the battle as a triumph. They did not even begin to try to understand that their presence at the Rufus River was the desecration of a region which for tens of thousands of years had been sacred to the Dreamtime hero Nurelli.

The battle for the Lower Darling area was over. During the next five years, although the white protector could boast that 'not a single case of serious injury or aggression ever took place on the part of the natives against the Europeans', Aboriginal people languished. Drunkenness and disease became commonplace. The settlers who moved into the area were, for the most part, inflexible and racist. They killed Aboriginal people in ones and twos to 'teach them a lesson'. They poisoned the flour they gave to Aboriginal people and, when cattle and sheep went missing, they went out on human hunting expeditions.

From 1845 to 1865 the movement was inexorable. The pastoralists followed the explorers into the area. Their advance was greatly assisted by the steamers which plied the Murray and the Darling, bringing supplies to the outback stations and shipping out the produce to the coast. By the time the squatters arrived, the Aboriginal population was cowed and subdued. The explorers, the overlanders and the troops had 'pacified' the whole area. Aboriginal people no longer had the heart to fight back.

The squatters and pastoralists developed a powerful hold over the Aboriginal people who had survived the diseases and the massacres. Life around the Darling River was hard. It was, at best, marginal pastoral land. The average rainfall rarely exceeded 250 millimetres and the characteristic vegetation was low scrub and hardy grasses. The pastoralists had trouble attracting white labour to the area and so a kind of mutual dependency developed between the local Aboriginal population and the station owners. The arrival of sheep and cattle ensured that the area's very precarious ecology was destroyed. Aboriginal people were forced to rely on white handouts which they saw as a kind of meagre compensation for the use of their tribal lands.

The pastoralists began to employ Aboriginal men as shepherds and stockmen. The men proved reliable and their knowledge of the local area was an invaluable asset.

The need for survival played havoc with traditional Aboriginal life. An entire family group would move into a station. This meant instant dependence on the station owner and this dependence caused problems because transport in the area was unreliable and costly. The station owner was at the mercy of erratic food deliveries. If the bullock team did not arrive with supplies of flour and tea the Aboriginal people, unable to survive on the ever diminishing native fauna and dependent upon the station owner's generosity, simply starved.

Major Mitchell was convinced that a corroboree, held on the banks of the Murray River on 26 May 1836, was a prelude to an attack.

The change in diet also had disastrous consequences. It is now widely recognised that while massacres killed large numbers of Aboriginal people, disease and starvation induced by the substandard European diet caused many more deaths.

As 'civilisation' arrived on the Darling River it became accepted that Aboriginal people were there to be exploited. Each new group developed different modes of exploitation. The men who wandered through the area, moving restlessly from one goldfield to another, exploited the women and persuaded the Aboriginal shepherds to 'sell' the sheep. The contractors who opened up the Murray to steamboats paid Aboriginal people with blankets for the work they did removing snags from the river. Pastoralists and squatters paid them meagre allowances to look after the sheep.

By the mid-1850s the rough justice of the native police came to the Darling River. In a series of confrontations, which they conveniently failed to report, the native police killed dozens of Aboriginal people (the figure may have reached into the hundreds) and opened up the frontier so that new settlers could move in.

The true scale of the killings along the Upper Darling between Menindee and Wilcannia can only be guessed at. Like so much of the killing on the frontiers, it was never reported. Like so much casual slaughter, in a few generations it faded from white memory. All that is left are incomplete references which hint at the slaughter — a letter to a friend with a passing reference, a report from a missionary, a note scribbled hastily by a settler or an explorer and hidden for over a century in family papers, a skull or some bones dug up by a farmer or exposed by a storm or a flood, a remark obliquely reported by a curious traveller. There is no coherence. The vital pieces have been lost. The jigsaw puzzle will never be completed.

The area was settled by Scots and the Scots, both in Australia and in the USA, had a reputation for both racism and brutality. They protected their land with a dour meanness which was notable only for its intolerance and inflexibility.

Through the memories blurred by time we hear of a massacre at Mount Murchison, of settlers shooting Aboriginal people like dogs, of one family shooting at some Aboriginal people who were committing no greater crime than swimming in the river, of a widely held belief that shooting was quicker and easier than capture, of poisoned flour being an effective way of reducing the Aboriginal population who were dependent on station food, and of skulls being found along the riverbank with bullet holes clearly indicating how they had died.

By the 1860s the area had been conquered. The settler Simpson Newland of the Marra station has left a melancholy image of the way the Aboriginal people were repressed and destroyed. In his journals he describes a tribal elder named Barpoo who refused even to talk with the hated white man:

> . . . much less work for him, wear his clothes, or even eat his food . . . On the few occasions we met, the proud savage took not the slightest notice of the stranger other than the Aboriginal's silent sign of aversion, spitting on the ground as he passed him. More he dared not do — scarcely that much as time went on, for the whip might find even his sacred shoulders . . . What he must have felt when he saw the detested interloper take possession of all his country after slaughtering many of his people in their vain attempts at resistance . . . then later to see them wither and die. There was clearly nothing left for him but to die too, and die cursing the white man.

CHAPTER 6

MAJOR NUNN'S CAMPAIGN — 1838

There are a thousand Blacks there, and if they are not stopped, we may have them presently within the boundaries.

Lieutenant-Colonel Snodgrass's instructions to Major Nunn

There was no law and no morality on the frontier. It was a shifting territorial cliché where men were men, life was tough, loneliness was normal, and fortunes were carved out of the virgin bush with bare hands.

Truth and cliché were indivisible. The men who pushed at the edges of white settlement were, for the most part, simple and hardworking. They came from lowly origins. Often some petty crime had given them free passage to Sydney. Those who arrived as free settlers were not so much entrepreneurs seeking new lands to conquer as they were people who had absolutely nothing to lose. They were hardworking, hard living men, unencumbered by women and families. Many were social misfits seeking to distance themselves from easiness and security.

At first they clung to the edges of the Sydney basin. The settlements at Sydney Cove and Parramatta were never more than a day's ride away. It was easy to get supplies. If a convict labourer escaped into the bush, more were available. If the local Aboriginal population became difficult, help was never very far away. Then the explorers pushed beyond the rims of the basin, moving north and south along the coast and, after crossing the Blue Mountains, fanning out across the slopes and the tablelands beyond the Great Dividing Range. They searched for fertile valleys and grass plains where livestock could be grazed. They returned to Sydney with stories of rivers and valleys and plains so fertile that men with little farming experience sold up in Sydney and headed west.

The river systems to the north, the Gwydir, Macintyre, Barwon and Namoi, attracted a different kind of settler. For the most part, the men who loaded flour and tea and axes, picks and shovels on to bullock drays and headed north-west from Sydney were true Australians. They were second-generation locals who had been born on the rural fringes of Sydney; sons of Hawkesbury River farmers, sons of the small holding who had been raised in a tent or a crude wood-and-bark hut. They were very short on book learning but they had learnt the skills of bushcraft from birth. They knew the hardships of the bush.

These pioneers had very clear and uncomplicated ideas about Aboriginal people. They had witnessed the 'battles' between their fathers and the Hawkesbury tribes. Most had been raised to accept the assumption that Aboriginal people were the lowest form of life. 'How is it that the abject animal state in which the Aborigines live should place them at the very zero of civilisation, constituting in a measure the connecting link between man and the monkey tribe — for really some of the old women only seem to require a tail to complete their identity,' asked Peter Cunningham, an early settler in the Hunter Valley. 'They are a filthy disagreeable race of people; nor is it my opinion that any measures that could be adopted would ever make them otherwise,' observed another settler.

Under no circumstances were Aboriginal people to be trusted. They were, according to the precepts of frontier society, known for their ability to steal, lie, cheat, deceive, kill stray animals, harass settlers and aggravate peace-keeping farmers who were trying to lead a quiet, hardworking life. They never even began to see things from the Aboriginal viewpoint. They didn't see their settlement of the land as dispossession. They didn't see their rape of Aboriginal women as a crime. They didn't see the killing of possums and kangaroos as theft. The law of the frontier, although it wasn't the law of Parramatta or Sydney Town, was not a law which needed to be questioned or challenged.

So it was that these young, hardy bushmen rode north and settled the rich valleys of the Namoi and the Gwydir. There was Archibald Bell with his holdings at Manilla, Barrabah and Bengari. There was Thomas Simpson Hall at Wee Bella Bolla and Bingara. There was John Fleming at Mundie Bundie and George Bowmen at Terri Hie Hie. There was Andrew Eaton at Biniguy and Cobbadah, and John Cobb on the massacre site he named Gravesend with macabre humour. There was James Cox at Moree and the stockyards of John Crawford at Ardgowan Plains.

By the late 1830s all the prime grazing sites along the two river systems had been taken. The young graziers brought convict shepherds and workmen with them. They fenced off some of the land, built rude, clay-floored huts, survived on damper and boiled meat, and bartered a sheep or a tomahawk for an Aboriginal woman when their sexual impulses became unbearable.

The Aboriginal communities in the area — the Kwaimbul, Weraerai and Kamilaroi — responded to the arrival of the whites with remarkable flexibility. The whites who respected Aboriginal people were, in turn, respected. The whites who carried with them the baggage of nineteenth-century cynicism and brutishness inevitably attracted reprisals and the killing of livestock. It is ironic that the Aboriginal people, the so-called primitives, learnt to discriminate while the whites tended

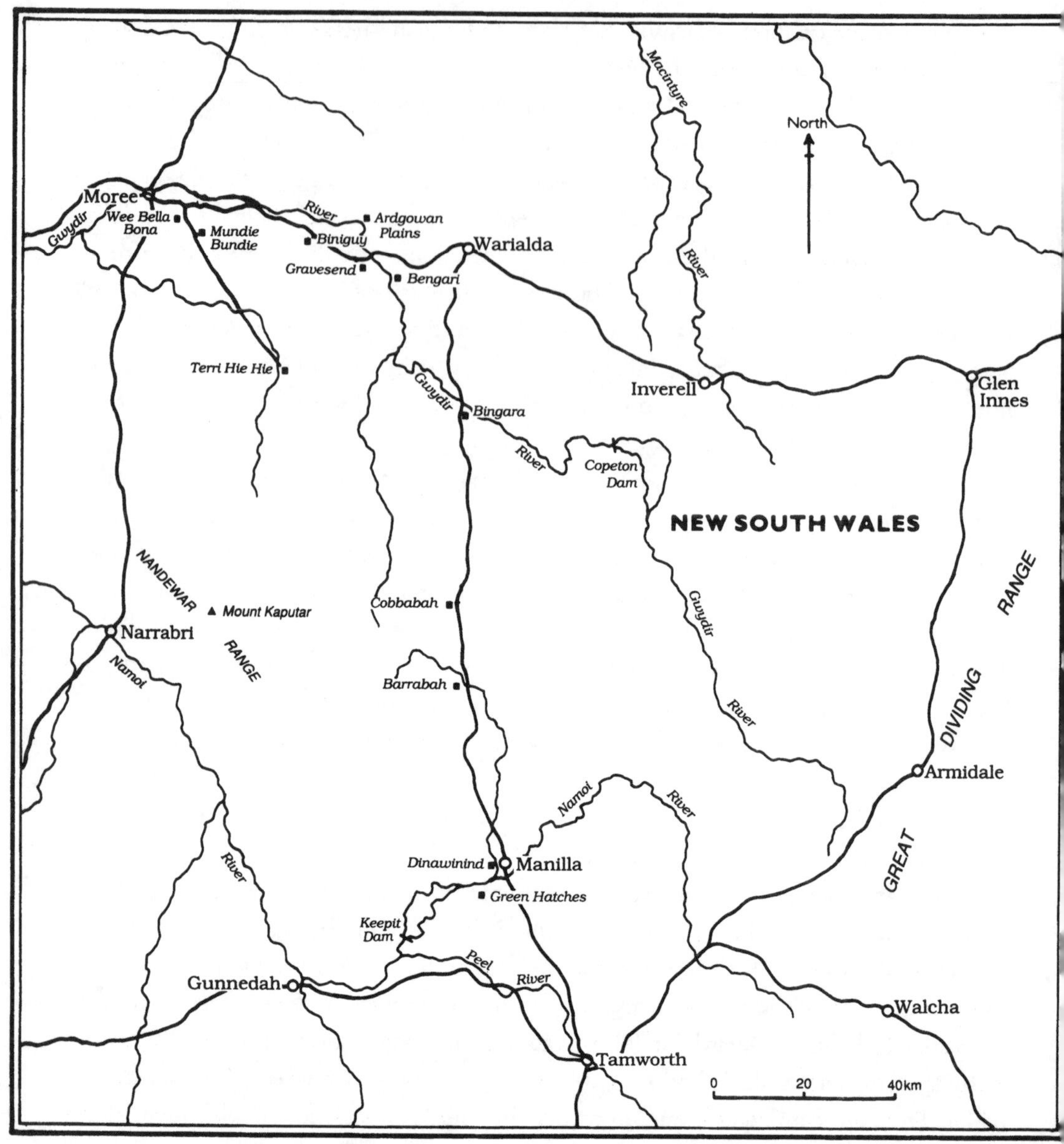

North-western New South Wales, scene of Major Nunn's campaign.

to see all Aboriginal people as one amorphous band of troublemakers.

It was inevitable that conflict would occur. By 1836 the area was supporting about four thousand Aboriginal people, as well as over twenty well-stocked cattle and sheep runs. At first the conflict was the usual low-level frontier confrontation — a black shot here, a shepherd speared there; a woman raped, a sheep speared; cattle and sheep rushed, blue pellets of arsenic in the damper.

The settlers were always on the alert for trouble and they acted with speed and viciousness. Throughout 1836 and 1837 the frontier skirmishes reached a level which the settlers found unacceptable. They felt that too much effort was being expended in removing Aboriginal people from the land; the settlers were constantly seeking new runs and Aboriginal people were constantly resisting.

In April 1836 Thomas Hall, who was already established at Barraba, decided to move some cattle north to the Gwydir River. During the journey his Aboriginal guide became nervous as the cattle moved into an area inhabited by a reputedly 'wild tribe' of Kamilaroi. Hall was furious at what he saw as the guide's cowardice and fired buckshot at him, discharging 'small shot in the Buttocks of the Black!' The guide responded to the attack by rushing off into the bush where he met and joined the Kamilaroi. Hearing of Hall's treatment of the guide the Kamilaroi attacked the party, killing one stockman, rushing the cattle and wounding Hall. Hall was forced to abandon his plans and retreat.

In July Hall formed a posse to avenge his humiliation. Accompanied by a number of local squatters, some stockmen and farmhands, and a contingent of mounted police from Jerrys Plains, he returned to the area determined to teach the Kamilaroi a lesson. In a two-week period the posse hunted and shot a large number of Aboriginal people. They returned to Barraba victorious. An estimated eighty Aboriginal people were killed.

In September, convinced that the Kamilaroi resistance had been quashed, Hall and others sent cattle and sheep over the ranges and a number of runs were established on the Gwydir plains. For the next year life along the Gwydir was quiet. The Aboriginal communities accepted the inevitability of their unhappy circumstances and the white settlers, having forced peace upon the area, felt no need to exacerbate the situation.

The problems really started the following September, in the spring of 1837. The Aboriginal population of the region had been accustomed to a highly structured annual cycle whereby they varied their living and hunting locations according to the seasons. They moved away from the river valley in winter to hunt possums and wallabies in the mountains. In the spring they moved back to the river where the eggs from nesting birds, the wildfowl in the marshes, and various shellfish which could be collected from the lagoons and billabongs, offered a rich variety of delicacies. That year when they returned to the Gwydir Valley the Aboriginal people immediately observed the havoc which white grazing had wreaked on the delicately balanced ecology. Drought and overstocking had ruined the marshy banks of the river. The cattle had polluted the water. The reeds which had been home to the wildfowl had been trampled by cattle grazing at the water's edge.

The stockmen, shepherds and hutkeepers made few concessions to Aboriginal people. When a group settled beside the river, they were hunted off lest they interfere with the cattle or the dwindling supply of water. When Aboriginal people came to a hut or station seeking flour or tea or beef, they were sent away empty-handed. When they asked for recompense for sexual favours, they were laughingly dismissed. The whites should have realised that the Aboriginal population, driven by hunger and anger, would retaliate. Their ignorance had its own reward.

At Terri Hie Hie, when a request for recompense for the sexual favours provided by a Kamilaroi woman was ignored, a large number of cattle were speared and two shepherds were killed. Predictably the whites formed a posse and rampaged through the surrounding country killing indiscriminately. A number of Aboriginal people were killed on Crawford's Ardgowan Plains property. Again, no-one bothered to record the actual numbers killed.

The Aboriginal population retaliated in the only way possible: they moved up the Gwydir River rushing sheep and cattle, living off animals which they speared and, when they reached John Cobb's property, Gravesend, they killed two more shepherds. Now numbering well over one hundred, the Aboriginal people crossed the Nandewar Range and began a process of harassment in the lower Namoi River valley, spearing cattle and intimidating isolated whites. Once again a mounted posse retaliated and once again a large, but unrecorded, number of Aboriginal people were killed.

Although the attacks on both sides were on a small scale, the frontier along the Gwydir and Namoi was on permanent alert and a quasi-war was being waged with considerable antagonism on both sides. By November the local white landholders were demanding military protection. Letters were sent to Sydney requesting a strong military presence. The newly appointed Crown Land Commissioner, Alexander Paterson, wrote to Sydney declaring that the area had no protection and the Aboriginal population were behaving in an outrageous manner. Wealthy landowners in the area, who it was suspected were encouraging their men to go on Aboriginal hunting expeditions, publicly dissociated themselves from the actions of their employees while calling upon the government for assistance. One landowner, James Glennie, actually blamed Aboriginal violence on the excessive kindness and humanity of the local

Conflict between Aboriginal people and whites was inevitable. When Aboriginal people attacked sheep, whites replied with rape, poison and musket fire.

stockmen. Another landowner, Robert Scott, claimed that the fault lay with the stockmen and shepherds, who he described as 'unprincipled men'. He explained to the governor that these men 'proceed to lengths which would probably be found unnecessary and avoided by responsible and unprejudiced persons'.

Their complaints fell on sympathetic ears. From 6 December 1837 to 23 February 1838 the colony was under the administration of Lieutenant-Colonel Kenneth Snodgrass who, as a landowner at Raymond Terrace on the north coast, was eager to assist troubled property owners. He ordered the Commander of the New South Wales Mounted Police, Major James Nunn, to organise a force and to sort out the problems in the area. 'You are to act according to your own judgement,' he commanded, 'and use your utmost exertion to suppress these outrages. There are a thousand Blacks there, and if they are not stopped, we may have them presently within the boundaries.'

It is ironic that had the letters from the landowners arrived two months later, Governor Gipps would have ignored them. As the governor who confronted the landowners over the Myall Creek massacre he would almost certainly have shown little sympathy towards men who were requesting a government organisation to legitimise their killing.

Major Nunn arrived at Fitzgerald's station, Green Hatches, 40 kilometres north-west of Tamworth on the Upper Namoi, in early 1838. Having reached the frontier, he discarded the propriety of British law and allowed his party of twenty-three mounted police to join a posse made up of local stockmen. Nunn was later to claim that he had joined the posse because a stockman had promised to lead him to the murderer of one of Thomas Hall's shepherds. This explanation was rather hollow. A few days later the posse headed out with the clear intention of rounding up all the Aboriginal people in the area. Over forty strong, all armed and all on horseback, they were a fearsome force.

There was only a hint of light on the eastern horizon when Nunn and his men saddled up and headed down the northern bank of the Namoi. They had received news the previous night that a group of some fifty Aboriginal people were camped about 15 kilometres downstream. Just as the sun was touching the upper branches of the gum trees along the river, the party arrived at a slight embankment above the camp. Below they could see the dying embers of the night fires still glowing and the blue eucalypt smoke wafting through the scrubby riverbank acacias. Nunn was too cautious and military-minded to charge the camp. He signalled to some of his troopers to ford the river upstream and position themselves on the southern bank. No Aboriginal people were to escape.

Nunn insisted that there should be no charge on the camp until the Aboriginal people spotted the posse. The riders moved slowly along the riverbank, all the time edging closer to the camp. Suddenly there was a wild yell of alarm from the

Aboriginal people. The troopers dug their spurs into the flanks of their horses and instantly the air was alive with Aboriginal yells of fear and aggressive whoops from the soldiers. Some Aboriginal people dived into the river; others ran into the scrub. Most huddled by the fires waiting in terror for their unknown fate. The troopers wheeled their horses around. Some galloped through the scrub in search of people trying to escape; others headed for the river. Shots were fired. One trooper charged his horse into the river after the fleeing Aboriginal people.

When the Aboriginal people had all been rounded up, Nunn announced, through an interpreter, that they were all being charged with the murder of white shepherds and the killing of cattle. 'There is,' Nunn continued, 'a way by which these charges can be dropped. If the guilty parties are identified, everyone else can go free.'

What Nunn failed to realise was that the Aboriginal camp had comprised two separate groups. An enterprising man from the 'tame' group, who had been in contact with the whites in the area, immediately accused fifteen men from the 'wild' group. They were, he assured Nunn, all guilty of cattle spearing. To complete the charges he accused an Aboriginal man, nicknamed Doherty — the hapless individual who had fled two years previously after being shot in the buttocks by Thomas Hall — of murder. Nunn accepted this implausible accusation. Doherty was immediately arrested and handcuffed. The 'wild' Aboriginal people were herded together and marched back to Green Hatches as prisoners. Nunn destroyed all the weapons in the camp and told the 'tame' Aboriginal people to be on their way.

Back at Green Hatches, Doherty was shot under questionable circumstances and buried in a hastily dug grave in a nearby paddock. Believing that his threats had taught the 'wild' Aboriginal people a lesson, and confronted by the tyranny of distance, Nunn let his remaining prisoners go.

The next day the posse pushed north across the Nandewar Ranges through Archibald Bell's Barrabah station and on to Thomas Hall's new station, Bingara, on the upper reaches of the Gwydir River. His aim was to catch and rout the local Aboriginal people. At Barrabah Nunn heard that the local Aboriginal people had recently been in the area threatening lives and cattle. He gave chase but he had been outwitted. He followed them into a narrow chasm only to find that they had clambered up the cliff face and were gazing down at him from unassailable parapets. Their laughter and derisory yells echoed across the gorge. Nunn had no alternative but to retreat.

Refusing to admit defeat, Nunn became convinced, after talking to the local stockmen, that the majority of the 'troublesome Aborigines' were moving along the Gwydir River valley. Before leaving Barrabah he added a number of local stockmen to his posse and took provisions to last a fortnight.

Nunn clearly had little understanding of the way Aboriginal resistance worked. All his actions suggest that he expected to engage in some kind of formal battle with a large, well-armed force. Instead of this very British scenario, five days out from Barrabah the posse came upon a single Aboriginal man sleeping under a tree. The terrified man told the posse that the Aboriginal people responsible for the murders were some days away and heading south. They had left the Gwydir valley and were cutting back towards the Namoi across the foothills of the Nandewar Range.

Assisted by two trackers, Nunn and his posse made contact with the group at Snodgrass Lagoon on a creek midway between the Gwydir and the Namoi. This was the moment Nunn had been waiting for. The Aboriginal people were camped beside the creek. Behind them lay a thick scrub of eucalypt and acacia. The creek was between them and Nunn's men. The posse attacked. A number of men, forming a pincer movement, galloped across the creek in an attempt to encircle the camp. Realising what was happening, the Aboriginal men grabbed their spears and rushed for the scrub. As the troopers' horses broke through the bushes, spears were thrown. One trooper was injured in the leg. The Aboriginal people retreated back towards the creek bank. As they came into the clearing the remainder of Nunn's troops, positioned on the opposite bank beyond the reach of spears, opened fire. The troopers in the bush began slashing at the fleeing Aboriginal people with their swords.

The battle, or massacre, was over in ten minutes. Nunn was to claim in his report that only 'a few' Aboriginal people had been killed. It was another frontier cover-up. He knew the humanitarians and do-gooders in Sydney Town would be appalled if the real death toll was revealed. Over the next decade, as the covenant of frontier silence was slowly peeled away, it became clear that 'a few' was, in fact, forty or

Aboriginal people retaliated — they began attacking shepherd's huts in the lower Namoi River valley.

fifty. In 1849 an account of the campaign in the *Sydney Morning Herald* described the deaths in terms of 'shot like crows in the trees'.

Not happy with the massacre, Nunn and his men rampaged back across the foothills for the next three days, killing many Aboriginal people along the way. Nunn was to remain dishonest in his reporting of the killings. Although he was to claim that at one point he had been faced with a force of one thousand Aboriginal people (a highly improbable figure), and although he was to claim that he had solved the 'Aborigine problem' in the area, he was to insist that all his killing could be measured in single figures. The more plausible truth is that, having killed forty or fifty Aboriginal people in a single encounter at Waterloo Creek, Nunn and his men engaged in a typical frontier-style mopping-up operation which meant that any Aboriginal person they came in contact with, they killed.

After the massacre they hunted the survivors through the riverbank scrub, shooting and slashing at them. Those Aboriginal people who tried to swim to freedom were shot midstream. The creek ran with blood. The women who had been at the camp were captured and forced to lead the troopers to other camps where similar massacres occurred. Nunn kept no record. The details and the scale remained imprecise.

After several days Nunn and his party arrived back at John Cobb's Gravesend property to a hero's welcome. Nunn bragged of his conquests. He depicted himself as some kind of swashbuckling Wild West hero; a man who shot to kill and who shot from the hip. Somewhere between the Gwydir and the Namoi Nunn had left the niceties of British law behind him. He had arrived at Gravesend full of swaggering braggadocio. 'Whenever a black popped out from behind a tree,' he declared to his admiring frontier audience, 'I'd reach for my holster pistols and dispose him like this.' And he'd flick his pistols out of their holsters and point them menacingly at his imaginary black enemies.

He was lionised all the way back to Sydney. At Tamworth the employees of the Australian Agricultural Company cheered him. He was told over and over again that he had rid the area of the 'black menace'. By the time he arrived in Sydney his ego had been so well massaged by enthusiastic rural supporters that he had forgotten that a different set of values operated around Port Jackson.

His report of the 'campaign' was full of bloodthirsty heroics. Governor Gipps, who had arrived in Sydney during Nunn's absence, was not amused. The report was his first contact with frontier violence and in Gipps's eyes it showed a vicious disregard for the rule of law. The memory of Nunn's campaign would loom large when Gipps insisted, less than a year later, that the perpetrators of the massacre at Myall Creek be treated as common murderers. Gipps was unambiguous: there was only one law and Aboriginal people and whites were equal in the eyes of that law.

CHAPTER 7

THE MYALL CREEK MASSACRE — 1838

I look on the blacks as a set of monkies, and the earlier they are exterminated from the face of the earth the better. I would never consent to hang a white man for a black one.

A letter in the Australian, *18 December 1838*

In early May 1838 a group of some forty Kwiambal moved south and set up camp on Henry Dangar's Myall Creek station. Already the nights were getting cold. The air was crisp and fresh, the hills around the Gwydir River were smudged with a smoky blue during the warm, dry days and the night skies were so sharp that the stars flickered like precious gems in a setting of sheer black silk.

The stockmen on Dangar's property quickly learnt that the Kwiambal were friendly and gentle. They showed no desire to rush the cattle or spear the sheep. Their traditional foods, possums, which they used for both clothing and sustenance, and fish from the river, were in ready supply and the station hands were happy to supplement this with small gifts of tea, sugar, flour and tobacco. Over the next month relations between the Kwiambal and the workmen on the Myall Creek station developed into an easy live-and-let-live situation which was mutually beneficial.

The station was run by William Hobbs with the assistance of two assigned convicts, both of whom had been transported for life — George Anderson, who was working as a hutkeeper, and Charles Kilmeister, a stockman. The station also had two Aboriginal servants named Davy (Yintayintin) and Billy (Kwimunga) and two hired hands — Charles Reid and Andrew Burrows.

By June relations between the stockmen and the Kwiambal were close. Anderson, the hutkeeper, was occasionally sleeping with a young Kwiambal girl, Impeta. It was common for the stockmen to join the Aboriginal people after work. There was much dancing and singing. Particularly sociable among the Aboriginal people were the huge white-haired man the whites named Daddy and the amusing three-year-old Charlie, who was universally seen as a clever and entertaining child.

Everything was friendly and amicable between the stockmen and the Aboriginal people when, on 5 June, Hobbs decided to move about one hundred head of cattle down river to Ponds Creek. It had been a dry summer. The grass at Myall Creek had been eaten to the ground and Hobbs hoped that there would be more feed on the Ponds Creek run. The plan was simple. Anderson, Kilmeister and Yintayintin would remain on Myall Creek and look after the property, Reid and Burrows would drove the cattle and Hobbs would follow on 7 June and pick up any cattle which had strayed from the main herd.

Burrows and Reid made good progress and on 7 June they spent the night at Bengari, a station owned by Archibald Bell about 60 kilometres south of Myall Creek. At one of the huts on Bengari they met what appeared to be a posse of six men. The group, who were heavily armed with muskets and swords, had been hardened by long gaol sentences in both England and Australia. The apparent leader was John Russell, an emancipated thief who was working as the overseer on Bengari. He was supported by George Palliser, an emancipist who had been transported for robbery. The other four men were all assigned convicts from the Lower Gwydir. There was the black Liverpudlian, John Johnstone; the handsome young Irishman, Ned Foley, who'd been transported for 'assaulting a dwelling'; and two rag-trade men — Charles Toulouse, a one-time glover, and James Hawkins, a draper.

It was clear that the men were planning something. Both Burrows and Reid noticed that they were cleaning their weapons and the talk inevitably turned to Aboriginal people. Casually, Russell asked the two drovers if there were any Aboriginal people living on the Myall Creek property. They replied that there were about twelve women, twelve children and sixteen men. 'How long had they been camped there?' Burrows, eager to protect the Aboriginal people on Myall Creek against even the chance of reprisal, lied and said they had been there for at least the last five

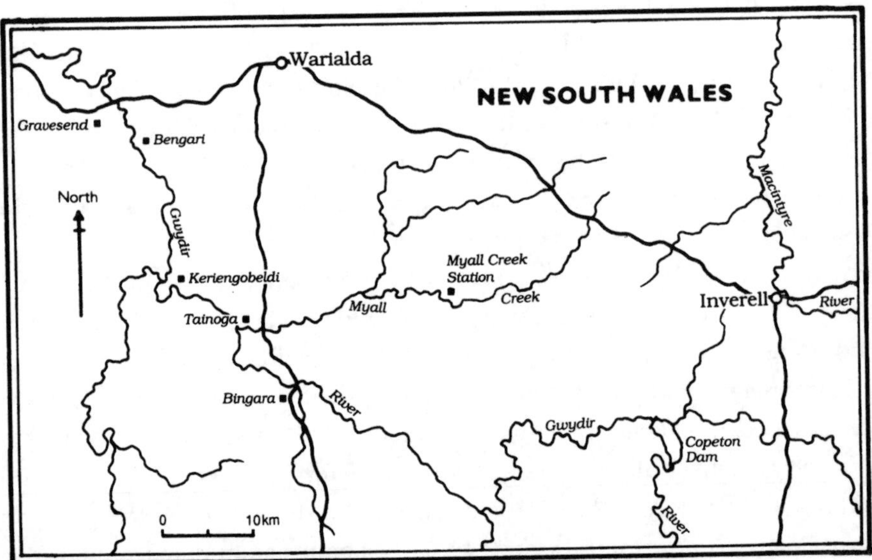

Northern New South Wales, scene of the Myall Creek massacre.

weeks. 'Then,' said one of the men, 'they couldn't be the blacks who caused the trouble down the river.' It seemed to Burrows and Reid that the posse were hunting some Aboriginal people who had been rushing cattle on the various runs on the Lower Gwydir. They never really found out. The conversation moved on. In the morning they departed without ever pursuing the question.

A few hours after they left Bengari they met John Fleming, the manager of the Mungie Bundie station. Unlike the other members of the posse, Fleming had been born in New South Wales and had worked and lived on properties all his life. He talked to Burrows and Reid, told them he had been out hunting Aboriginal people and, on hearing that the posse were only a few hours away, expressed the hope that his horse would be strong enough to catch up.

Over the next twenty-four hours the posse were joined by Fleming, an overseer 'Jem' Lamb, a young man named James Parry and a man named John Blake. By the time they reached Tainoga on the confluence of the Gwydir and Myall Creek they were a formidable and ugly force — ten men on horseback, armed with swords and guns, and ready to kill any Aboriginal people unlucky enough to make contact with them.

On 9 June two men arrived at Henry Dangar's Myall Creek run. They were Thomas Foster, the superintendent on Dr Newton's run at Tainoga, and William Mace from Keriengobeldi, about 10 kilometres downstream from Tainoga. It had been an informal tradition on the Upper Gwydir that station owners who needed short-term help would find a group of Kwiambal and employ them for a few days. Foster and Mace needed some bark cutters. They met with the Kwiambal at Myall Creek and it was agreed that ten men, including the 'leader', whom the whites had dubbed King Sandy, would travel downstream that day.

Later that day the posse, who had travelled up the Gwydir and cut across to Myall Creek, arrived at Dangar's station. They had spent the day hunting Aboriginal people but so far had been unsuccessful. As the horsemen approached the Myall Creek station they divided into two groups and galloped towards Anderson's hut. The noise of the galloping horses filled the evening with a sense of danger and foreboding. The Aboriginal people, fearful of some kind of attack, left their camp and raced to Anderson's hut believing that their white 'friends' would protect them. The intentions of the posse were clear. They reined their horses in and dismounted. Kilmeister, who had been living in the area for some years, went out to meet the men. He knew them and he greeted them in a friendly, relaxed way. Anderson was less enthusiastic. He had only been on Dangar's run for five months. The men were strangers. It was obvious from the swords, pistols and muskets that they carried, and from the terror of the Kwiambal, that the posse were bent on revenge and murder.

As he talked to Kilmeister, John Russell unhitched a long tether rope and began to untie it. With the Kwiambal huddling behind him, Anderson asked Russell what he was planning. Russell indicated that he was going to tie all of the Aboriginal people up and take them away. 'We're going to take them over the back of the range to frighten them,' he said ambiguously. Russell and Lamb then pushed their way past Anderson and went into the hut. The Kwiambal, anticipating their fate, began weeping and wailing and crying. Ned Foley stood in the hut doorway. His gun was drawn. He was determined that no-one should escape. Anderson felt the overwhelming frustration of helplessness. The plaintive voices in the hut were calling out for his help. What could he do against ten armed men? The voices inside the hut also called to their 'friend' Kilmeister to save them. Kilmeister stood by indifferent to the fate of the people who only the previous night he had sung and danced with.

Anderson became more and more agitated. He liked the Kwiambal. He had not been corrupted by the jaundiced view of Aboriginal people which prevailed on the frontier. He was, in his own strange way, emotionally committed to Impeta and his attitude was that the Kwiambal were people, not pests.

The men in the posse were worried about Anderson. He looked at them with a mixture of disdain, fear and horror. He touched their consciences at a time when they didn't want any 'moral' interference. They sent him off to get some milk. When he returned, he was confronted by a miserable pathetic line of Kwiambal, all roped together and weeping uncontrollably. There was the giant figure of Daddy with tears

This photo gives a unique view of the life of the early settler — the simple hut, the crude fences, the Aboriginal woman for sexual purposes, and the group of Aboriginal men as casual labour.

In May 1838, a group of forty Kwaimbal set up camp on Myall Creek station. They often visited the stockmen's huts in the evening.

streaming down his face. There were women with their babies wrapped in possum coats. There were people looking bewildered and trying to understand what was happening. Little Charlie, the three-year-old who had been a favourite with the stockmen, ran behind trying to catch up with his mother.

Only five were to escape. A woman was left behind for Yintayintin. Another, not Impeta, was left to appease Anderson. She was left, as Russell later admitted, 'because she was good looking'. Anderson managed to keep a child in his hut and later two young boys appeared who, upon hearing the galloping horses, had hidden in the creek.

The sun had set and the cold night air was rising from the creek as Anderson watched the hapless group make their way slowly towards the hills. Kilmeister hastily saddled his horse, grabbed his pistol and a sword, and galloped off to join the men. A few minutes later the Kwiambal prisoners, flanked on every side by stockmen, disappeared from sight. About twenty minutes later, the forlorn watchers at the hut heard two shots. Then silence and darkness fell upon the valley.

Yintayintin was determined to see what had happened. He followed the party at a safe distance. The moon came out and swathed the bush in a ghostly light. A couple of kilometres from the hut was a newly built stockyard. As he approached it, he was confronted by a gruesome sight. Near the stockyard was a pile of twenty-eight bodies lying in a lake of blood. It seemed that the murderers, not wanting to waste ammunition, had drawn their swords and cut the Kwiambal to pieces. They had decapitated most of the babies and children. Heads had been hurled far from the bodies. One man had been burnt to death. Sickened by what he saw, and terrified that the same fate may be his, he fled. Arriving back at the hut, he blurted out the news to Anderson.

A few hours later the Kwiambal who had been bark cutting with Foster and Mace returned to Myall Creek. News of the posse had spread quickly through the area. They had rushed back to their families in an attempt to avert disaster. Sensible to the possible dangers which awaited them, the ten bark cutters approached Anderson's hut cautiously. They had already established that their own camp was deserted. Their cooees carefully melted into the night sounds. Anderson, by now completely terrified, clutched his blankets and refused to leave the hut. The women, recognising the voices of the men, called back. The men were out of breath. They had run all the way back from Tainoga. They stood gasping and sobbing as Yintayintin, Anderson and the two women poured out the details of the massacre. Their first thought was to go straight to the stockyards and bury the members of their family. Wisely, both Yintayintin and Anderson persuaded the men to take the women and the three children and seek refuge on Andrew Eaton's run on the Macintyre River, about 40 kilometres to the east.

The murderers had not finished their work. They had kept one of the attractive young Kwiambal women alive. She had been forced to stand by and watch as twenty-eight members of her kin were killed — shot, decapitated and stabbed. After the killing the men turned on her and, with the blood of her family on their hands, they raped her over and over again.

On Monday morning they rode back down the Myall Creek to Tainoga searching for the ten Kwiambal bark cutters. They confronted Thomas Foster and demanded the whereabouts of the cutters. Foster, who had accurately guessed what they had been up to, refused to tell them anything. He noticed the bruised and abused Kwiambal girl in their midst. He also noted Charlie Kilmeister and, recalling his previous friendliness towards the Aboriginal people, gazed at him and disdainfully asked, 'Well, Kilmeister, are you after the blacks?' Kilmeister had no reply. To cover his guilt, and to rationalise his position before his angry inquisitor, he declared that the Kwiambal had rushed his cattle. Foster knew it was a lie. His withering look was unambiguous.

The posse were not deterred by disapproval. They felt that, according to the non-laws of the frontier, their actions were justified. They saw themselves as heroes — not as murderers.

They left Tainoga and rode to Keriengobeldi where they boasted of the massacre.

They were relaxed about their killings. Over breakfast with John Bates, a hutkeeper on the station, they quickly forgot the massacre and started comparing horses, boasting about their horsemanship and generally ranging across a number of subjects as though the massacre of the previous night was unimportant.

After breakfast they rode back to Anderson's hut on the Myall Creek run. They were still looking for the ten cutters. Back in what they regarded as safe territory, the posse began to talk about the massacre. They were all proud of their killings. They compared notes, boasted of their bravery and worked out plans regarding the bodies. Anderson listened to them with a mixture of horror and disgust. He heard them boasting about the woman they had raped. Somewhere between Keriengobeldi and Myall Creek they had disposed of her. Anderson wondered whether she had been Impeta.

The men rose early on Tuesday morning and, after breakfasting with Anderson, rode across to the stockyard. It seemed that the enormity of their crime was beginning to register with them. Guilt can insinuate itself with potency and persistence into the most hardened and confident of minds. Even these men, all of them ex-convicts and most of them outwardly proud that they had 'settled the blacks', could not escape the moral consequences of their actions. They were haunted and possessed. Three of them took sticks from Anderson's fire. They looked at Anderson and suddenly saw his fear as wrathful judgement. 'You stay with him. Keep him out of the way,' Russell said to Ned Foley.

Leaving Foley and Anderson behind, they rode off. They collected logs and branches, bracken and leaves, and piled them against the rotting bodies. Soon Foley, who had been showing his bloodied sword to Anderson in a mock-heroic-threatening way, noticed a dull pall as smoke rose from the various pyres.

Once the fire was alight they returned to the hut. Kilmeister was ordered to stay behind and tend the pyre until the bodies were reduced to ashes. The other men, driven by an impossible and irrational need to kill the remaining Kwiambal, forced Kwimunga to tell them where they had fled to.

The bark cutters had arrived at Eaton's station on Monday night. He had fed them and sheltered them but he knew that he was powerless against Russell's band. When, on Wednesday morning, the sound of the posse was heard in the Macintyre Valley, Eaton sent the Kwiambal into the hills. It was all he could do. The Kwiambal fled. The posse hunted them down. A child was shot. The two women were recaptured. Three of the men were shot. The other seven men, including King Sandy, managed to escape into the bush. By Thursday the massacre was over. The posse broke up and the men, including Kilmeister, headed back to the various runs and stations on which they were employed.

Word and rumour travel quickly in the bush. No-one quite understands the process but in a matter of hours a news item can travel hundreds of kilometres. By

14 June, having delivered the stock to Henry Dangar's Lower Gwydir run, William Hobbs had heard of the massacre on the land he oversaw. He didn't know the details. The story was imprecise. But he did know that a lot of Aboriginal people had been killed.

Hobbs arrived back on the Myall Creek run shortly after noon the following day. He rode immediately to the place where the Kwiambal had been camped. He knew instantly that something was wrong. The camp was still there — the clothing, the blankets, the nets, the trinkets, the stores — but the Kwiambal had vanished. He returned to the station where Anderson and Yintayintin met him. Hobbs was blunt with them. He told them that he knew of the massacre. He then started, in his coldly relentless way, to cross-examine them. He was dragging the details out, building up the gruesome picture, when Kilmeister, fresh from the killings on the Macintyre, arrived back.

Hobbs looked at him. 'I know,' he said in a slow, measured voice and choosing his emphasis carefully, 'they were murdered. I know all about it.' He started to question Kilmeister. Hobbs was the overseer, the employer, and he wanted to know the truth. He wanted to know why a hired hand, an assigned convict, had left the property when he had quite explicitly been instructed to help mind the run. Kilmeister protested, claiming that he had been looking for stray cattle. It was a transparent lie and Hobbs was not fooled.

Later that afternoon Yintayintin, who had abandoned all pretence at lying, took Hobbs to the stockyard. As they moved up the ridge Hobbs discerned the footmarks of the Aboriginal people and the hoofmarks made by the posse's horses. As they moved around the ridge towards the stockyard they came upon the scene of the massacre. It was, as Hobbs was later to describe it, horrible beyond description. The fires had been only partially successful. Spread around the stockyard were piles of half-burned bodies. The stench of death and decay was overwhelming. Daddy was nothing more than a torso. His head, legs and arms had all been cut off. All the children had been decapitated and their heads tossed away in a frenzy of blood-lust. The ground was caked hard with dark pools of coagulated blood. The sound of flies and insects filled the air. Overhead crows and hawks, disturbed by the arrival of the men, circled lazily, waiting to return to the bodies.

Hobbs attempted to count the bodies but decapitation and dismemberment made the task an impossibility. He counted twenty-eight bodies before the stench and the awfulness of the place sent him reeling away to vomit in the bush. He returned to the station determined that the massacre would not go unreported. He called Anderson and Kilmeister and began to question them again. He was certain that Kilmeister had been involved in the murders but, though he accused him directly, Kilmeister denied all involvement.

That night Foster visited Hobbs. They talked about the massacre and decided that

Supposedly a photograph of Kwaimbal men, the caption 'Myall Aborigines' was often used to distinguish between 'wild' and urbanised Aboriginal people.

Dangar should be informed. The next morning the two men rode across to the stockyards. They gazed at the carnage until Foster could stand no more.

In the days that followed the massacre preyed on Hobbs's conscience. He did not know what to do. He vacillated between silence and outrage. He wrote a letter to Henry Dangar but did not send it. He tried to confirm Kilmeister's claim that the cattle had been killed but even though he scoured the run he could find neither skeletons nor carcasses. He repeatedly quizzed Kilmeister who repeatedly protested his innocence. Anderson claimed that he knew none of the men.

Eventually Hobbs's conscience overwhelmed all other considerations and he wrote letters outlining what he knew of the massacre to Edward Denny Day, the police magistrate at Muswellbrook, and to his boss, Henry Dangar. The letter sent to Day was duly reported to the Colonial Secretary who, in turn, brought it to the attention of Governor Gipps.

Gipps saw himself as the moral arbiter in New South Wales. He stood, as his office demanded of him, as the bastion of British law and morality in a community which had little respect for such precepts. He decided that the events of Myall Creek were an opportunity to reassert British law on the lawless frontier. He ordered Day to investigate the massacre with a view to prosecution.

On 28 July, six weeks after the massacre, Day, accompanied by a trooper, arrived at Myall Creek. Hobbs and Kilmeister were repairing a fence as the two men approached. Kilmeister blanched and began to tremble. 'Why are you frightened?' queried Hobbs, 'You say you're innocent.' Kilmeister looked at him despairingly. 'It's enough to make anyone frightened,' he protested. 'I could be sent back into government service. I don't like the police. Never have.'

Day was made welcome by Hobbs. Kilmeister quietly moved away. When he felt they were not noticing, he fled to Anderson. 'For God's sake,' he pleaded. 'Mind what you say. Don't say I went with them. Say I left a quarter of an hour later.'

For all his fear Kilmeister could not escape. That afternoon Hobbs took Day to the ridge. Hobbs had not revisited the scene since he had taken Foster there in mid-June. He noticed that things had changed considerably. The ground looked as though it had been swept and most of the bones removed. It was only when they raked through the ashes that the three men managed to find a jaw bone and the bone of a child. It was obvious that someone had been trying to remove the evidence.

Over the next seven weeks Day, in the slow, methodical and thorough way of a police magistrate, began to accumulate evidence. Carefully he pieced the puzzle together. In the end he had a detailed account of the massacre from George Anderson and he had eleven men whom he charged with murder — Charles Kilmeister, John Russell, George Palliser, John Johnstone, Edward 'Ned' Foley, Charles Toulouse, James Hawkins, John Blake, Charles 'Jem' Lamb, James Parry and James Oates.

Public opinion, and private opinion, on the Gwydir strongly disapproved of what Hobbs had set in motion. Henry Dangar, although he publicly declared 'You can depend on Hobbs and everything he says', immediately informed Hobbs that his term of employment would not be renewed after October. Day, realising the public animosity, took Anderson to Sydney to protect him from local reprisals.

The arrival of the murderers in Sydney brought frontier lawlessness face to face with the precise and pedantic British rule of law. It immediately exposed the hypocrisy which underpinned the fragile assumptions of the system. The theorists could protest that under British law both blacks and whites were equal. The reality was that, with a disturbing unanimity, the citizens of New South Wales agreed that no white man, not even an assigned convict, should be tried for the murder of a black. Such was the public antagonism to the arrests that public committees were formed to raise money to defend the prisoners.

The men were tried at the Supreme Court in Sydney on 15 November 1838. The central charge was the murder of Daddy. Evidence of the massacre and the guilt of the men seemed so overwhelming that the chief justice, in summing up the case against the men, told the jury:

> It is clear that the most grievous offence has been committed; that the lives of nearly thirty of our fellow creatures have been sacrificed, and in order to fulfil my duty I must tell you that the life of a black

> is as precious and valuable in the eye of the law, as that of the highest noble in the land.

The jury listened but the weight of public opinion overwhelmed the Chief Justice's logic. It took them only fifteen minutes to consider that all the eleven men were

The Myall Creek massacre, as published in The Chronicles of Crime or the New Newgate Calendar *in London on 1841.*

not guilty. The court burst into loud applause. Frontier law had overwhelmed British justice. The jury had implicitly endorsed the indiscriminate killing of blacks.

Then, to the amazement of everyone in the court, it was announced that the eleven men would be held in custody and re-tried using the same evidence. The public was outraged. Gipps was reviled. Newspapers called for the release of the prisoners. On 27 November a second trial was held. This time only seven of the men — Kilmeister, Russell, Foley, Oates, Johnstone, Parry and Hawkins — were charged with murder. The jury returned a verdict of 'guilty on the first five counts, of the murder of a child unknown'.

On 7 December Governor Gipps, after lengthy consultations, agreed with the verdict and sentenced the men to death. They were to hang.

Before their execution the men confessed to their crime. Their defence of their actions, a pitiful plea on their part, was that, because killing Aboriginal people was a common frontier sport, they did not realise that it was illegal. They certainly did not realise that it carried the death penalty. It had never occurred to these men, brutalised by the values of the society in which they lived, that the real rule of law actually existed. They were victims of their society; a society which suffered ethical schizophrenia. Laws were bent into fantastic shapes by expediency and a class-ridden autocracy.

They were hanged on 18 December. The repercussions of their executions reverberated up and down the frontier for the next fifty years. Myall Creek may have been British justice vindicated but it was also a warning to all squatters and frontiersmen.

The government hoped that the lesson was 'Don't kill Aboriginal people'. The message received on the frontier was translated as 'If you kill Aboriginal people don't, under any circumstances, let the authorities know.' The result of the trial and the executions was that nearly all further massacres in New South Wales went unrecorded and, as recorded in one Sydney newspaper, the whites turned to more devious means of ridding themselves of the 'black menace'.

> 'Have they hanged the men?' asked the countryman.
> 'Yes,' replied the city citizen.
> 'It's a damned shame,' went on the countryman. 'However, we have a safer technique in our part of the country.'
> 'Indeed,' said the city citizen curiously. 'What is that?'
> 'Oh!' replied the countryman with sly enthusiasm, 'We poison them and have done so to a good many already. Serves them right, too.'

Thus the history of thousands of Aboriginal people was determined, in part, as a result of the Myall Creek massacre. A new, unwritten law emerged: death by stealth.

CHAPTER 8

MASSACRES IN A COASTAL PARADISE — 1830S AND 1840S

'A lot of them were shot. It's a pity they didn't shoot all the bastards,'

The wife of a grazier in the Three Rivers district

Imagine this:

> The alluvial banks of the river and its tributary creeks (now bare) were then covered to the water's edge with dense brush, characterised by an extraordinary luxuriance and denseness of growth, a great diversity of species, and an almost tropical aspect, most of the trees being of lofty and fine proportions, with an abundant undergrowth of tree and other ferns, and clothed and adorned above with an almost infinite variety of beautiful mosses, orchids' climbers twiners and creepers; some of the huge fig trees being literally draped with ivy, and intermixed here and there with graceful, feathery-fronded palms, some of which attain a height of over one hundred feet, the whole with the river and creek running between forming glorious winding avenues, and open vistas of surpassing beauty.
>
> Nor were there only scenes of floral beauty, but of animation of life and sound, for these jungle forests were literally alive with birds — some of them of great beauty — of pigeons of many kinds — some of them with rich plumage — besides doves, Regent birds, Dragoon birds and Lyre birds and a host of others now very rarely seen.
>
> The water was also teeming with aquatic birds, with swans, ducks, Teal, shags, divers and Pellicans; while the reeds and other cover, as well as the trees, which adorned the banks, revealed the Red-Bill, Nankeen birds and Water-hen. The White-headed Eagle, and the Osprey (the latter now very rarely seen) with many hundreds of

> cranes, some of them snow-white, were also often to be seen quietly perched in some neighbouring trees, or fishing in the water. The water itself was literally swarming with fish of all kinds . . .
>
> Nor was this all, for the Blacks — then in considerable numbers — were often to be seen in their little bark canoes, moving slowly along which added considerably to the picturesqueness of the scene, usually one man in each canoe standing with a long slender pole in hand, plying it with alternative strokes on either side, his lubra, generally with her picaninny, squatting behind him before a little smouldering fire on the bottom of the canoe resting on a protecting basement of clay; both of them with eyes intent upon the water, when if a shoal of fish was approaching, the man with catlike stealth and motions would, stooping and crouching, reach for his (usually) five pronged spear and, with eager eyes intent upon his prey, suddenly launch it . . .
>
> I must also speak of the countless flocks of beautiful parrots to be seen or heard in those days — constantly passing with a rush, or joyously screaming while busily engaged gathering honey from the flowers of the forest trees, the wedge-tailed eagle soaring far above us in the heavens . . . large flocks of pigeons in dense vine-draped bush, and at night thousands of flying foxes on the wing . . . the sparkle of innumerable fireflies, while the voice of the More-pork, the scream of the curlew, the screech of the 'possums, the howl of the dingoes, and the croaking of frogs in chorus, with at times the mirthful shouting of the poor Blacks heard from their distant camps — then unsuspicious and in happy ignorance of their future.

This idyllic vision of the mid-north coast of New South Wales (quoted in Geoffrey Blomfield's *Baal Belbora: The End of the Dancing*) is from Augustus Rudder's article 'Sixty Years a Settler' which was published in the *Town and Country Journal* in January 1902. It sets the scene for the massacres which took place in this region. The world that Rudder was describing was a world which was enjoyed by most Aborigines along the East Coast of Australia. The weather was, for most of the year, warm and pleasant. The basic necessities of life — fish, berries, nuts, small animals, shelter, the full array of bush food — were in such rich supply that life was easy. There were rarely arguments because everything was in such abundance. Then Europeans entered this rural paradise where the three rivers — later to be named the Hastings, the Macleay and the Manning — cascaded over the steep mountains of the Great Dividing Range and made their way towards the Pacific Ocean, only slowing briefly to meander across the narrow coastal floodplains for thirty or forty kilometres.

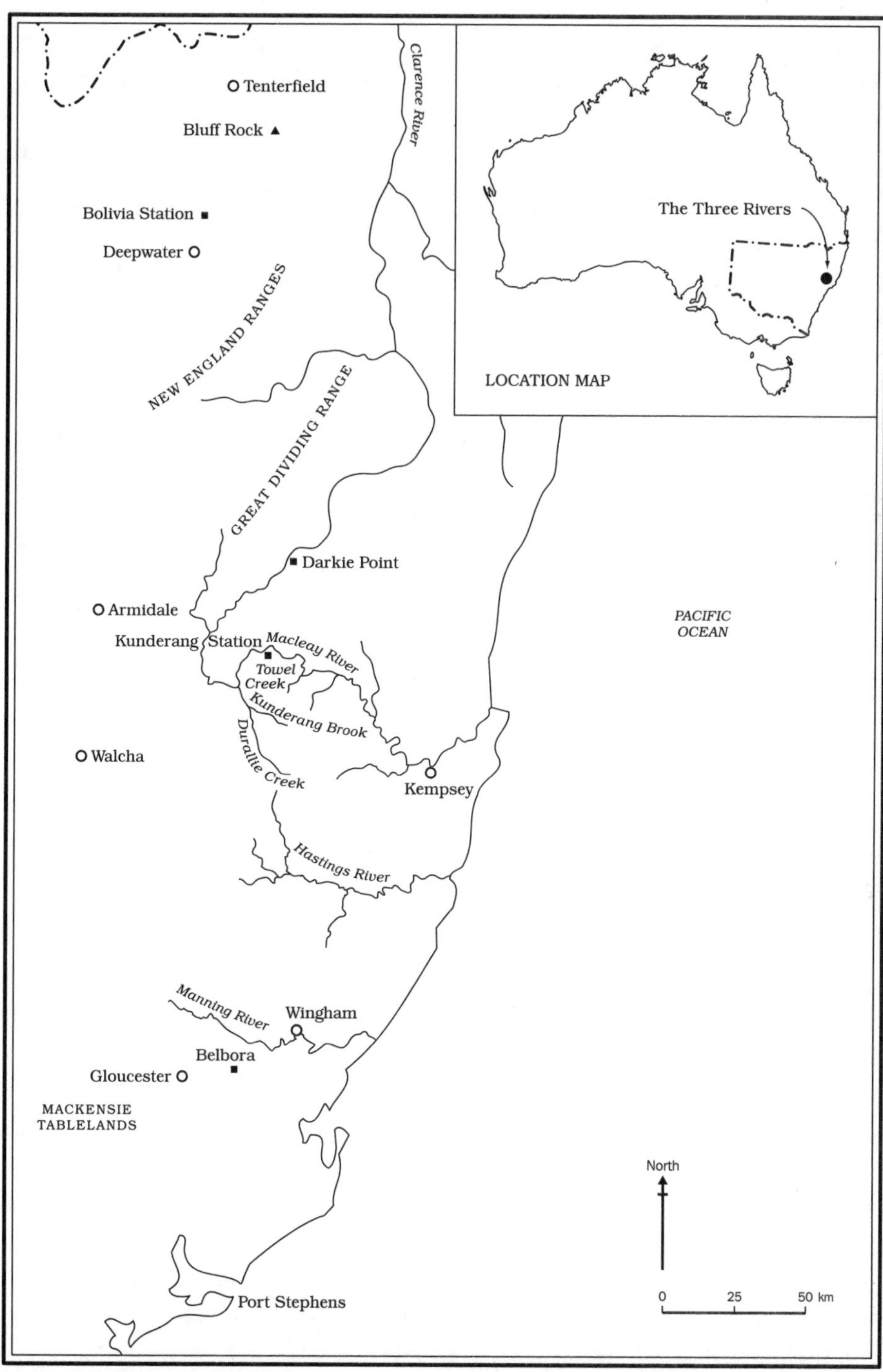

The Three Rivers region on the New South Wales Mid North Coast, scene of numerous massacres in the 1830s and 1840s.

The first Europeans arrived in the area as early as 1821 but serious and systematic European settlement did not start until 1828. By 1836 the white occupation of the land was all but completed. Cedar cutters and farmers had claimed every hectare of land which, if they had ever stopped and asked who owned it, they would have realised they were stealing from communities — the Birpai, the Ngaku and the Thungatti groups — who had occupied the area for tens of thousands of years. The town of Macleay on the Macleay River was surveyed in 1842. As settlers moved into the area the conflicts between the original occupants and the new settlers started.

Typical of the conflicts was a massacre which occurred on the Upper Macleay River in May 1840 and which was so widely reported in the colony that it made the pages of the *Sydney Herald*. The story goes that a large herd of sheep was brought overland from Bathurst — across the mountains and down into the coastal valley of the Macleay River — for Messrs Betts and Panton of Long Flat station on the Macleay. The overseer of the sheep, a certain Sergeant Freer, noted that during the trip down the steep valley of the Upper Macleay River an estimated 370 sheep had gone missing. Believing that they had been stolen by the local Aborigines Freer established a small scouting party comprising himself, a mounted Aborigine and a stockman. The trio headed back up the valley to find the sheep. The tracks were obvious. It was quickly established that the sheep had been cornered by local Aborigines who were, by the time Freer and his posse arrived, herding them off towards the hills. After riding a further thirteen kilometres Freer reached a vantage point where he could see a group of between two hundred and three hundred Aborigines who had started a large cooking fire and were roasting and eating some of the sheep.

Freer and his two colleagues were sighted by the Aborigines who immediately prepared to defend their catch. The Aborigines, thinking they were being followed by a large posse, hastily retreated into the cover of the bush. However when they realised that Freer's party consisted of only three men they attacked and forced them out of the valley. Freer rode to Towel Creek station where he raised the alert. A larger posse was formed. They returned to the place of the first sighting only to find that the Aborigines, having consumed some sixty sheep, had already left. Following the tracks (there were still over 300 sheep left) made by the sheep, Freer chased the Aborigines, caught them beyond Kunderang Brook and fired upon them with the result that some 220 sheep were recovered. No one recorded how many of the Aborigines were killed.

This was only shortly after the Myall Creek massacre and Freer, in the report in the *Sydney Herald*, recalled nothing more serious than 'upon being fired upon they speedily decamped'. This is one of the earliest examples of the frontier going silent and euphemisms being used for harsh and murderous reprisals. Writing about this

An Aboriginal family living along the banks of the Macleay River towards the end of the nineteenth century.

massacre in 1851 Lieutenant John Henderson claimed that as a result of the theft of the sheep 'two or three dozen men were slaughtered later'. If this is true, and there is no reason to doubt it, then only two years after the Myall Creek massacre another killing of the same scale occurred and, even though the crime by the Aborigines was reported, the revenge killings by Freer and his party were neither recorded nor punished.

Given the values of the time it was natural that papers like the *Sydney Herald* would report the white side of the conflict. They didn't seem prepared to acknowledge that the local tribes in the three rivers area were not going to relinquish their lands without a fight. Over the next decade a kind of war raged in the district. Europeans who were foolish enough to be isolated (either because they were out working the land or because the regular inhabitants of a station had departed) could expect no mercy. There are numerous stories of the determination of the local Aborigines to rid themselves of these undesirable invaders. At Kunderang station, for example, two shepherds and their wives were killed by Aborigines who successfully stole some 800 head of sheep.

Lieutenant Henderson described the Aborigines as courageous in their attacks but also hinted at the level of the reprisals describing the behaviour of the settlers as:

> Many treacherous murders, however, had been committed without suffering the punishment due to their misdeeds, for, from the state of the laws, the difficulty of catching them, and the almost impossibility of identifying the guilty, they could seldom be brought to justice, or even summarily punished.

There was a state of lawlessness and the 'war' was totally unequal. Sooner or later guns and posses travelling on horseback were going to win against the low level guerrilla forays pursued by the local Aborigines.

Perhaps the best example of the complexity of 'truth' and 'myth' lies in a story recounted by Mrs H A McMaugh in her *Early Settlement of the Upper Macleay*. Mrs McMaugh tells how a white woman named Pearl Duffy (or Dufety) was kidnapped by a group of local Aborigines and taken to an area near Walcha. She survived for three weeks with the local community until she was eventually rescued by the local police. Given the anger and distress which must have been felt by the woman's husband and the rest of the local European community it is significant that Mrs McMaugh makes no mention of any kind of reprisal. This simply beggars belief. In other accounts of the event, which was widely known and quite widely reported, there are suggestions of a very major massacre with the bodies being piled up and allowed to rot. Why does Mrs McMaugh not mention the massacre? Because at the time there was a code of silence.

The Towel Creek Massacre

Another large-scale slaughter shrouded in 'frontier silence' is the story of the Towel Creek massacre. At the time of the massacre, relations between the newly arrived settlers and the local Aborigines were really no better than undeclared war. The Aborigines were unhappy with the white settlers. They constantly harassed any settlers they could find and, when they knew the men had gone away, they had no hesitation coming out of the bush to terrify the white women. Consequently many of the settlers quickly adopted a policy of 'shoot on sight' when any Aborigines were seen near white settlement.

The Towel Creek massacre probably occurred in 1856. At the time the local Aboriginal group had been doing everything to scare the settlers away. One white settler, hoping that the local Aborigines would believe she was a man, had taken to dressing up in men's clothing in order to protect her seven small sons and two daughters. One time when her husband had to leave the area it had been agreed that an old station hand, Scotchie Gray, would stay with the woman and protect her from possible attack. Scotchie was no hero. When two Aboriginal men arrived at the front and back doors of the settler's home demanding food Scotchie headed for the bedroom and was later found under the bed. He was dismissed in disgrace.

Shortly after this farcical event the settler was working in his cornfield when he was approached by two Aborigines who asked for a pumpkin. When he leaned down to get the pumpkin one of the Aborigines hit the man on the head. The man survived but became convinced that all the local people were dangerous and untrustworthy. He started a campaign of 'shoot upon sight' and, with another local settler, decided to rid the area of all Aborigines by raiding and 'shooting up' a nearby camp. The two men spent the night making lead slugs for their muzzle-loading guns. Fortunately for the local Aborigines there was an Aborigine named Jimmy Taylor working for the squatter. When he heard the massacre plans he slipped out of the house and warned the local group who fled upriver and hid in the trees and undergrowth of the rainforest in the headwaters of Towel Creek.

The next morning the two settlers accompanied by a small posse headed for the Aboriginal camp. Finding it abandoned they headed up the valley until, by accident, one of the hiding Aborigines either coughed or laughed (the stories differ) allowing the men in the posse to shoot randomly at any of the group they could spot. No one knows how many Aborigines were killed in this poorly reported massacre. One thing that is known is that a baby was later found still suckling his dead mother's nipple. He was taken in by the Scott family, named Jack, and subsequently became a horseman of local repute. His descendants still live in the area.

The Durallie Creek Massacre

There is perhaps no better example of the silence of the frontier than the Durallie Creek massacre. There is no written record of the event and yet, for over a century, it was an integral part of the oral tradition of all the Aboriginal groups who lived within the Three Rivers district. The story will probably never be proved but it fits with the behaviour of so many of the early settlers. The setting was the junction of the Durallie Creek and Kunderang Brook. Two graziers from further down the valley, tired of the incursions of local Aborigines and determined to 'teach them a lesson they will never forget', formed a posse which included such unsavoury local characters as a large, brutish farm worker who was simply known as Big Red Ted. The posse rode up the river and, with the kind of luck that evil so often has, came across a large group of Aborigines swimming and relaxing around a pool at the junction of the creek and Kunderang Brook. Without hesitation they fired on everyone they could see. Those closest to the far side of the pool fled and started clambering up the rocks only to be shot as they tried to escape. Their bodies fell back into the bloody waters of the pool. A small group of children hid beside the pool but were attacked and killed by Big Red Ted who, rather than using a firearm, used a stirrup iron attached to a long piece of leather. This particularly ugly weapon was commonly used for killing dingos. One girl who was hiding in a tree was shot and for days after her body hung from the tree, her ankle had been caught in a fork as she fell. A man who had been up a tree collecting honey when the massacre started was able to hide until the killing had stopped. It was he who escaped and was able to tell the story in such detail. No one knows for sure how many were killed. The best estimate is that probably as many as sixty people were killed in this single massacre. Certainly it was known for decades afterwards that the area was littered with the skulls and bones of the dead. It is said that in the language of one of the local groups the word 'durallie' means 'they fight us'.

Bluff Rock Massacre, Tenterfield

Go to Tenterfield today and the local Bundjalung people will still tell the story of the Bluff Rock massacre. It is, by sharp contrast with the Durallie Creek massacre, an event which has been well recorded by both local Aborigines and white historians. The massacre occurred at Bluff Rock near Tenterfield around October 1844. As far as anyone can tell it was a case of competition for land and food. The early settlers to the area brought sheep. The sheep ate the native vegetables, grasses and seeds indiscriminately. Settlers did not seem to realise that sixty to seventy per cent of the Aboriginal diet on the New England Tablelands was made up of the wild vegetables and seeds which were now being eaten by the herds of sheep which covered the

The Avengers; or, Settlers Tracking the Blacks.

It was widely known in the cities that settlers, once they had come in bloody conflict with the local Aboriginal communities, would organise posses and seek revenge. This engraving entitled 'The avengers or settlers tracking the blacks' was published in the Illustrated Melbourne Post *on 18 April 1865.*

grasslands. Retaliation of some sort was inevitable. The most vulnerable people were the shepherds who tended the sheep and were often forced to go far from the safety of the homestead. In October 1844 a shepherd named Robinson on the property known as Bolivia, which was owned by the Irby brothers, was found beaten to death and floating naked in a local creek. This was a very serious act of reprisal by the Bundjalung. The Irby brothers, furious at the killing, were determined to revenge the death. They gathered a posse of four men which included station hands from Bolivia as well as some riders from Deepwater which was owned by the Windeyer family. There would be no 'innocent until proven guilty' concept of British law applied here. There would be no 'onus of proof' on the part of the posse. All they wanted was revenge and consequently all they did was chase after any Aborigines unlucky enough to come into their sights. The result was a massacre of huge proportions.

The Irbys and Windeyers found some Aborigines who were fleeing towards the high country near Bluff Rock. The posse fanned out so that the Aborigines could be herded in front of them. Slowly and systematically they pushed the Bundjalung towards Bluff Rock. The Bundjalung group comprised men, women and children. The posse closed on the group until they had no alternative. They would be shot if they moved towards the posse and tried to escape. Instead they threw themselves off Bluff Rock. For decades afterwards it was said that the posse saved one small child and he was raised by one of the Europeans who had been instrumental in killing all his family.

Later Edward Irby was to write:

> The blacks saw us coming and hid themselves among the rocks. One, in his haste, dropped poor Robinson's coat so we knew we were onto the right tribe. If the natives had taken to their heels they might well have got off safe. Instead of doing this, however, they got their fighting men together to attack us, so we punished them severely and proved our superiority to them.

If this sounds like someone who was driven to violent actions by frustration it is worth recording that Lieutenant Colonel Godfrey Charles Mundy, who rode through the New England area and recorded his impressions in a book published in 1855 wrote:

> It was common after an inroad of the blacks upon the sheep and cattle, for men of two or three adjoining stations to assemble for a regular and indiscriminate slaughter in which young and old were shot down . . . Reprisals were undertaken on a large scale — a scale which never reaches the ears of the Government . . . or if it reached them at all, finds them conveniently deaf . . . Men, women and children are butchered without distinction or stint . . . it becomes by practice a pleasurable excitement.
>
> Occasionally bush gossip let out that the 'blackfellows were going to get a dose': and indeed, in more than one known instance, 'damper well hocussed' with arsenic or strichnine was laid in the way of the savages, whereby many were killed.
>
> Some attempts were made to bring justice to the perpetrators of this cowardly as well as barbarous act; but, in the bush, justice is too often deaf, dumb and lame as well as blind.

The Clarence River Massacre

Massacres of large numbers of Aborigines were occurring from the New England ranges down to the sea throughout the 1840s and 1850s as the white settlers tried to purge the area of its 'troublesome blacks'. The scale of the killing was so great, and the silence imposed by the executions resulting from the Myall Creek massacres was so complete, that it is now quite impossible to estimate how many people were killed. Perhaps the most disturbing aspect of the massacres was the willing participation of some of the government's officials. In 1839 a part-time poet James George 'Humpy' Macdonald, who was acting as the Commissioner of Crown Lands, named the area now known as the City of Armidale after his clan's baronial estate of 'Armadale' on the Isle of Skye. Around this time his acting appointment became official. Officially Macdonald was a representative of the NSW government and, therefore, was obliged to uphold the law of the colony.

In 1845 Macdonald reported to the NSW Legislative Council that 'the Aborigines have been for the last three years in friendly relations with the Europeans in the district'. It was a typically dishonest sleight-of-hand. They may have been 'friendly' from 1842 to 1845 but in 1841 Macdonald had actually led a posse against a group of Aborigines who had been camped on the banks of the Orara River near Grafton. So much for the 'friendly relations'. Macdonald and his posse had surrounded the large camp during the night and at daybreak, when the Aborigines were still asleep under the trees by the riverbank, the posse had charged into the camp indiscriminately shooting men, women and children. In the melee that followed some Aborigines were lucky enough to reach the river where they tried to swim to safety only to be shot as they fled. It was said that for some days afterwards bodies of murdered Aborigines floated down the river past the settlement at South Grafton. The cruel irony of the situation was that Macdonald claimed that the attack was to revenge a theft from Remornie station. Hardly an offence worthy of a massacre. Subsequently the theft was discovered to have been committed by a white person, a hut keeper named Lynch. The Commissioner of Crown Lands had murdered a large number of totally innocent Aborigines. He was never prosecuted.

Darkie Point Massacre

There are very few really detailed first person accounts of the massacres which occurred in the mid-nineteenth century. However, in *Baal Belbora* Geoffrey Blomfield reveals that while trying to track down the events which inspired Judith Wright's poem, 'Nigger's Leap' he came across F Eldershaw's 1851 publication *Australia As It Really Is* in which Eldershaw, who moved to the New England ranges in 1841, recalls in great detail how three of his workers were killed and 2000 of his sheep

Local Aborigines spearing fish on the Bellinger River around 1845.

were stolen by some local Aborigines. Written in the cumbersome and florid style of the mid-nineteenth century, and obviously eager to explain how a massacre was necessary and, indeed, beneficial for both blacks and whites, Eldershaw's account of the Darkie Point massacre is a remarkable first person account. It offers a rare opportunity to look into the mind of a white settler who, confronted with a crime beyond the limits of the colonial legal system, simply took the law into his own hands. Eldershaw's attitude to the massacre is probably best summed up in the title of the piece — 'An Adventure with the Blacks'.

An Adventure with the Blacks

Far away from the busy haunts of civilised man, unprotected by military or police, an adventurous band of 'Squatters', hemmed in by the daily encroachments of their agricultural neighbours, bought out by monied land proprietors, or pressed by their own rapidly-increasing flocks and herds; sought in more distant regions of the interior of this great 'terra incognita' those broad acres of hill and plain, so absolutely essential to the success of pastoral avocations.

Among this little band the writer of these pages journeyed forth, and after a long and arduous search selected as his squattage a very nice piece of country on the north-western skirts of the fertile district of New England. Rough and horribly tedious were our first struggles with the daily hardships and privations of this enterprising undertaking. Gradually, however, its difficulties began to lessen, its more pressing privations to decrease; our prospects of eventual success, by slow but sure degrees, assumed a brighter promise, huts had sprung up, sheds had been built; outstations formed; and the ordinary routine of a Squatter's life was beginning decidedly to resume its old accustomed regularity.

Numerous depredations, however, on the part of the 'Blacks', accompanied with acts of more or less violence, had frequently and seriously warned me, as well as others of my co-adventurers, of the imminent risks we were still daily incurring in these first efforts to people and subdue the solitude and savages of this vast wilderness.

Cattle had been speared and driven from our runs; sheep had been rushed and slaughtered; shepherds and stockmen hunted for bare life: but hitherto, in our immediate neighbourhood, no human blood had happily been shed, and sanguine hopes, in spite of conflicting experience, began to dawn upon our minds, that by patience and conciliating care we might yet be spared the horrors and atrocities of these vengeful collisions of the Aborigines, which ever result from this peculiarly treacherous and unequal warfare. But herein our hopes were destined to be rudely undeceived — our peaceful efforts to reclaim these wandering hordes were all delusive.

Towards the close of the autumn of '41, after a beautiful and most prosperous season, we were miserably startled from the unconscious lull of security which long-continued impunity from harm invariably produces, by the appalling intelligence that one of my out-stations had been attacked, its three unfortunate occupants brutally massacred, and the sheep, two thousand in number, carried off as spoils, together with whatever stores and implements the station had been provided. Accompanied by three neighbours, I immediately proceeded to reconnoitre the spot of this atrocity. The tracks, camp fires, and numerous gunyahs, indicated clearly the recent presence of a tribe of natives numbering, we surmised, at least two hundred. The hut was empty, but we could plainly perceive, by blood and other evidences of deadly struggle, that one at least of the unfortunate fellows had here met his dreadful end. A still further and more minute examination of every track and indication around revealed to our practised eyes, mysteriously but unmistakeably, full evidences of the conduct of the whole catastrophe. The watchman, it was

A vital record of the Aborigines of the Grafton area was made by J.W. Lindt who took these two women to his studio and photographed them against a natural backdrop in 1875.

apparent, had been sneaked upon in his hut, and while in the act of turning or in some way attending to 'damper' baking in the ashes, speared in the back. The shepherds had been waylaid on their return with the flocks, and destroyed probably without the chance of an effort for their lives.

Our subsequent discovery of the bodies tended to verify the accuracy of these observations; we dragged the unfortunate fellows from a neighbouring waterhole, and buried them with such decent rites as our limited means permitted; two of them, the shepherds, were literally riddled with spear-wounds; the watchman had received four spears in his loins, and in addition, the back of the skull — the occipital and posterior face of the sphenoid bones — was completely smashed to fragments by the waddies of these brutal savages.

Possessed of all the information which it was possible thus to obtain, we returned to arrange a party for immediate pursuit. Each of our men was savagely anxious and eager to be chosen for this painfully imperative task; the thought of their butchered comrades, with sundry vivid reminiscences of personal escapes from a fate as dreadful, made them pant for an opportunity of vengeance on the heads of their wily and dangerous enemies. We made our selection from among them, however, upon other and I hope sounder grounds than could be gathered from the noisiest ebullition of excited feeling. Including my neighbouring friends, we mustered a party of ten, well mounted and accoutred, and taking with us ten days' provisions, we started at daybreak on the following morning in pursuit.

From all appearances the murderous villains must have had at least a five days' start of us; but the broad track of two thousand sheep gave small occasion to halt upon our progress, and the third day's journey brought us evidently very close upon their heels. We had by this time passed eight of their nightly camps, at each of which fresh witnesses to their plunder were abundantly apparent. Well remembered pass-boxes, the recent property of the murdered men, boots, scraps of paper, torn rags, old sugar bags, and other useless refuse of their spoils, were discarded; while the remains of the numerous carcases of sheep, bones, heads, etc., bore ample testimony to the extent of their nightly meals. During the latter part of this day's journey we perceived with much annoyance that they had headed us more and more for the broken country, near the main dividing range, in the direction of the heads of the south branch of the Clarence, and towards night we were scarcely able to make headway, for the roughness and steepness of the broken ground over which they had passed. Still we struggled on as best we could, anxious to obtain a position close to their this night's camp, fearing from the altered and difficult road they were now pursuing, that they must have observed or in some way suspected our approach. We were compelled to halt, however, without obtaining more substantial evidences of their proximity than could be gathered from the recent sheep-tracks over which we were passing, and which were clearly not many hours old. We chose our camp in the bed of a deep gully at the foot of the mountain over which the Blacks had steered their course. In this selection we were influenced mainly by the desire of concealment, the night being somewhat too chilly to dispense with fires. There was in our immediate neighbourhood also an abundance of pure water, plenty of long but rather too dry grass, for the use of the cattle, and the encircling mountains, thickly covered with scrub and dry timber, afforded us no lack of fuel. Here, then, we arranged our quarters, refreshed our inner man, talked over our plans, and resolved upon the details of the morrow's contemplated attack.

No sooner, however, had the twilight shadows faded and the darkness of a moonless night fairly enshrouded us, than we had reason to apprehend that the spot of our selection would turn out neither one of refuge nor of rest. It was very evident we had been discovered or observed; the affrighted snorts of horses, an occasional cracking of dead timber, as if being trodden down by some passing foot, the harsh rustling of dry underwood, the startled fluttering of birds, were sounds sufficiently ominous to arouse our utmost vigilance and anxiety.

Our horses were quickly gathered together; each looked to the priming of his gun; the fires were extinguished; watch parties posted; and everything as far as possible prepared to guard against surprise. Hour after hour we waited, however, without attack, the scouts came in, and feeling somewhat ashamed of our apparently groundless apprehensions, we began to think our nerves must have been too much unstrung after our late excitement, we therefore deemed it incumbent to seek some rest preparatory to the labours of the ensuing day. Fixing a regular watch, and advising the utmost caution, we at length betook ourselves to repose. The briefest possible slumber fell to my individual lot, for suddenly an alarm of 'fire', and the startling cry of 'the Blacks! the Blacks!' effectively dispelled all feeling of drowsiness. For some moments, however, we were utterly unable to perceive or appreciate the exact nature of our hazardous position. A bright and rapidly increasing glare of light, pouring down in circling eddies from the hills, and sweeping the grassy gullies at our feet, surrounded us and effectively excluded every distant object from our observation. In this perplexity two or three heavy spears darting amongst us sufficiently indicated the whereabouts and intentions of our agile though invisible foes; we discharged four barrels in their direction, and immediately a yell, the wildest and most frought with fear ears every heard, rang through the burning forest. No time was evidently to be lost; a moment's delay might for aught we knew prove fatal. By one portion of the party our horses were saddled and all prepared for immediate movement, while the other, with leafy boughs of trees, set vigorously to work to stop the approach of the raging element, which every moment came more near with fierce and rapid sweeps, blinding our eyes to all beyond its livid circle of flame. This at length, but with much difficulty, was accomplished, and lighted by the now extended circle of blazing timber that spread on all sides like a bright horizon round us, we proceeded in search of the late intruders, but in vain, no trace of their existence could be discovered; they had vanished as effectually as if they had never been in the land of the living.

In an incredibly short space of time the whole range of mountains was on fire; miles of long dry grass, thousands of huge trees, and all the dense mass of withered underwood by which they were encompassed, were enveloped in one enormous unapproachable flame: to proceed through this vast burning mass was obviously impossible; retreat, however, seemed equally hazardous; no course apparently was left but to await the coming day and force our way, if practicable, towards where some creek or water-course might reasonably be expected to have intervened to check the spread of this disastrous fire. If no such spot should be discovered, farewell to all prospect of regaining the lost flocks. The case was nearly hopeless; we could not help calculating somewhat, however, upon the peculiar ingenuity of our enemies, nor herein were we much deceived, for when the sun was fairly up we faintly descried through the dense clouds of lurid smoke that almost quenched the light of day, a wavy line of clearer atmosphere, towards which, at imminent hazard from the falling timber that blazed and burst in every direction round us, we urged our anxious way. All tracks of sheep, of course, were lost in this black and dismal spot; but pushing on, we at length descried, to our inexpressible joy, an open mountain spur, divided from us by a rocky creek, running at right angles with our former course, untouched by the ravaging flames, and standing out like a bright and beautiful oasis in the black and calcined desert by which it was surrounded. As we approached, a wider prospect opened around us; far away in the grassy valleys to our left our sheep were feeding onwards, tended and driven apparently by the Gins and Picannies of the tribe. But what of the Blacks themselves? Where could they be? We knew too much of their habits not to suspect the approach of mischief, even from this slight appearance of incautious exposure. The question, unhappily, was soon resolved, a shower of spears and boomerangs came flying into our party, four or five of the former striking with deadly aim the unfortunate fellow, who, in charge of the commissariat, was bringing up the rear. On three sides we were beset; each tree appeared to have produced its man, so sudden and startling was their apparition like approach. Exasperation broke all bounds of prudence and order, and dashing at them, each man as he listed, I soon found myself alone, flying up the scorching hills in wild but profitless pursuit of the quick and snakelike savages, for upon our first discharge they had dispersed in every direction. Searching with reckless haste, I climbed the steep and rugged tracks which wound upwards round the side of the next adjacent mountain, until the ascent became so steep my panting horse could barely stand. No sooner had I fairly halted, than a yell of exultation rang in my ears, and descending towards me from two opposite sides of the mountain, with rapid strides, fierce gleaming eyes, and weapons quivering in their excited hands, a party of these frightful savages were hurriedly approaching. The moment was a fearful one; the almost perpendicular side of the mountain open to my retreat was thickly strewn with large and rugged granite boulders, the deep sand in which they were but partially imbedded, unstable as water, scarce needed the lightest pressure of the foot, the slightest conceivable impulse, to release them for their tottering height, and hurl them thundering into the deep abyss, through which the sparkling waters of the surrounding hills found egress to the plains. Upon the opposite side of this terrific gorge a mass of rock opposed its rugged face to my escape. Destruction seemed inevitable, but any death was preferable to that of butchery at the hands of these insatiate wretches; so with what coolness I could command, and with an aim as steady as circumstances would admit, I discharged one barrel at each mass of my approaching foes, wheeled round my brave old horse, and dashed headlong towards the yawning chasm beneath. At three bounds he was down the mountain, the huge boulders crashing at his heels, the yell of death and disappointed rage still ringing in my ears: the terrific gorge gaping to receive my bruised lifeless form still rivetted my fascinating gaze; nearing it, until its terrible depths became apparent to my bewildered brain. Involuntarily I closed my eyes; my dizzy senses reeled — I held my failing breath like one falling in a frightful dream from giddy heights, expecting momentarily the fatal crash that should at once annihilate me.

Not so the gallant steed, whose sinewy limbs had borne me thus far scathless; with measured stride and powerful bound, he flew at the terrific gulf, cleared the adjacent rocks, and with tremendous leap landed me unharmed and safely on the opposite bank. By this time our party had again assembled, and, directed by the infuriated shouts of my savage pursuers, arrived in time to ward off further attack, and to chastise them soundly for their unwonted temerity.

I experienced much difficulty in escaping from the rocky perch whereon my noble horse had landed me, the descent from which was truly hazardous. However, I at length got safely down, and having reached the plains, arranged operations for the night, and taken a slight refreshment, we pushed on in the direction of the sheep. Towards evening their tracks led us again in the direction of the mountains, to a gap, or bog, in one of which, for the night's encampment, they were evidently tending. The utmost circumspection here appeared to be imperative; it was obvious to any practised observation that all our steps were closely watched, and their every moment regulated by our own. We determined, therefore, to proceed slowly and cautiously direct towards the gap, into which the sheep, at least, had certainly preceeded us, until darkness should permit a change of course without immediate chance of observation. We then proposed taking a circuit from our apparent course, and endeavour to obtain a higher point on one of the adjacent hills, whence we might securely view their force and contemplate operations.

Towards nightfall we described their fires; the bleating of the sheep and the yelping of their dogs became also distinctly audible. Dismounting at this point, and leaving a strong party in charge of our horses, with strict injunctions to push forward in the event of any skirmish, the remainder of our party crept into the Bush, and taking a wide and ascended circle mounted the jagged rocks which overhung their camp. Here a scene of most astounding wildness was presented to our gaze; a perfect amphitheatre lay beneath us, formed by a mass of perpendicular rocks, whose bare and rugged faces would have afforded scarcely sufficient room for an eagle's nest; except that about midway from the smooth bottom of the glen, on which the camp fires dimly blazed, and the height on which we stood, there appeared to be a rough projecting ledge running round nearly the entire of the two opposite curves of this strange and quarry-like spot. A few moments' careful examination revealed to our wondering senses the wily stratagem by which these savage warriors had intended to beguile us into almost inevitable destruction.

The projecting ledge of rock, which was about a hundred feet below us, and apparently about a similar height above the floor of the gap, was thickly thronged with the fighting men of the tribe, each armed powerfully with heavy spears, but most of them carrying a boomerang and waddie. Huge stones, also, lay piled about, apparently from their position destined for warlike purposes; and had we but in this instance approached with the incautious haste which usually distinguishes the white man's mode of dealing with these much despised Aborigines, our total destruction could hardly, in all human probability, have been avoided. Hurriedly edging our way towards the mouth of the apparent ascent to the rocky platform, we were startled by the discharge of a gun proceeding from the party below. An ominous stir among the Blacks in the direction of this spot alarmed us for the safety of our friends, and reminded us of the necessity for immediate action.

Pouring in, therefore, upon the eager but unconscious crowd below the contents of ten barrels, a fearful change was effected in their savage glee; a scream of mingled consternation and surprise, a rush in reckless despair towards the only means of escape from their exposed and dangerous elevation; a murderous and tumultuous struggle amongst themselves; their yells of mingled hate and agony, as grappling together in the last grasp of death the foremost of them fell, urged over the ledge's brink by the pressing crowd behind that madly hurried on, into the yawning sepulchre beneath, was all of the horrid scene that the increasing darkness of the night enabled us clearly to perceive.

We had now reloaded, and our party from below pushing forward to the scene of conflict, poured in a deadly volley upon the thronging crowds that lined the rocky entrance to this fatal ledge — back flew the despairing wretches from that dreadful spot — again a volley from our party on the heights dealt frightful havoc in their ranks. The utmost wildness of despair now seized upon them all; some actually dashed themselves in frantic violence to the depths beneath, in utter heedlessness of life. One solitary tree grew in this fatal glen; its topmost limbs reaching almost to the level of their feet; with faint remains of hope, some of the youngest and most active of the tribe sprang at its fragile boughs in vain — few grasped its treacherous aid, where, quivering for a moment on its yielding branches, their latest shrieks of dying agony, mingling with the mass beneath, too plainly told the dreadful fate they sought to shun, but only had anticipated. Sick of the horrid carnage below, I fain would have retired from the dreadful spot, but all my efforts, entreaties, threats, were utterly useless. Shot after shot with curses wild and deep, the excited fellows launched at their hated foes — their butchered comrades' blood was that night fearfully avenged!

It is by no means my intention to dwell upon the subsequent details of this miserable catastrophe; its salutary consequences were, however, sufficiently apparent, not only in the future safety of the Squatter's life and property, but also in the comfort and security of the numerous native tribes that dwell in the mountain ranges of that district. Deeply impressed with a mysterious and superstitious fear of the stupendous power of the white man, they at once renounced all thought but that of serving or conciliating him; and from that day, and in that particular district, scarcely a depradation of any consequence has been committed, and human life has almost invariably obtained that sacred reverence so essential to mutual safety.

On the other hand, the formerly wild and savage Blackfellow, now harmless, tractable, and subdued, soon gained for himself, first the toleration, then the kind regards of all his white brethren with whom he came in contact; and, as a necessary consequence, those barbarous and inhuman secret murders, by poison, or by some violent and remorseless treachery, of which in preceding times I had so frequently heard and read, were happily now abolished.

With the occasion for fear, the persecution of these roving tribes entirely disappeared, and a good and kindly feeling has grown up on all hands, brought about in some measure, I have no doubt, either by the dreadful and apparently inauspicious commencement, of which

COPYRIGHT REGISTERED.
AUSTRALIAN ABORIGINALS.
J. W. LINDT, PHOTOGRAPHER.
MELBOURNE, VICTORIA; AND GRAFTON, NEW SOUTH WALES.

The Aborigines lived peacefully on the riches of the local rivers. This photograph of a local fisherman was taken in the 1870s by J.W. Lindt.

> the above presents some of the leading features, or of other such affrays probably somewhat similar in their nature, conduct, and result.
>
> Of my flocks in this adventure, about seventeen hundred were recovered; and without any further molestation we retraced our steps to those quiet humble roofs, which, by a figure of speech not unfrequent even among the dwellers in bark huts and tents, we find ourselves occasionally denominating HOME!

Mount Mackensie Massacre

The Australian Agricultural Company (AAC) was formed in England in 1824 with the object of raising fine wool and agricultural products for export to England. The company was granted one million acres on the northern side of Port Stephens and, impressed by the 'romantic scenery' of the river valley, the first manager Robert Dawson established an outstation which he named Gloucester after the English town. He claimed the landscape reminded him of Gloucestershire. The Gloucester and Avon valleys were soon full of sheep and a dairy was established on the estate around 1831 for the supply of AAC employees.

Dawson was, according to most contemporary accounts, a broad-minded man who admired the local Aborigines and was eager to establish harmonious relations with them. However it was quite impossible to turn one million acres of Aboriginal land into a sheep and cattle property without conflict occurring. By the early 1830s a heifer station had been established at Belbora between Gloucester and Wingham and the local Aborigines, probably the Kattang people, were killing the heifers for their own consumption. This, predictably, led to the AAC employees leaving damper infused with arsenic in the huts around the outstation. The deaths that followed were inevitable. It was typical rough frontier injustice.

After these murders relations between the Aborigines and the AAC employees degenerated into the inevitable tit-for-tat with the Aborigines spearing and killing five convict shepherds on Wattenbakh station which was adjacent to the AAC holding. This, in turn, provoked a counterattack by a large posse of whites. The posse was drawn from the AAC employees, some settlers from as far away as Port Stephens and some soldiers who were working for the AAC.

Locating the tracks of the Aborigines, who fled into the mountains beyond Gloucester, the posse followed. By nightfall they had tracked the group to a rocky outcrop on the edge of the Mackensie Tableland. Unaware they were being followed the Aborigines made camp for the night. The posse waited. As dawn smudged the horizon shots rang out. The Aborigines, frightened by the sounds and realising that they were surrounded, attempted to escape from the gunfire. They found the routes away from the cliff edge were blocked. They were left with two equally grim alternatives — head towards the posse and be shot or jump off the cliff and die in the bush and undergrowth below. Most of them chose to jump. For decades later the bones of the massacred Aborigines lay beneath the cliff as a grim reminder of the inevitable consequences of trying to resist European invasion and settlement.

The truth about these massacres is now hidden forever in the craggy slopes and valleys. Who can ever know how extensive the killings were? Certainly the local Aborigines were prepared to kill anyone they considered to be an invader — although, significantly, they did have good relations with those rare squatters and graziers who respected their culture and their lifestyle. The occasional killing of shepherds inevitably led to reprisals which always greatly outnumbered the original killing. 'So many of the wild savage tribe were killed that day that the place was ever after called Waterloo,' wrote Mary McMaugh in *Days of Yore*.

The information in this chapter has been taken from *Baal Belbora* which, sadly, is now out of print. The author Geoffrey Blomfield was a meticulous local historian who, to the best of his ability, tried to apply rigorous historical methodology to an aspect of local history which had been poorly reported. His skill in finding people within the local Aboriginal communities who would tell him their massacre stories, then matching those stories with contemporary newspaper accounts and local histories as told by white settlers, sets a standard which makes much of his book a genuinely valuable contribution to the history of massacres and maltreatment in this country.

CHAPTER 9

MASSACRES IN THE GIPPSLAND REGION — 1840 TO 1851

Some escaped into the scrub, others jumped into the waterhole, and, as fast as they put their head up for breath, they were shot until the water was red with blood.

The reminiscences of a 'Gippslander' in 1925

The frontier was silent. Seven men had been hanged in Sydney for killing Aboriginal people. Everyone who had ever dealt harshly with the Aboriginal people, and that meant almost everyone beyond the reach of the law, breathed a sigh of relief and muttered, 'there but for the grace of God go I'. Around the camp fires, in the crude wattle-and-daub shelters and in the shacks that passed for pubs, the conversation turned again and again to the men who had killed twenty-eight Aboriginal people at Myall Creek. The settlers, itinerants, convicts and labourers who made up the frontier population looked with disdain and disgust on the moral self-righteousness of the governor and the city do-gooders.

Hanging certainly was a deterrent but so too, in the simple brutish minds of the frontiersmen, was shooting Aboriginal people. If the Aboriginal people rushed the cattle — shoot them; if they speared a sheep — shoot them; if they protested over the rape of a woman — shoot them. Only now if you shot them you had to make certain that no-one knew.

Secrecy about killings and massacres took a variety of forms. The most popular methods were either for each participant to swear allegiance to the other 'hunters' involved in the massacre or for an agreement to be reached that no-one would talk about the massacre. It worked. For over half a century men along the frontier continued to kill Aboriginal people with impunity. No records were kept; no details were revealed. The gentle eraser of time did its work. The smudgy details were cleaned away.

A so-called do-gooder who travelled through the Gippsland area of Victoria in 1846 noted the silence of the locals. Hearing of the Warrigal Creek massacre, which had occurred only three years earlier, he wrote, 'I have protested against it at every station I have been to in Gippsland, in the strongest language, but these things are kept very secret as the penalty would certainly be hanging'.

His oblique and incomplete report is typical of the way information leaked out. No-one involved in a massacre ever sat down and recorded the details of the event. The result is information which is unreliable and often based on third-hand or even fourth-hand accounts. In the case of the Warrigal Creek massacre no-one will ever know how many Aboriginal people were killed (reports range from sixty to one hundred and fifty) and although it is called the Warrigal Creek massacre, it may well have occurred at Gammon Creek or Freshwater Creek or Red Hill.

The whites arrived in the Gippsland area in the mid-1830s. Settlement occurred quickly and by 1842 there were 7000 head of cattle, 3500 sheep, 150 horses, 225

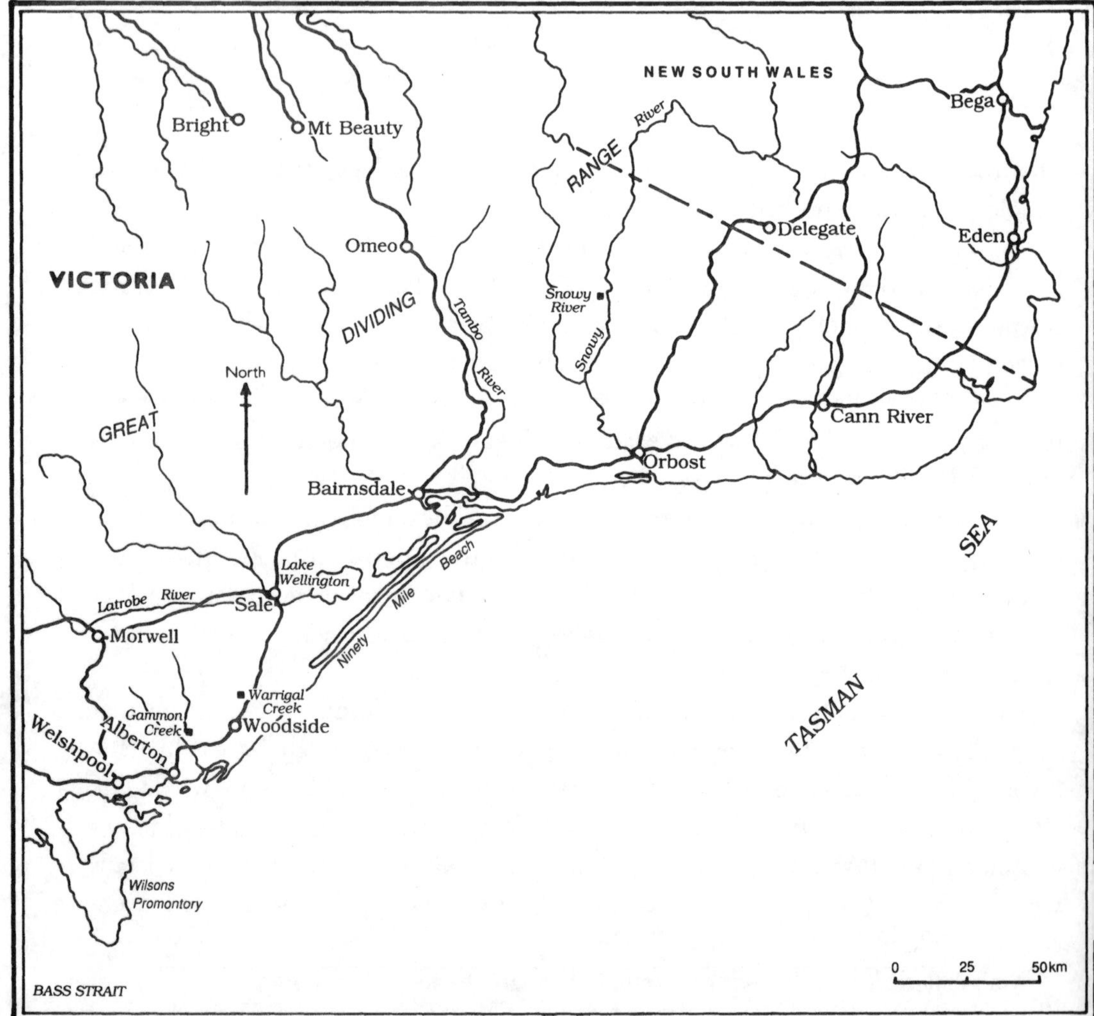

The Gippsland region in eastern Victoria.

free settlers and an unknown number of escaped convicts. Settlement had been too hasty and the Kurnai, realising that their lifestyle was being destroyed, fought back.

Massacre after massacre occurred. The area bounded by the Great Dividing Range to the west, Wilsons Promontory to the south and Ninety Mile Beach to the east ran with blood. The Kurnai, trying vainly to protect their lands, killed the occasional shepherd or lonely traveller. The white settlers formed posses and went on killing sprees.

As early as 1840 Angus McMillan, a thirty-year-old Scot in the employ of Captain Lachlan Macalister, decided to teach the Kurnai a lesson in frontier law. McMillan had moved cattle into the area convinced of the huge pastoral potential of the Gippsland region. The Kurnai, probably aware of the damage wrought by cattle upon the native ecology, attacked the stock and dispersed them into the bush. McMillan's response was immediate. He formed a posse from his stockmen and for the next few days marauded across the countryside killing many Aboriginal people — men, women and children. He kept no record of the killings. It was estimated later that fifty or sixty Aboriginal people were killed. McMillan had hoped that his massacre would teach the Kurnai a lesson. In fact, it had little impact. The Kurnai had no options. They were fighting for their survival. Between the winters of 1842 and 1843 at least five whites were killed in the Gippsland area.

Then, in July 1843, the Kurnai killed Donald Macalister, the nephew of Lachlan Macalister, one of the most powerful property owners in the region. It was a reprisal killing. Some days before, a shepherd, possibly young Donald Macalister, had thought it a huge joke to throw a shovelful of hot ashes on the feet of a Kurnai warrior. There was also a rumour at the time that some local stockmen, full of alcohol and racial bigotry, had gone out hunting Aboriginal people and had killed a number of friendly Kurnai who had been living on the outskirts of Port Arthur. Whatever the reason, it was clear that in killing Macalister the Kurnai were reacting to specific provocation.

Frontier mythology has played strange games with the Warrigal Creek massacre. It predates any concept of investigative reporting. Thus it is a springboard from which 'creative' journalists can dive into an elaborate world of innuendo and suggestion. The circumstances surrounding the actual killing of young Macalister are shrouded in a series of widely varying reports. One particularly ghoulish report has the Aboriginal people spearing Macalister and removing his kidney fat. Another, reported in the *Port Phillip Patriot*, claims:

> Mr. Macalister was dragged off his horse and cruelly murdered in the township of Alberton, his head being so totally disfigured that his countenance could not be recognised amongst his most intimate friends (this outrage being committed) by these harmless innocent

> citizens of the wilds of Gippsland bearing the anomalous cognomen of Her Majesty's most liege subjects (we give it as our gratuitous opinion, most bitter enemies).

Once again it was Angus McMillan, self-appointed scourge of the Kurnai, who decided to teach Aboriginal people a lesson. Young Macalister had been his friend. He was driven as much by revenge as by any dubious 'educational' sense.

McMillan let it be known that he was forming a posse and that those interested should meet at his property, Nuntin. Within twenty-four hours stockmen and property owners were riding in. Old Lachlan Macalister, with his huge double-barrelled Purdy under his arm, arrived with most of his station hands. Other men joined the party. Before they departed from Nuntin, McMillan warned them of the Myall Creek massacre and the subsequent hangings. They were all sworn to secrecy. It was a secrecy so binding that the true facts of the massacre died with the perpetrators and their victims.

The posse, probably numbering as many as twenty, rode out in search of Macalister's killers. In his *Book of the Bush*, George Dunderdale puts the posse's rationale succinctly: 'It was, of course, impossible to identify any blackfellow concerned in the outrage and therefore atonement must be made by the tribe.' The posse found a large group of Aboriginal people camped beside a waterhole on Warrigal Creek. Their intention was to avenge the death of Donald Macalister. No hostages were to be taken; no member of the group was to survive.

McMillan gave the instruction to surround the camp. The posse split. Some

Angus McMillan (centre) led massacre posses against the Kurnai in the 1840s and by the 1860s was the local Protector of Aborigines.

men rode upstream; others downstream. In twenty minutes the camp was surrounded. McMillan gave the order and simultaneously, from every direction, the men opened fire.

The Kurnai attempted to escape. Some raced into the scrub only to be met by stockmen who gunned them down. Others jumped into the waterhole. McMillan and his men positioned themselves around the waterhole 'and, as fast as they put their heads up for breath, they were shot until the water was red with blood'.

The massacre lasted less than half an hour. No-one bothered to count the bodies but it became folklore in the area that up to one hundred and fifty men, women and children had been killed. McMillan and his men had learnt the lesson of Myall Creek. No pile of half-burnt bodies was left at Warrigal Creek. For the next few hours they did a careful mopping-up operation. The bodies of their victims were thrown into the waterhole. Years later the bones of some of the victims would be found.

Those who had been injured or captured were used as spies. One account, told over eighty years later, recalled, 'I knew two blacks, who, though wounded came out of that hole alive. One was a boy at the time about 12 or 14 years old. He was hit in the eye by a slug, captured by the whites, and made to lead the brigade from one camp to another.'

Over the next couple of days the posse moved through the area leaving a trail of bodies and blood. They killed at every opportunity.

The covenant of silence was not broken. McMillan, who had opened the Gippsland region up to white settlement, went on to become a respected and prominent citizen. For many years he was the president of the Gippsland Caledonian Society. In 1859 he became the first representative for South Gippsland in the Victorian Legislative Assembly. Ironically he also became Protector of Aborigines and gained such a reputation that his entry in the *Australian Dictionary of Biography* records that he 'took a sympathetic interest in the welfare of the Aborigines'. Silence and position had allowed him to rewrite history.

The killings and the code of silence continued. Occasionally over the dinner table or when the beer and spirits were flowing freely, there'd be some talk of massacres and of 'teaching the Aborigines a lesson' but mostly the events were forgotten. Every once in a while a curious traveller would hear of some outrage but the details were scanty and often the event had occurred years before.

The issues were land ownership and appropriate remuneration. It was self-evident (although few white landowners recognised it) to write, as Dunderdale did in his *Book of the Bush*, that, 'It is absurd to blame the Aborigines for killing sheep and cattle. You might as well say it is immoral for a cat to catch mice. Hunting was their living; the land and every animal there-on was theirs . . . to seize their lands by force and to kill them was robbery and murder.'

The Kurnai of Gippsland, Europeanised and living on a reserve near Lake Tyers in 1886.

Hugh Buntine established a property run near Port Albert on traditional Kurnai land. The Kurnai sought suitable recompense and Buntine's wife provided them with flour, beef, sugar and tea. As Buntine's herd grew larger and demands on the land became greater so the Aboriginal people demanded more and more stores. Finally Buntine's wife, who refused to see the logic of the barter, decided to rid the property of the Aboriginal population. She took her stockwhip, saddled her horse, and proceeded to round up all the Kurnai who had ever come to her demanding supplies. Her skills as a stockwoman were considerable and to her Aboriginal people were little better than cattle. She rounded them up and headed them towards the dunes and lagoons of Ninety Mile Beach. If any Aboriginal person attempted to escape through the bushes, she galloped after them cracking her whip and cutting pieces out of their flesh with her lash. On the beach she drove them into the sea and waited till they drowned.

Throughout the rest of 1843 more and more whites arrived in Gippsland. The conflicts between Aboriginal people and whites increased until, in 1844, the white landholders, tired of the skirmishing, appealed to the government for help. Their pleas, obviously exaggerated to garner support, mentioned cattle which had been killed, complained of Aboriginal people rushing livestock, and claimed, in spite of Warrigal Creek, that all white attempts at reprisals had been unsuccessful.

Charles Tyers, the newly appointed Commissioner of Crown Lands, took up the landholders' cause. At one point he wrote to the government describing an incident where the local landholders had chased two hundred Aboriginal people and, amazingly, had killed none of them. 'Mr. McMillan and others pursued them and came up with them on the ranges. Blacks poised their spears — party fired — not known if any blacks were killed — number of natives said to be two hundred.'

In the wake of the Myall Creek massacre a new frontier strategy was emerging. First the settlers complained. They moaned and groaned and wept and wailed. Here they were, brave pioneers who had conquered the harshness of the Australian bush, Godfearing men who had forded flooded streams and trudged long distances behind herds of smelly livestock, and their intentions were entirely honourable. They were carving a life for themselves out of a new country and these wicked blacks, these subhuman and vicious creatures, were doing everything in their power to destroy all their hard work. How dare the blacks kill their cattle! How dare the blacks come on their land! 'Please, Mr government officer, we need military protection. We are simple farmers. We can't defend ourselves against savages.'

Well, of course, it was just good old rural chicanery. A bunch of insincere platitudes and clichs masquerading as self-righteous innocence. It was a strategy which could not fail. If the government did not provide assistance, then any massacre could be justified with 'Well we asked for help . . . you knew how desperate we were . . . we had no alternative . . . ' If the government responded, which they did in part with the formation of the border police and the native police, then the problem of Aboriginal attacks was removed. And if the government police didn't do a good job, which was inevitable given the size of the frontier, then the settlers had a convenient whipping boy to lacerate when the Aboriginal community killed men or livestock.

It began to seem as though every night, after the boiled beef and dumplings had been eaten, the frontier became alive with epistlers, all hunched over rudely made desks with candles flickering beside them, furiously writing lengthy complaints to every government officer who was likely to be swayed by them. These ill-educated men, after a hard day clearing land or herding cattle or shooting at Aboriginal people, would stagger in, pick up a quill and start complaining. 'My neighbour, William

Pearson, has had ten cattle speared between the Thomson and La Trobe Rivers,' moaned Brindsley Sherridan, the manager of Strathfieldsaye on the shores of Lake Wellington. 'Cattle have been speared at Mr. Tom's on Tom's Creek,' and 'Stock has been driven off the Heyfield run by Aborigines,' wrote Sherridan in another letter. 'Fifty calves are missing from John King's Fulham station,' wrote another aggrieved correspondent. 'Spear wounds have been seen in the sides of the steers at Mewburn Park.' 'Steers have been killed at Macalister's Boisdale station.' 'The Aborigines have killed some of the pigs at Merton.'

It was unambiguous lobbying. Straight political manipulation. Tyers had little alternative but to bow to the force of the lobby group. The letters of complaint reflected badly on all government officers in the area. They were pouring in. He could not ignore them.

In February 1844 he decided to diffuse the landholders' anger by forming a posse of such strength that it would dispose of the 'Aboriginal problem' in less than a week. He persuaded the border police, the native police and a strong contingent of local landowners and their stockmen to join forces and rout the recalcitrant Kurnai. It was an unholy and highly illegal alliance. It had long been agreed that police and civilians should not join forces because of the legal complications. Tyers simply ignored this precept.

On 11 February Tyers, the notorious Angus McMillan, a contingent of the border police under the command of Sergeant Peacock, some stockmen from Lachlan Macalister's Boisdale station, Commissioner Frederick Powlett with a number of members of the native police, and various trackers and squatters, including John King and Edward Hobson, all gathered at a pre-arranged meeting place on the banks of the La Trobe River. The party divided with one group keeping close to the river and another group spreading out in an arc to cover the scrubby hinterland. They travelled all day without sighting a single Kurnai. The following day they came across a Kurnai camp in the late morning. Tyers, who was now in charge of the operation, instructed the men to surround the camp. In the official report he recalled that at this point 'I issued orders to both the Border Police and the Blacks not to fire except in self-defence — but to rush upon them and take them by surprise.'

Official reports are rarely more than a carefully fabricated miscellany of lies, justifications and omissions. The men did fire. Tyers claimed that he couldn't see whether it was in self-defence or not. The report managed to omit whether any Aboriginal people were killed. If the rest of the frontier was any kind of precedent, there was killing. As usual the truth was covered up by bureaucratic detail. The official report included a list of weapons and an estimate of the weight of beef found — six English tomahawks, twenty-six stone tomahawks, sixty spears, thirty nets filled with beef, twelve hundred-weight of smoked beef . . . but no bodies. With a peculiarly moral Victorian sensibility Tyers earnestly reported that as a punishment

Skirmishes involving the mounted police and Aboriginal people were rarely reported by the police. Many reports managed to omit whether Aboriginal people were killed.

'I caused their spears and the beef they had taken to be burnt on the spot'. Then, with astonishing audacity, Tyers went on to report that his antiseptic mopping-up operation, in which few guns had been fired and no loss of life had occurred, was a total success.

A month later Lachlan Macalister and Angus McMillan were once again complaining about the Kurnai attacking their livestock. So much for the total success. Once again it was the settlers who decided to sort out the Kurnai. A new arrival in the region was a man named Patrick Buckley who was working a run called Coady Vale, just north of Warrigal Creek. The property ran for nearly 10 kilometres along Ninety Mile Beach. Buckley was a cold, hard, poorly educated man. He had been born in Newgate Prison in 1817 and had been transported with his mother to Botany Bay. He was a giant of a man, standing two metres tall. He had little respect for the Kurnai and he expected them to keep well away from his land. He was furious when he found that sheep had been taken from the paddock adjoining his hut.

Determined to rid 'his' land of Aboriginal people and to recover his sheep, he joined forces with a friend, Len Mason, and the two men, both armed with double-barrelled shotguns, went in search of the culprits. They spent the whole day in a fruitless search and it wasn't until evening that they discovered a group of Kurnai. They fired upon the group, who fled into the bush. Buckley claimed that the carcasses of two sheep were found at the abandoned camp. He used this to justify his attempted murder of the Aboriginal people and to demand immediate government action from Sergeant Peacock and the border police. A posse was formed and for the next week Buckley, Peacock and a number of other squatters scoured the area, intending to kill any Kurnai they made contact with. The Kurnai outwitted them. The men spent a week searching the area without sighting a single Aboriginal person. Instead, with comic irony, they got lost, became bogged in the coastal marshes, lost their horses, and were drenched by a number of unseasonable downpours. Buckley rationalised the failure by declaring, 'We must have struck terror in them the first evening we went up'.

Undeterred by the failure, when he found one of his cows and a steer dead on Ninety Mile Beach he decided once again to try and find the culprits. This time he found an old man and woman walking along the beach. Angered by his previous lack of success, he made scapegoats of them. In his diary he recounted his treatment of his helpless victims with considerable relish:

> I saw two blacks coming along the beach from near the Creek. I waited behind the sand hammock until they came opposite me. I then rode down toward them and they took to the sea. I had a pistol with me and fired blank shots to keep them in the sea which I did for about four hours and drove them along in the water to near the mouth of Merriman's Creek which is about a mile. The blackfellow got very weak, the gin seemed to be quite strong. I called to her several times to leave but she stuck to the blackfellow faithfully but at last she thought there was no chance for him consequently she left him. At this time he seemed nearly drowned in the breakers. I rode into the surf after him, got a rein round his neck and pulled him out and nearly hanged him, whilst doing so. When I got him out on the sand he pretended to be dead but when I pulled out his hands to look at them he used to jerk them in again. I planted him back of the Hammock for some time but he would not move so I came away and left him. Only my Mare was too frightened I would have brought him home to the hut. The Blackfellow must have been very weak for being so long nocking about amongst the Surf.

Buckley continued with his undeclared war on the Kurnai. It was a war of attrition which Buckley won by force of arms. He kept no records of how many Aboriginal people he killed but it is certain that dozens, maybe even hundreds, died at his hands over the next decade.

To the north of Buckley's run lay the large holding of Lindenow, owned by Henry Loughnan and managed by Fred Taylor. Taylor had arrived in Gippsland with the first settlers in 1842. He was a hard man with a reputation for massacring any group of Aboriginal people who interfered with 'his' land. As early as 1843 his reputation was well established. G A Robinson, Chief Protector of Aborigines, had written of Taylor that he 'was notorious for killing natives . . . I found a tribe, a section of the Jarcoots, totally extinct and it was affirmed by the natives that Taylor had destroyed them.' He was the kind of quasi-criminal who was attracted to the frontier. His behaviour, which was always on the edge of the law, was unconstrained in a society where the few policemen were overworked.

For twelve years Taylor hounded the Kurnai from his land. He gained a reputation as a landowner and manager who was hated by the Aboriginal community. He never recorded his killings but it was clear that between 1842 and 1860 dozens of Kurnai lost their lives because they accidentally wandered on to one of his runs.

Taylor and Buckley were typical of the well-established frontier belief that massacring groups of Aboriginal people in the immediate vicinity was the most effective way to assert ownership of a region. Their behaviour was illegal. It almost always involved the killing of a large number of innocent women and children but it was 'effective'. The authorities simply turned their backs on the murders.

As the squatters continued to kill the Kurnai, so they were joined by the native police. The native police's rationale was always self-defence. They rarely killed in large numbers. Their commanding officers knew that it would be hard to rationalise a massacre of forty or fifty people with an explanation of self-defence so killings were restricted to twos and threes. The policy was to be judge, jury and executioner at the one time.

The modus operandi of the native police was well explained by George Dunderdale in *Book of the Bush* when he recalled:

> I heard Mr. Tyers relate the measures taken by himself and his native police to suppress their irregularities. He was informed that some cattle had been speared, and he rode away with his force to investigate the complaint. He inspected the cattle killed or wounded, and then directed his black troopers to search for tracks, and this they did willingly and well. Traces of natives were soon discovered, and their probable hiding-place in the scrub was pointed out to Mr. Tyers. He therefore dismounted, and directing two of his black troopers armed with carbines to accompany him, he held a pistol in each hand and walked cautiously into the scrub. The two black troopers discharged their carbines. The commissioner had seen nothing to shoot at, but his blacks soon showed him two of the natives a few yards in front, both mortally wounded. Mr. Tyers sent a report of the affair to the Government, and that was the end of it.

The native police were always happy for an excuse to kill Aboriginal people. To the

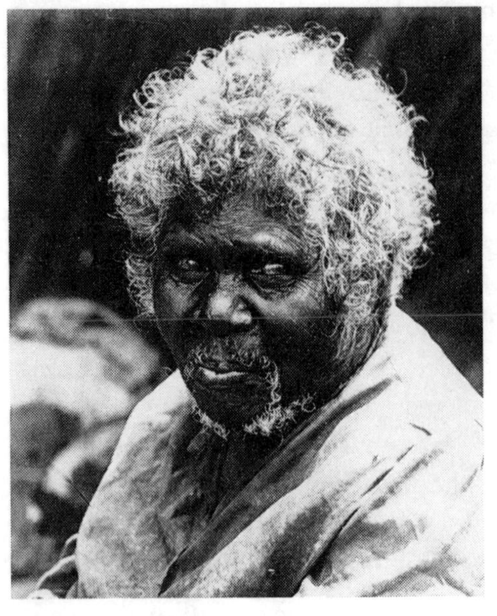

One observer noted of the Kurnai: 'It is a great pity that powder and ball seems to be their fate, as the settlers think no more of shooting them than they do of eating their dinners.'

white settlers they were an efficient force above criticism; to Aboriginal people they were a scourge.

An opportunity for large-scale killing by the native police came in late 1846. For some years rumours had drifted through Gippsland, from camp fire to camp fire and from hut to hut, that a shipwrecked white woman was living with the Kurnai. If there is anything guaranteed to stir racial hatred it is the notion that a woman is being sexually attacked by racially inferior men. It was all right for the settlers to rape Kurnai women but it was morally outrageous for the Kurnai to take a shipwreck victim and offer her care and protection.

Some Aboriginal prisoners confirmed the existence of a red-haired white woman. She was said to be living somewhere in the foothills of the Snowy Mountains with a Kurnai warrior named Bunjil-ee-nee.

Charles Tyers decided that Bunjil-ee-nee and his white mistress could be lured out of the mountains with promises of clothing and blankets. Five Kurnai prisoners were sent to barter with Bunjil-ee-nee. They returned some weeks later somewhat chastened. Bunjil-ee-nee had cracked two of them over the head with a large waddy and sent them scampering back to their white masters. Tyers wrote of the incident:

> I need scarcely observe that the nature of the country is such that should force have to be resorted to, a strong party would be required, which should be divided into five or six parties, to cooperate by land and water, to insure the probability of success.

The wildness, the sexuality, the adventure, the intrigue of the whole incident was like heavenly manna to the Port Phillip yellow press. It was precisely the kind of story which increased readership. It was a story for the prurient, a story loaded with unstated sexual possibilities. Public meetings were held. Funds poured in from well-wishers. Newspapers editorialised.

In October 1846 a search party, the Gippsland Expedition, led by Christian De

Villiers, a former commandant of the native police, and including ten Aboriginal people, left Port Phillip. They had supplies for three months. They sailed around the coast and arrived in Gippsland in November. Within a week of their arrival they were engaged in an acrimonious brawl with W Walsh who commanded the local native police. In an attempt to diffuse the situation Tyers, who had received information that Bunjil-ee-nee was moving up to the headwaters of the Snowy River, sent a contingent of native police lead by Walsh and some border police under the command of Captain William Dana to find the elusive Aboriginal husband.

De Villiers and his men searched fruitlessly along the coast. They came upon evidence of a vast number of unrecorded massacres but made no contact with the white woman. One of De Villiers's men, after coming across a second mound of bones, rather wistfully wrote of the Kurnai:

> They certainly are a very fine race, few under six feet and stout in proportion. It is a great pity that powder and ball seems to be their fate, as the settlers think no more of shooting them than they do of eating their dinners and from what we can learn some fearful slaughters have taken place.

De Villiers learnt of the whereabouts of the white woman and sent her a letter, which was delivered by two old Kurnai men. The men were captured by Walsh and Dana and returned to Tyers. The whole operation was becoming ludicrous. Instead of co-operation to bring the woman out of the mountains, the two expeditions were warring with each other.

Knowing that the white woman was somewhere in the general area of the Snowy River, both groups set off to find her. It was the accident of having Walsh and Dana's frontier-style patrol in the same area as De Villiers's very humane, almost citified, expedition which provided one of the few well-documented accounts of the massacres of the Kurnai people.

Dana, Walsh and their contingent of native and border police reached the Snowy River ahead of De Villiers. It was clear that the discovery of the white woman was important but the massacre of any Kurnai was also part of their plan. As a member of De Villiers's expedition was cynically to observe, 'So long as such persons as Messrs. Dana and Walsh are in command of the Native Police nothing can stop the extermination . . . nothing gives them so much pleasure as shooting and tomahawking the defenceless savages.'

It was late afternoon, the sun was still touching the ridges and a hint of evening coolness was drifting off the fast-rowing, icy river, when Dana, Walsh and their men sighted the smoke which was the certain sign of a Kurnai camp fire. The Aboriginal people saw the police approaching and fled. The police opened fire and a number of Aboriginal people were killed. Dana and Walsh slept near the riverbank that night and the following morning pushed north. They found more Kurnai camps, which they attacked. The scale of their killings was large.

Late on the second afternoon they saw a large camp of Kurnai settling in for the night. Although Dana, Walsh and the police had already killed dozens of Kurnai and rushed and destroyed a number of camp sites, these Aboriginal people felt secure because they had retreated up a stream which was a minor tributary of the Snowy River.

Dana and Walsh decided to wait until darkness fell. The police, trained for silent movement through the bush, slowly surrounded the camp. Through the branches of the tea trees and acacias they could see the men building up the night fires. The Kurnai wrapped themselves in their possum coats and nestled against each other to protect themselves against the cold night air. The spears and waddies were piled up against a nearby tree. Silence, broken only by the rustling of night animals and the doleful 'Mopoke, Mopoke' of the owls, settled over the camp.

The signal for the attack was given. Suddenly the silence was ripped by gunfire and bloodcurdling yells as the native police broke from their cover and charged the camp. Swords, the effective close-range weapons which had gained notoriety after the Myall Creek massacre, were wielded. Gun butts were brought down with sickening force on the heads of women and children. The Kurnai, with sleep and terror mingling, attempted to escape. Babies were hurled onto the camp fires. Limbs were severed. Moaning and wailing began to fill the night air. Dana and Walsh did not bother to count the dead. They grabbed three children and an old man and woman who were cringing in terror, chained them together, and headed back to the main river where they camped for the night.

In the morning De Villiers and his expedition caught up with Dana and Walsh. They had twice heard gunshots but thought they were no more than an attempt to flush the Kurnai out of the hills and head them back to the lakes. De Villiers was surprised by Captain Dana's demeanour. The officer seemed ill-at-ease and uncomfortable. De Villiers, not realising that he was only a few kilometres away from the scene of a massacre, interpreted Dana's reticence as residual resentment dating back to their earlier disagreements. He asked Dana if he could question the prisoners about the whereabouts of Bunjil-ee-nee and the white woman. Dana begrudgingly agreed and De Villiers took the five Aboriginal people back to his camp for questioning. It was during the questioning, and away from the terrifying influence of the native police, that the old man and woman revealed the details of the massacre. De Villiers was cautiously circumspect. He realised that the story was almost certainly true but was loath to confront Dana with the accusation. The prisoners were returned. De Villiers set up camp about a kilometre further downstream. During the night, although secured together by handcuffs around the ankles, the old man and woman escaped.

The next day the two groups parted company. De Villiers was determined to move further upstream. Dana and Walsh were returning to the police station. De Villiers asked for the key to the handcuffs so, if he came across the old man and woman, he could set them free. His request was refused. As far as Dana and Walsh were concerned the Kurnai escapees could spend the rest of their lives handcuffed together.

Dana went to some trouble to ensure that De Villiers didn't travel up the creek where the massacre had taken place. He pointed out that the creek led nowhere and that if Bunjil-ee-nee was still in the mountains, he would be somewhere up the Snowy River valley. De Villiers took little heed of Dana's advice. By mid-morning the expedition had reached the site of the massacre. The Kurnai had removed most of the bodies but in the reeds De Villiers found:

> . . . the body of a fine strapping Aboriginal about twenty-five to thirty years old. The head was cut in two places and the skull split as if by some sharp instrument; there was a mark on the chest and one on the leg, both appeared like gun-shot wounds. I was informed after examining the body, that four more men had been shot and that it had been done by the narran [police] black and white fellows.

Later that day they found the old escapees and although they didn't have the key, they did manage to unlock the handcuffs. As he moved back downstream De Villiers found more evidence of killings by Dana, Walsh and the native police.

Immediately upon their return, Dana and Walsh filed a report insisting that they had sighted the white woman during their expedition and that any shooting the native police had done had been aimed at saving the woman.

De Villiers was determined that Charles Tyers know the details of the whole affair. It probably would have all been hushed up in Gippsland had not one of De Villiers expedition, a man named James Warman, written a letter to the *Port Phillip Herald* in which he bluntly spelt out the barbarous behaviour of the native police. He claimed that the Aboriginal people had offered no resistance to the 'wanton barbarity' of this slaughter 'by these harpies of hell, misnamed police' and concluded 'I almost blush to say that one or two Europeans were not a whit behind these demi-civilised wretches . . .'

Tyers, aware of the possible repercussions, called Dana, Walsh and their 'harpies of hell' off the case. The last thing he wanted was dozens of city do-gooders bringing a moral microscope to bear on the carnage which had characterised nearly a decade of settlement in Gippsland.

De Villiers returned to the mountains and although he met a group which claimed that the white woman was one of their number, he was never allowed to see her or talk to her. The men in the group assured De Villiers that the woman, who they named Lohan-tuka, was loved by them all. He deduced that she had given birth to a boy who was accepted by the tribe. Although he tried everything from threats to gently cajoling, the group refused to let him see the woman. He abandoned the search in late January and was back in Melbourne in early February 1847.

The saga of the mysterious white woman dragged on. Bunjil-ee-nee was captured and questioned but he never produced the mysterious Lohan-tuka. He died on 21 November 1848 and the secret died with him. Amongst the Kurnai the legend of Lohan-tuka lived on. The shipwreck and the life with Bunjil-ee-nee were forgotten. In the folk memory of the tribe she was simply 'a big pale-coloured woman with long flowing red hair who lived by herself. She came out of her cave to frighten the people and the little children'.

The whole of the Gippsland area had been won by violence. The settlers just killed and killed and killed. Massacres, rapes and casual killings were so normal, so commonplace, they barely deserved discussion. The squatter Henry Meyrick, who was as likely to kill Aboriginal people as any of his bloodthirsty neighbours, left a unique record of the scale and brutality of the killings in his letters to his mother. In them he makes mention of squatters who would ride into a Kurnai camp and kill everyone who was too slow to escape from the sword and the gun. At various times he wrote, 'I have heard tales and some things I have seen that would form as dark a page as ever you read in the book of history, but I thank God I have never participated in them' and vainly, but wisely, reflected 'if I could remedy these things, I would speak loudly though it cost me all I am worth in the world, but as I cannot, I will keep aloof and know nothing and say nothing'. The things he was loath to mention were hinted at when he wrote, 'No wild beast of the forest was ever hunted down with such unsparing perseverance as they are . . .' and 'but what can urge in their excuse, who shoot the women and children, I cannot conceive'.

The last major massacre recorded in the Gippsland area occurred in May 1851. It was a typical piece of frontier law. An example of unjustified white viciousness.

In the late 1840s, a ticket-of-leave man named Dan Moylan arrived in the area. He was a small, pugnacious, stocky Irishman who was variously known around the camps and stations as Little Dan or Dan the Cook. In 1850 he got a job as cook and general labourer on Archibald Macleod's Orbost station. He quickly adopted the values of the whites in the area. He treated the Kurnai with disdain and whenever the opportunity arose he was only too happy to go on a 'black hunt'.

On 2 May 1851 Little Dan managed to capture a young Kurnai girl who he dragged to his hut. He tied her up and, for the next three days, raped her over and over again. The girl's family group attempted to recapture her but Moylan fired at them and at night he laid a moat of hot coals around the hut. Desperate to save the girl, the Kurnai waited for Moylan to leave the hut unarmed. On the third day he walked out the front door of the hut. Spears showered down upon him until he

Kurnai fishing on Lake Tyers. In less than fifteen years, a proud race of over two thousand was reduced to one hundred and twenty six.

stood lifeless and propped up. The Kurnai freed the girl and fled to Milly Creek knowing that white reprisals were inevitable.

The settlers, ignoring the fact that Moylan was hardly a person deserving of their ire, eagerly formed a posse to avenge the murder of Little Dan. They saw no reason to wait for the arrival of either the native police or the border police. Accompanied by two trackers, they arrived at Orbost station to find that Moylan's hut had burnt to the ground. They gave chase and at Milly Creek found a family group whom they routed. Few escaped. Some of the men swam to safety. Some boys hid in the reeds. A woman with a baby on her back was shot such that the ball passed through both the mother and child.

The men showed little interest in counting the dead. They rode on to the Snowy River where another group were caught on the high rocky outcrop known as the Pyramids. The settlers advanced and those Kurnai who weren't shot, fell to their deaths.

It was the last major massacre. A hint of civilisation was beginning to reach Gippsland. While most of the settlers approved of the Milly Creek massacre there was now a significant group of whites who recognised Moylan's death as retaliation and were loath to endorse the actions of the posse. They knew that the Kurnai had acted against a man who had committed a vicious and unprovoked crime.

Gradually the dwindling number of Kurnai gave up their resistance. The landowner Edward Curr saw the changing face of the frontier:

> A considerable portion of the males of the tribe having been shot down the black learns the uselessness of his resistance and sues for

> peace. When the white man is of the opinion that the tribe has been so weakened and subdued that his small party has no longer anything to fear if moderate precautions are taken, peace is granted and the tribe is allowed to 'come in' as it is termed; that is to make its home at some appointed place at or near the establishment of the station-holder. From this epoch a few of the men of the tribe receive occasional employment on the station for which they are paid in food. The refuse of animals slaughtered for station use is also generally given over to the tribe.

When gold was discovered near Omeo in late 1851, the area was changed for ever. The possibility of Aboriginal resistance vanished as gold-diggers poured into the area in their thousands.

The end of the Kurnai was inevitable. The squatters, settlers, stockmen, border police, native police, disease, poison, rape, massacres and casual shootings had, in less than fifteen years, reduced a proud race of over two thousand people to one hundred and twenty-six. It was destruction which equalled the near genocide in Tasmania in its scale and viciousness.

CHAPTER 10

The Massacre at Kilcoy

That blackfellow been eatim damper. Then plenty that been jump about all the same fish, when you catch im, big mob been die — him dead all about . . .

an unnamed Aboriginal person recalling the arsenic deaths at Kilcoy

The structure of Aboriginal society was simple, pragmatic and effective. For most of the year small groups, rarely more than twenty, established themselves in particular areas where the food was adequate and plentiful. If a group lived on the coast their primary concerns were fresh water, reasonable shelter and ready access to fish, molluscs and crustaceans. Those who lived away from the coast mixed berries, fruits, nuts and vegetables with a variety of animals. Ecology was everything. Replenishment was essential and it was necessary to keep moving so that the flora and fauna were allowed to re-grow and mature.

But everywhere there was excess. At certain times of the year areas were impossibly rich with food. Such was the case on the Blackall Range which rises behind what is now the Sunshine Coast in Queensland. Each year the pine cones from the bunya trees were heavy with succulent nuts.

A complex social pattern, which had been in place for hundreds of years, existed when the first Europeans arrived in Australia. Each year (sometimes, if the food took longer to replenish, the interval would be every two or three years) groups of Aboriginal communities would gather to enjoy the rich supply of food. It was a time for sharing and celebration. Beyond this it was a time to tell stories, to engage in the trading of goods such as ochre, and to dance and laugh and sing.

By the 1820s there were two tribes, the Nalbo and Dallambara, who lived and ranged across the hinterland behind the Sunshine Coast. The Nalbo lived on the eastern slopes of the Blackall Range while the Dallambara had settled in the Conondale Range and survived on the rich provisions offered by the rainforest in the upper reaches of the Mary and Stanley rivers. Both groups were part of a larger language group, the Jinibara, which, by this time, probably numbered around 500 and were spread throughout the mountains.

Further south, around the present site of Moreton Bay, the Ngundanbi and Yagara lived along the banks of the Brisbane River.

In September 1822 the British Government instructed the governor of the colony of New South Wales, the Scottish astronomer and administrator Sir Thomas Brisbane, to send out exploration parties to Moreton Bay, Port Curtis and Port Bowen with a view to finding a suitable place for a new penal colony.

In November 1823 the explorer John Oxley reached the waters of Moreton Bay. Within days of his arrival he chanced upon three escaped convicts — Thomas Pamphlett, Richard Parsons and John Finnegan. The convicts claimed that, while on a wood-cutting expedition, they had been swept out to sea. Their small vessel had floated north and eventually been washed up onto the lonely sands of Moreton Island. They had been found by the local Aboriginal people who had shown them the closest source of fresh water. This the convicts duly showed to Oxley who named it the Brisbane River after the governor.

Oxley immediately returned to Sydney Town with news of the discovery. The next year Governor Brisbane sent the explorer back to Moreton Bay accompanied by 29 convicts, 14 soldiers, botanist Allan Cunningham, a surgeon, a storekeeper named Walter Scott, and the settlement's first military commandant, Lieutenant Henry Miller. Before the small sailing ship *Amity* left Sydney Cove, Brisbane told Oxley:

> The *Amity* is placed under orders for the purpose of crowning your late discovery of a large river flowing into Moreton Bay with the formation of a new settlement in its vicinity. The spot which you select must contain three hundred acres of land, and be in the neighbourhood of fresh water. It should lay in the direct course to the mouth of the river, be easily seen from the offing of ready access. To difficulty of attack by the natives, it ought to join difficulty of escape for the convicts.

The first settlement was at Redcliffe on Moreton Bay. Three months later the site was moved to North Quay on the Brisbane River. When Chief Justice Forbes arrived in December 1824 it was decided that the colony should be called 'Edinglassie' but this was soon rejected for Brisbane, in recognition of the governor's important role in the founding of the colony.

Although it was to remain a closed colony (no free settlement was allowed in the immediate area) it certainly was not a very effective prison. Like Pamphlett, Parsons and Finnegan before them, two convicts, James Davis and David Bracewell, managed to escape and move north where they were taken in by the Dallambara who named them Duramboi (James Davis) and Wandi (David Bracewell). It would seem from the available evidence that Davis-Duramboi had escaped around 1828 and had been living with the Dallambara for fourteen years. Bracewell-Wandi was a recidivist. Between 1828 and 1839 he escaped from Moreton Bay four times. He accompanied

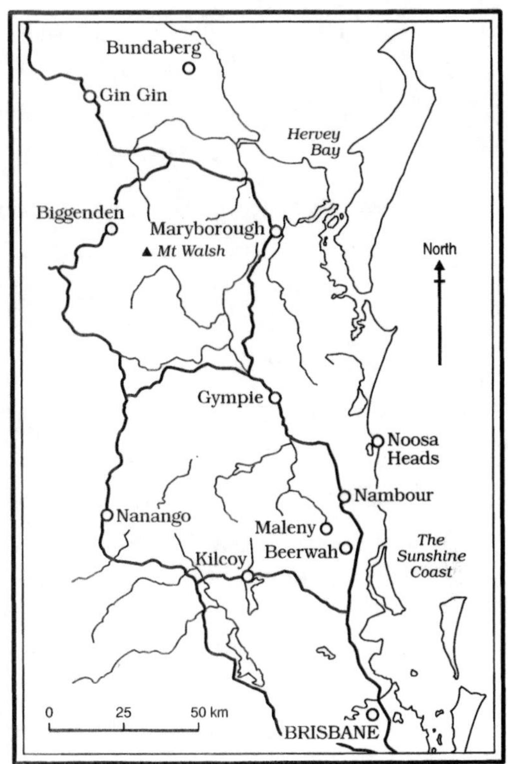

Andrew Petrie's exploration of the coast in 1842 and was involved in the rescue of Eliza Fraser on Fraser Island.

It was almost certainly Bracewell-Wandi who first alerted the authorities to the great gathering which became known as the Bunya Feast or the Bunya Festival.

In 1842 Stephen Simpson wrote a report for the colonial secretary about the area to the north of Moreton Bay. In it he described 'the great Bunya Scrub, called Booroom, lying N.W. about 2 days journey from the Glass House Mountains' and explaining that 'Here the Bunya is plentiful & in the month of January the blacks assemble for hundreds of miles round and partake of the fruit'.

As a result the Colonial Secretary's Office in Sydney issued a clear instruction on 14 April 1842:

> It having been represented to the Governor that a District exists to the Northward of Moreton Bay, in which a fruit-bearing Tree abounds, called Bunya, or Banya Bunya, and that the Aborigines from considerable distances resort at certain times of the year to this District for the purpose of eating the fruit of the said Tree: — His Excellency is pleased to direct that no Licenses be granted for the occupation of any Lands within the said District in which the Bunya or Banya Bunya Tree is found. And notice is hereby given, that the several Crown Commissioners in the New England and Moreton Bay Districts have been instructed to remove any person who may be in the unauthorised occupation of Land whereon the said Bunya or Banya Bunya Trees are to be found. His Excellency has also directed that no Licenses to cut Timber be granted within the said Districts.
>
> By His Excellency's Command, E. DEAS THOMSON.

The Bunya Festival was an extraordinary gathering. People came from up to 200 kilometres away and certainly the groups of Aboriginal people who lived on Bribie

Island, around Moreton Bay, and as far north as Fraser Island and beyond, saw the gathering as a vital part of the tapestry of their lives.

By the early 1840s the Bunya Festival was known widely within the European community. Ludwig Leichhardt visited it in December 1843 and wrote of it:

> There is a little valley, an open plain, in the midst of these brushes which cover, perhaps, an extent of 50 miles long and 10 miles broad. This plain they call Booroon, and it seems the rendezvous for fights between the hostile tribes who come from near and far to enjoy the harvest of the Bunya.

But the most authoritative report is from Tom Petrie, a remarkable young man who arrived at Moreton Bay with his engineer father, Andrew Petrie, in 1837 when he was only eight. Young Petrie was fascinated by the local Aboriginal community and by the time he was a teenager he was speaking the local dialect fluently.

Petrie first visited the Baroon Bunya Festival in the summer of 1845–46 when he was only 14. He accompanied a group of around 100 Aboriginal people from Brisbane who travelled up the coast and then, knowing the terrain from centuries of making the journey, made their way up a ridge in the Blackall Range until they arrived at Baroon. When Petrie and his group arrived they were greeted by between 600–700 Aboriginal people from the surrounding region. This was a major festival. While it seems that smaller festivals were held each year, the major one was held once every three years so the bunya cones could ripen.

Strictly speaking the bunya, which Petrie referred to as *bonyi* and which was probably pronounced *barnji*, is not a pine. Its botanical name is *Araucaria bidwilli* and it belongs to the Southern Hemisphere *Araucaria* conifer family. In the summer months the tree produces large cones (similar to pine cones) which have seeds which are rich in carbohydrates and protein.

It seems that the Dallambara and Nalbo groups controlled the Bunya Festival and, through the complex web of communication which existed between the groups in the area, they would notify everyone when the trees were ready for picking. Consequently the 'harvest' could be as early as December or as late as January or February. Certainly it seems to have lasted for a minimum of a month and, when the harvest was particularly good, for as much as three months.

The Dallambara and Nalbo were the hosts. They climbed the bunya trees and knocked down the cones. The people below would break open the cones and collect the nuts in bags. Once they had been collected they were roasted, some people ate them raw and, for the older people and the babies, the roasted nuts were ground into a paste and cooked in small cakes. It was a wonderful time. A time for celebration, joy, lots of eating, lots of games. Petrie recalled:

> Great times those were, and what lots of fun these children of the woods had in catching paddymelons in the scrub with their nets, also in obtaining other food, of which there was plenty, such as opossums, snakes, and other animals, turkey eggs, wild yams, native figs, and a large white grub, which was found in dead trees.

The inevitable result was that everyone got fat and the adolescents developed acne because of the high levels of oil they were consuming.

At the same time the gathering was a perfect opportunity for the groups to reaffirm their friendship and for goods to be traded. Bags, dogs, shells from the coast, red ochre, cockatoo feathers, weapons carved from special timbers and bunya nuts were exchanged.

The Bunya Festival was vital to the fabric of life for all Aboriginal people living in south-eastern and central Queensland. Information, goods, family ties, food, celebration and happiness were all part of the event.

Tom Petrie's explanation of the way the festival was communicated seems like an early description of what, in recent times, has been called 'the songlines':

> The Bribie blacks (Ngunda tribe) on receiving their invitation would perchance invite the Turrbal people to join them, and the latter would then ask the Logan, or Yaggapal tribe, and the other island blacks, and so on from tribe to tribe all over the country, for the

In 1842, Stephen Simpson described 'the great Bunya Scrub, called Booroom, lying N.W. about 2 days journey from the Glass House Mountains'.

> different tribes were generally connected by marriage, and the relatives thus invited each other.

As far as he could work out the Aboriginal communities who he joined at Baroon were from 'Burnett, Wide Bay, Bundaberg, Mount Perry, Gympie, Bribie, and Fraser Islands, Gayndah, Kilcoy, Mount Brisbane, and Brisbane'.

Inevitably, with such a wide spectrum of people coming together, there was a lot of shared information. And, in 1842, the information coming from the groups from the Kilcoy area was terrifying. Suddenly the idyllic life of the Kilcoy people had come to an end and it was clear that life in the district would never be the same.

The first settler in the Kilcoy region north-west of Moreton Bay was Sir Evan Mackenzie. He was the son of Colin Mackenzie (who was created a baronet in 1836) and Isabella Cameron. The family were part of the Scottish aristocracy. Young Evan was educated in Europe and by the time he left school he could speak German, French and some Greek. Instead of returning to Britain he joined the Austrian army, was promoted to second lieutenant in 1838 and resigned in early 1840. That same year Evan and his brother Colin emigrated to Sydney Town. Almost immediately Evan headed off for the 'frontier' and by 1841–42 he had taken up land which he called 'Kilcoy' after his family estate in Scotland. He lived in the area for only three to four years during which time he built the first house in Ipswich, established a village at Kangaroo Point where he built a boiling-down works, married Sarah Anna Philomena Parks, and became a prominent squatter and a friend of Ludwig Leichhardt. When his father died in 1845 he sold Kilcoy and his other interests and returned to Scotland.

No-one knows exactly what happened on Kilcoy station during Mackenzie's ownership. Some sources are eager to point out that the massacre which occurred cannot possibly be linked to this enterprising Scottish aristocrat. But the pattern is there and it is hard to imagine that the usual frontier mixture of frustration, malevolence and indifference to the lives of the local inhabitants was not at play.

Tom Petrie recalled that the Baroon Bunya Festival was like some huge council meeting. It was an opportunity for members of every group to air their opinions, give voice to their grievances, and explain what had been happening in their district. He noted of the meeting he had witnessed:

> One man would stand up and start a story or lecture of what had happened in his part of the country, speaking in a loud tone of voice, so that all could hear. When he had finished, another man from a different tribe stood forth and gave his descriptions, and so on till all the tribes had been represented.

When the groups gathered for the Baroon Bunya Festival in the summer of 1842 the Inwoorah and Tombarah people had a tale to tell but, instead of one of the elders standing and simply recounting the events, they acted it out. The festival that year had attracted fourteen or fifteen different groups. As was the tradition the women had dug a large circular ditch where the meetings were to be held. No-one knows whether the Inwoorah and Tombarah waited for the festivities to begin, or whether they acted out their story as soon as they arrived.

The story was strange and mysterious. They entered the ring and, in a group, they acted out a scene which started with people finding some food, some 'white man's flour', and preparing a damper over the fire and then everyone sitting around and starting to eat it. At this point the mime must have seemed strange. This was what everyone at Baroon was doing. There was probably a fire already alight with dampers made from crushed bunya nuts cooking for the old people.

Then slowly the image of the massacre unfolded. The people held their heads as though they were swelling to a point where the eyeballs rolled and it seemed as though their skulls were about to explode. They coughed and mimicked foam and spittle coming from their mouths. Their bodies convulsed with agony and they mimed violent vomiting. They cried out for water and twisted with pain. Then their bodies started trembling uncontrollably, they jumped around like fish taken out of water until, exhausted from their agony, they fell prostrate and feigned death on the ground.

Shortly after, as they told of what had happened at Kilcoy Creek, they explained that one group who had always attended the festival were absent this time because they had been destroyed by the poisoned flour.

Years later an old Aboriginal was to recall the event: 'That blackfeller been eatim damper. Then plenty that been jump about all the same fish, when you catch im, big mob been die — him dead all about.'

No-one knows how many people were killed in the Kilcoy massacre. The lower estimates are thirty men, women and children. The upper estimates put the number up around fifty or sixty.

This woman from the Maryborough region is carrying a bag which would have collected the bunya nuts in preparation for the feast.

No-one knows the exact circumstances. Was Evan Mackenzie active in the massacre? Did the massacre occur before Mackenzie arrived in the district? Was the massacre a result of itinerant shepherds, looking for new pastures for their sheep, who felt threatened by the local Aboriginal population and decided to add arsenic to the flour so they could eliminate the problem? It is impossible to say.

What is very clear is that the 'death pudding', as squatters and settlers came to call flour and poison (usually strychnine or arsenic), became commonplace in Queensland and was still being used as recently as the turn of the century.

In 1885 Harold Finch-Hatton, in his book *Advance Australia: An Account of Eight Years Work, Wandering and Amusement*, wrote:

> The rations contained about as much strychnine as anything else and not one of the mob escaped. When they awoke in the morning they were all dead corpses. More than a hundred Blacks were stretched out by this ruse of the owner of Long Lagoon.

Kilcoy was the start of a wholesale reign of terror in Queensland which, although poorly documented, indicates that probably thousands of Aboriginal people were killed by poisoning between 1842 and 1900.

In the disturbing book *Race Relations in Queensland*, Raymond Evans records:

> James Demarr records the poisoning of an unspecified number near Laidley in the 1840s, while both Tom Petrie and Edgar Foreman give evidence of arsenic placed in food killing 'fifty or sixty' at Whitesides Station on the Upper Pine River. Foreman recalled finding some of the ghastly remains of this feast: 'I, as a little boy, rode through a small pocket of what was called Rush Creek and saw scores of bleached bones including a complete skeleton.' There are also mentions of poisoning along the Macintyre and in the Warrego District, of an attempted poisoning on the Maroochy River, of a successful one at Maryborough in 1854, and of another, large distribution of toxic food 'at Christmas', in the Burnett District sometime afterwards. There are reports of other poisonings in the Dawson River region, at Apis Station near Marlborough, and in the Cardwell District. There are undoubtedly numerous poisoning cases which, through guilt and shame, were never reported at all. In North Queensland, E W Docker claims, such poisonings were 'almost a commonplace occurrence', whilst as late as 1908, an alarmed Reverend Campion was told here: "Why, if you give the blacks phosphorous in their flour it only makes their eyes water, but if you mix arsenic with the flour, that'll stretch them out."

Those who survived the shootings and poisonings could only look on as the new settlers built huts on what had been old camping grounds.

What is also clear is that the Aboriginal people at Baroon who witnessed the Kilcoy massacre re-enactment, and who spoke to the people from the Inwoorah and Tombarah groups, swore vengeance on all Europeans.

In his *History of Queensland* William Coote concluded that 'from all I have learned I can arrive at no other conclusion than that very many of the murders perpetrated by the blacks for years afterwards were more or less in direct consequence, or in revenge, of the wholesale poisoning at Kilcoy'.

So it was that over the next twenty years, until they had been cowed into submission, a war raged in southern Queensland as the Aboriginal population fought an unequal battle against the might of the colonial forces and their very superior firepower.

CHAPTER 11

MASSACRES BY THE NATIVE POLICE

Nothing gives the Native Police so much pleasure as shooting and tomahawking the defenceless savages.

The journal of James Warman, 1846

A certain kind of person becomes a policeman. The duties, the uniform, the discipline, the authority, the carrying of arms, the small-scale power, the security, the 'respect' draw people who find these attributes of the job attractive. Policemen are not moulded by their colleagues or the job; they are drawn to the job because it fulfils deep needs. The native police were, in essence, no different to policing forces anywhere else in the world.

Created in 1848 they were a typical product of ruthless frontier pragmatism. The aim was simple: set an Aboriginal person to kill an Aboriginal person. The method was to flatter Aboriginal men by providing them with a horse, local women, plenty of booze, an attractive blue and white uniform, blankets and a double-barrelled carbine and pistols and, in return, ask them to track and kill Aboriginal people with whom they had neither kinship nor allegiance. The result was a despised force, who were known chiefly for their brutality and for the frequent brawls they became involved in over local tribal women.

When Frederick Walker, one-time Clerk of Petty Sessions at Tumut on the edge of the Snowy Mountains, was appointed commandant of the newly formed corps of native police, he knew that he'd have no trouble recruiting from the local tribes. Certainly there'd be those Aboriginal people who would look with horror on the idea of donning a uniform and marching off to subdue other Aboriginal people. But, equally, there'd be plenty of Aboriginal people for whom the kudos of a uniform, a horse, a gun, regular wages and white tucker would be irresistible. By March 1849, after visiting four tribes in the Murrumbidgee–Murray area, Walker had fourteen recruits and was riding north to bring law and order to a frontier which now stretched in a huge, gracious arc from the Macintyre, through the Darling Downs and back across to the coast through central Queensland.

While this was the first major native police force, it was not the first Aboriginal police force to be recruited in the colony. As early as 1839, as a direct result of the Myall Creek massacre, the border police (a quasi-native police force) had been formed. Originally this force was supposed to be operational for only two years but it was not disbanded until 1846.

The border police–native police force operated on the Darling Downs, in the newly settled areas west of Moreton Bay, and, to particularly brutal effect, in the Gippsland area of Victoria. They were, at best, a very ad hoc organisation made up of ex-convicts, any Aboriginal men who wanted to join, stockmen, shepherds and itinerant whites seeking regular pay, food and lodgings. Their grasp of the niceties of British justice was, at best, tenuous. They certainly would have shown little interest in Governor Gipps's arguments about the foundation of a frontier police force:

> The vast interests, which have grown up in those distant parts of the Territory, and the number of persons of all classes now engaged in depasturing Sheep and Cattle beyond what are called the Boundaries of Location, might be sufficient themselves to call for the protection of a Police Force; but the necessity of it is rendered far more urgent by the frequent aggressions made of late by the Aboriginal Natives upon Flocks and Herds of Stockmen, by the outrages which have been committed on the Aborigines as well as by them, and particularly by one atrocious deed of blood for which seven unhappy men have suffered death on the scaffold.

The aim of the native police was simple — set an Aboriginal man to kill an Aboriginal man. The force was a product of ruthless frontier pragmatism.

While Gipps could rationalise the need for a border police force the truth was that the practice of squatting (taking sheep or cattle beyond the limits of land ownership and declaring a run on Crown land claimed by dint of possession) had forced circumstances upon the government which the government simply could not avoid. The squatters and the new frontiersmen had become an immensely powerful lobby group. These were the glory boys. They were the sons of the landowning class which had consumed all the usable land around Sydney. They had moved beyond the boundaries of the initial nineteen colonies knowing that fortunes awaited those who grabbed vast tracts of land and managed to keep the Aboriginal population at bay. As William Forster eloquently put it to the 1858 Select Committee on Native Police:

> Enterprising men, induced by the large profit or appearance of profit held out in undertakings of the kind, will always go beyond any protection the Government can give them; and, in that case, murders will be committed by the natives, and upon the natives, in spite of any force you can organise.

It had been these 'enterprising men' who had, almost certainly, encouraged their labourers and station hands to commit the slaughter at Myall Creek. It was these 'enterprising men' who had joined forces with the border police and the native police to wipe out the Kurnai in Gippsland. And now it was these 'enterprising men' who eagerly lobbied the government in Sydney for the establishment of a police force to protect their sheep and cattle against attacks from local groups of dispossessed Aboriginal people.

It is a comment on the greed and ruthlessness of these pastoralists, all of them committed to making a fortune and maximising their profits, that not once did they consider conciliation as a solution. Realistically a group of Aboriginal people, given the right to move freely across a vast 8000 hectare run and given the right to kill livestock when native fauna was not available, would have made little impression on the profits of a successful white landholder. Ironically the cattle killed, livestock rushed, and man-hours involved in hunting Aboriginal people was almost certainly more expensive than a policy of live and let live. But this was not to be.

As the frontier moved out, like some huge tidal wave, across New South Wales and north and south into what was to become Queensland and Victoria, Aboriginal people tried unsuccessfully to hold the line.

It was not, as some people have suggested, organised warfare. It was too random and haphazard for that. It was not in the nature of Aboriginal society to organise military-style operations; they were simply fighting for their right to exist.

In spite of the inequality produced by the superiority of guns, Aboriginal people developed highly effective means of harassment which in some areas, most notably the Upper Darling around the modern-day site of Wilcannia, actually drove white

The history of the native police is an ugly chapter in the expansion of the white frontier in Queensland.

settlers off the land. The most successful technique was the rushing and slaughter of cattle and sheep. Stations had to be large. It was impossible to patrol and guard livestock day and night and sheep and cattle were easy targets for spears and clubs. As Aboriginal communities began to interfere with the livestock herds, the settlers began to demand protection. It was out of these requests that the native police corps was formed. The rationale, according to the Moreton Bay Police Magistrate, Captain John Clements Wickham, was based on the argument that 'it was well known that the natives of one tribe would destroy those of another, upon the slightest provocation'. This claim probably had no basis in fact although the native police did carry out their duties with unnerving enthusiasm.

So it was that the first corps of native police was formed under Frederick Walker on 6 December 1848.

Immediately settlers in outlying areas — the Darling Downs, Lower Condamine River region and the Macintyre River — started requesting police protection. Walker and his men went about their task of suppressing Aboriginal aggression with such viciousness that they quickly gained a reputation which resulted in white admiration and black fear.

In 1849 Walker and his police force arrived on the Macintyre River. A local landholder, William Tooth, had complained that the local Aboriginal people were killing his cattle. Walker and his force found the local tribe and in the massacre which followed they so terrorised the Aboriginal population that Tooth later reported:

> The blacks were so completely put down on that occasion and terrified at the power of the Police, that they never committed any more depredations near there. The place was quiet at once, and

> property became fifty per cent more valuable . . . Larnach sold the station at a sacrifice, as the blacks had been very troublesome. Scarcely a man would go into the district for double the wages paid anywhere else and no woman would go near it at all. The hutkeepers would not venture to go down to a waterhole without being armed with gun or pistol. In three months after the police came, the district was so quiet a man could walk about anywhere.

This first encounter had exactly the effect that the landholders had hoped for. The land increased in value, the labourers felt secure and the Aboriginal population was removed.

Walker and his men garnered more popular support with their next massacre. The local Aboriginal population had been attacking the bullock drays bringing food and supplies into the area. The drays moved slowly and were poorly guarded. Rumour in the area was that a bullock driver nicknamed 'the Smiler' was to be the next target of an attack. The native police and Walker agreed to help him. They hid in the back of one of the Smiler's drays and when the group of Aboriginal people accosted Smiler and asked for tobacco, the native police opened fire. The Aboriginal people fled with the native police in pursuit. Upon their return the native police conveniently failed to report how many Aboriginal people had been killed. It was a dangerous precedent. One white observer remarked that 'the number they killed no one but their commander and themselves ever knew'.

Within weeks of their formation, the native police had adopted the frontier strategies of silence and omission. Thus most of their actions would remain unrecorded.

In June 1849 Walker received a request from a number of squatters who had taken up land along the Condamine River. Leaving part of his force to police the Macintyre, he moved to the Condamine where two major attacks (or massacres) took place. In his report of the incidents Walker described groups of Aboriginal people up to one hundred and fifty strong. With a coyness which refused to mention the actual numbers killed, he wrote, 'on the first occasion, the FitzRoy Downs tribes (who had killed seven men of MacPherson's on Mount Abundance, a shepherd of Blyth's besides spearing Blyth himself, and two men of Hughes's) suffered so severely that they returned to their own country, a distance of eighty miles'.

In early 1850 Walker, after continued demands from landholders across the frontier, expanded the native police by employing two lieutenants, Richard Purvis Marshall and George Fulford.

Marshall was left in the Condamine–Macintyre area with a force of ten native police. He had learnt all the tricks from Walker. When, in February 1850, complaints came through from landholders in the Lower Condamine he moved his troops into the area, picked up the trail of an Aboriginal group, and in three days had attacked

The Black Police, published in 1890, exposed the brutality and barbarism which characterised the native police.

their camp, shooting at random. A number of Aboriginal people were killed but Marshall conveniently forgot to keep a record of the killings and when an inquiry was held into the massacre his defence was that warrants had been issued for the arrest of twenty Aboriginal people in the area. He did not say whether he had killed any of the Aboriginal people charged and the inquiry did not bother to ask.

For every massacre by the native police there were literally dozens of single killings. It was not uncommon for a totally innocent Aboriginal person, terrorised by the very presence of the native police, to attempt to run for cover. Running away, in the eyes of the police, was effectively an admission of guilt. On one foray in search of Aboriginal cattle killers, Marshall and his men found an abandoned camp fire. As they rode away they saw an Aboriginal man named Talbot fleeing into the bush. The police gave chase, assuming the man was guilty. When Talbot refused to give himself up, one of the police shot him.

On another occasion, on 1 December 1851, Marshall and his men killed an Aboriginal man named Milbong only to find out subsequently that they had shot the wrong man.

The police had little need to worry about such 'errors'. When Walker sent in his report on Marshall's activities the Governor, Sir Charles Augustus FitzRoy, bluntly observed that 'A great many blacks are reported as having been killed by the Police but I think that the depositions when received will prove these acts of severity to have been unavoidable'.

The native police were 'successful' largely because they removed the most potent weapon Aboriginal people had. As FitzRoy observed, 'It requires people of their own class who can make their way through dense scrubs and creeks and places where a white man encumbered with clothing cannot travel.' This was no more devastatingly demonstrated than in the massacres at Fraser Island. For some years the whites had been attempting to remove Aboriginal people from the island but with little success. The local Aboriginal population used the terrain and tropical vegetation to avoid capture. The arrival of the native police destroyed this advantage.

Both Marshall's force and Walker's force sailed to Fraser Island in late December 1851, landing on the island on 27 December. The weather and the terrain were unbearable. It rained every evening, the humidity was debilitating, the island's freshwater streams became swollen and, worst of all, the sticky air was alive with mosquitoes and sandflies.

After two days Walker and Marshall were exhausted. They had been forced to walk through dense jungle and they needed rest. Two of the native police sergeants, Edgar and Willy, sought permission to continue the pursuit of the island's Aboriginal population. For the next four days the native police, unencumbered by horses and set free from the constraints which Walker and Marshall would have placed upon them, rampaged across the island.

Walker made little mention of the massacres which occurred. He mentioned the deaths of only three Aboriginal people and complained about the hardships which the expedition had experienced. Governor FitzRoy commented on Walker's report:

> The Commandant has, I conclude, observed the rule which must invariably be followed when deaths occur in the collisions which may take place between the Native Police and the Aborigines [sic], of making and sending to the Attorney General depositions as to the facts of each case. The Commandant's movements appear to have been conducted with much judgement.

The 'facts of each case' were certainly never told. By this time the reputation of the native police was such that every 'collision' was nothing more than a euphemism for a large-scale massacre.

If the evidence of Charles Eden, who claimed that the native police loved to kill, is anything to go by, then the unreported massacre on Fraser Island would have involved anywhere up to one hundred innocent Aboriginal people. Eden wrote of the native police:

> It is a rash thing to rob a lioness of her whelps or a tiger of his prey, but I doubt if either would be attended with more danger than interfering between the troopers and their foes when once their blood is up. Then is the only time the officer loses his control over them.

Walker and Marshall were busily rewriting the history of their corps. Everyone on the frontier knew of the real brutality of the native police but the official records portrayed this band of licensed murderers as models of probity and conservatism.

There is a pointed story about these officially sanctioned lies in A J Vogan's book *The Black Police: A Story of Modern Australia*:

> A young 'sub', new in the force . . . used the word 'killed' instead of the official 'dispersed' in speaking of the unfortunate natives left hors de combat on the field. The report was returned to him for correction with a severe reprimand for his careless wording . . . The 'sub' being rather a wag corrected his report so that the faulty portion now read as follows. 'We successfully surrounded the said party of aborigines and dispersed fifteen, the remainder, some half dozen, succeeded in escaping . . .'

Is it reasonable to assume that every time a native police report mentions 'dispersal' that the sub-text means that there was a massacre of fifteen Aboriginal people? Is it in the spirit of these lies that the history of the native police has to be interpreted? Walker always portrayed the native police as men of conscience and moral character. When Walker went to Sydney in early 1852, he addressed his troops in the following ludicrous manner:

> The Governor will ask me all about you, mind, and I am obliged to tell him everything. There is one thing that you must all mind and this is never to tell a lie. The old policemen have been with me now three years and they never told me a lie, never drink grog, never swear, and never quarrel. I want you all to be the same.

What the men made of such nonsense was never recorded.

While Walker was away, the native police once again went on the rampage. In the course of their duties they travelled to the Maranoa district to investigate some cattle stealing. For some reason Sergeant Dempster, the officer in command, allowed the police to be led by a civilian named Johnson. Dempster later argued that Johnson had known 'the near ways through the bush'. Whatever the reasons, the result was that Johnson led the police to an Aboriginal camp only a kilometre away from the local Court of Petty Sessions at Surat. There the police, with their usual brutal efficiency, set about slaughtering men, women and children. If it had been in the bush the incident would have been forgotten — or treated as a 'dispersal' or 'collision'. Because it was so close to white settlement, it presented problems. Lieutenant Fulford wrote to Sergeant Dempster in harshly unambiguous terms.

> . . . I am sorry to say there is a very strong case which I should not be at all surprised, will lead both myself and you, with Mr. Johnson into a mess. The Police must not on any account whatever be permitted to go after Blacks without an Officer with them, not even

> in the case of murder, because they may be induced by either foolish or designing persons to fire on Blacks who are perfectly innocent of the offences laid to their charge.

It was nothing more than a word of caution. The 'dirt-throwing philanthropists' and 'Negrophiles' must never know what really went on at the edges of the frontier.

If the native police and their officers were unwilling to report large-scale massacres, they were not as reticent about individual shooting which they passed off as self-defence. Their reports had a peculiar monotony which smacked of cover-up. The Aboriginal person always attacked the policeman. The policeman always did everything in his power to exercise restraint. The policeman was 'forced' to shoot the Aboriginal person. Trooper Rinaldo ducked as a boomerang was thrown. He ordered the Aboriginal person to stop. The Aboriginal person reached for his spears and nulla-nulla. Trooper Rinaldo shot him. Another Aboriginal person threw a nulla-nulla. He was shot, too. An Aboriginal man named Oromondi was to be arrested. Trooper Donald found him in the scrub. Oromondi threw a boomerang which narrowly missed Donald. Meanwhile three more Aboriginal people had come to Oromondi's aid. Donald shot all four of them. Behind little truths great lies are hidden. In spite of the continuous killing the settlers and landholders were never satisfied. It never occurred to them that if any real morality operated on the frontier, the native police should be protecting the Aboriginal population. It never occurred to them that it was a strangely inverted morality which argued that the invaders should be protected.

The settlers were greedy. They wanted continuous protection. Governor FitzRoy agreed to increase the native police by forty-eight men in 1852. What was never asked was where the new men came from. It was one thing to bring men from the Murray and the Murrumbidgee which was hundreds of kilometres away. It was another thing altogether to recruit men from the local area thus fuelling old tribal animosities.

It was common practice to offer Aboriginal men in prison the chance to serve out their time in the native police force. In 1883 the *Queensland Figaro* reported, with a tone which suggested that the practice was not uncommon, that 'The Aboriginal, Dicky, who murdered his gin at Coreena isn't to be hanged. He's wanted as a policeman and should prove a good one in cases having a tendency to the homicidal . . .'

When Walker tried to curb the indiscriminate killings by the native police, particularly the killings which occurred on stations far removed from 'civilisation' the settlers and station owners complained to the governor. The result was that, in 1854, Walker was removed from the position of commandant.

If the native police had been under some modicum of control with Commandant Walker, this disappeared with his dismissal. By 1864, after the newly formed Government of Queensland had assumed control, the force was really little more

than a brutal collection of killers led by sadists. Violence breeds violence. It is impossible to say whether the brutish officers bred brutal policemen or whether the vicious environment which was the Queensland frontier acted like a magnet and attracted the very worst people to its lands. Certainly, as one critic has observed, 'the Native Police offered a perfect niche for the sadist'.

Not only did the police massacre Aboriginal people but the white officers seemed to get particular pleasure out of oppressing and maltreating the Aboriginal police below them. In 1875 two Aboriginal policemen died after being flogged for disobedience by Sub-Inspector Carroll. In the subsequent inquiry Constable John Thomas described what happened:

> On the morning of the 26th December, Sub-Inspector Carroll directed me to bring Echo from the dray to which he was handcuffed to the parade ground; the boy was then handcuffed to a tree . . . Mr. Carroll . . . brought out two stockwhips and gave me one of them and told me to 'wire in'. I struck the trooper twice on the back with the whip. Mr. Carroll then flogged him . . . until the boy fainted . . . I do not know the exact number of lashes but it was over thirty . . . his head was hanging back and his eyes were set. I poured some water down his throat — it seemed to run down his throat without his attempting to swallow it . . . he was then handcuffed to the limb of a

A native police camp on the Herbert River in north Queensland.

> tree standing on his feet, while he was in this fainting fit, Mr. Carroll struck him three times with the whip. I took the key . . . to release the boy when Mr. Carroll told me to let him there for two or three hours it would do him good . . . about a quarter of an hour afterwards I missed the boy from the tree and never saw him again. I did not report this matter as I was told that it was a general occurrence in every Native Police Camp and not to mention the subject anywhere as people would call us tyrants . . . I have seen troopers on a former occasion flogged quite as much by Mr. Carroll with wire.

In the final analysis it is impossible to measure the deaths which resulted from the activities of the native police. It is impossible because the police themselves kept no records and because their actions, for the most part, were endorsed by the white settlers.

For fifty years, from the 1830s to the 1880s, the native police were a convenient tool of government policy. The Aboriginal communities of Queensland had no intention of giving their land up without a fight. In many ways they resisted white settlement more effectively than the Aboriginal communities in New South Wales, Victoria or Tasmania. They formed large and effective fighting forces and they had few qualms about attacking huts and stations.

The history of the native police is an ugly chapter in the expansion of the white frontier in Queensland. It is a history of the kidnapping of Aboriginal women and children, the casual shooting of prisoners, and the indiscriminate butchering of innocent Aboriginal people. The details are shrouded in silence. All that is left are the oblique hints of the carnage. No-one recorded what really happened, all that is left is the bigotry which goaded and encouraged the native police. 'I should like to see the last of them hunted down by their own people, the native police,' said a Queensland mail contractor, 'and there is nothing those beauties like doing half as much as shooting 'em down.'

When John Douglas called for a royal commission into the behaviour of the native police his request was greeted with laughter from fellow parliamentarians. 'If the honourable member wanted to bring charges,' laughed one politician, 'he ought to have gone back to the origin of the black police, when Robinson Crusoe and his man Friday went out together to kill blacks.'

The epitaph for the force was written in a letter to the *Queenslander* in 1880 which poignantly captured the scale and the anonymity of the carnage — 'I have seen their tracks, and on their tracks I have seen the dead bodies of their victims . . .'

CHAPTER 12

THE MASSACRE OF THE YEEMAN PEOPLE — 1857

Suppose you don't kill piccaninnis, in time they become warriors and kill you. If you kill the women no more piccaninnis are born.

A native policeman, 1857

The Australian frontier did not breed characters of legendary stature. The national mythology, once Ned Kelly has been accounted for, lacks men of the illusory stature of Wild Bill Hickock, Wyatt Earp, Davy Crockett, Jim Bowie or Billy the Kid. The frontier was not really conducive to myth-making. Even Harry Redford, who rustled a thousand head of cattle and drove them from western Queensland to South Australia through country which had killed Burke and Wills four years earlier, is nothing more than a footnote in Outback history.

For a couple of decades, from 1857 until the early 1880s, William 'Billy' Fraser looked as though he might be writ large in the history of central Queensland. He became a talking point in bars, around the camp fire, and in the shearing shed. He became a symbol and a focus for all the misguided frontier animosity which whites felt towards Aboriginal people. The image that was kindled and fuelled by frontier bigotry was that of a man who, standing at the grave of his mother, sisters and brothers, raised a tomahawk aloft and swore he would not rest until its razor-sharp blade was embedded in the skull of the Aboriginal people who had killed his family. To the minds of the white settlers on the frontier it was an image of heroism, justifiable revenge and a kind of romantic vengeful wrath which they endorsed and applauded. The fact that the legend also embraced the killing of at least one hundred Aboriginal people, thus making Billy Fraser the largest mass murderer in Australian history, seemed not to tarnish the heroic image. The fact that Fraser's murders were almost entirely of innocent men, women and children doesn't seem to have troubled his admirers. Similarly, the fact that he was never arraigned or criticised or brought to justice for his crimes seemed unimportant.

History plays strange tricks with fame and infamy. Billy Fraser is forgotten today. The details of his massacres are blurred and smudged by time. The memory of his atrocities has conveniently slipped from white consciousness. The people whom he killed, the Yeeman of the Upper Dawson River area, have disappeared. A man who spearheaded the genocide of a group totalling over three hundred people has been expunged from the history of Queensland. Yet, for a brief moment, he symbolised all that was ugly about the frontier conflict between whites and Aboriginal people, all that was unjust about the rough justice handed out by the pastoral invaders.

By the 1850s the frontier of settlement and squatting was reaching far beyond the fertile river valleys and plains of eastern New South Wales, Victoria and Queensland. Settlement was occurring along the great western rivers. Isolated homesteads were being built along the banks of the Condamine and Macintyre rivers. Squatters, greedy for ever-larger tracts of land, were pushing further and further westward.

It was a well-established frontier law that Aboriginal people were a nuisance and that death — either by shooting or by poisoning — was the only solution to the problem. It was well known on the frontier, and often discussed with a good deal of laughter and approval, that after Aboriginal people had killed a couple of outriders and a prize bull on Sir Evan Mackenzie's Kilcoy station, the old man had added arsenic to the flour and killed nearly thirty of them. That was the kind of lesson that never quite managed to be reported to the local police.

The people on the frontier liked that story. They chuckled at the fact that it had occurred only four years after Myall Creek and that it had occurred not far from the settlement at Moreton Bay. Aboriginal people could still be killed with impunity so long as the murderer was discreet and the bragging was done to people who 'understood' the rules of the frontier.

As the whites began to settle southern Queensland, conflict with the Aboriginal population became intense. It was the same story which had been enacted on every other Australian frontier. The shepherds, the outriders, the labourers, all the whites least able to protect themselves, were killed in clashes with Aboriginal people. In turn Aboriginal people were raped, slaughtered, maltreated

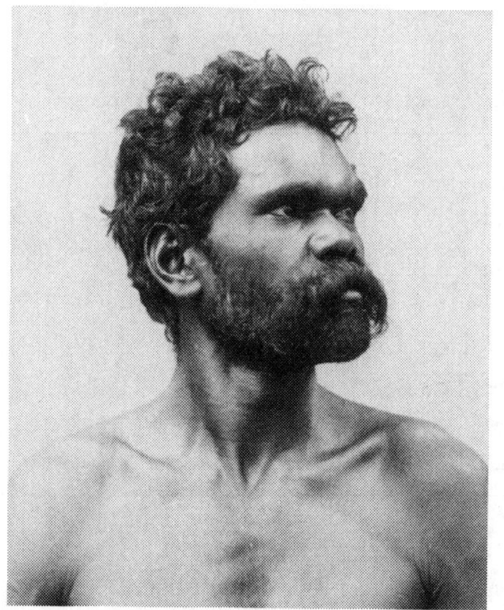

This man, photographed in Roma in 1824, may have been a member of the Yeeman tribe. The tribe was wiped out in 1857 and it is therefore impossible to know what they looked like.

and abused. One observer of the brutal excesses of the frontier reserved much of his vitriol for the emancipated ex-convicts who saw Aboriginal people as the lowest form of life and proceeded to treat them as such. 'It was no unusual thing,' he wrote in *Adventures in Australia Fifty Years Ago*, 'to hear these ruffians in conversation with one another, boasting of the blacks they had slaughtered, and when relating the particular qualities of a savage brute of a dog, say, he would pull down a blackfellow, and tear his entrails out.'

Treated as animals, it is hardly surprising that the Aboriginal population began to retaliate.

In the vast amphitheatre formed by the headwaters of the Dawson River and the streams and creeks which flowed into it there lived a group of Aboriginal people, probably called the Yeeman, who were noted for their impressive physique and their skills at hunting and fighting. They were a justifiably proud people whose adornments included crescent-shaped scars on their chests.

White settlers started moving into the Dawson River basin in the mid-1840s. The land parcels were large. A sheep to every four acres (1.6 hectares) meant a grazier needed 16 000 acres (6475 hectares) to run 4000 head of sheep.

Andrew Scott arrived in the area in 1853 and founded a station at a place Aboriginal people called Gaganybilany. He called it Hornet Bank after the hornets which abounded in the area. Scott was a cautious man. He came from a lowly Scottish background. He was dour and unassuming; a man who brooked no trouble from the local Aboriginal population and saw constant vigilance as the only way of protecting the land he had assumed as his own.

Sometime in late 1853 a group of Yeeman killed one of Scott's shepherds and attempted to rustle 1400 sheep. Scott immediately called in a detachment of the notorious native police who were stationed nearby. The police arrived, tracked the Yeeman, and, euphemistically 'The killing of the shepherd was duly avenged'. The actual scale of the massacre is unknown but it undoubtedly involved dozens of Yeeman, including women and children. The scar that was left on the group's memory was not to be easily assuaged.

By 1856 the Dawson River basin was not for the faint-hearted. The white encroachment and partition of the land had not been accepted by the Yeeman who took every opportunity to snipe at the unwelcome invaders. Still this had not deterred the large family of John Fraser who were currently leasing Hornet Bank station and who had been in control of the property since 1854.

In 1856 John Fraser died of dysentery. His eldest son William, known in the area as Billy, took over the lease. To supplement his meagre income he also became a bullock driver. He took wool from the Dawson River basin across the Great Dividing Range to Ipswich. This meant that although he was the eldest male in the family, Billy Fraser was often away from Hornet Bank for months at a time. Billy was not

Andrew Scott arrived in the area in 1853 and called his station Hornet Bank after the hornets which abounded in the area.

in a situation where he could monitor or control the relationships between the Yeeman and the graziers and police in the area. During his long absences the vigilance which Andrew Scott had been so adamant about began to slacken. The primary offenders were the native police.

The presence of the native police in the vicinity of Hornet Bank station in early 1857 raised tensions in the area considerably. Yeeman women were attracted to the camp. Yeeman men who attempted to retrieve their women from the native police were frequently attacked and humiliated. The Yeeman saw Hornet Bank, with its obvious shortage of white adult males, as a place where they could avenge their humiliations without fear of a battle. On 15 June the Yeeman gathered to attack the station but they were dispersed at the last minute by an emergency call which brought the native police to the station. The Yeeman now had little fear of the native police. The force was becoming casual and ineffective. From July to August six shepherds were killed. No real attempt was made to locate the Aboriginal people who had committed the murders. For a brief moment it looked as though the Yeeman were going to reassert their rights over the land.

On Hornet Bank station at the time lived 43-year-old Martha Fraser and her eight children — Elizabeth, 19; Mary, 11; Jane, 9; Charlotte, 3; John, 23; David, 16; Sylvester (known as Wessie or West), 14; and James, 6. There was also a 27-year-old tutor, James De Lacey Neagle, at least four shepherds, and an Aboriginal man, variously known as Bahlee, Boney or Joey, whom Andrew Scott had brought from the south.

It is impossible to know for certain why the Yeeman chose Hornet Bank for their first attack in what was planned as a war but, God knows, they had reason enough. It was well known that the Fraser boys were wont to forcibly kidnap and rape the Yeeman women. It was likely that Hornet Bank station was a sacred site which was being despoiled by Scott and the Frasers. Recently a station overseer had shot a Yeeman after accusing him of theft. For the past three years the area had been the scene of a number of atrocities — at least a dozen Aboriginal people had been killed in a reprisal raid after some cattle had been speared, another group of Yeeman had been poisoned nine months before with a strychnine-laced Christmas pudding, the native police had recently used Hornet Bank as a base for their murderous sorties and rape was now commonplace. If it wasn't the Fraser boys, it was the shepherds or the native police. The Yeeman had every reason to strike back. It became imperative that they match rape with rape.

On the night of 26 October the Yeeman surrounded the Fraser hut. They had already convinced Bahlee to help them. Around midnight Bahlee took a heavy piece of wood and killed all of the station dogs. The way was clear for a Yeeman attack. At dawn a group of about one hundred Yeeman, guided by Bahlee, attacked. James was beaten to death. Wessie was beaten to unconsciousness and, somehow, in the darkness managed to fall between his iron stretcher and the wall. The Yeeman, believing him to be on the stretcher, beat it until they were convinced he was dead. The attackers then moved on to the lean-to where John and David were sleeping. The noise of the group woke John who came out, undressed and rubbing the sleep from his eyes, to argue with them in the pale dawn light. He offered them anything they wanted. They listened for a minute before one warrior raised his nulla-nulla and clubbed John to death. A small group moved into the room and disposed of David.

As the terrified and bloodied Wessie regained consciousness, he could hear the war party arguing with his mother. Martha was pleading for her life and desperately attempting to save the lives of her children. The Yeeman dragged Martha and all the girls out of the house and ransacked it. Then, after brief deliberations, they raped Martha, Elizabeth and Mary and clubbed all three and the remaining children to death. Wessie could do nothing. He ached from the battering he had taken and his head had a deep gash in it from a glancing blow.

As he lay waiting for the Yeeman to retreat he heard two hired hands, Bernangl and Newman, who had been sleeping some four hundred metres from the station, carefully approaching the carnage. He lay silently, not knowing where the Yeeman were. His caution was well founded. The departing Yeeman, noticing the two hands, raced back. A desperate fight ensued but the hands were no match for the warriors and in moments they both had been killed.

The bloody rays of the early morning sun had disappeared and the flies were already hovering around the bodies when Wessie finally dragged himself out from under the bed. He was bruised, bloody and terrified. He surveyed the carnage and wept. Then, with a pistol in his hand, he ran 16 kilometres to Euromah station. It was morning tea time at Euromah and all the shearers were sitting in the shade outside the huts when the shoeless, bedraggled and blood-stained figure of Wessie

Fraser staggered into their midst. In a delirium of terror and exhaustion he blurted out the story of the killings.

The news spread rapidly through the valley. Shepherds abandoned their huts and flocks and fled. Graziers and station owners attempted to muster forces but agonised over whether to protect their own properties or ride at once to Hornet Bank. Those who went were horrified by the scale of the carnage. Eleven bodies were lying in and around the station. Blood was everywhere. The three eldest women had been raped; James Neagle had been castrated. The storehouse had been ransacked and the sheep rustled.

The authorities were slow to act. The Dawson River stations were on the very edge of the frontier. The men who worked for the station owners were unwilling to form posses. The thought of a spear in the back or a nulla-nulla crashing down on the skull was enough to send most of the hired hands rushing back to the coast. Distances were vast; life was lonely and isolated. The policing of the area was inadequate.

On 28 October young Wessie watched as a few brave shearers dug a hole in the dry earth and buried most of his family. There had been no inquiry. No minister was in attendance.

On 30 October Second-Lieutenant Walter Powell and a small police contingent caught up with a group of Aboriginal people on the slopes below the gorges of the Upper Dawson. They shot five. The rest of the group fled into the bush.

There is not much room for rationality in a world fuelled by fear, anger and revenge. None of the whites in the Dawson River area acknowledged that the Fraser massacre was a natural, if bloody, reprisal for attacks on the local Aboriginal population, which had been a hundredfold more vicious and more unjustified. No-one paused to consider the fundamental principle of British law — innocent until proved guilty — and no-one declared that only those members of the Yeeman who had killed, raped and plundered should be brought to justice. Frontier law did not recognise such niceties. In the vengeful minds of the whites all Aboriginal people in the region were responsible. The crime was the result of collective collusion. Therefore all Aboriginal people in the area must be punished — and the only appropriate punishment was death.

Wessie, having buried the rest of the family, rode 515 kilometres in three days until he reached Ipswich where he found Billy loading stores and supplies on to a dray. Billy was distraught when he heard the news. He abandoned his dray and the stores, borrowed a horse and within hours was riding back to Hornet Bank. As he rode his mind became obsessed with revenge and reprisal. He composed a letter to the Ipswich magistrate in which he argued that 'unless the most stringent measures are resorted to, the aboriginals of the Upper Dawson will only be encouraged to perpetrate similar, and if possible more terrible, atrocities'.

But Billy's revenge was not going to be salved by letters to the authorities. In his mind he went over and over the murders. He grimaced and tears rushed to his eyes every time he thought of the fate of his sisters and his mother. He knew that he could not take the law into his own hands, but he knew that he would not rest until he had destroyed the Yeeman.

Billy's vengeful impulses were matched by those of the other settlers in the valley. Within days a number of posses had been formed. The reprisals were bloody and indiscriminate. Posses, the native police and detachments of mounted police used the Fraser massacre as an excuse to shoot as many Aboriginal people as they could.

The most notorious posse was known as the Browns. 'It consisted of McArthur from Bungaban, Serocold and his overseer from Cockatoo, Piggott and a black boy from Auburn, Thomas from Dykehead, Horton and myself with Ernest Davies and Billy Hayes and Freddy, my two black boys,' wrote Thomas Murray-Prior, friend of Ludwig Leichhardt and owner of the Hawkwood station.

In the weeks after the Hornet Bank massacre the Browns rode through the Upper Dawson valley shooting every black they could find. They hunted the Yeeman ruthlessly. Near Piggott's station they caught a group of Yeeman who had Bibles and prayerbooks from Hornet Bank. The Aboriginal people fled and for the next six weeks the Browns hunted and shot them. They were acting totally outside the law but they seemed to be oblivious to such constraints. Ernest Davies was convinced the posse had 'got the right men' and was proud of his efforts. He later wrote that 'they got their deserts at our hands, so far as it was within our power to deal out rough justice'.

At Redbank station the Aboriginal station hands fled to the owner seeking protection only to have the Browns literally drag them out of the station and shoot them. Although the Aboriginal station hands at Redbank had clearly not been involved at Hornet Bank, they were twice attacked by vengeance parties. The Browns rounded them up and shot a large number of the men. Then, some weeks later, the native police came through and took the remaining men into the scrub where they were shot.

These were small massacres in comparison with what William Fraser was planning. Shortly after arriving back in the Upper Dawson, he joined up with the native police and went on a bloody rampage. At one place they came across a group of Aboriginal people and without even questioning them they opened fire. Nine were killed; the rest fled into the bush. Troopers led by Second-Lieutenant William Moorhead arrived soon after and shot and wounded another group of Aboriginal people — they did not even bother reporting the number killed. Another group of troopers came upon some Aboriginal people and shot four of them. A further detachment of troopers found a group of Aboriginal people and shot three and wounded 'a considerable number'.

In spite of these bloody reprisals the squatters in the Upper Dawson became convinced that Aboriginal people had embarked on a systematic campaign of terror and murder. They had no evidence for such a claim but it did manage to fuel the paranoia of the area and it was a perfect excuse for indiscriminate reprisals. This paranoia was further fuelled by the local papers which, with the solitary exception of the *Moreton Bay Courier*, all demanded revenge.

The frontier simply bent the law to ensure that Billy Fraser was given every opportunity to assuage his grief through murder. Aboriginal people, whether innocent or guilty, fled the area. This did not stop Fraser, who by now was being actively supported by troopers and the native police. In his mind every Aboriginal person he saw had been involved in the rape and murder of his mother and sisters. At Euromah, on 27 November, Fraser and some troopers surrounded a group of Aboriginal people and shot six of them. Three of those killed were women. Fraser claimed he recognised two of the victims. The other four had been shot on the premise that they were 'guilty by association'.

In December Fraser and the troops reached King's station at Rochedale. Once again they made a dawn raid on an Aboriginal camp. Fraser's rationale this time was that some of the men in the camp had been 'always in the neighbourhood at Hornet Bank'. On that evidence seven Aboriginal people were shot. On 4 January Fraser, supported by the troopers, shot fourteen Aboriginal people (eleven men and three women) at Cockatoo. Fraser claimed they had all been involved in the Hornet Bank murders. No-one questioned this claim.

Hornet Bank station in the 1880s. The main house at the time of the massacre is second from the right. The kitchen and tutor's room were in the small building third from the right.

Fraser was now driven by an irrational bloodlust. At Juandah, by some judicial miracle, a group of Aboriginal people were brought before five magistrates. The magistrates listened carefully to the evidence before agreeing that there was no evidence on which they could convict the Aboriginal people, who were duly set free. Unhappy with the verdict, Fraser and the native police simply ignored the ruling. As the Aboriginal people left the station in which the hearing had taken place, they were gunned down. Some were shot on the verandah. Some were shot in the kitchen in front of one of the magistrates who had just declared them innocent. Frederick Walker, the first commandant of the native police, subsequently wrote to the Queensland Attorney-General to complain about the massacre. 'Two Blacks,' he wrote, 'who had by some whim been spared were then made to bury the victims, and one Ruffian said to the other, 'What shall we do with the sextons?' The answer was, 'Shoot them.' One was accordingly shot, why the other was spared I know not, possibly the supply of cartridges was running short.'

Billy Fraser's exploits against Aboriginal people were applauded on the frontier. He became a hero and stories about him became legends in Outback Queensland. It was the nature of the frontier that exaggeration and viciousness were seen as virtues.

It was claimed that at Juandah station he massacred a group of Aboriginal people — men, women and children — as they tried to flee across a lagoon. Subsequent evidence suggested that none of the Aboriginal people he killed had been involved in the Fraser murders. A similar story exists which has the native police killing another group as they swam across the lagoon and then wading into the reeds on the edge of the lagoon to shoot those who were attempting to hide.

The story of Billy Fraser's revenge was obviously served well by the camp-fire desire to spin a 'good' tall tale. Looked at in hindsight Billy Fraser is not the hero the frontier wanted to portray. He was a cold-blooded, lawless killer. Stories, like the following one, began to circulate about the killing of innocent blacks:

> The following episode, Mr. Jones informed me, he had heard from the only white man who had witnessed what took place. I am informed that this man is still living in the Burnett district. He was driving through the bush with a black boy whom he had himself raised from infancy. The boy had been brought up on the station and was employed at stock-riding and accompanying his master on his journeyings throughout the district. They were travelling through the bush, when suddenly they met 'Big Fellow Fraser', as he was called, who ordered a halt, saying, 'I am going to shoot that black' . . . It was useless expostulating. Fraser was informed that the black boy had been brought up like a white boy, that he had lived nearly all his life

By March 1858 over one hundred and fifty Aboriginal people had been killed in the Upper Dawson area by posses of squatters, the Browns and the native police.

> on the station, and that he had nothing to do with the blacks who had murdered the family, but all to no purpose, for the cruel brute began to threaten, 'I may put a bullet through you if you hinder me in carrying out my purpose.' And there and then the poor cowering innocent black boy was shot through the body repeatedly, and thrown into the gully like so much carrion. The terrible vengeance which the black police had already wreaked upon the actual murderers should have been sufficient. It was a disgrace to the surviving son and his name has been rendered infamous.

To this legend can be added two further Aboriginal deaths. In the main street of Rockhampton, Fraser supposedly shot an Aboriginal woman who he later claimed had been wearing a dress similar to his mother's. He was never tried for the murder. In Toowoomba, he reportedly shot an Aboriginal strapper at a local race meeting. He was never charged.

By 1858 the frontier stations were awash with stories of massacres. The area was now being ruled by the gun and no Aboriginal person was safe. In his memoirs one squatter, George Serocold, recalled:

> When the news of the Hornet Bank massacre went around the district, all the squatters turned out and the Native Police from different tribes acted with us, and a considerable number were shot. It was necessary to make a severe example of the leaders of the tribe and about a dozen of them were taken into the open country and shot. They were complete savages and never wore any clothes, and were so much alike that no evidence could ever be produced to enable them to be tried by our laws. These men were allowed to run and they were shot at about thirty or forty yards distant.

Serocold's memoirs offer a rare insight into a rationalisation for the killing of Aboriginal people which, although common, was infrequently articulated. To the racist perception of British migrants all Aboriginal people looked the same. This was rarely vocalised because it made a nonsense of the claim that a specific Aboriginal person could be identified positively.

In February 1858 a party of ten police, accompanied by Billy and Wessie Fraser, moved into the Lower Dawson. It was here that a massacre which became legendary amongst the local settlers occurred. By early 1858 the Aboriginal population was very wary of any whites. They would hide in the bush knowing that contact with whites usually resulted in death. The troopers and the Frasers decided to strip off their clothes and weapons and, by friendly gestures, persuade the Aboriginal people to join them in a hunt. One family, comprising a father and eight sons, joined the

hunt and later participated in a feast organised by the troopers. Midway through the feast the troopers and the Frasers grabbed their guns and shot the father and seven of the sons.

Years later a squatter recalled the killings as 'a most treacherous affair' but defended Billy and Wessie Fraser on the grounds that 'a portion of their sister's clothing' was in the Aboriginal camp. It never seemed to occur to the Frasers or the squatter that a piece of clothing was not the kind of evidence which justified the cold-blooded murder of eight people.

By March 1858 over one hundred and fifty Aboriginal people (probably as high as three hundred) had been killed in the Upper Dawson area. The killings were being carried out by posses of squatters, the Browns and the native police.

It was clear that what little law there was on the frontier was being ignored. Any Aboriginal people who were suspected of being associated with the Hornet Bank massacre were shot. This led to totally unjustified random killings. At one station an old blind Aboriginal man who couldn't possibly have been involved in the massacre was shot by whites. A young Aboriginal boy sent on an errand from one station was shot upon his arrival at his destination.

This group of Aboriginal people near Charters Towers would have gathered annually with the Yeeman, however, by the 1880s the Yeeman had been totally wiped out.

As a result of these random killings the Yeeman moved away from the Upper Dawson and headed east towards the coast. This did not ease the pressure. They were followed by the native police and sniped at by squatters. In Maryborough the local police raided a camp on the outskirts of the town, burnt all the Aboriginal people's clothing and possessions, and shot a twelve-year-old boy. A few weeks later, the native police raided a nearby camp and shot three Aboriginal people.

The war, for it had been a clear battle in which the Aboriginal people had tried to hold the conquering squattocracy at bay, was nearly over. The Yeeman had fought back. They had tried to match killing with killing and rape with rape. In the end it was the effectiveness of the gun and the single-minded aggressiveness of the whites which won. In 1871 the Englishman George Carrington, after spending some years in Queensland, summed up the war strategy succinctly when he wrote:

> There is a steady, but irregular, guerrilla warfare going on, the blackfellow having, on his side, cunning and knowledge of the country, and the other side depending on their superior weapons and skill. There can be no doubt, however, about the final result, as for every white man killed, six blackfellows, on an average, bite the dust.

By the 1870s the only Aboriginal people remaining in the Upper Dawson region were the casualties from the war — people who could not flee from the region. A decade later there was no evidence of the Yeeman in the area. They had either been dispersed or killed. The result of eleven white deaths had been the wholesale slaughter of an entire Aboriginal group with the consequent obliteration of their language and culture. For a brief moment the Yeeman had held back the tide of white settlers. In the end they knew the battle was a lost cause.

Murray-Prior recalled in his memoirs that he once asked one of his Yeeman station hands why the war between Aboriginal people and white settlers had stopped after the killing of the Fraser family:

> The squatters were puzzled that the Aborigines, with the exception of certain ringleaders who were well known, did not follow up the attack on Hornet Bank by raiding other stations, many of which would have been at their mercy. I often afterwards met one of the leaders, Cockatoo Billy, who, although he had been in the front, had managed to keep out of the way during the war. As he had been a long time with the whites and understood English well, I asked him how this was. He explained that after the first party [the Browns] had been out, they had had a 'corbon woolla' [conference of chiefs]. Some wished to attack the station — others to keep as clean as they could and, as Cockatoo Billy said, even suppose they were able to kill all the whites that were in possession of their land, there were any number more in Sydney to come on. Sydney was their idea of the habitat of the white man. Cockatoo Billy said that if all the blackfellows were killed, there would be no more blackfellows; they trusted that if they separated and kept quiet the white man's anger would pass.

Cockatoo Billy is the solitary voice left to us by the Yeeman. He cries across the centuries. How wrong he was. The Yeeman were wiped out long before the white man's anger had passed.

CHAPTER 13

THE MASSACRE AND THE REPRISALS AT CULLIN-LA-RINGO — 1861

Unhappily hundreds of Aborigines have been killed and many of them are still so killed. Yet I have never heard of the execution of a Colonist for the murder of a native in Queensland.

Reverend Duncan McNab, 1881

The frontier was changing. No longer was it the exclusive preserve of males. The family, the large and cumbersome Victorian family, was moving out. In the past Aboriginal communities had been restricted to livestock and lonely, isolated males when they had sought revenge. Now, by accident, they found themselves confronted by entire families.

The advent of family life should have brought a level of cautious rationality to the frontier. Kidnapping and raping Aboriginal women, forming posses to go on black hunts, making poisoned dampers, maltreating those Aboriginal people who worked on, or lived near, the stations, should all have declined. If the men on the frontier had thought about their actions against the Aboriginal population, they would have realised that every rape, every killing, every act of humiliation endangered their women and their children. It required no great display of intellect to realise that there was a law of cause and effect which operated in the case of Aboriginal reprisals. Aboriginal people rarely attacked without motive. They usually attacked when the provocation was such that tribal law demanded some kind of retribution.

In the tangled web of reasons for the massacre of the Fraser family at Hornet Bank, it was clear that the Yeeman had not arbitrarily chosen the station and it had not been a spur of the moment decision to rape the three women. They were exacting revenge for crimes which they believed the white community en masse, and the Fraser family specifically, had committed. On one level these crimes were clearly sexual. It was well known to the landholders in the area that the older Fraser boys, and the other whites at Hornet Bank, had been in the habit of kidnapping and raping Yeeman women. Stories had circulated that two Yeeman girls had been brutally whipped and raped. Lieutenant Francis Nicoll, an officer with the native

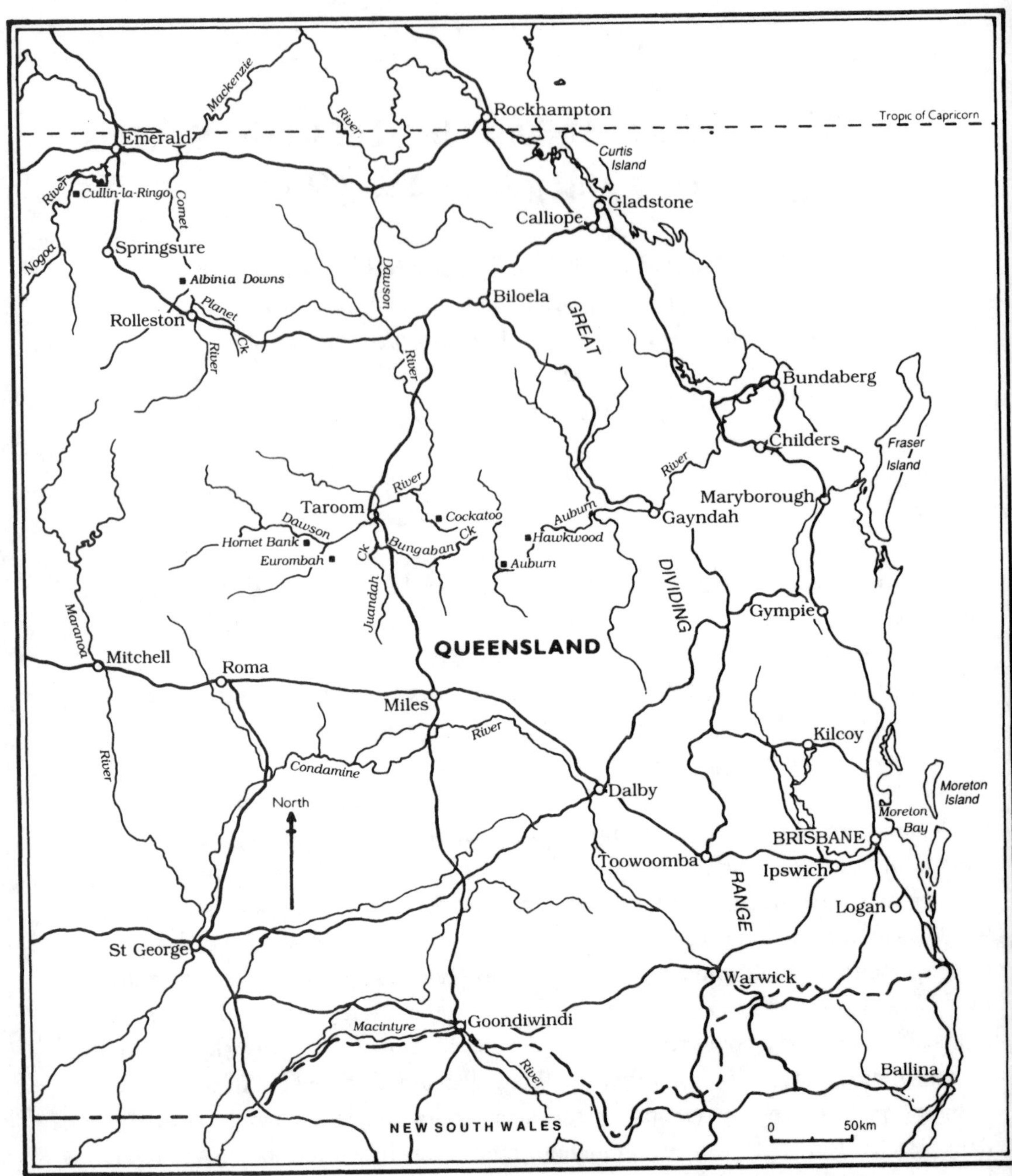

Central and south-eastern Queensland, showing the scene of the massacre of the Yeeman people at Hornet Bank station, and the massacre at Cullin-la-Ringo and other stations in the region.

police, was later to give evidence that some months before the massacre at Hornet Bank Mrs Fraser had begged him to speak to her sons 'for forcibly taking the young maidens'. Mrs Fraser had the foresight (although it did her no good) to admit that 'she expected harm would come of it, that they were in the habit of doing so, not withstanding her entreaties to the contrary'. She had pleaded with her sons who had laughingly ignored her.

In retrospect it is hard to imagine what sort of muddled logic drove the young Frasers. Did they really believe that the Yeeman men would submissively stand by while their young women were raped and tortured? Did it ever cross Billy Fraser's mind as he rampaged across the country in search of the men who had raped his mother and his sisters that his own acts may well have sparked their deaths?

It was also true that Aboriginal people sought revenge against the native police. The reputation the native police had acquired in central Queensland was one based on indiscriminate murder and constant assaults on local Aboriginal women. Aboriginal communities saw the native police as a tool of the white settlers. They made no distinction between native police and settlers. Revenge for crimes by the native police could, quite reasonably, be exacted on white settlers. At the time of the Hornet Bank massacre the native police had been camped in the Upper Dawson and a number of confrontations over women had occurred between the police and Yeeman men.

In theory the lessons of Hornet Bank were obvious. If whites and native police were going to attack the local Aboriginal people there would inevitably be retaliation. The lesson was there. The settlers took no notice whatsoever.

The 1861 Select Committee into the behaviour of the native police in Queensland tells the story of the events which culminated in the massacre at Cullin-la-Ringo. In the four years between Hornet Bank and Cullin-la-Ringo the native police on the frontier had acted with no regard for any law. A string of massacres was reported. The younger brother of Lieutenant-Commander Morisset had been sent to the Mortimer's station near Maryborough with instructions to investigate complaints about the killing of livestock. Upon their arrival at the station the native police had ridden to the nearest camp and shot and killed a number of totally innocent Aboriginal people. On 3 February 1860 a corps of native police, under the command of Lieutenant John O'Connell Bligh, had fired upon a harmless and unarmed group of Aboriginal people in the main street of Maryborough. Four of the group were killed. Bligh claimed that one of the men was under suspicion of attacking a white woman. While travelling through the Logan district, Second-Lieutenant Frederick Wheeler had ordered his men to kill a number of innocent Aboriginal people, including a woman. His defence was that they may have been involved in the spearing of some cattle. At times it seemed as though the native police were almost goading the Aboriginal population.

The problem with the native police was a problem of power without responsibility. Anyone could join the force and there were few constraints upon the behaviour of the white officers or the Aboriginal troopers. A uniform was a licence for unimportant men to wield large amounts of power over helpless Aboriginal people.

Second-Lieutenant Alfred Patrick was one such 'unimportant man'. In the summer of 1861 he brought his troopers to Henry Dutton's Albinia Downs station on the Comet River in central Queensland. He had no particular reason to be in the area. It was a routine visit not prompted by complaints or problems. Relations between Dutton and the local Aboriginal people were amicable.

A minor altercation between the cook and some Aboriginal people over the carcass of a sheep was enough to galvanise Patrick and his men into action. Without consulting Dutton, he rode out to the nearby camps and demanded that the Aboriginal people leave immediately. Patrick's bluntly officious manner provoked an attack. This was hardly surprising given that Henry Dutton had specifically given the Aboriginal people permission to remain on his land until a bullock dray with supplies arrived. Dutton had promised the Aboriginal people a number of tomahawks.

Quite by accident Dutton had made a fool of Patrick. Patrick had tried to assert himself against Aboriginal people who were on the property with the express permission of the owner.

Unwilling to admit his error, Patrick believed that the only response he had left was an impetuous display of force. He marched out to the Aboriginal camp and ordered his troops to open fire. The troops were unwilling, knowing that the Aboriginal people had committed no crime. The Aboriginal people, realising what was happening, fled into the bush. Patrick grabbed all the spears and waddies at the camp site and burnt them.

Dutton, who was furious, intervened. He ordered Patrick and his native police off his property and that night penned a savage indictment of Patrick's behaviour which he sent to Lieutenant-Commander Morisset, the head of the native police.

'Here,' he wrote, 'a small lot of peaceable blacks who came in at my request to receive a gift of tomahawks and blankets, were rushed out of their camp by the Police, threatened with shooting if they dared to stand, their implements of chase carried off and destroyed.'

Dutton knew that the frontier was always delicately balanced and that provocative actions had predictable violent consequences. He may not have been a bastion of racial tolerance but when he wrote, 'These creatures, wretched and debased and brutal as they are, have still one feeling common with whites . . . that of deep implacable revenge for unprovoked injuries. They ask me why they are shot. They say "bail no me kill white fellow . . . bail take ration, what for shot him?" How are they to be answered, how appeased?' He was sensitively understanding the situation in a way that Patrick, with his ego and his petty power, could never comprehend. He was also articulating the central cause for the massacre at Cullin-la-Ringo.

Patrick's troublemaking in that area didn't stop with this first altercation at Albinia Downs. He was the kind of thuggish character that the force all too frequently

'The Avengers' by S T Gill depicts the settlers' response to Aboriginal people. Attacks upon Aboriginal camps were often unprovoked and unjustified.

attracted. It was officers like Patrick who prompted one Queensland parliamentarian to observe that 'the black troopers were less culpable than the men under whom they acted . . . men in the force whose careers were long records of crime sanctioned by the Government . . . He knew of such men who went patrolling through the country shooting the unfortunate blacks wherever they met them . . .'

In early March 1861 Patrick and his troopers moved across to Planet Creek, a tributary of the Comet River and, with no justification at all, dispersed a camp of friendly Aboriginal people. They then moved on to Rolleston station where 'dispersal' again became a euphemism for massacre as they rode into an Aboriginal camp shooting and killing indiscriminately.

Frederick Walker, the first commandant of the native police and now a landholder in the area, complained that Patrick was provoking trouble. He wrote to Lieutenant O'Connell Bligh pointing out that the local Aboriginal people were protesting that they were being attacked without cause and that, as they saw the native police as an arm of white law, they were accusing all whites in the area of treachery. Walker was so annoyed by Patrick's actions that he demanded his immediate removal from the area. He demanded protection for the Aboriginal people and threatened that, unless something was done, he may have to create a force of local settlers to remove the native police.

Bligh was unmoved. He said Patrick's actions were justified and that most of the settlers endorsed them. He refused to withdraw Patrick.

Patrick continued to wreak havoc. His actions were on such a scale that Henry Dutton was later to write that all that was needed was to 'secure to the Blacks in future a recognition of their rights as human beings, which the whole conduct of the Native Police has ignored'. The native police under Patrick must, in part, have agreed with these sentiments. In early June they all deserted and Patrick had to spend some days convincing them to continue in his service.

But these were all minor in comparison to the attack on the Aboriginal people which occurred in early July 1861. It was an attack which highlighted the need for caution and careful judgement on the frontier.

Ten months before, an English-born overseer named Jesse Gregson had started out from the New England area to move five thousand sheep to a run called Rainworth near the Comet River. Gregson's attitude to Aboriginal people had been hardened by five years of frontier living. When he arrived at Rainworth on 24 June 1861 he made it clear to the local Kairi tribe that he wanted them off 'his' land. The Kairi, used to this kind of treatment, quietly departed.

Curious about any new whites in the area, Patrick visited Gregson in early July. Patrick's native police made a camp beside the river and the two men spent the evening around the camp fire, yarning and drinking. A few days after the arrival of Patrick and the native police, Gregson noticed that about three hundred of his sheep were missing. The police, Gregson and his men went looking for the sheep and found a group of Aboriginal people herding them.

Apparently the sheep had separated themselves from the main herd and when the Kairi had spotted them they had assumed that Gregson had 'thrown them away'. It was a typical misunderstanding caused by a huge cultural gulf. The Aboriginal people were so convinced that the sheep now belonged to them that they herded them back to camp where a few were slaughtered in anticipation of a feast.

When Gregson, Patrick and the men arrived the Aboriginal people welcomed them and asked if they would like to share in the feast. Instead the whites stormed the camp shooting indiscriminately. A number of Aboriginal people were killed but in the chaos some of the native police were injured and Gregson accidentally shot Patrick in the leg.

For the Kairi the massacre was the culmination of a series of unwarranted attacks. They had attempted to accommodate the white invaders and the only response they had ever had was killing. They now, as Dutton had predicted, had a desire for 'deep implacable revenge for unprovoked injury'.

It was agreed amongst the tribal elders that the Kairi people should strike back. As so often happened on the frontier, the people who were to become the target of the Aboriginal people's attack had not been involved in the crimes they were attempting to avenge. It happened that Gregson's Rainworth station was adjacent to Cullin-la-Ringo, a station owned by a Victorian squatter named Horatio Spencer Wills. Wills, accompanied by a large contingent of workers and their families, arrived in the area three months after the massacre on Rainworth station. It is not known whether he knew of the killings. His party came via Henry Dutton's Albinia Downs station, stayed there for a few days, then moved on across the Nogoa River to a station they were to call Cullin-la-Ringo. What they didn't know was that Horatio Wills looked disarmingly like Jesse Gregson. They wore similar clothes and rode horses which had similar colourings.

Hundreds of Kairi men had gathered at Separation Creek on the border of Rainworth and Cullin-la-Ringo stations. They were determined to avenge the massacre of their people which Patrick and Gregson had committed.

Wills and his men arrived at Cullin-la-Ringo in early October. They immediately set to work building slab huts and stockyards. The weather in central Queensland, even in October, was such that the Victorians, used to a cooler climate, needed to take a siesta in the middle of the day. They started early in the morning, broke for a long lunch, and resumed in the afternoon after the heat had gone out of the sun.

On 16 October Wills sent his son, Tom, and two station hands back to Albinia Downs to collect some things which had been left there. Travelling at night, the three men noticed the full moon which gave the gums a ghostly appearance and threw eerie shadows across the grasslands.

The morning of 17 October saw the mercury climbing rapidly. The sky was cloudless and the humidity and the flies were constant irritants. About ten o'clock a dozen Kairi wandered casually into Cullin-la-Ringo and watched with a kind of

The graveyard on the Cullin-la-Ringo property. The massacre on 17 October 1861 was the largest perpetrated by Aboriginal people.

idle curiosity as the sunburnt, sweating whites laboured to put poles into the ground and to nail sheets of slab and bark to rudely constructed frameworks. They stayed for about half an hour and left as quietly as they had arrived.

By noon most of the workers were exhausted. They drank some tea and chewed on pieces of damper and salted beef before collapsing into heavy noontime sleep in any comfortable, shady spot they could find. As they slept the Kairi silently circled the camp. An old man gave the signal — a loud squawk of a black cockatoo — and suddenly the silence was alive with yelling and screaming.

It is likely that most of those killed scarcely realised what had happened. The attack was lightning fast and little resistance was offered to the spear and the nulla-nulla. Old Horatio Wills managed to draw his revolvers, fire a couple of shots, and mount his horse before a well-aimed spear saw him tumbling lifeless to the ground. The main overseer, a man named Baker, had been working through the heat of the day with two helpers. Unarmed, they tried to fight off the Kairi with fence poles but they were beaten to death with nulla-nullas. Three shepherds, who had gone unnoticed by the raiding party, managed to escape. One of them, John Moore, escaped by hiding among his flock. When he was safely out of sight, he fled to the riverbank and began running the 30 kilometres to Rainworth. He arrived there the next morning.

The other shepherds, Edward Kenny and Patrick Mahoney, hid until the Kairi had departed. They returned to the station where Kenny immediately saddled a horse and headed for Rainworth to raise the alarm. That evening, as the sun was setting, Gregson, accompanied by nine shearers who had been working at Rainworth, arrived at Cullin-la-Ringo. Gregson was later to write in his memoirs: 'The bodies of men, women and children were lying in positions and attitudes which showed, as the shepherds had supposed, they had all been killed on the instant without any struggle on the part of the men.'

In total nineteen people had been killed. It was the largest massacre of whites by Aboriginal people.

Even in their wildest imaginings the Kairi could not conceive what they had set in motion. The massacres of Aboriginal people which were to follow would reach into the hundreds. One estimate would actually reach three hundred.

If the native police had provoked the attack, then the native police would lead the reprisals. Within three weeks there were no fewer than seven separate contingents of native police in the general area of the Nogoa and Comet rivers. Their instruction was that the 'murderers of the Wills party' must be 'thoroughly pursued and punished for their misdeeds'.

Upon seeing the scale of the killing, Gregson immediately decided to form a posse. Within hours most of the settlers in the area, with the notable exceptions of Dutton and Walker, had gathered at Cullin-la-Ringo. The victims were buried and

An Aboriginal tracker in native police uniform. Within three weeks there were no fewer than seven separate contingents of native police in the area.

the posse, numbering in excess of thirty, set off to do battle with the fleeing Kairi. The next morning the posse came upon a camp with over one hundred Aboriginal people. The battle that followed resulted in a considerable, but unrecorded, loss of Aboriginal life.

The first troop of native police to arrive in the area came from the Dawson River area and were led by Second-Lieutenant William Cave. They set off immediately to avenge the killings and for the next month travelled through the area indiscriminately killing Aboriginal people. Soon after their arrival they picked up some tracks which they followed day and night for four days. They cornered the Aboriginal people and started firing. In a desperate attempt to escape, the Aboriginal people climbed up a hill but the police shot them off the ledges and cornered them in the gullies. An estimated thirty Aboriginal people were killed in this one encounter.

Second-Lieutenant Moorhead and six troopers were moved from the Maranoa and stationed in the Nogoa for two months. His instruction from his commanding officer was 'not to allow any Blacks to remain at the Stations in their District, but to send them away without violence if possible, that is to say except in self-defence'.

Another troop led by George 'Black' Murray arrived in the area and 'shot a large number of aboriginals and recovered firearms and other property which had been stolen from Cullin-la-Ringo'.

Apart from the native police, the area was alive with posses. There is evidence of settlers riding hundreds of kilometres to help avenge the Cullin-la-Ringo deaths. There is even some evidence that Billy Fraser rode in to lend a hand.

By late 1862 Second-Lieutenant William Cave, who had remained in the area, could report that the killings were over. In fact the killings had been so complete that Cave claimed that there were few Aboriginal people living in the area.

Sir George Ferguson Bowen, the first Governor-in-Chief of the Colony of Queensland, reported to the Colonial Office in London that about one hundred members of the native police had taken part in the Cullin-la-Ringo reprisals. He also claimed that about seventy Aboriginal people had been killed in retaliation. His figures seem to be conservative and they ignore the posses raised by the settlers.

Cullin-la-Ringo is just one more episode in the history of the white frontier. It may have been the most powerful act of Aboriginal retaliation but it was also met

George 'Black' Murray, with seven of his 'boys' and two junior officers, was responsible for the deaths of a number of Aboriginal people in the area.

with a series of massacres which probably saw the deaths of three hundred people.

Nothing changed. The frontier pushed forward. The violence and the viciousness remained. Four years after Cullin-la-Ringo the *Rockhampton Morning Bulletin*'s editorial was moved to comment:

> There is already too much indiscriminate shooting of the blacks, and while the practice is continued outrages may be expected in retaliation. No sooner is an outrage by the blacks reported than troopers and squatters set out equipped with fire-arms, and every blackfellow within reach is shot down, without inquiry, without a thought as to whether provocation has previously been given.

CHAPTER 14

THE MASSACRE AT PIGEON CREEK — 1862

My saintly creed is: if the Myall (Aborigine) takes the initiative in transgression bung into him straight away — a timely shot or two can save a lot of trouble — but if he holds aloof and is unoffending let him rest at that

Blagden Chambers in his book Black and White.

The frontier continued to nudge further and further into the inhospitable grasslands and deserts of western Queensland. Entrepreneurial squatters and graziers claimed vast tracts of land watered by the rivers which flowed west and south into the mighty Darling-Barwon-Murray river system. This was good grazing land — scrubby, flat, lonely but with enough grass and enough winter rains to feed herds of cattle and sheep. It was beyond the Great Dividing Range. The western foothills were a distant memory to the men who boiled in the unforgiving summer heat and froze in the clear, icy winter nights.

There was always a problem with the local Aboriginal communities. They didn't welcome the arrival of the new settlers. They recognised that the men who were grazing sheep and cattle on their land were not itinerants. These people had come to stay and their claims upon the land meant that the previously uncomplicated activities of hunting and gathering gave way to fences, shepherds and herds of animals being fattened for their meat.

Pigeon Creek, a huge run straddling a tributary of the Warrego River, lay to the west of the Dawson River and Hornet Bank station. It was assumed that, after the massacre of the Fraser family, many of the Yeeman had moved westward and were now living on the eastern edges of the property.

Blagden Chambers was only nineteen when he was given charge of the property which, according to the official records was 'twelve hundred square miles, more or less, approximately sixty by twenty, and estimated to comprise the whole watershed of Pigeon Creek, which takes its rise in the main range westerly from Mount Hope, and the Angellala watershed, and is a tributary of the Warrego River'.

It was difficult country. At its best, towards the east, it was rolling grassland. At its worst it was useless brigalow — scrubby, sandy and lacking regular water supplies. The owner, A S Darby, had tried to eke a living out of it from 1860 to 1862

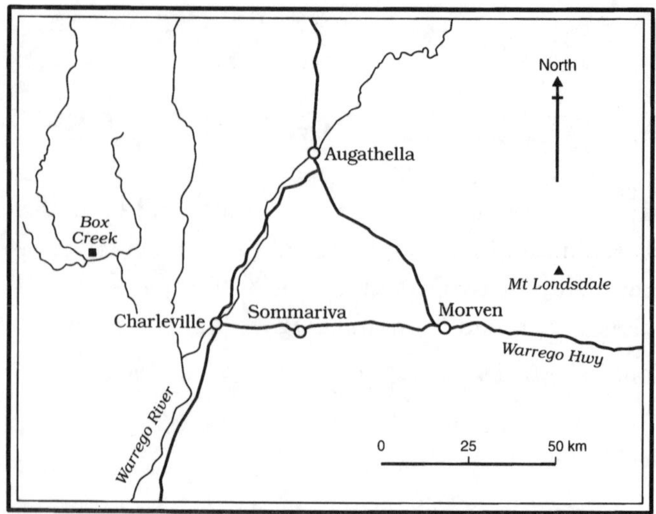

The area of western Queensland where the Pigeon Creek run was located.

but had abandoned it to a workforce of fifteen comprising Chambers, ten shepherds (there were 13 000 sheep on the property), a cook, two general rouseabouts, and a young Englishman named James or Jim who had washed up in this distant colonial outpost.

If this sounds strange it is worth remembering that Chambers, for all his youth, was a 'gentleman', having been born the son of Joseph Chambers, a Member of Parliament who had been the first solicitor in East Maitland. He had been educated at the Reverend John Pendrell's Perdue School at Glebe in Sydney. Chambers was one of those people who, when he died at the age of 97, could say with certainty that he had lived life to the full. When he left school he worked as an articled clerk in his father's office before heading for Queensland where, after a brief period, he was placed in charge of the Pigeon Creek run. Some years later he moved south to manage one of Darby's properties in the New England district before taking up land near Barraba in northern New South Wales. Like 'Banjo' Paterson he was an interesting combination of bushman and creative artist, writing articles and verse for various Sydney-based publications and becoming one of the founding members of the Art Society of New South Wales.

This complex, almost citified, background produced a sophisticated response to the Aboriginal people on the Pigeon Creek run. As he was to later remark: 'My saintly creed is: if the Myall (Aborigine) takes the initiative in transgression bung into him straight away — a timely shot or two can save a lot of trouble — but if he holds aloof and is unoffending let him rest at that.'

By late twentieth century standards this 'compassion' seems barbaric. It seems like the kind of attitude which led to the deaths of thousands of Aboriginal people on outlying stations and properties. It suggests that so long as the Aboriginal people stayed away from the cattle and the homestead they were alright. But, in an area like Pigeon Creek, the danger was always that the Aboriginal people would kill a sheep or, worse still, spear a shepherd who had wandered too far from the safety of the homestead.

Mercifully Chambers had no problems with the local Aboriginal people. Their traditional food was in abundance in the Pigeon Creek area. In fact, even today, the road between Charleville and Blackall is thick with kangaroos at dawn and dusk. This was country where the grasslands, and the winter rains, ensured abundant wildlife.

Chambers was acutely aware of the reputation the native police had acquired in the local area. By 1862 there were groups of native police stationed strategically throughout western Queensland. In the case of Pigeon Creek there was a group, under a white lieutenant, stationed at Charleville camp to the west and Mitchell Downs to the east. If there was any trouble with the Aboriginal population help was less than 100 kilometres away. Still, Chambers was wary. The native police had a reputation for stirring up, rather than solving, trouble. They were known to rape and kidnap the local women; they were always eager to kill, or fight with, the local men; and their basic attitude to their fellow Aboriginal people showed no compassion. In most cases they had been recruited from New South Wales and Victoria and their sympathy for the local people was non-existent.

As Chambers explains in his book *Black and White*: 'The presence of these bloodthirsty, uniformed blacks, led by a white man, terrorised the wild Myalls, scattered families, and drove the remnants of them off their usual beats, causing hunger and privation which often led to thieving and the spearing of cattle, as well as fanning the flame of hatred of the whites in the breast of the unfortunate Myall.'

Given that Chambers had experienced no problems with the Aboriginal people who moved around his property, he was less than pleased when, one Sunday in September 1862, he was confronted with the local commander of the native police accompanied by eight trackers and three packhorses. Chambers took an instant dislike to the lieutenant. Here was the epitome of quasi-military arrogance and power in a place where neither were qualities of any value. The man boasted a blond moustache, a supercilious air, a silk shirt and coat (it is worth remembering that the station was nearly 700 kilometres from Brisbane) and carried himself as though he was the officer of an important regiment about to go into battle.

Chambers, and his right-hand man, whom he called 'Jim', rose to meet the stranger. They were courteous. The man was rude, pompous and arrogant. When he asked where the owner was, Chambers informed him that he was in charge. The lieutenant looked at him, weighed up his obvious youthfulness, and said dismissively:

A family camp in western Queensland. Camps like this were regularly invaded, or 'cleared up', by squatters and the native police. The unstated policy was that sheep were more important than the local indigenous community.

'Oh Lord, you don't say so? Why, I understand the manager here was a big man over six feet high, with a large iron-grey beard.'

Chambers did not rise to the bait. He patiently explained that Darby had left three months ago, that he was now living in Brisbane, and that he, Chambers, was in charge. Embarrassed, the lieutenant, was beginning to apologise when Chambers, with typical bush hospitality, asked him if he would like to stay the night. The offer was accepted. The native police, 'boys' as the officer referred to them, were given some food and told to make a camp down by the creek.

'Scottie', the camp cook, turned on a decent meal. At that time, and under such circumstances, this was probably little more than boiled mutton in a glutinous gravy with flour dumplings. Certainly both Chambers and Jim were spending all their time putting up fences and outbuildings. It is unlikely that they'd had time to grow vegetables.

During the course of the evening the lieutenant asked Chambers if he was having any problems with the local Aboriginal people. Chambers explained that none of them had come near the station but he was aware of their presence in the upper reaches of Pigeon Creek because there were numerous tracks around the waterholes and fires were regularly seen in the distance. He invited the lieutenant to do a little 'clearing up' because, being towards the end of winter, he was planning to take the ewes up the creek for lambing and he knew that the heat and dryness of summer would place burdens on the property's limited water supply. He did not want the Aboriginal people killed. He simply wanted them moved off his land. They might kill the occasional sheep and they might want some of the limited supplies of summer water. It never occurred to him that these Aboriginal people, who had been living on this land for thousands of years, might have some rights. Both Jim and Chambers drove home the message that they did not want the police attacking the Aboriginal people. All they wanted was the presence of native police in the area. If the troops could go and camp in the area for a couple of days then they were confident that the Aboriginal people would be so terrified they would move out. Such was the fear of the native police.

As they sat around the fire they talked about the role of the native police. Jim explained that they were widely seen as doing more harm than good. He recalled the Hornet Bank massacre and blamed it squarely on the excesses of these poorly controlled Aboriginal troopers. He reminded the lieutenant that the runs on the Dawson and Fitzroy rivers had been beset with problems after the native police had moved through the area.

Typical of the mindset of those in authority, the lieutenant insisted that the stories from the Dawson and Fitzroy river areas were 'infernal lies'. He was only too eager to blame the slaughter of the Fraser family on the local Aboriginal people and to see the native police as totally innocent.

Chambers would not be dissuaded. 'Lies or no lies,' he retorted, 'that sort of thing is against my creed, and I hope nothing of the kind will occur on Pigeon Creek while I'm in charge.'

The lieutenant was derisory. He suggested that Darby should have taken Chambers back to Brisbane where he would have been usefully employed teaching Sunday School. Sorting out Aboriginal people was rough work for a tough man — not one with scruples. Then, in a moment of rare revelation, he added, 'I believe a good-looking gin would scare the life out of you'. It was all about sex and power, exploitation and rape. The lieutenant could protest that he had little control over the native police; he could protest that the native police were innocent of all the charges levelled against them; he could insist they were vital for keeping the frontier safe; but he was also admitting that they were an anarchic, evil and exploitative force with neither ethics nor morality.

Chambers was furious. 'It's all very well for your sort,' he said, barely capable of hiding his anger, 'here today and gone tomorrow, surrounded by a cut-throat bodyguard no individual of which dare disobey you, under peril of being triced up to the nearest tree by his fellows while you carve Roman numbers on his buttocks with a stockwhip. You and your company patrolling the scrubs, unembarrassed by the presence of undesirable witnesses, may do as you please with these little scattered mobs of Myalls. You are a law unto yourself as far as those poor devils go, against which they have no appeal, and over the execution of which you are not likely to be questioned. You then have the sanctuary of your Native police station, perhaps a hundred miles away, to which you can retreat, leaving the settler upon whose run your exploits were achieved to make peace as best he can with the injured and irritated Myall round him, who regard your act as countenanced and approved by him. How is the Myall to discriminate between you and the settler? You are a white man like him and have camped and associated with him. So naturally the Myall regards you as 'brother belonga' and of the same tribe. By and by, the savage instinct rancouring in the breast of the wild nigger, a chance comes and he takes revenge upon the unoffending settler for the injury you inflicted.'

In spite of this verbal attack the evening ended pleasantly with all three men drinking a tot of rum before retiring. In the morning, before sun up, they were preparing for their day's activities. Additional supplies were offered to the police; Chambers and Jim bid the lieutenant a friendly farewell; there was no discussion of the native police's plans for the day but, as Chambers started working, he noticed they were heading towards the upper reaches of the creek.

During the course of the day Chambers rode up the creek looking for a couple of draught horses. They had strayed away from the home paddock attracted by the new green shoots growing along the banks. Around midday he heard shots further up the creek. Jim turned to him and declared that the noise would have to be from the carbines carried by the native police. They both realised that the police were almost certainly firing on some Aboriginal people they had found. They decided to see if they could catch them. As they turned their horses and headed up the creek they realised that the shots had come from the Top Plain area. They wheeled their horses around and, making their way across the plain and through a myall forest, reached a section of dense brigalow forest. It was difficult terrain and they were concerned that they would not be able to get through the dense undergrowth and reach the native police when, in front of them, they noticed a huge kurrajong tree with an Aboriginal man hanging lifeless from one of the branches. Below, close to the butt of the tree, were a further five Aboriginal men who had been recently shot. No more than sixty metres away there were three more victims lying in the long grass.

It was clear that the dead, all of whom were males, had tried to escape by climbing the tree and the native police, almost at their leisure, had shot them out of the branches. Those who had survived had tried to run away only to be chased on horseback and shot in the back. None of the victims were carrying weapons. They had been shot at the whim of the police for reasons which seemed to be nothing more than cold-blooded viciousness.

Chambers and Jim rode on until they came to a large clearing they knew as Top Plain. There were some clumps of trees — silver-leaved box gums, rosewoods and buddas. Under one of the clumps of box gums they could see some twenty-five women and children with the lieutenant, his 'sergeant' and another native policeman guarding them. Beyond the open plain, somewhere in the brigalow, they could hear the sound of gunshots as the rest of the troop hunted down the men who had managed to escape. And some distance off, in the high grass, a solitary policeman was riding round and round in circles as though he was mustering sheep or cattle.

The two men decided that, although they were outnumbered, the very least they could do was set the women and children free while the bulk of the troops were away hunting down the remaining men. They approached the lieutenant who protested that he was 'just trying to get some information out of them'. Carefully Jim distracted him while Chambers, in a neat movement, grabbed his pistol and threatened to tie him to his horse if he did not co-operate. They also managed to relieve the 'sergeant' of his carbine by insisting the lieutenant instruct him to hand over his weapons.

Soon after this was completed the third policeman, who had been riding around in circles, arrived with a teenage woman, handcuffed and hobbled, lying across the pommel of his saddle. Again Chambers forced the lieutenant to command the kidnapper to hand over his weapon and to give up his prisoner. The trooper dropped his weapon but, seeing that he could possibly win in a contest with Chambers and Jim, he placed his foot firmly on it and challenged them to come and take it off him. He was not going to be intimidated by two young white men. It was a mistake which he later regretted because Jim, who was hardened from long hours of building huts and constructing fences, also happened to be an accomplished boxer. When the young policeman raised his fists, Jim simply strode up to him and with a swinging left uppercut nearly knocked him out.

The Aboriginal women, who had been cowering under the box gums, let out a roar of applause and support. Here, for the first time, was a white man prepared to beat and humiliate the dreaded native police. As Chambers was later to write, 'The prompt hiding Jim had given the trooper showed them that we were actually befriending them and their jabbering and their demonstrations of joy were evidently their method of barracking.'

Shortly afterwards Chambers freed all the women and children, led them into the brigalow, and, with signs of gratitude, they fled the scene. They left behind the carnage. Nine men and one woman (she had been carrying a baby and had obviously tried to escape with the child) had been killed. The lieutenant knew enough to realise that Chambers and Jim, if they could provide hard evidence of the crime, were capable of destroying his 'career' and, probably, if he was taken back to Brisbane and tried, he would hanged. It was one of the cruel ironies of Queensland in the

This old lantern slide, titled 'A Group of Gins', gives an impression of the sight that greeted Jim and Chambers when they came out of the brigalow and saw twenty five women and children.

1860s that if you could get away with murder, as the native police regularly did, then nothing happened. If, however, you were caught, then the punishment was hanging. With this in mind Jim and Chambers constructed what they called 'Silvermo's death warrant' which read:

> I, -----, Lieutenant of native police stationed at ----- in the colony of Queensland, do hereby solemnly declare that on the ----- day of September, eighteen sixty-two, I was present at Top Plain, Pigeon Creek Station, and there did see Thomas ----- and James ----- of that station by means of strategy disarm and arrest two troopers of my company, take from them and set at liberty twenty-eight wild female Aborigines, three of whom, between the ages of twelve and sixteen years, had handcuffs upon their ankles, and nineteen children; that the said gins and piccaninnies were being detained by the said two troopers, while the remaining six troopers of my company were pursuing and shooting the adult male Aborigines of the same mob or part tribe as the aforesaid gins and piccaninnies; and that after the said Thomas ----- and James ----- had fully effected the escape of the said female Aborigines and their children they did then release the two troopers aforesaid.

The lieutenant begrudgingly signed it and promised to return to his barracks. The following day Chambers rode out to the site of the massacre and recorded the full scale of the sad slaughter. The mother of the baby had been shot in the head by a bullet which had clearly been fired by a person on horseback. In the scrub, where the native police had been while Chambers and Jim had been freeing the women, they found five more bodies of males and, at intervals for the next five kilometres, they found a further eleven bodies. There was evidence that some of the men had been wounded and then viciously beaten to death. In total the native police, without any controls from their white lieutenant, had killed twenty-five males ranging in age from around sixteen to one grey-haired old man who Chambers estimated as probably being nearly eighty. Only one woman had been killed. By the creek they found a teenager whose leg had been broken. They took him back to the homestead.

Blagden Chambers' story is full of the contradictions that characterised the frontier. Here is a civilised man prepared to bring a wounded Aboriginal boy back to his homestead where he could nurse him back to health. Here was a man who was deeply disturbed by the bloodthirsty, anarchic behaviour of the native police. Yet here was a pragmatist whose main interest was to protect his property, whose driving motivation was to ensure that the Aboriginal people on his property stayed away. His story is typical of the complexity of the situation. He was no humanitarian but, in comparison to the lieutenant and his native police, he was a true protector of the local groups.

CHAPTER 15

THE FORREST RIVER MASSACRE — 1926

Nowadays . . . you can hear ghosts crying in the night, chains, babies crying, troopers' horse, chains jingling . . . We were there sleeping, still. It was all silence. You could hear woman rocking her baby to sleep, 'Wawai! Wawai! Wawai!' . . .

Daniel Evans's account of the massacre quoted verbatim in Randolph Stow's To the Islands

Who knows why Hay attacked Lumbia? Some say it was over a woman. Some say that Hay, who was a boundary rider on Nulla Nulla station in the East Kimberley, came to Lumbia and said, 'Bring that woman here to work for me. I want her to make my camp. I want her to water my garden, watch my place, sweep the house'. And the woman went but soon she returned to Lumbia. Then the next time Hay came to get the woman Lumbia said, 'No! She can't go. She stays with me,' and Hay got angry and attacked Lumbia.

Others say that one morning in late May 1926 Hay went out to check the boundaries to ensure that the cattle were okay. After checking the boundaries, he cut back to the station and on the way back noticed two old Aboriginal women beside a billabong. He rode up to them and called out, 'What are you doing here?'

The old women looked at him incomprehensibly; they did not understand English. All they were doing was cutting some lily roots for the evening meal.

Hay spoke to them in pidgin, 'Which way you husband?' he asked. They guessed his meaning from his gesticulations and pointed to a nearby gum tree where Lumbia had been sleeping. At the sound of the horse's hooves he had woken and was now leaning against the bole of the tree, gazing idly at Hay. He saw no danger. This was tribal land and the women were gathering lily roots just as they had done last year and the year before that.

'What are you doing here on the cattle boundary? What are you doing on the cattle run?' barked Hay.

The queries were incomprehensible. Lumbia looked at the wiry, red-faced boundary rider who loomed over him and explained that, as any fool could see, the women

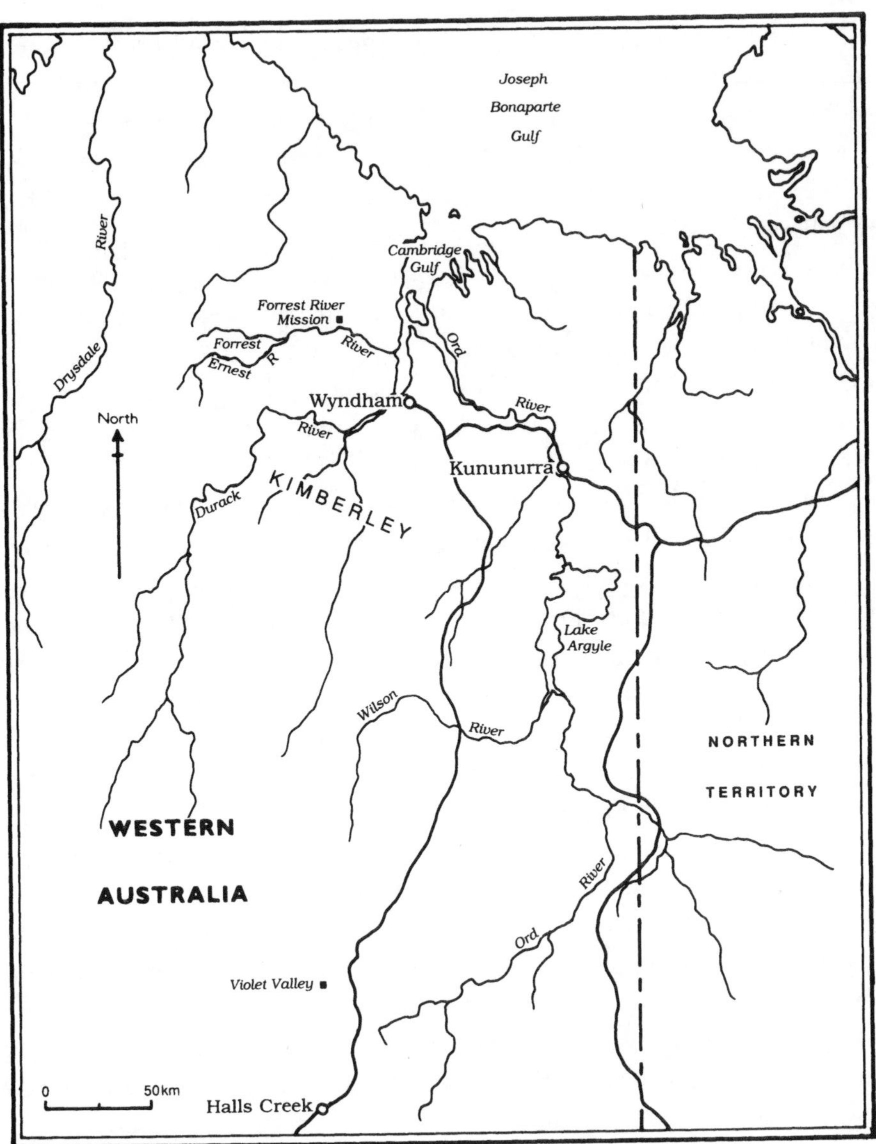

The Kimberley region in north Western Australia where many Aborigines from the Forrest River mission were massacred.

were collecting lily roots. He spoke in his own language. Hay didn't understand.

Who knows why Hay attacked Lumbia? But he did. He dismounted, carefully and slowly unfurled his stockwhip, and proceeded to flog the old man who covered himself defensively and tried to escape. Hay must have landed twenty or thirty lashes. He had cut Lumbia on the back and the arms and the legs and a thick welt, with blood seeping from it, ran across Lumbia's face just below the eyes. Then Hay, driving home his 'lesson', grabbed Lumbia's spears and started breaking them. As Hay remounted, Lumbia reached for his shovel spear and with unerring accuracy hurled it at his attacker. It went through Hay's chest and punctured his lung. The horse galloped away but before it had gone 20 metres Hay's grip on the reins weakened and he fell off dead. The terrified horse, its saddle covered with Hay's blood, galloped back to Nulla Nulla.

Lumbia moved across to Hay's body. He checked the dead boundary rider's pockets and helped himself to Hay's tobacco and matches before covering the body with a couple of branches and departing.

As the Reverend E R Gribble, Protector and head of the Forrest River Mission, was later to report: 'As a matter of fact, it was simply a dispute between an armed white man and, at the outset, an unarmed savage. The savage won.'

That night, when he did not return for his evening meal, Hay's two colleagues began worrying about the missing boundary rider. It was feared that he had fallen from his horse. They decided to search for him at first light.

As they were saddling up their horses in the cold dampness of the dawn the two men noticed that during the night Hay's horse had found its way back to the station. When they looked closer they noticed blood on the horse's saddle. They spent most of the day searching for Hay. They rode around the boundary of Nulla Nulla not realising that Hay had been killed taking a short cut back to the station.

It wasn't until mid-afternoon that some crows circling lazily near the billabong attracted their attention. By the time they reached the billabong little was left of Hay. The carrion-eaters had been at his corpse for nearly twenty-four hours. It was hard to tell whether the remains were those of an Aboriginal man or a white man.

It became folklore amongst the local Aboriginal communities — among the Gadjerong, Djangada, Wurangangari and Wiladjau — that the only way the stockmen knew that the remains were those of Hay was because the crows had pecked around a gum leaf which had stuck to the body and when the gum leaf was removed it revealed a small piece of white flesh.

That night the stockmen got out their motor launch and set off down the Forrest River to Wyndham. On about 6 June a party of four whites, two mounted constables and two policemen named O'Leary and Jolly who had been specially sworn in to participate in the investigation, left Wyndham. They were accompanied by seven Aboriginal trackers. It was, by any measure, a strange force to hunt a single Aboriginal man. Apart from the thirteen men, there were forty-two horses and mules. An estimated five-hundred rounds of ammunition were taken. It was clearly, as was later observed, 'a punitive expedition rather than one intended merely to capture a criminal native'.

It was a simple lesson in the mentality of the frontier. It may have been the twentieth century. It may have been the era of the movie, the motor launch, the aeroplane and the radio but on the frontier — now in the far northern tip of Australia — the mentality which had been in the Sydney basin in the late eighteenth century, at Myall Creek in 1838, and in northern Queensland in the late nineteenth century, still prevailed. An Aboriginal man had killed a white man and therefore a lot of Aboriginal people had to die.

The frontier code of silence still operated. No-one knew how many were killed. Professor Elkin, who travelled through the area two years later, said, '20 or more'. The Reverend E R Gribble wrote, 'There are some thirty native men and women missing.' Daniel Evans said, 'So many hundred . . . women, men and children'. And old Grant Ngabidj, who was twenty-two at the time, and who really knew, said, 'They shootim that lot now, piccaninny, old old woman, blackfeller, old old man, somewhere about hundred'.

It was cold and calculated slaughter. The posse arrived in the area and moved systematically from camp to camp, killing as they went. Their system was to move into a camp and shoot all the dogs and break all the spears before setting on the people. In one camp a policeman shot a dog and the bullet passed right through the dog and killed an old woman named Nyuwi who was sleeping in a humpy.

At one place on the Ernest River the posse constructed a main base from which they could attack nearby Aboriginal camps. They would ride out in the morning, move into a camp, capture as many of the inhabitants as possible, chain them together, and bring them back to the base camp. They would then separate the men from the women. The men, still chained together, were led away from the camp to a lonely place on the edge of the Forrest River where they were tied to a tree and shot.

The posse were thorough and very cautious. The police boys dug a huge hole in the soft sands of the riverbank, piled in large amounts of dry wood, and created a huge bonfire. On to the fire they threw the bodies of the Aboriginal men. Someone sat and waited and, as the fire died down, he threw more wood on until the pyre was nothing more than a large patch of glowing embers. On top

'Cumjam, murderer of Ferguson, 1894.' Like Lumbia at Forrest River, Cumjam was caught and chained to a tree.

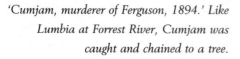

of the embers large stones from the river were placed to keep the heat in and to hide the evidence of the massacre.

The women, who had been chained to a nearby tree, were forced to witness the death and cremation of their menfolk. They were then marched for another 10 kilometres along the riverbank. No-one knows if they were raped or how they were killed but they were all executed and once again the police boys dug a hole and the bodies were burnt.

For over a week the troopers moved slowly up the bank of the Forrest River. The process was always the same: capture the Aboriginal people, kill them, burn the bodies and hide all the evidence. At times it seemed as though they were making no serious attempt to capture Lumbia.

On 21 June, thirteen days after they had left Wyndham, the posse reached the Forrest River mission. There they told Reverend Gribble, who had a reputation as a 'hardworking, obstinate and tactless man', that they had travelled up the river but they had seen no Aboriginal people. At this point Gribble had no reason to disbelieve them. He explained that Hay's murderer was well known to most of the Aboriginal people in the area and that it was recognised by the local black community that Lumbia would have to stand trial under white man's law.

Gribble sent two men from the mission to escort the posse and help them find Lumbia. The group left on 26 June and returned to the mission on 4 July with a group of some twenty to thirty Aboriginal men, all chained together. The group included Lumbia.

Gribble was not amused. Accompanied by his Aboriginal pastor, the Reverend James Noble, he rode down to the posse's camp and demanded an explanation. 'What,' he asked, 'are you intending to do with those prisoners?' Some five days earlier, word had drifted into the mission of the massacres. Gribble may have been tactless but he was not going to accuse a group of policemen of murder without evidence. At this stage all he wanted was to ensure that no more Aboriginal people were killed unnecessarily. He told the police that as Protector of Aborigines and as a Justice of the Peace he would not allow any innocent Aboriginal people to be taken off the mission.

Gribble then rode back to the mission and collected James Noble's wife who acted as an interpreter. From Lumbia and his wife and another woman he got the same story. Lumbia told of how Hay had attacked him with the stockwhip and how he had retaliated by spearing Hay with his shovel spear. Lumbia stated that he had been the only man involved.

The police were forced to accept the story. In due course Gribble, the witnesses, Constable Regan, two Aboriginal trackers and Lumbia travelled to Wyndham. 'Then,' according to the Aboriginal folklore of the area, 'a good while after, Reverend Gribble dreamed a dream. In his dream he saw the figure of a native getting shot.

Aboriginal pastor, the Reverend James Noble, and his wife with some mission boys.

He was a real holy man. God must have told him to go Onmalmeri [on the Forrest River] way.'

By now rumours of the massacres were widespread in the Kimberley but no-one connected with the killings would talk. The Sergeant of Police at Wyndham tried to investigate the rumours but was met with typical frontier silence.

After Lumbia had been committed for trial on the charge of murder, Gribble returned to the mission. It was there that the rumours of the massacres persisted to a point where they could not be ignored. A man came to Gribble with a list of Aboriginal people who had been killed. Other Aboriginal people arrived at the mission to report the massacre.

Gribble took the challenge tenaciously. On 12 August, accompanied by a number of Aboriginal people, Gribble rode out to investigate the rumours. In a few hours they located the base camp the posse had used. They found clear evidence of native prisoners but no evidence which supported the massacre rumour.

On 18 August, while Gribble was in Wyndham, Reverend James Noble and a group of local Aboriginal people, who were experienced trackers, returned to the posse camp and followed tracks which led to a place

> . . . where a number of native men had been killed and their bodies burnt. He also found tracks of three native women who had been chained to a tree a short distance from where the men had been murdered. Their tracks were also in evidence right up to the spot

On 4 July 1926 the posse returned to the Forrest River mission with a group of twenty or thirty Aboriginal men chained together. The group included the accused, Lumbia.

> where the men had been butchered . . . Mr. Noble brought back a parcel of charred bones.

On 22 August Gribble took the bones to the medical officer in Wyndham. He returned to the mission on 25 August, accompanied by a man named Mitchell, a government officer from Wyndham. Mitchell reported that:

> We went straight to the spot, being guided by Noble. Where the men had been done to death was a small tree to which the prisoners had evidently been fastened. Round this tree was a ledge of rock about a foot high. Dark stains were still visible, though great efforts had been made to clean up the declivity. Stones had been removed and the edges of the rock had been chipped. About forty feet away to the north-east from this spot in the midst of the rocky bed of the flood-waters of the Forrest River was a large hole where a large fire had been . . . In the ashes were found a quantity of fragments of charred bones and other matter. In a shallow pool about 20 or 30 feet to the north of where the fire had been were small heaps of charcoal and in these we found small portions of skull and other

> bones. We then followed the tracks of three native women and three shod horses. We followed them about six miles up the bed of the Forrest River. Both Noble and myself had come to the conclusion that these women had been liberated and I said, 'Well, we will follow on to the top of the sandbank'. We did so and, as we surmounted the bank, we all received a shock for there, facing us, were the remains of a large fire at the foot of a tree . . . Searching among the ashes we found a quantity of teeth and fragments of charred bones.

Daniel Evans's version of the story includes the detail that Gribble 'stooped down and scratched the grave to see if any body remained. So he couldn't find any bones — he picked up a teeth, one teeth . . . He put it in his pocket, held a burial service, and they left the grave'.

Gribble returned to the area on 30 August. This time he was accompanied by Inspector Douglas. 'We went over the same ground and, where the women were burnt, we found a large stone behind the tree near where the fire had been, and on this stone dark stains and a few human hairs.'

To this gruesome evidence Gribble was able to add many examples of Aboriginal people who, in the weeks after the posse had passed through the area, had come to the mission to have medical attention for their wounds. One Aboriginal person had

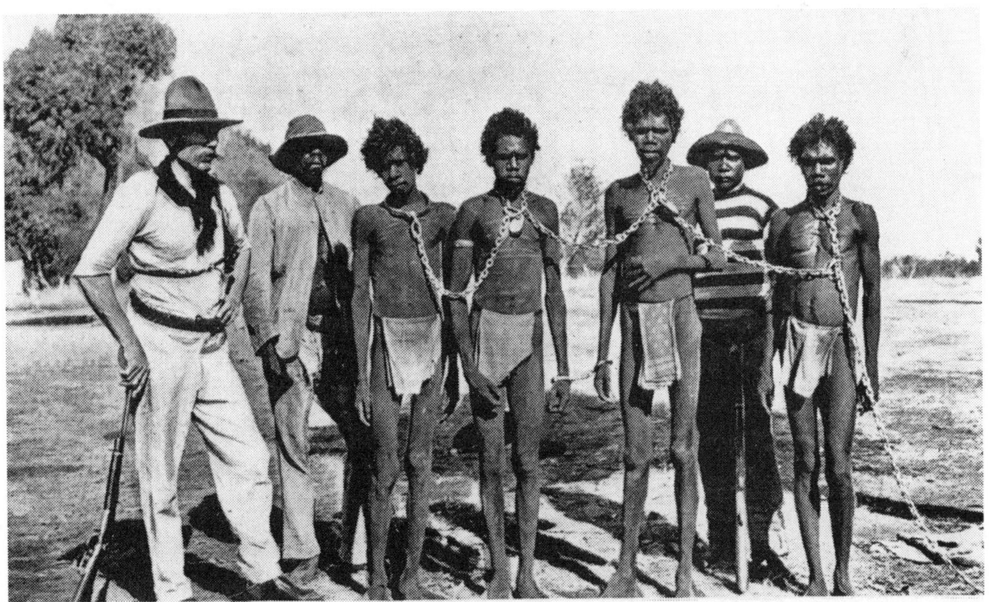

The Reverend Gribble told the police that as Protector of Aborigines and as a Justice of the Peace he would not allow any innocent Aboriginal people to be taken off the mission.

come in with a bullet wound in the leg. A woman came in with a bullet in her thigh. A sister of one of the Aboriginal people on the mission was reported dead. It was accepted that she had been shot by one of the trackers with the posse and that her baby had been bashed to death. Gribble's tenacity was finally rewarded. By January 1927 the evidence was overwhelming and the West Australian Government was forced to establish a royal commission under the magistrate, Mr T G Wood. The commission, which reported to Parliament in 1928, was titled the 'Royal Commission into the Killing and Burning of Bodies of Aborigines in East Kimberley, and into Police Methods when Effecting Arrests'.

The results of the commission were inconclusive. Commissioner Wood's investigation was blocked at every turn. Public sympathy in the local white community was such that funds were raised for legal representation of the posse. The only action taken against the posse was that two of the police officers were arrested for murder. They were tried and acquitted. The government promoted them out of the area.

And what of Lumbia? The story is that he served three or four years in Fremantle gaol before returning to settle down on the Violet Valley mission. In the late 1950s, Daniel Evans told Randolph Stow:

> Nowadays, now, at Onmalmeri, you can hear the ghosts crying in the night, chains, babies crying, troopers' horse, chains jingling. I didn't believe it, but I went there, mustering cattle for droving to the meatworks, I heard it, too. We was camping at Onmalmeri Station couple of weeks. We were there sleeping, still. It was all silence. You could hear woman rocking her baby to sleep, 'Wawai! Wawai! Wawai!' like this, rocking the baby to sleep . . .

CHAPTER 16

THE CONISTON MASSACRE — 1928

What use is a wounded black feller a hundred miles from civilization?

Mounted Constable William George Murray in evidence in a Darwin Court

The drought was now in its fourth year. The grass was bone brown and lifeless. Wild animals were scarce. Many of the waterholes were no more than sticky, cracking bowls of mud. The carcasses of cattle littered the large, and once overstocked, properties to the north and west of Alice Springs. The land was a wilderness of red sand, withered mulga trees and crackling spinifex. The winter skies of the western desert were cloudless and intensely blue.

These were the times which reminded the Ngalia and Walbiri people of the damage white grazing had wrought upon the delicate balance which sustained life on the edges of the desert. There had been droughts before. Life had never been easy in the desert beyond the Lander River and Hanson Creek. But, even in the most savage drought, there'd always been food and water. The grass seeds had been scarcer and small animals harder to find but, with a sense of ecological balance nurtured by an understanding of the land, life had continued. Now, with the added demands of the cattle, some of the waterholes had dried up. The people of the area had been forced to congregate around the larger waterholes. Occasionally, due to a lack of 'bush tucker', the men would spear one of the undernourished steers grazing nearby.

By the winter of 1928 some thirty or forty Aboriginal people were camped around a soak on a dried-up riverbed about 20 kilometres south of Coniston station. Into their midst on the evening of 2 August came Fred Brooks, a wiry, tough sixty-seven-year-old dingo trapper. Brooks was a drifter. About thirty years before he had turned his back on city life and wandered into the Outback where he'd worked at anything which offered food and a place to sleep. At various times he'd been a station hand, camel driver, fencer, boundary rider and general rouseabout. Now, in the middle of a drought which had seen less than 25 millimetres of rain fall in the previous six months, he'd bought a couple of camels, employed two Aboriginal boys whom he called Dodger and Skipper, and was going to try to eke out a living from dingo trapping. It was steady money; the government was paying ten bob a head.

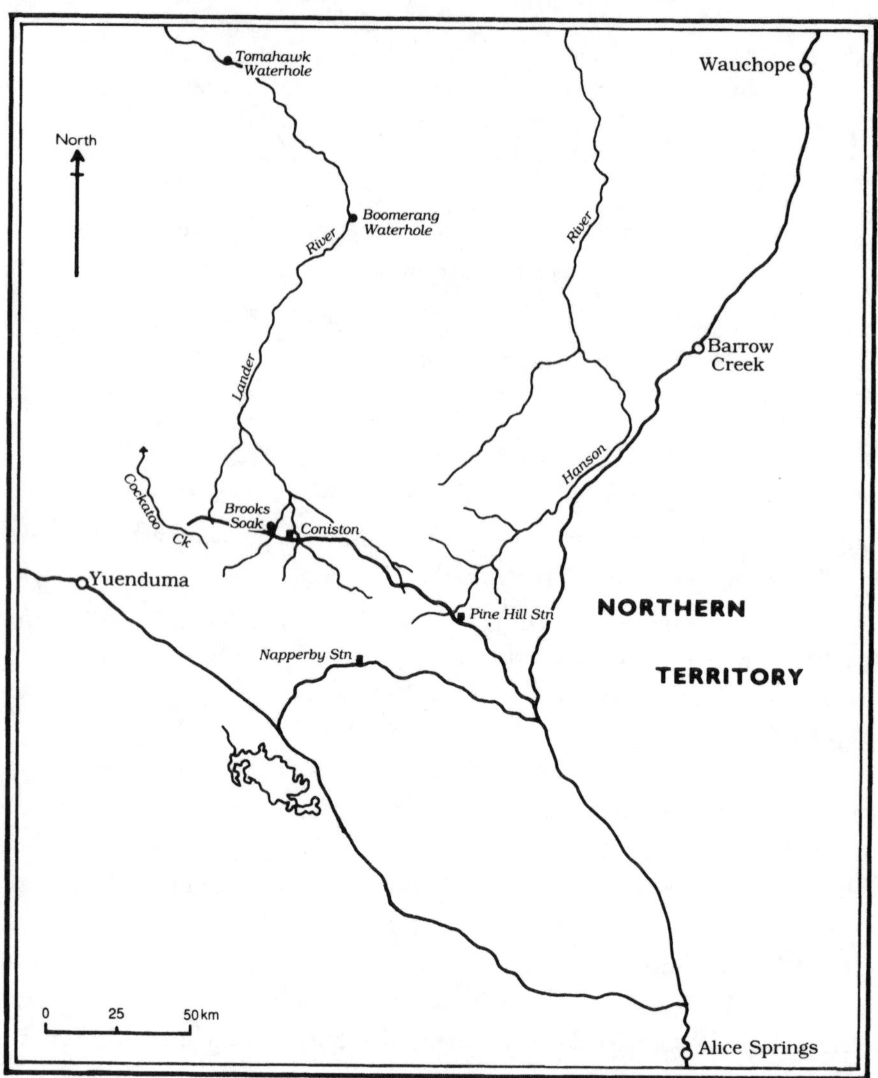

The Alice Springs region in central Australia.

Brooks was a cross between a swaggie and a bushie. His body, hardened, tanned and leathery, belied his age. He was strong and steeped in a bushcraft learnt from hard-won experience and Aboriginal teaching. He was not an overt racist. His attitude to Aboriginal people was a complex mixture of respect for their skills, exploitation of their women, frontier chicanery and a quiet confidence produced by his own, perceived, superiority.

Somewhere in the back of his mind Brooks must have known he was riding into trouble. He spent a couple of days at Coniston station with his old friend Randal Stafford. Stafford warned him that the drought had driven the local tribes to an unprecedented level of aggression. Food shortages meant Aboriginal people were fighting for their own survival. Ignoring Stafford's warnings Brooks left Coniston station on 2 August and that evening set up camp at the far end of the soak. Over the next couple of days he set traps, caught a number of dingoes, and had Dodger and Skipper successfully dig a rabbit out of its hole.

Two days later a mining engineer, Charles Young from the Mid-Australian Exploration Company, saw Brooks and warned him of the potential danger. Once again Brooks ignored the warning.

The next day Brooks struck a deal with an Aboriginal man named Bullfrog. In exchange for tobacco and sugar, Bullfrog's woman, Marungali, would wash Brooks's clothes. Implicit in the transaction was the not uncommon agreement that Marungali would spend the night with the trapper.

On the night of 6 August, Marungali came to Brooks's camp; Bullfrog had honoured his side of the deal. Brooks was aware that payment was due but he ignored Bullfrog. Throughout the night Bullfrog waited. He sat with his uncle Padirrka and, as he realised that the white man was not going to honour the agreement, he became increasingly more angry and frustrated.

By dawn his fury was uncontrollable. With Padirrka he marched on Brooks's camp seeking revenge. Brooks attempted to leap from his bed but retribution was swift. Bullfrog slashed Brooks's throat with his boomerang and, while Marungali held him down, Bullfrog and Padirrka beat the trapper to death with stone axes and knives. After collecting tobacco, tea and sugar, they stuffed Brooks's body in a hessian bag and half-buried it in the rabbit hole which Dodger and Skipper had dug a couple of days earlier. Bullfrog threatened Dodger and Skipper with their lives if they told anyone and sent them to Coniston station to tell Randal Stafford that Brooks had died mysteriously in the bush.

Realising the seriousness of what they had done, and reprimanded by the tribal elders, Bullfrog and Padirrka left the soak and disappeared into the vast, inhospitable anonymity of the Western Desert.

Dodger and Skipper, who were barely teenagers, arrived at Coniston station to find that Stafford was away in Alice Springs buying supplies. Although sworn to secrecy, the boys couldn't resist telling the Aboriginal workers at the station about the murder. Their fear, and a typically adolescent sense of the macabre, embroidered the killing and made much of the fact that Old Fred's leg was protruding from the hole.

A day later a half-caste named Alex Wilson arrived at the soak just on nightfall. Stumbling around in the twilight he saw Old Fred's leg. Terrified he hastily remounted his camel and rode through the night scarcely daring to look behind him. Shortly after dawn on 8 August he arrived at Coniston station. He had not slept for over forty-eight hours and, with a mixture of tiredness and hysteria, he told of how a white man had been chopped to pieces and left to rot in a hole. He, too, made much of the protruding leg.

By the time Stafford returned from Alice Springs the bush telegraph had weaved its spell on Coniston. He was greeted by Aboriginal station hands who told of the murder and dismemberment of Brooks in graphically elaborated detail. Stafford was furious and vengeful but he was unwilling to act without police support. While he had been in 'the Alice' he had visited Mr Cawood, the Government Resident, and demanded a police presence in the area to curb cattle killing. He realised that the drought was pushing everyone to the limit. Fred Brooks's death was a powerful confirmation of his fears.

Stafford's request for proper policing had not gone unnoticed. On 11 August, totally unaware of Brooks's murder, Cawood sent Mounted Constable William George Murray to investigate Stafford's complaints.

Murray had that peculiar frontier police mentality which constructed the world in simplistic terms: Aboriginal people needed to be controlled; white settlers needed to be protected. A fist or the butt of a rifle was easier justice than dragging some minor offender hundreds of kilometres to the Alice Springs lockup. Crime prevention could be achieved by 'making examples of offenders' and 'teaching people lessons'. Simplicity and necessity would always take precedence over the niceties of the law. He was a simple and brutal man charged with dispensing law in a vast, unmanageable territory. Like law officers in the Wild West he had never received a day's instruction.

Murray had been born in rural Victoria. His early life and military service at Gallipoli had given him the skills of marksmanship and horsemanship which the Northern Territory police force prized. He had joined the force in 1919 and by 1928 was in charge of the Barrow Creek police station, a position which included the paternalistic title of Chief Protector of Aborigines for the area. His career had not been meteoric but he was regarded by his superiors as conscientious and efficient.

By mid-afternoon he arrived at Coniston with an Aboriginal tracker named Paddy. Stafford met them with a version of the events at the soak which had been warped and contorted by imagination and rumour. Fred Brooks, he reported, had been murdered and chopped up by some thirty or forty Aboriginal people. His remains had been shoved down a rabbit hole. No-one was game to go to the soak for fear of further attacks; no-one was prepared to retrieve Fred's body so that it could be buried.

At the time, there were no Aboriginal people at the soak. Murray, however, was in no mood to check the accuracy of Stafford's account. He drove back to the Alice Springs road and telephoned Cawood with news of the murder. Cawood refused to send reinforcements. Instead he gave Murray a free hand to deal with the Aboriginal people in any way he saw fit.

Returning to Coniston station on 12 August, Murray was determined, in his own brutally methodical way, to teach the Aboriginal people in the area a lesson about the sacrosanct nature of white life which they would never forget.

The owner of Coniston station, Randal Stafford, felt guilty about Murray's treatment of Aboriginal people on his station.

During the afternoon he began organising a posse of eight which included himself, the tracker Paddy, the half-caste Alex Wilson, Randal Stafford, a station Aboriginal man named Major — the older brother of Skipper, Jack Saxby and Billy Briscoe — two itinerant whites who were working for Stafford at the time, and Dodger.

Murray had no love for Aboriginal people. He may have wanted to find out the truth about Brooks's murder but the punishment he was preparing to mete out to the Walbiri was a reaction constrained neither by law nor by the most rudimentary principles of justice, humanity or fair play.

During the day he questioned Dodger and Skipper. Bullfrog's threats were no match for Murray's cold and ruthless presence. The boys outlined the events which had led to the murder of Brooks and laid the blame on Bullfrog, Padirrka and Marungali. Murray listened. He must have realised that, at the most, three Aboriginal people had been involved in the killing of Old Fred Brooks. However, as far as he was concerned, all the Aboriginal people in the area were guilty by association. He could see no reason why he should restrict his attentions to the three offenders.

Mid-morning a dingo trapper, Bruce Chapman, rode in to Coniston. Murray sent Chapman, Paddy and Alex Wilson off to 'Brooks's Soak' to determine what had really happened. The three men disinterred the body (which hadn't been dismembered) and buried it on the bank above the soak.

During the afternoon two Walbiri, named Padygar and Woolingar, who were obviously oblivious to Brooks's murder, wandered into Coniston station hoping to trade some dingo scalps. Paddy saw them first and, believing that they had been involved in the killing, tried to arrest them. He grabbed them and dragged them to Murray's truck. He had managed to get the police chains out of the truck and was trying to drag the two suspects to a nearby tree when Woolingar managed to break free. Paddy swung a punch and Woolingar went sprawling.

Hearing the noise of the fracas, Murray raced out only to be confronted by a chain-swinging Woolingar. Murray drew his revolver and fired. Woolingar fell to the ground with a bullet wound to the temple. Murray was convinced he'd killed him but a few minutes later Stafford arrived and delivered a kick which not only determined that Woolingar was alive but also broke the man's rib in the process. Woolingar was to lie chained to the tree for the next eighteen hours.

The following morning the posse, comprising fourteen horses, food supplies and eight men — with Padygar and Woolingar stumbling along behind — left Coniston and headed for the soaks along the Lander River. They moved slowly and didn't arrive at the Walbiri camp until early afternoon. Murray insisted that no shooting should occur. He was keen to take about twenty prisoners. Instead of approaching directly, the party split up and began to encircle the camp. Paddy and Alex Wilson rode around the flanks while Briscoe, Stafford and Saxby spread out to the left and right of Murray.

Somewhere in the parched desert between Coniston station and the Walbiri camp Murray had forgotten the law he was supposed to be administering. Upon sighting the camp, which was nothing more than a few lean-tos of bark and branches in which twenty-three innocent Aboriginal people were living, he charged. The others followed. Suddenly the peacefulness of the camp was filled with the sound of galloping horses and yelling, yipping riders. Murray rode into the middle of the camp, dismounted, and within seconds was surrounded by a group of very angry, very frightened and very confused Aboriginal people all screaming abuse and threatening him with yam sticks and boomerangs. Suddenly Briscoe started shooting. Saxby and Murray joined in. Within a minute the 'battle' was over — the gun rarely loses in a competition with sticks. Three men and a woman had been killed. Another woman, who had been badly injured, was to die within the hour.

Stafford, who had managed to avoid being involved in the shooting, was horrified. He began to realise that circumstances were beyond his control. He had sought only to protect his cattle. Now he was associated with the murder of five innocent Aboriginal people.

He challenged Murray's right to shoot. Murray replied curtly that he had fired in self-defence. In his world of right and wrong there was no room for doubt or interpretation. With cold matter-of-factness he collected up all the spears, boomerangs, yam sticks and nulla-nullas and burnt them. His search for weapons also uncovered Fred Brooks's coat, shirt, quart pot, blanket, tobacco and some knives and singlets. Murray showed these to Stafford as evidence justifying the murders. Stafford remained guilty and unconvinced. The next day he returned to Coniston alone. He wanted no part in the killings.

That night Murray set up camp where the killings had taken place. Padygar was fed but by now Woolingar was too weak to eat. During the night Wilson captured three young Aboriginal boys, including a boy named Lolorrba, known as Lala, who would later become a key witness for Murray.

The three boys had been sent by their tribes to assess and report on the police party. Now, having been captured by Murray, they faced the impossible dilemma of divided loyalties enforced by threats. If they told Murray where the rest of the Walbiri were hiding, they faced punishment when they returned to the camp. If they didn't tell Murray, they would face a beating from the policeman and his tracker. Their solution was to smash their feet with rocks so they could not lead Murray to the tribe's camps. Murray was furious but the boys would not betray the tribe. The policeman forced the crippled boys to lead the party but the boys headed off into the desert.

By nightfall they had reached Cockatoo Creek, about 30 kilometres north-east of the previous day's murderous activities. As twilight fell on the desert and the wintry night air began to cool and sharpen, Paddy sighted four Aboriginal people on a nearby ridge. Murray spurred his horse on and galloped towards them. Paddy circled across to a narrow gully. Seeing the men approaching, the Aboriginal people started to run. Word had spread quickly and they had heard that white men were moving through the area killing indiscriminately. This was no time to wait and find out what the men galloping towards them wanted.

Paddy cornered two of the men and called to them, in a language they did not understand, to stop. He leapt from his horse and was endeavouring to handcuff the men when one, with a strength driven by fear, slipped the handcuffs and began to run for freedom. Murray fired two shots at the man but missed. Paddy dropped to his knees, aimed his rifle at the man who was ducking and weaving through the bush, and shot him in the back. The man pitched forward into the sand of the gully bed. He was dead.

The killing was now without motive or sense. The Aboriginal people had not attacked. There was no evidence to link them with Fred Brooks's murder. They were being killed simply because they were Aboriginal people. After questioning the other three for a couple of hours, Murray let them go. His reputation as a crazed, vengeful and irrational killer spread up and down the soaks and camps along the Lander River. Fearful for their lives, Aboriginal people decamped and headed north along the riverbed or into the dry wilderness which lay to the west of the river. It was better to die of thirst and starvation than to be gunned down for no reason by a demented policeman.

The next two days saw the police party make no contact with any Aboriginal people. Confident that he had brought order to the region, Murray turned his police party around and headed back to Coniston. By now Woolingar was dying from his wounds and Lala's self-inflicted injuries were infected. As the party passed through Coniston, Lala, Woolingar and Padygar were left in Stafford's custody.

The party, unencumbered now by their prisoners, moved to the north. They knew that if the Walbiri were anywhere they'd be moving north along the bed of the Lander River. By early afternoon they reached the bank of the river, which was now no more than a series of isolated soaks and muddy holes. They dropped down to the wide, dry riverbed and before they had travelled more than a few kilometres, Paddy had picked up fresh tracks.

Murray spurred his horse into a gallop. The others followed. The five men — Murray, Saxby, Briscoe, Paddy and Alex Wilson — spread out across the dusty riverbed and moved rapidly through the scrubby terrain. At dusk they rounded a huge dry meander and in front of them, in the scrub along the bank, was a Walbiri camp. Murray yelled out instructions. They must surround the camp. No-one must escape. There were only twenty or thirty Aboriginal people in the camp and most of them were women and children. This made no difference to Murray. Old Fred must be avenged. Who was there to say these Aboriginal people weren't responsible for his death?

The women and children ran for cover. The men, who had heard of the other killings, grabbed their spears and boomerangs prepared to fight to the death. Murray called on them to drop their weapons. The instruction was incomprehensible. Paddy repeated the call. His instruction was equally meaningless. The Aboriginal men charged. Murray leapt from his horse and shot a charging warrior. Paddy charged the warriors, shooting indiscriminately. Briscoe and Saxby stood their ground firing at random.

Once again spears and boomerangs were no match for rifle power. The 'battle' was over in five minutes. Three men had been killed. Three had been injured. No-one knew how many injured men had managed to escape. By morning two of the injured had died. The third prisoner was dead by noon.

Murray had now killed twelve Aboriginal people. Yet they were pointless killings. Bullfrog and Padirrka were now far beyond the reach of the police party. He was slaughtering innocent people. The whole campaign was becoming bloody and irrational. How could he return to Alice Springs? He still did not have the murderers.

This did not deter the party. For the next week the killing went on. Murray's philosophy, as he was to tell a court months later, was, 'What use is a wounded black feller a hundred miles from civilisation?' All members of the party shot to kill. No-one kept a record of how many they killed. Aboriginal people, be they men, women or children, were shot on sight.

The Walbiri were later to estimate that between sixty and seventy of their people were shot as the party roamed up and down the Lander River.

By 24 August, after nine days in the desert, Murray called a halt to the killings. He captured a suitable scapegoat named Arkirkra who could be blamed for Brooks's murder and headed back to Coniston station. That night Woolingar died in chains under a tree at the station.

The official count was seventeen dead. The luckless Padygar and Arkirkra were marched back to Alice Springs and charged with the murder of Fred Brooks.

Murray returned to Alice Springs on 1 September and was immediately hailed as a conquering, local hero. News of his 'work' along the Lander had filtered back to the town and he was greeted with admiration and approval. Once again white justice had been brought to the recalcitrant blacks.

The forty people living in Alice Springs in 1928 were, for the most part, hardened, practical frontier battlers who in their ultra-conservative, pragmatic way felt that they 'knew about what was best for the blacks'. They cracked jokes about Aboriginal sexuality, dismissed Aboriginal alcoholism as 'a weakness of the race' and deemed most Aboriginal people, who they variously called abos, boys, niggers, bucks, lubras, gins, and piccaninnies, as either lazy or stupid. They could never understand that their so-called 'practical knowledge' lacked even a hint of humanity or a scintilla of awareness that Aboriginal society was neither better nor worse, it was simply different.

In their own simplistic way they equated different with dangerous. Thus Murray, who by his own admission was bragging around town that 'the number shot was closer to seventy than seventeen', was a hero, not a cold-blooded killer.

In early 1929 the *Adelaide Register-News Pictorial* would echo the sentiments of Alice Springs when it wrote of Murray: 'He is the hero of Central Australia. He is the policeman of fiction. He rides alone and always gets his man.'

Murray submitted his report to Government Resident Cawood. It was brief. Seventeen Aboriginal people had been killed. All had been shot in self-defence. All had been involved in the murder of Fred Brooks. Two days later he was to turn back towards Coniston intent on wreaking even greater havoc on the Walbiri.

Only a few days later, just as Murray was returning to Alice Springs, another series of events were unfolding to the north of Coniston station.

William John Morton was the kind of violent, brutish man who is attracted to those areas beyond the reach of the law. A one-time circus wrestler, he was a short, squat man built and trained for violence. He was known in the Territory as Nugget. As the co-owner of Broadmeadow station which adjoined the Lander River, he had a reputation for violence towards his workmen, maltreatment of the local Aboriginal people, and rampant sexual exploitation of most of the Aboriginal women who were unlucky enough to cross his path.

On 27 August Morton, accompanied only by two horses and two dogs, left his main camp and travelled north along the dry bed of the Lander River. His mission was simple. He was bent on punishing those members of the Walbiri who were killing his emaciated, drought-starved cattle. Forty kilometres to the north he came

Aboriginal men from the region north of Alice Springs. It was men such as these whom Mounted Constable William George Murray and his posse hunted down in 1928.

upon a large Walbiri camp on the riverbank above the Boomerang waterhole. He challenged them, accused them of killing his cattle, and rode off to inspect the area for any signs of freshly killed carcasses.

The Walbiri had every reason to hate Nugget Morton. He was the kind of white man who treated Aboriginal people with undisguised loathing and, through his pastoral ignorance and negligence, he was systematically destroying the delicate ecological balance of the whole area.

That night the Walbiri decided that Morton should die. During the night they tracked him and by morning they had surrounded his camp. As Morton was eating breakfast three Aboriginal men approached him. They had been designated to lead the attack. Morton was not to be killed so easily. The three men attacked him and immediately found themselves being savaged by his dogs. The fight was on. As Morton, supported by the dogs, fought for his life, some fifteen Walbiri men armed with boomerangs and yam sticks charged the short, muscly ex-wrestler.

Somehow Morton managed to get to his rifle. He shot one Aboriginal person and the rest, realising the danger, retreated. Morton managed to drag himself back to his main camp, from where he was taken to the inland mission base at Titree Well. The nurse removed seventeen yam stick and boomerang splinters from his head and managed to bandage his skull which had been seriously fractured. It was a mark of his remarkable fitness and hardiness that he was still alive.

Morton's treatment by the Walbiri was only symptomatic of a larger problem. The area to the north of Alice Springs was becoming the last frontier. This was to be the last act of real defiance before the Aboriginal people living in the inhospitable desert finally succumbed, thus bringing to an end a process which had started exactly one hundred and forty years earlier.

The Aboriginal people, living on the edge of survival after four years of drought, were exhausted but determined. On 16 September Henry Edward Tilmouth, part-owner of Napperby station, shot an Aboriginal person. His later account of the event to the government inquiry is illuminating for its racism and its simple, frontier pragmatism.

> On 16 September, one nigger sneaked up near my bed at the well and my nigger ran up and told me the blacks were sneaking up. I walked out about 25 yards and fired one shot. The nigger did not move and I started to walk towards him. The dog also went after him. He ran a little way and I tried to load the rifle but the bullet jammed in the bridge. I took about ten minutes to get the bullet out. I could see the nigger coming up on the other side. I called on him to stop. As soon as I spoke he raised his boomerang to throw it. I had the rifle at my shoulder, I fired at him. The bullet entered his body over the heart. I had no further trouble with the blacks.

Around this time Randal Stafford once again called for police assistance and Tom Moar at Pine Hill station was complaining about problems. On 19 September Murray brought two Aboriginal prisoners in from Pine Hill station. Five days later, at the request of Government Resident Cawood, he went to Broadmeadow station. His brief was an ambiguous request to 'sort things out'.

Murray reached Broadmeadow station on 24 September. That afternoon, along with Morton, two half-castes — Alex Wilson and Jack Cusack — and fourteen horses, Murray moved north along the Lander. For the next three weeks Murray and Morton were to engage in a ruthless killing spree. They kept no records. They took no prisoners. They simply rampaged up and down the riverbed killing just about every Aboriginal person they saw. The brutality of the two white men knew no bounds. At Tomahawk Waterhole, at the northern limits where the Lander River disappears into the desert, they killed four Walbiri. At Circle Well one Aboriginal person was shot and Murray beat another one to death with an axe. They moved east across to the Hanson River where another eight Aboriginal people were killed.

A mounted police constable bringing Aboriginal prisoners into a local lockup.

They then rode back to Broadmeadow where they replenished their food supplies before heading south to Tippinba. In 1977 Martin Jampijinpa, who was only a small boy in 1928, recalled the events:

> When I was a little boy . . . I seen him. Murray grabbed me then and he's hold me on the shoulder. There was a big camp there. They [the tribespeople] was getting in all the bush tucker. But he shot about ten o'clock in the morning, eight o'clock in the morning. Shot at seven, eight, that way . . . They yardem round, bringem to one mob . . . and they shot it two or three shot guns going, people was going. Wilson was there, Nugget Morton, what's his name was there too, Jack Cusack and Murray . . . they all sit round here, all the old people was sleeping here. Round 'em up, just like cattle . . . and bringem to one mob this way just suddenly. And shot it there.

Later they moved on to Dingo Hole where they stumbled upon a corroboree. According to Walbiri folk memory, four men and eleven women and children were shot there.

Murray's official report did not mention the actual number of Aboriginal people killed. The two men were later to admit in court to killing fourteen people. The Walbiri were to claim that the real number was closer to one hundred.

The killings were over. No-one was to ever find out how many Aboriginal people had been killed. And it was not until 1982, when a land rights hearing took evidence from the Walbiri, that any Aboriginal accounts of the massacres were recorded.

The episode was to end in a typically unsatisfactory way. Murray's case against Padygar and Arkirkra fell apart in the Darwin court and was dismissed through lack of evidence. Murray, who had gone to Darwin convinced of the rightness of his actions against Aboriginal people and basking in the halo of heroism bestowed on him by the people of 'the Alice', was humiliated in the court by the judge, Mr Justice Mallam.

'Constable Murray,' asked the judge, 'was it really necessary to shoot to kill in every case? Could you not occasionally have shot to wound?'

'No, Your Honour,' replied Murray with a confidence bred of Outback support, 'What use is a wounded black feller a hundred miles from civilisation?'

The judge looked at the policeman coldly, 'How many did you kill?'

'Seventeen, Your Honour.'

'You mean,' replied the judge with measured and ill-disguised contempt, 'You mowed them down wholesale.'

A Methodist lay missionary, Athol McGregor, managed to generate enough national and international interest in the case to force a government inquiry. It was clear from the outset that the inquiry was designed to placate liberal sensibilities rather than attempt to come to grips with the truth. The appointment to the Board of J C Cawood, who many saw as the bureaucratic architect behind the massacres, left little doubt that an official cover-up was to be the primary outcome of the inquiry.

The cynics were not disappointed. The Board had been convened to investigate the deaths of seventeen Aboriginal people. By the completion of the sittings it was known that at least thirty-one had been killed and there was a strong feeling that not all the story had been told. The Board travelled thousands of kilometres and heard evidence from all the whites involved. However, no evidence was called from Alex Wilson, Skipper, Dodger or any Aborigine who may have been able to offer an alternative eyewitness account.

On 7 February 1929, six weeks after the hearings had begun, the *Finding of the Board of Enquiry concerning the killing of natives in Central Australia by Police Parties and others and concerning other matters* was submitted to the Federal Government. The conclusions were:

> a. In respect to the shooting of seventeen natives in pursuing the murders of Brooks the evidence of the following reputable settlers i.e. William Briscoe, Randal Beresford Stafford, and John Saxby corroborated the account given by Mounted Constable Murray which shortly is to the effect that, on each of four separate occasions, the pursued natives who had been identified by Tracker Major as being

implicated in the murder of Brooks, after being repeatedly warned to lay down their weapons, were the aggressors and attacked Mounted Constable Murray who, on each such occasion, was endeavouring to effect the arrest of the guilty natives and for that purpose was on foot and his horse had galloped back to where the packhorses were camped. Each of the witnesses was subjected to a rigorous cross examination and each of them emphatically stated that the shooting was absolutely necessary to save their own lives . . .

b. Respecting the shooting of fourteen natives implicated in the attack on W. Morton, the evidence of Mounted Constable Murray is corroborated in every detail by Mr. Morton. Morton can speak the 'lingo' of that particular tribe. This tribe was also implicated in the murder of Brooks. Morton swears he warned the natives repeatedly, on each occasion, to sit down and put their weapons down on the ground; that they refused; and that on each occasion when Constable Murray dismounted to endeavour to effect an arrest, the natives attacked with boomerangs, spears, nulla nullas and a tomahawk and it was necessary, in order to save their lives, that the blacks should be shot.

Morton knew each of the blacks who attacked him as they had at times worked for him and he identified them on each occasion and in some instances blacks were allowed to go free as they were not implicated in the attack on him . . .

c. Respecting the shooting of an Aboriginal by settler H. Tilmouth, the Board examined Tilmouth and an intelligent Aboriginal in his employ who corroborated Tilmouth's story, and has no hesitation in finding that the shooting was justified in this case . . .

The Board unanimously answers the first three questions as follows:

(a) The shooting was justified:

(b) The shooting was justified:

(c) The shooting was justified . . . In conclusion, the Board wishes to state that there is no evidence of any starvation of blacks in Central Australia. On the contrary, there is evidence of ample native food and water.

Chairman: A H O'Kelly

Members: J C Cawood, Government Resident

P A Giles, Police Inspector

It was an extraordinary judgement which once again showed that the rule of law was a tissue of hypocrisy and dishonesty as far as Aboriginal people were concerned.

Murray was quietly removed from the area shortly afterwards. He died in Adelaide in the 1960s. So did Randal Stafford who retired south after World War II. Morton sold up in the 1930s and moved out of the area.

And what of Bullfrog? He outlived them all. He died of old age at Yuenduma in the 1970s.

CHAPTER 17

MASSACRES, MASSACRES, MASSACRES

We are indeed a civilizing race . . . when we came here, the aborigines covered these wide plains in thousands. Where are they today? We have 'civilized' them — they are dead.

David MacDonald in Gum Boughs and Wattle Bloom

So many of the massacres have been forgotten. So many live on as memories and folklore. So many have simply been dissolved by time. That was the way it was on the frontier. A few blacks killed over there. A few blacks killed here. It was a good story for ten or maybe twenty years, then the whites conveniently forgot about it.

It lived on in the Aboriginal memory — if the tribal group survived. At night, beside the camp fire or under the stars, the story would be told and retold. The massacre, or massacres, became tribal history. They were told in the peculiarly clipped, and poetically repetitive, style which characterises so much Aboriginal storytelling. The central truth of the tragedy is revealed and the details are spun around it like a beautifully symmetrical spider's web. It is only when someone — an Aboriginal person, a researcher, a government officer — records them in print or on tape that they are revealed to people outside the tribal group. They are like fossils. They lie dormant, waiting to be exposed.

The massacre at Hodgson Downs

In 1973 an old man named Isaac Joshua, reputedly the last fluent speaker of the Warndarang language, sat down with a researcher at the Ngukurr settlement in Arnhem Land and told a story which white history had conveniently forgotten.

Isaac Joshua was born in 1904. The events he described had occurred before he was born but they were part of his tribal history and had been told to him by his father. They were events which would have simply been dissolved by time had they not been recorded and published.

An Aboriginal man whom the whites called Long Peter was sent, sometime in the 1880s or 1890s, into Queensland to collect a number of horses and overland them to Hodgson Downs in the Northern Territory. On the way back to the station

One of the most famous photographs of Aboriginal prisoners, this was taken in the late nineteenth century in Western Australia.

Long Peter met a number of his friends and they decided to kill and eat some of the horses. After the feast a corroboree was held. Before long all of the horses in Long Peter's care had been consumed. Realising what he had done (and the likely repercussions), Long Peter went back to Hodgson Downs.

Suspicious that something was wrong, the Queenslanders came looking for the horse thief. 'Where is he? Where is Long Peter?' the posse asked any Aboriginal people they met.

One group told them that Long Peter had gone to Hodgson Downs and was staying there. The posse rode to Hodgson Downs where they found Long Peter with a group of Aboriginal people in a camp beside the Roper River. 'Did you kill our horses?' the head stockman demanded.

'No!' Long Peter replied. 'They just died.'

The head stockman looked at Long Peter sceptically. He was unpersuaded by this answer. He turned to the other Aboriginal people in the camp and started to question them. 'What did this man do to the horses?' he asked.

One of the old women, fearful of the posse, blurted out, 'He and the others ate them until they finished them off.'

The head stockman and the posse grabbed Long Peter and tied him to a huge ghost gum which stood on the banks of the river. The men from the posse then rounded up the Aboriginal people from the camp and sent them off to cut and collect firewood.

The Aboriginal people did not question their orders until one old man, an elder of the tribe and a man who knew something about the nature of magic, asked: 'Why are we cutting this? Maybe they are going to shoot us and burn us.' And then, as if by some dreadful premonition, he cried out, 'Something terrible is stabbing at me, something awful is cutting into me.'

The posse rode down to where the Aboriginal people were cutting the wood. The horses encircled the group. Some of the old men picked up sticks to protect themselves. The old man who had mysteriously anticipated the event kept crying out, 'Something terrible is cutting into me! Baga arungal jaljngara janjani narilamangani rabalwayi! Something terrible is cutting into me! Look at them! Just as I told you! Here come the white men!' Another old man took his stick and stuck it into the eye of one of the horses. The horse reared back in fright and bolted.

Seeing the gap in the circle, the old men tried to escape. It was the excuse the posse had been waiting for. They wheeled their horses around, dug their stirrups in, pulled their rifles out of the saddle holsters, and gave chase. The old men ran in every direction in a desperate attempt to escape. The men in the posse opened fire. A number of the old men fell. Some tried to escape up a stone hill but they were caught and killed. No-one ever bothered to count the dead.

In the end the whites piled up all the firewood that the old men had been collecting and set it alight. When the pyre was ablaze, they threw the bodies of the Aboriginal people on it. They also shot Long Peter and threw him on as well. By evening the fire was nothing more than a few glowing coals and charred bones.

The story of the massacre disappeared from white history but in the Warndarang folk memory it lives on.

The massacres around Lake Eyre and the Simpson Desert region

No official enquiries were ever held into these massacres, which appeared to have been the common morality of the day.
G. Farwell, *Land of Mirage*

By the 1880s the frontier of New South Wales and Queensland was reaching into the harshness of the central desert. The outposts of civilisation were little one-horse, one-house towns, like Maree on the edge of that flat wasteland known as Lake Eyre and Clifton Hills on the banks of the huge and intermittent Diamantina River. This was not marginal country: it was desert. To the west lay the no-man's-land which was the Simpson Desert. To the east lay country in which the temperatures soared into the fiery forties every summer.

Why the massacres continued in this hellish wasteland is a mystery — but they did. In fact, the three major massacres which occurred in the 1880s in the area — the massacre of the Mindiri people at Koonchera Point, the massacre of the

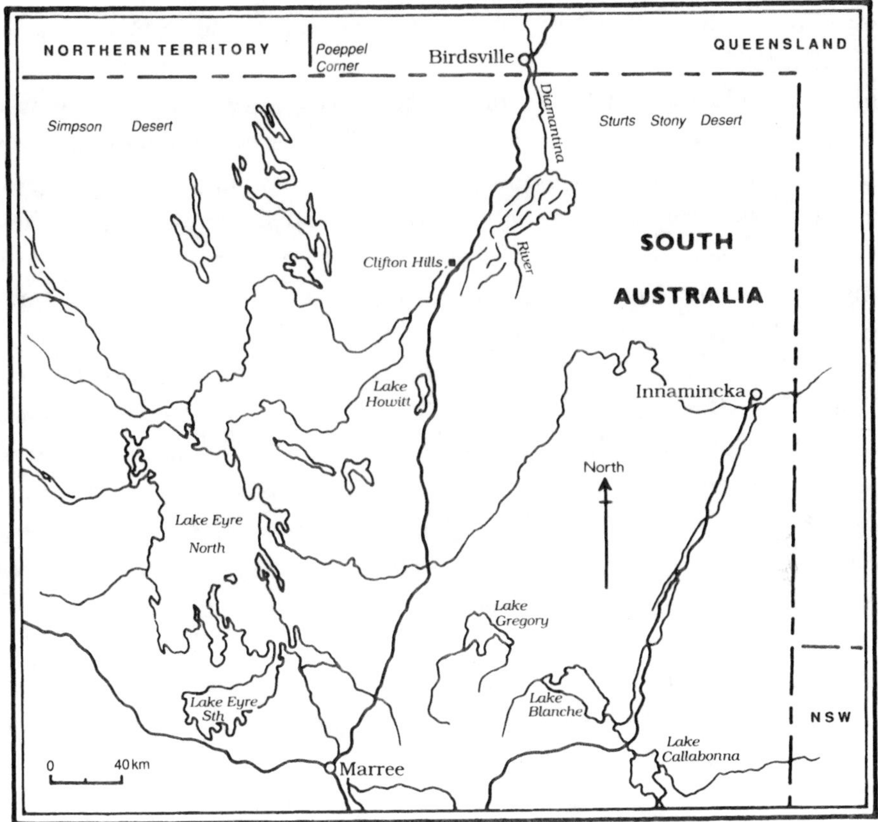

The Lake Eyre and Simpson Desert region in central Australia.

Wardamba people in the eastern Simpson Desert and the massacre of the Yaluyandi, the Garanguru and the Yawarawarga at Wiyirbi near Clifton Hills — are massacres which make all the other known killing expeditions look minor by comparison.

It is probable that as many as five hundred people were killed during the Simpson Desert and Clifton Hills massacres. The reason these massacres were so spectacularly larger than all others was that they coincided with major Aboriginal annual festivals which drew distant tribes to the area. The result was that many of the tribes in the area were driven to the edge of extinction.

The massacre of the Mindiri at Koonchera Point

The people had been walking for days. This was no ordinary gathering but an annual corroboree. The Ngamani came, and the Yawarawarga, the Yandruwanta and the Bugadji. They had walked these same paths to dance these same dances for thousands of years. This was a sacred time. It was a time when all those people who lived in the lands where the ancestral emu had once wandered came together to sing and dance and celebrate.

The Mindiri Hole, the main site for the corroboree, was prepared. It was at Mirra Mitta, or Lake Howitt as the white people called it, that the celebrations started. It was here that the preliminary ceremony, the Idigaru ceremony, was held. They drew the marks of the emu's feet on the ground and painted the markings of the emu chicks on their bodies. First the men danced, then the women. The celebration went on long into the night. The next day they moved on to the Mindiri Hole but they never danced there.

It seems that someone, possibly one of the hundreds of Aboriginal people coming to the corroboree, had shot a bullock at Koonchera and this had been enough to bring the police and their Aboriginal trackers out in force. No-one ever knew where the police came from. They could have come from the stations at Andrewilla or Birdsville or Karathunka Waterhole, just south of Birdsville. They could also have come from any one of a dozen stations in northern South Australia or far western Queensland. Wherever they came from, they did not file a report of the massacre upon their return.

Over five hundred people had gathered around the old tree on the flats between the waterhole and the sand dunes of the desert when the police and their trackers rode in. There was no discussion or warning. The police officer called out, 'Let'm all get killed! Let them get killed! Let'm get shot!' and the trackers and troopers carried out the instructions with deadly enthusiasm.

They fired again and again. They killed all the women and the old men. They killed the young men who were about to participate in their first corroboree. In the

This posed photograph, titled 'Taken by Surprise', was taken near Kalgoorlie and depicts a goldminer being attacked by local Aboriginal people.

end the lifeless, sandy soil was littered with bodies and stained with blood. There were two hundred, maybe three, four or even five hundred people killed.

Mindiri legend has it that only five people escaped. Four of the young men — Waya-Waya, Guranda, Niba and 'Charlie' — managed to slide into the reeds at the side of the Koonchera waterhole and escape. They made their way cross-country to the Diamantina River and never returned to Koonchera.

The fifth survivor, old Charlie Ganabidi, became part of the folklore of the area. It was said that he went back to where the bodies were lying and smeared the blood of his maternal grandmother on his forehead. Then, hearing the white policemen approaching, he lay down and pretended to be dead.

Some of the whites walked by and noticed Charlie. 'Poor old Charlie,' they said to each other, 'he got shot, too! Old Charlie. He was a good tracker. What a pity. Well we can't do anything for him now.'

Afterwards the whites sat down under the tree to rest and Charlie managed to sneak away across the waterhole. Before they left, the whites burnt all the bodies. It was only because of old Charlie Ganabidi that the story of the massacre lived on.

The massacre of the Wardamba people near Poeppel Corner in the eastern Simpson Desert

The details are blurred by time. It appears that a white man, probably a station hand at Nappamanna station, rode into one of the Wardamba camps and kidnapped a Wardamba woman. He took her back to his hut where he raped her repeatedly before letting her return to her family group. The Wardamba did not passively accept the attack upon the woman. They hunted the rapist and killed him.

News of the murder of the white man took some days to filter back to the police forces stationed on the edge of the desert. During this time the tribes in the area — the Midaga, the Wanganguru, the Nyulubulu, the Wangamadla and the Yaluyandi — had joined the Wardamba people for a corroboree. They had gathered near Poeppel Corner to the west of the Diamantina River in the vast wasteland which is the eastern Simpson Desert.

The festivities were well underway when the police and their trackers arrived. Once again the opportunity for a large-scale slaughter was there. Driven by irrational hatred and revenge, the police shot randomly at the gathering. Large numbers of innocent people were shot. No-one knows how many. The police did not worry about a body count.

As so often happened, the Ngulubulu man who had killed the rapist escaped.

The massacres near Clifton Hills

Clifton Hills was one of those Outback places which, in the 1890s, was nothing more than a couple of huts on the Birdsville Track somewhere between Sturt's Stony Desert and the Simpson Desert. It was, and still is, inhospitable land prone to extremes of temperature and waiting silently to consume the unwary traveller.

It was here in the 1880s that the native police and some trackers fought a bloody battle with the Yaluyandi, the Garanguru and the Yawarawarga which resulted in hundreds of Aboriginal deaths. No-one knows what happened. All that is certain is that the trackers had a grudge against the local people.

Some years later, as old Ngadudagali (which means 'he spears you in the ribs') told it, another smaller massacre occurred. He couldn't remember exactly where or when it happened but it was in the Clifton Hills area and it was sometime in the early 1890s.

A group of Aboriginal people had killed a bullock. They knew that if the whites discovered what they had done they'd be in big trouble. They knew that the whites thought nothing of shooting ten or twenty Aboriginal people if they found that a bullock had been speared. So they were careful. They decided to cook the animal where it had been killed and take the cooked meat to a distant place to eat it.

They thought the plan through very carefully. They dug a huge cooking pit in an area where the cattle often came. The idea was that after the bullock had been cooked, the fire pit could be covered with sand and the trampling of the cattle would totally hide the 'crime' from the white settlers.

The Aboriginal people duly dug the pit, filled it with wood and got a good fire going. Then they chose a bullock and drove it towards the fire. A number of men followed behind with boughs, dragging them over the ground to cover the tracks. When the bullock reached the cooking pit, it was killed with a war spear, pushed into the pit, and covered with hot coals so that it cooked right through.

They left the bullock to cook for most of that day and all of the following night. In the morning the men returned and removed all the cooked meat. They then got some sand and fresh soil and covered the pit totally. Then they built a rough windbreak and a small camp fire to give the impression that a group of Aboriginal people had camped in the area.

After a few hours the other cattle came along the track and trampled over the cooking pit. Later the white stockmen came looking for the missing bull.

'They've been camping here,' said one stockman. 'This is definitely a blackfellow's camp. They must have killed a bullock — but where is the evidence?' The Aboriginal people had been very thorough. The stockman could find no blood, no tracks, no hide and no bones.

By now most of the Aboriginal people, laden down with meat, were a long way away. They had put as much distance as possible between themselves and the stockmen. Unfortunately some of the Aboriginal people decided not to leave the area. Some went only as far as they thought they had to, and Ngadudagali and his young wife, full of the misguided bravery of youth, remained quite close to the site where the bullock had been killed.

When the stockmen came riding up, Ngadudagali hid in the reeds beside the swamp but his young wife, curious about the strangers and oblivious to the possible dangers, sat on the top of a sandhill and watched them approach.

'I'll bet she's got some of that bullock meat in her bag,' called out one of the stockmen and he rode up to where the young woman was sitting. He grabbed the woman's bag, opened it, and called back to his colleagues, 'This is the one, mate. She's got a big chunk of bullock meat here. She's one of the mob that killed the bull. Shoot her.'

One of the stockmen raised his rifle and fired.

Ngadudagali heard the shot and guessed what had happened. He was well hidden in the reeds beside the waterhole. Commonsense overruled his concern for his wife and he remained hidden. Eventually the stockmen rode off. Ngadudagali came out of hiding and crept up to the top of the sandhill where he found his wife lying dead. Without ceremony, he dug a grave in the sand and buried her.

Grief-stricken, he followed the posse. On the way he kept saying to himself, over and over again, 'Alas, they killed her just like that! They killed her just like that!' They'd kill anyone!' He tracked the posse fearful of what they might do.

Out on the plains the posse caught up with the second group. They drove their stirrups into the flanks of their horses and the silent, empty plains came alive with heavy, galloping thuds as the horses and their riders charged towards the defenceless group. The stockmen wheeled their horses around and encircled the group of twenty or thirty Aboriginal people.

'There's bullock meat here!' called out one of the men and the other men lowered their rifles and fired. They shot them all. Babies and old women were shot. Old men and young mothers were executed without a second thought.

Ngadudagali saw what was happening and hid in a nearby creek bed. He crouched under the debris left by the last flood — branches and grass and soil which had built up behind a tree near the riverbank. He heard the cries and again knew the feeling of utter helplessness.

The group who had walked far out into the desert just kept walking. They never returned to the area. And Ngadudagali, now a solitary figure in that vast shimmering wasteland, followed them for he had nowhere else to go.

The reprisals in King Sound in the 1890s

Relations between the pearl fishers and the Aboriginal population were never very good. The pearl fishers, working out of the thriving port of Broome, moved up and down the coast in search of shells and the wealth they contained. They were a strange lot drawn across the oceans by the possibility of fortune. They came from Ireland and Finland, from Japan, from the great port cities of Asia, from Malaya, Sarawak, Borneo, Timor, the Dutch East Indies and from Macassar. They were tough, greedy itinerants prepared to live rough, to stop only briefly for their pleasures, and to demand virtual slave labour from the Aboriginal people, whom they exploited ruthlessly.

The first pearlers arrived in the area in the early 1860s. By the 1890s their reputation for prostituting Aboriginal women, spreading venereal disease, forcing Aboriginal men to become divers, and killing Aboriginal men with 'the bends' was well established. The Seaman Aboriginal Land Inquiry 1983–84 vividly describes the condition which prevailed around Broome at the end of the nineteenth century:

> Aborigines were confined between seasons on islands such as the Lacepedes from which they could not return to the mainland and where, if they survived, they could be picked up again by the pearlers for the next season.
>
> Despite the attempts by the legislature to outlaw the cruel abuses of the pearlers the industry was to have a dramatic effect on Aboriginal society until well into the twentieth century. Constable Zum Felde reported to the Aborigines Department in 1901 that for a distance of 100 to 150 miles from La Grange Mission Aboriginal women from between 10 to 40 were traded as prostitutes to men on pearl shelling boats with the result that nearly all the women suffered from venereal disease. The Constable grimly recorded that there was one camp where he saw nine Aboriginal women: 'Everyone of them with sores all over their body dying a miserable and slow death.'

Such was the environment on the coast and around King Sound in the 1890s.

There were two brothers, known to the local Aboriginal people as the Bilikin brothers, who drifted up the coast from Broome searching and diving for pearls. Eventually, hundreds of kilometres north of the noise and bustle of Broome harbour, they rounded Cape Leveque and sailed into the waters of King Sound. At the mouth of the sound a small archipelago of islands — Tyra Island, Allora Island, Sunday Island and a dozen lesser outcrops — were inhabited by small groups of Bardi-speaking Aboriginal people. The Bilikin brothers, with a Chinese diver, hauled their small boat ashore at Bargoran and decided to rest up for a couple of days while they scraped the molluscs and peeling paint off the hull and painted the cutter red and white.

No-one knows why the Bardi turned against the Bilikins but a meeting of the locals decided that the pearl fishers should be executed.

The Bardi had noticed that the Bilikins were sleeping on the beach at night. One day, when the Bilikins rowed out to dive for pearls, the Bardi came to the beach and hid a number of spears in the sand. The Bilikins returned to the beach, dragged their rowboat up above the tidal line and had started to paint their cutter when a group of Bardi wandered along the beach. Noting that the group were unarmed, the brothers took little interest in them and continued their work. Suddenly the Bardi reached down into the sand, grabbed their spears, and hurled them at the Bilikins. One of the brothers died instantly. The other brother was wounded. He reached for his rifle and managed to fire one shot before he was speared to death.

Although the Bardi hurled a number of spears at him, the Chinese diver managed to escape. He rowed around the coast, found another pearling lugger, and raised the alarm. The lugger abandoned its diving and set sail for Derby to alert the police. Realising what they had done, the Aboriginal people made preparations for the arrival of the police.

Within days a number of police arrived in the area. They rode across the rugged terrain on donkeys. The Aboriginal people, who had never seen such strange animals before, called them dogs. The bells which hung around their necks jangled eerily in the humid, tropical silence. The approaching policemen could be heard all over the island. Anticipating violence, the Aboriginal people fled from the island. They jumped into the water and swam across to the Giban Reef. The policemen saw them escaping and fired at them. They fired hundreds of rounds but the Aboriginal people were out of range. They managed to escape and they stayed on Giban Reef until the policemen left.

Determined to avenge the deaths of the Bilikin brothers, the policemen then sailed across to Tyra Island. By now they had been joined by a number of whites including sailors and pearl fishers. They anchored off the tiny island and rowed ashore. Sensing an attack, the Bardi fled to the far side of the island and hid in a large cave which they called Larmada.til the policemen left.

The white posse scoured the island. They searched the rolling undulations of the sandhills, clambered up the scrubby slopes and eventually reached Monna Hill, the island's highest point. They were about to abandon their search when they noticed three Aboriginal youth — a child and two teenagers — walking along a beach. They immediately opened fire. The two teenagers fled along the beach only to find that they were caught between two groups of whites. Caught in the crossfire, the boys dived into the sea. One of them was shot and killed. The other managed to avoid

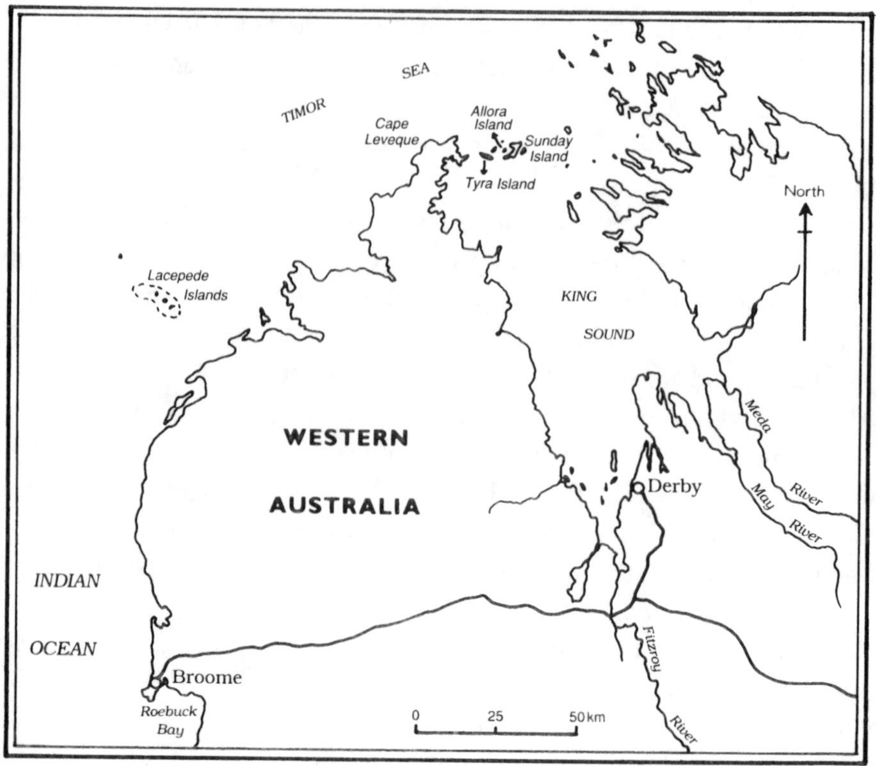

The King Sound region in northern Western Australia.

being shot but was chased for some hours by the men. He eventually managed to run along the reef, double back to the shore, and escape into the hinterland.

The white posse then moved on to Allora Island. They anchored offshore and within hours saw three Aboriginal men — two young men and an old man — signalling from shore. The men were unaware of the deaths of the Bilikin brothers and had no fear of the whites on the lugger.

A Chinese diver rowed to shore to pick up the three men. The whites, eager for some revenge and 'target practice', ensured that the Aboriginal people were seated at the front of the rowboat. As the boat approached the pearl lugger the whites took aim. Seeing what was about to happen, the old man hurled himself to one side of the boat. The boat capsized. The whites fired. The two young men were killed instantly. The old man held on to the capsized boat until it had floated back towards the shore. He duckdived and swam to shore. Each time he surfaced the men on the lugger shot at him. It was only when he had reached the shore that a stray, ricocheting bullet clipped his shoulder. The old man, whose name was Gawiri, looked back at the lugger and called out loudly in Bardi, 'I am still alive and have escaped'.

This story was told to a researcher by a Bardi elder, Tudor Ejai, in February 1970.

Some Aboriginal men of the north-west of Western Australia. It was people from this area who were massacred at Forrest River and King Sound.

The massacre at Mowla Bluff — 1916

Will anyone ever get an appreciation of the true scale of the massacres and maltreatment of Australian Aborigines? When I wrote the first edition of this book I scoured the libraries for books and journals recording any and every massacre. Some, like the Myall Creek massacre and the Coniston station massacre, were well reported. They had found their way into the courtrooms of white Australia and consequently the records were detailed and accurate. But, over and over again, the stories keep coming. There are literally dozens of massacres recorded in Geoffrey Blomfield's *Baal Belbora* and, as I continue to read local histories from around the country, I keep finding reports of killings ranging from minor skirmishes involving one or two people through to massacres of unknown numbers. Consequently this book just grows and grows.

One such recording of a massacre occurred when my colleague at the *Sydney Morning Herald*, Tony Stephens (a fine writer who has always taken a deep and compassionate interest in Aboriginal affairs) rang me and asked: 'Have you ever heard of a massacre at Mowla Bluff in the Kimberley?' I admitted that I hadn't and promised that, after scouring through my now substantial library on Aboriginal massacres, I would get back to him. I hunted and hunted and came up with nothing.

The reason? The killings had occurred at Mowla Bluff on the edge of the Great Sandy Desert in Western Australia in 1916. It was a time and a place where people could get away with crimes, particularly crimes against Aborigines, and no one really cared too much. Add to that a so-called police investigation which found that no crimes had been committed and all you had left was the tribal memory of the group whose brothers and fathers had been killed. The tribal group, obviously traumatised by the killings, had complex emotions. They wanted to remember the dead and they wanted the world to know that there had been crimes committed which had never been acknowledged and no one had ever been punished for.

So, in late 2000, two tribal elders — Peter Clancy and John Watson — led the people of the Nyikina, Mangala and Karajarri groups of the Kimberley to Mowla Bluff to try and find the places where their ancestors had been murdered. They travelled to a place which the locals call Jarinyadum — a deep and rocky amphitheatre with sheer red rock walls nearly 100 metres high. It is a stark and isolated place with that kind of hot, rugged beauty which characterises so much of the Kimberley. Red rocks. Impossibly blue skies. And these colours cut by the birds and the trees which survive in this harsh environment. It was here probably in September 1916, according to tribal memory, that Burrungu (a relative of John Watson) and Banaga (a relative of Peter Clancy) were pushed to their death.

But this wasn't just the death of two men. Nearby at Longanjully the tribe memory believes that three men were shot and their bodies thrown into crevices in the rocks where they were left to rot. And at Mowla Bluff a total of six men, probably part of a group of nine, were chained together and shot.

How did it happen? What prompted the white settlers in the area to seek such revenge? The likely explanation, which seems to have been common in the Kimberley, is that a white boundary rider, a man named George Wye, had been forcing himself onto some of the local women. The men of the group, irritated by Wye's unwelcome advances, decided to take the law into their own hands. They found Wye and gave him a good beating.

The local authorities decided that, regardless of what Wye had done, the local Aborigines needed to be taught a lesson. The police records actually list the Aborigines wanted for beating Wye. A posse comprising some local station managers, some of the police working in the area and some black trackers raided one of the local campsites some time in September 1916 and removed nine Aborigines. We do not know all their names but we do know that among them, and involved in the massacre to a greater or lesser extent, were Cadgery (also known as Mick), Nanya (also known as Dick), Nullagumban (also known as Moon), Winga, Myolil and Chandil.

We know this because the first reports of the killings came when Cadgery and Nanya went to a local doctor, Dr. A.R. Haynes, with bullet wounds. Haynes extracted a bullet which had penetrated below Nanya's shoulder blade. Cadgery's wound was more serious. He had been shot in the mouth. Haynes, unwilling to apportion blame, would later tell the police that the bullet 'could have entered when the patient was kneeling with the head thrown back'.

Whenever a 'crime' was committed the West Australian police would round up a number of Aborigines, chain them together and take them to the nearest police station or lockup. This was commonplace in the Kimberley. Here over twenty men have been taken prisoner for an unknown crime.

It is clear that the survivors knew exactly what happened. A subsequent police enquiry in 1918 records that Nanya named the six men who were chained together and recounted how they had been chained together and shot. He was also able to recall that their bodies had been burnt on a rock near Geegully Creek and that the killers had 'raked up all the ashes, bones and pieces of unburned wood together.'

That same police enquiry also records that both Nullagumban and Nanya knew the three men who had been shot at Longanjully. Nullagumban reported that 'The bodies of Winga, Myolil and Chandil were just thrown into a deep crevice.'

It says something about the lack of acceptance of Aboriginal evidence and the inability of the police in the Kimberley in the 1910s to prosecute their duties, that the massacre, in spite of an inquiry, was dismissed.

In 1918, Inspector O. Drewry reporting upon the disappearance of the nine men declared that 'there is nothing to support the allegations of Dick and Moon' and in May 1919 an Inspector T. Houlahan wrote to the West Australian Police Commissioner declaring: 'If the natives named have not been murdered as alleged there should be no difficulty in finding them.' They were never found.

Today Mowla Bluff is part of Mowla Bluff Station which is now owned by the local Aboriginal community. They know the truth and are determined to preserve this shadowy event so it does not disappear as the older members of their community die. They have built a stone memorial with a polished plaque which, in part, reads 'The Mowla Bluff incident was closed and forgotten by the authorities but never forgotten by us, and is supported by the evidence presented in the 1918 inquiry. This plaque is in memory of all our family members who had their lives taken away in the massacre.'

The massacre on Bentinck Island — 1918

Some were shot high up on the sandhills, shot with their babies.
Roma Kelly, recalling the massacre

Roma Kelly was born at Mambunki on Bentinck Island in 1917. Her parents named her Dibirdibi Mambunkingathi.

The small Aboriginal community on the island probably numbered slightly over one hundred. Because of their isolation in the southernmost corner of the Gulf of Carpentaria, Roma Kelly's people, the Kaiadilt, had been little affected by the white conquest and settlement of Australia. Few whites showed much interest in the Wellesley Island group of which Bentinck was a part. And even when whites, by some strange accident, did briefly stop, the Kaiadilt were happy to hide themselves.

Bentinck Island is about 20 kilometres long and, at its narrowest point, is only about four kilometres across. It lies at the same latitude as Cairns and consequently its climatic year is divided into a time when the rains fall with heavy tropical regularity and a nominal 'dry' season.

When he circumnavigated Australia, Matthew Flinders did not land on Bentinck Island. He did, however, land on nearby Allen Island in 1802. Here he met six Kaiadilt people. It is likely that news of the visit by the strange white man spread to Bentinck Island.

By 1910 there had probably been no more than five visits by whites to the island. In 1841 Captain Stokes explored the island without making contact with its indigenous population. In 1880 Captain Pennefather, another explorer, landed on the island. The Kaiadilt avoided him. In 1901 Roth and Howard, the Northern Protectors of Aborigines, visited the island but their contact was brief.

Some two kilometres to the east of Bentinck lies Sweers Island. It's a narrow strip of land about a kilometre wide and five kilometres long. The island was occupied by whites in the 1860s. Conflicts occurred briefly between whites and blacks. By the 1880s the white settlement had been abandoned and the Kaiadilt had returned to their traditional lifestyle.

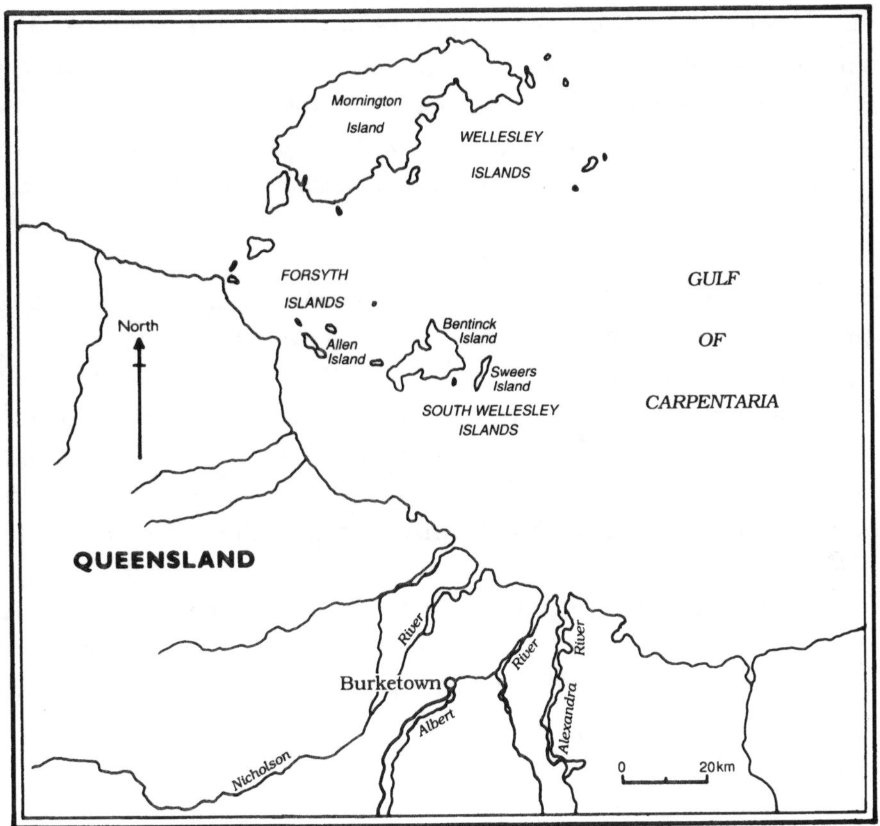

Bentinck Island off the coast of far northern Queensland.

In 1911 a man named McKenzie obtained a government lease which, according to Queensland law, gave him titlehold over all of Sweers Island and a large portion of Bentinck Island. Little is known of McKenzie. He seems to have been one of those elusive and brutal Scotsmen who pass briefly across the frontier of Australian history trailing rape, murder and mayhem in their wake. He was, according to those who met him, a large, heavy-boned Scot with a ruddy complexion, a dour manner and a ruggedness bred of frontier hardship. He arrived on Bentinck accompanied by an Aboriginal woman and some sheep. Near the Kurumbali estuary he built a hut. McKenzie knew that he was far beyond the reaches of the law. He also knew that the law would show little interest in his activities and would not disapprove of his actions.

McKenzie decided that the Kaiadilt living on Bentinck should be wiped out. The process was not systematic. When the whim took him he would saddle his horse, ride out, and shoot any Aboriginal people he could find. His sexual proclivities were such that whenever possible he would rape any young females whom he managed to capture.

In the early 1980s, while researching the language of the Kaiadilt people, Nicholas Evans met Roma Kelly and she told him the story of McKenzie's massacre. A little brutal moment of Australian history was recorded over sixty years after it occurred. She told of how McKenzie, accompanied by dogs and a party of unknown gun-happy murderers, had ridden to Rukuthi at the northernmost tip of the island and forced the fleeing Kaiadilt into the sea.

In the sand dunes and along the beach where the waves tumbled lazily on to the hot sands McKenzie and his men had found a group of Kaiadilt. Seeing the men galloping over the sand hunched behind the reins with their guns at the ready, Aboriginal people fled in every direction. Some fled into the sandhills and were caught by the men and shot. There were women with babies, pregnant women, grandmothers and grandfathers. They were gunned down and left to die in the hot, shadowless wasteland of the dunes. Some fled into the mangrove swamps where the horses could not follow them. They crawled in among the tangled roots and hid until the men had departed.

But the bulk of the Aboriginal people fled into the sea. They knew that beyond the line of breakers they could not be followed. McKenzie, seeing what they were doing, chased them. Spray splashed around the hooves as the horses galloped into the shallow water. The men raised their rifles and fired as they rode.

There were women running across the sandy beach dragging little toddlers behind them. There were old people and young people; people who could not run. Those who were not shot, drowned. Few escaped. 'Women drowned,' Roma Kelly recalled, 'with children in their bellies, or leading them by the hand . . . They swam along and dived under the sea. Far out to sea they drowned and died. They sank dead with their children there way out at sea.'

McKenzie and his men managed to capture some of the young women. They raped some of them on the sandhills amongst the dead bodies of their families. Others they took back to McKenzie's camp where they held them for three days, raping them repeatedly. Eventually they let the women go.

The authorities never heard of the massacre. McKenzie returned to his hut and continued to live on the island. Sometime later he moved to Sweers Island. On that tiny island, helped by two Aboriginal people from Mornington Island, he continued to run sheep and goats. He also established a kiln and produced lime which he sold to other settlers in the area.

After that he quietly vanished from the area. No-one knows his first name or where he was born or where he died. In the Gulf of Carpentaria his name is remembered only by the people of the Kaiadilt.

Outrages against Aboriginal Australians

The scale of the massacres never ceases to amaze. It seems as though images of the frontier seem to be consumed with blood and death. In 1879 George Robertson (of Angus & Robertson) published the *Australian Dictionary of Dates and Men of the Time*. Under the listing 'Aborigines — Outrages Against', appears the following entry:

> OUTRAGES AGAINST. — Violation and ill-treatment of five native women by a party sent to cut rushes in one of the bays adjacent to the settlement, 1788. Twenty-eight men, women and children barbarously murdered at Mr. Henry Dangar's station, Myall Creek, June, 1838.
> Konikoondeet (Jajowrong) and another man, name unknown, reported by the aboriginals to have been shot by two white men when exploring the country, March or April (so in official records) 1838.
> About fourteen men, names unknown, shot by a party of men from Bowman's, Ebden's and Yaldwyn's stations, in recovering a flock of Bowman's sheep, July, 1838.
> Noorowurnin and another Jajowrong, shot by Bowman's assigned servants at the Maiden Hills, February, 1839.
> Six men, names unknown, shot by the Mounted Police on the Campaspe, June 22, 1840.
> Pandarraagooendeet, a Jajowrong native, shot by one of Dutton's assigned servants, who afterwards absconded, August, 1814.
> Panumarramin, a Grampian native, shot by the late J. F. Francis in his sheepfold, September 1840.
> Bonnokgoondeet, Jojowl, Kombonngarramin, and Pertunarramin, shot by J. F. Francis in the Pyrenees, December 21, 1840.
> Gondu-urmin, a Kalkalgoondet native, shot by Dutton's assigned men near the Lodden, February 7, 1841.
> Mokfte (Jajowrong) shot near Mount Cole; it is said by a splitter, March 1841.
> Keonycrook, a Taoungurong, shot, it is supposed by Bennett's shepherd, who was found in a tree badly wounded, and died in Melbourne hospital, May, 1841.
> Two men reported by the aboriginals to have been shot near Hall's, at the foot of the Grampians, by Hall's hutkeeper, July, 1841.
> Kowarrimin, two other men, and a girl, reported by the aboriginals to have been shot by three white men near Kirk's, Purrumbeep, July or August (so in official record) 1841.

> Bood Bood Yarramin, reported by the aboriginals to have been shot by Captain Bunbury's storekeeper near Mount William, August, 1841.
> The bodies of three aboriginal women, and one male child, found dead, and an aboriginal wounded by a gun shot in a tea-tree scrub near the station of Messrs. Osbrey and Smith, Portland district (now Western Victoria), February 25, 1842.
> A tribe of about sixty slaughtered in return for Frazer massacre, Dawson River, 1857.
> About 170 blacks slaughtered in Medway Ranges, Queensland, by police and other, in return for Wills' massacre, Oct. and Nov., 1861.

To this list have to be added the nineteen massacres listed in the chapter titled 'Eliminating the Native Inhabitants' in Michael Cannon's excellent book *Life in the Country: Australia in the Victorian Age*. Apart from mentioning those massacres already covered in detail — the massacre of the Yeeman, the massacre at Cullin-la-Ringo, the mass poisoning at Kilcoy station, the 'Battle of Pinjarra', the Myall Creek massacre, and the Warrigal Creek massacre — Cannon ranges widely across Australia mentioning large-scale massacres which have never been treated in detail by historians.

He writes of the fifty Aboriginal people killed in reprisals after Aboriginal people attacked and killed seventeen white men near Benalla in Victoria. Then there was the massacre at Port Fairy in Victoria where, after four shepherds were killed and nearly four thousand sheep speared (at least that's what the settlers claimed in order to justify their killing), a posse rode out from Smith and Osbrey's station near Mount Rouse, found a group of Aboriginal people, and killed a number of women and children. Hearing of the outrage, Governor La Trobe demanded that the murderers be brought to trial and threatened to close down all the stations in the area. But his threats were to no avail — no-one was ever charged with the murders.

In 1840 in central Victoria, after the cook at Glengower station had attempted to poison the local Aboriginal people, there was a massacre in which Captain Dugald McLachlan and his station hands rode to the nearest Aboriginal camp and shot every Aboriginal person they could find.

At Konongwootong station near the modern-day town of Hamilton in Victoria about fifty Aboriginal people were killed in 1840. After a number of sheep had been killed the owners of the property, the Whyte brothers — George, Pringle, James and John — rode to a nearby camp and slaughtered all the men, women and children. An observer at the scene recalled that afterwards 'the bones of the men and sheep lay mingled together bleaching in the sun'.

Popular writer, Rolf Boldrewood, reported a story about a squatter named John Cox who ran Mount Napier station. Cox, finding that some of his sheep had been killed by Aboriginal people, gave chase and although he had never before killed anyone, he said that he did so without hesitation and that in a matter of minutes he had killed three blacks — 'two men and a boy, with one discharge of my double barrel'.

It has been claimed that Frederick Taylor wiped out an entire tribe while he was manager of Glenormiston station near Terang in Victoria. Taylor did not know how many he killed but a subsequent owner of the property found one mass grave in which twenty bodies had been buried.

In 1844 at Glen Innes in New South Wales, Edward Irby and his men chased a large group of Aboriginal people to a rocky outcrop called Bluff Rock where 'they threw the blacks off the rock onto the ground at the bottom . . . A lot of the blacks got killed and a lot more got crippled'.

At Ballina on the northern coast of New South Wales in 1846 over one hundred Aboriginal people were killed. After some station hand had been killed in the area a posse was formed and they rounded up all the local Aboriginal people, shot them, and threw them into the sea.

In Western Australia in 1864 an expedition leader named Maitland Brown took particular delight in teaching the local Aboriginal people a 'severe lesson'. In the space of ten minutes he shot and killed an estimated eighteen Aboriginal people.

'Do we shoot them? Of course we do . . . There is only one way to keep the beggars down: When they commit a murder, pay them out for it in their own coin' was the response offered by one of the officers who killed seven men, four women and five children in the Clarence River district of New South Wales in 1845. Their only crime had been the theft of a few sheep.

Near Grafton on the northern New South Wales coast some troopers came upon a large number of Aboriginal people camped beside the Orara River. The troopers opened fire indiscriminately. The crime once again had been cattle stealing. A local squatter grimly reported later that 'their dead bodies subsequently floated down past the Settlement'.

Around the Daly Waters and Roper River area of the Northern Territory in the 1890s it was estimated that Constable William Willshire, the officer in charge of the local contingent of native police, literally killed thousands of Aboriginal people. Eventually word of his atrocities filtered back to 'civilisation' in the south and the local magistrate attempted to have him charged with murder. But Willshire's actions had met with such local approval that no jury could be found who were prepared to convict him.

The massacres, the oblique references and the folk memories just keep on emerging. They will never all be documented. Some died with the killers and their victims. Some will reappear when a cairn of bones is found or when a researcher in some musty library stumbles upon a yellowing letter or diary in which a long-forgotten atrocity is recorded.

It is always dangerous to make generalisations; they are imprecise and open to

The homestead staff at Wonaminta, NSW, in 1892. As their livelihood was taken from them, Aboriginal people drifted into the stations.

criticism. However, on the basis of the evidence available and on the basis of an understanding of the nature of the frontier, it is hard not to conclude that Aboriginal blood has been spilt by white aggressors on every square kilometre of settled Australia. The whole complex truth, it would seem, is a wedge far more heinous than the thin sliver of truth revealed in these pages.

CHAPTER 18

THE STOLEN GENERATION

> This time I was raped, bashed and slashed with a razor blade on both of my arms and legs because I would not stop struggling and screaming. The farmer and one of his workers raped me several times. I wanted to die, I wanted my mother to take me home where I would be safe and wanted. Because I was bruised and in a state of shock I didn't have to do any work but wasn't allowed to leave the property.
>
> *Story of Millicent.* Bringing them Home: Report on the National Inquiry into the Separation of Aboriginal and Torres Strait Islander Children from Their Families.

It is a huge tome: 690 pages weighing 1.8 kilograms and titled *Bringing them Home: Report on the National Inquiry into the Separation of Aboriginal and Torres Strait Islander Children from Their Families*. It was formally released in April 1997 and since then, like so much Aboriginal history, it has been the subject of abuse, misinterpretation, argument and disputation.

To read it is to realise that the massacres, which constitute so much of this book, may have stopped in the 1920s but the maltreatment of Aboriginal people continued unabated and was still very much part of the legal and institutional fabric of most Australian states as recently as the 1980s.

'Bringing them Home' is predominantly a well-argued history of the way governments legislated to separate Aboriginal children from their parents. At various points in the text first person accounts, most of them confidential submissions to the inquiry, are used to drive home the painful, day-to-day human reality of the government policies. It is these stories which colour the whole report. To read them is to be shocked into a sense of outrage at the inhumanity of government agencies. To read them is to weep, as so many have done, at the stupidity of those people who were placed in charge of a program designed to integrate Aboriginal people into the larger fabric of white European-Australian society.

Here is the story of Millicent:

At the age of four, I was taken away from my family and placed in Sister Kate's home — Western Australia where I was kept as a ward of the state until I was eighteen years old. I was forbidden to see any of my family or know of their whereabouts. Five of us D. children were all taken and placed in different institutions in WA. The Protector of Aborigines and the Child Welfare Department in their 'Almighty Wisdom' said we would have a better life and future brought up as whitefellas away from our parents in a good religious environment. All they contributed to our upbringing and future was an unrepairable scar of loneliness, mistrust, hatred and bitterness. Fears that have been with me all of life. The empty dark and lonely existence was so full of many hurtful and unforgivable events, that I cannot escape from no matter how hard I try. Being deprived of the most cherished and valuable thing in life as an Aboriginal child — love and family bonds. I would like to tell my story of my life in Sister Kate's home — WA.

My name is Millicent D. I was born at Wonthella WA in 1945. My parents were CD and MP, both 'half-caste' Aborigines. I was one of seven children, our family lived in the sandhills at the back of the Geraldton Hospital. There was a lot of families living there happy and harmonious. It was like we were all part of one big happy family.

In 1949 the Protector of Aborigines with the Native Welfare Department visited the sandhill camps. All the families living there were to be moved to other campsites or to the Moore River Aboriginal Settlement. Because my parents were fair in complexion, the authorities decided us kids could pass as whitefellas. I was four years old and that was the last time I was to see my parents again. Because my sisters were older than me they were taken to the Government receiving home at Mount Lawley. My brother Kevin was taken to the boys home in Kenwick. Colin and I were taken to the Sister Kate's Home. We were put in separate accommodation and hardly ever saw each other. I was so afraid and unhappy and didn't understand what was happening.

We were told Sundays was visiting day when parents and relatives came and spent the day. For Colin and I that was a patch of lies because our family were not allowed to visit. We spent each Sunday crying and comforting each other as we waited for our family. Each time it was the same — no one came. That night we would cry ourselves to sleep and wonder why. We were too young to understand we were not allowed family visits.

A couple of years passed and I started primary school. It had been such a long time since I had seen my brother Colin. I was so helpless and alone. My brother had been taken away to the boys' home in Kenwick and now I was by myself. I became more withdrawn and shy and lived out in a world of my own hoping one day Mum would come and take me out of that dreadful place. As the years passed I realised that I would never see my family again.

They told me that my family didn't care or want me and I had to forget them. They said it was very degrading to belong to an Aboriginal family and that I should be ashamed of myself, I was inferior to whitefellas. They tried to make us act like white kids but at the same time we had to give up our seat for a whitefella because an Aboriginal never sits down when a white person is present.

Then the religion began. We had church three times a day, before breakfast, lunchtime and after school. If we were naughty or got home from school late we had to kneel at the altar for hours and polish all the floors and brass in the church. We had religion rammed down our throats from hypocrites who didn't know the meaning of the word. We used to get whipped with a wet ironing cord and sometimes had to hold other children (naked) while they were whipped, and if we didn't hold them we got another whipping. To wake us up in the morning we were sprayed up the backside with an old fashioned pump fly spray. If we complained we got more. Hurt and humiliation was a part of our every day life and we had to learn to live with it.

Several more years passed and I still had no contact with my family, I didn't know what they looked like or how I could ever find them. By this time I was old enough to go to High School. This meant I didn't have to look after several of the younger kids as I had previously done, bathing, feeding and putting them on the potty and then off to bed, chopping wood before school and housework which all of us kids done and the housemothers sat back and collected wages — for doing nothing. My life was miserable, and I felt I was a nobody and things couldn't get any worse. But I was wrong.

The worst was yet to come.

While I was in first year high school I was sent out to work on a farm as a domestic. I thought it would be great to get away from the home for a while. At first it was. I was made welcome and treated with kindness. The four shillings I was paid for the work I did at Sister Kate's so you don't miss what you didn't get, pocket money etc. The first time I was sent to the farm for only a few weeks and then back to school. In the next holidays I had to go back. This time it was a terrifying experience, the man of the house used to come into my room at night and force me to have sex. I tried to fight him off but he was too strong.

When I returned to the home I was feeling so used and unwanted. I went to the Matron and told her what happened. She washed my mouth out with soap and boxed my ears and told me that awful things would happen to me if I told any of the other kids. I was so scared and wanted to die. When the next school holidays came I begged not to be sent to that farm again. But they would not listen and said I had to.

Children were taken from their 'traditional' and 'family' environments and taught skills which would allow them to enter white society as labourers and servants.

I ran away from the home, I was going to try and find my family. It was impossible. I didn't even know where to go. The only thing was to go back. I got a good belting and had to kneel at the altar every day after school for two weeks. Then I had to go back to that farm to work. The anguish and humiliation of being sent back was bad enough but the worse was yet to come.

This time I was raped, bashed and slashed with a razor blade on both of my arms and legs because I would not stop struggling and screaming. The farmer and one of his workers raped me several times. I wanted to die, I wanted my mother to take me home where I would be safe and wanted. Because I was bruised and in a state of shock I didn't have to do any work but wasn't allowed to leave the property.

When they returned me to the home I once again went to the Matron. I got a belting with a wet ironing cord, my mouth washed out with soap and put in a cottage by myself away from everyone so I couldn't talk to the other girls. They constantly told me that I was bad and a disgrace and if anyone knew it would bring shame to Sister Kate's Home. They showed me no comfort which I desperately needed. I became more and more distant from everyone and tried to block everything out of my mind but couldn't. I ate rat poison to try and kill myself but became very sick and vomited. This meant another belting.

After several weeks of being kept away from everyone I was examined by a doctor who told the Matron I was pregnant. Another belting, they blamed me for everything that had happened. I didn't care what happened to me anymore and kept to myself. All I wanted now was to have my baby and get away as far as I could and try and find my family.

My daughter was born [in 1962] at King Edward Memorial Hospital. I was so happy, I had a beautiful baby girl of my own who I could love and cherish and have with me always.

But my dreams were soon crushed: the bastards took her from me and said she would be fostered out until I was old enough to look after her. They said when I left Sister Kate's I could have my baby back. I couldn't believe what was happening. My baby was taken away from me just as I was from my mother.

Once again I approached the Matron asking for the address of my family and address of the foster family who had my daughter. She said that it was Government Policy not to give information about family and she could not help me. I then asked again about my baby girl and told she did not know her whereabouts. In desperation I rang the King Edward Memorial Hospital. They said there was no record of me ever giving birth or of my daughter Toni. Then I wrote to the Native Welfare Department only to be told the same thing and that there were no records of the D. family because all records were destroyed by fire.

I now had no other options but to find a job and somewhere to live. After working for a while I left Western Australia and moved to Adelaide to try and get my life together and put the past behind me. I was very alone, shy and not many friends and would break down over the simplest thing. Every time I saw a baby I used to wonder, could that be my little girl. I loved her and so desperately wanted her back. So in 1972 I returned to Western Australia and again searched for my family and child. I returned to see the Matron from Sister Kate's. This time she told me that my daughter was dead and it would be in my best interest to go back to South Australia and forget about my past and my family. I so wanted to find them, heartbroken I wandered the streets hoping for the impossible. I soon realized that I could come face to face with a family member and wouldn't even know.

Defeated I finally returned to Adelaide. In my heart I believed that one day everything would be alright and I would be reunited with my family. My baby was dead. (That's what I was told). I didn't even get to hold her, kiss her and had no photographs, but her image would always be with me, and I would always love her. They couldn't take that away from me.

Confidential submission 640, South Australia: WA woman removed in 1949. In January 1996, Millicent received an enquiry from the South Australian welfare authorities. A woman born in 1962 was searching for her birth mother. This was Toni, Millicent's daughter. The two have since been reunited.

Maltreatment cannot be qualitatively measured but it would seem that Millicent, in the 1950s and 1960s, experienced treatment which bears a disturbing similarity to that of Truganini in the early 1800s. The same pattern emerges. In the case of Truganini there was the formal insistence that nothing be done to harm the local Aboriginal people. Van Diemen's Land's Lieutenant Governor Collins had issued a proclamation insisting that 'Any person whomsoever who shall offer violence to a native, or who shall, in cold blood, murder, or cause any of them to be murdered, shall, on proof being made of the same, be dealt with and proceeded against as if such violence had been offered or murder committed on a civilised person'.

And then there was the reality. By the time Truganini was seventeen she'd been raped (and probably contracted syphilis), her mother had been stabbed to death, her uncle had been shot, her stepmother had been kidnapped, her sisters had been enslaved by sealers, and her betrothed had been murdered.

Stories of Aboriginal suffering don't get much worse than Millicent's tale of maltreatment. On one level it is a personal tragedy lightened only by her extraordinary resilience. On another level, however, and this is the nub of the 'Stolen Generation' issue, there are the constant references to the way Millicent's journey into hell was effectively controlled by government agencies. This is not the story of some person who could not get their act together and who stumbled from one crisis to the next. That story exists in all cultures at all times. This is the story of a perfectly happy person who, like some character out of a Franz Kafka nightmare, finds that she has no control over her life as the insensitive and brutalising forces of bureaucracy and legislation conspire to turn an ordinary life into living hell.

There were a lot of complex reasons why governments decided to take Aboriginal children away from their parents and place them in institutions. There was the belief that the lives of Aboriginal people were so poor and unrewarding that life in an institution would provide opportunities and an environment from which Aboriginal children could easily make the transition to the more superior world of white Australians.

There was the belief that Aboriginal people were a blight upon the face of Australia and that the most effective way to eliminate them was to carry out an active program of 'integration' where children were taken from their 'traditional' and 'family' environments and taught skills which would allow them to enter white society as labourers and servants.

There was a belief that Aboriginal people were bad parents, that Aboriginal women did not look after their children, that marriages were too early and young Aboriginal women became pregnant in the most unsavoury of circumstances.

There can be no argument (and this has been central to the arguments of the apologists) that many of the people involved in this process — both the official government officers and the variety of people from social and religious organisations — believed that what they were doing was for the overall benefit of the children who came under their care and protection. There is a companion argument that these 'well-meaning' people were simply reflecting the attitudes and values of their time. 'They cannot be blamed for their actions,' say the apologists, 'at the time they believed that what they were doing was for the betterment of the Aboriginal children. They were providing them with food and shelter where previously they had lived in conditions of great poverty. They were offering them an education where previously their attendance at school was intermittent and the environment at home was not conducive to study.'

The problem is that, in the case of someone like Millicent, regardless of the so-called 'benefits', they were also offering rape, maltreatment, dislocation of family life, extraordinary institutionalised violence and a total lack of respect for the rights of the individual. In the 1950s and 1960s, when most of these acts occurred, they were illegal and totally against the prevailing values of Australian society. It was illegal to kidnap. It was illegal to rape. It was illegal to beat a person to a point where grievous bodily harm occurred. It was illegal to forcibly remove a child from its mother. They are rules which have been on the statute books of Australia, and most Western countries, for hundreds of years. They are deeply embedded in the Christian moral system which underpins much of our law.

As the report observes:

There was a significant divergence between the imported British notions of fairness and liberty and the treatment of indigenous peoples in Australia. The major components of forcible removal were,

1. deprivation of liberty by detaining children and confining them in institutions;
2. abolition of parental rights by taking the children and by making children wards of the Chief Protector or Aborigines Protection Board or by assuming custody and control;
3. abuses of power in the removal process, and
4. breach of guardianship obligations on the part of Protectors, Protection Boards and other 'carers'.

The structure of *The Stolen Generation* report is simple. It starts by declaring that 'grief and loss are the predominant themes of this report' and by pointing out that the dislocation and abuse of one generation, the 'stolen generation', resonates and impacts on the children and grandchildren of those who suffered. It then attempts to define the scope and terminology of the inquiry looking at terms like 'compulsion', 'duress', 'undue influence', 'justification', 'families' and then, statistically, analyses the consequences of taking children from their family environments.

The report is not cold and abstract. When defining the terms it provides frightening examples of the consequences of removing children from their families. At one point, driving home the message, an example is offered of an Aboriginal mother who 'didn't know how to hug her babies, and had to be shown how to do that'.

The inquiry took testimony from 535 indigenous people around Australia. This was the metaphorical tip of the iceberg. In Western Australia, for example, the local Aboriginal support organisations, eager to help the inquiry, collected 600 personal testimonies.

The centre of the report is the detailed, state-by-state analysis of the history of the stolen generation. It is a story of government legislation approving the establishment of institutions and, in the case of Queensland and Western Australia, giving the

Children at Deebing Creek mission in Queensland. Many Aboriginal children were told their families didn't want them and that they should be ashamed to be Aboriginal.

Chief Protector of Aborigines (was there ever a more ironic title?) the right to remove children from their mothers at the age of four.

It is a story of over 700 pieces of legislation (which makes it very difficult to argue that it wasn't government policy) and 67 definitions of 'Aboriginality' which led to nearly one half (47 per cent) of all Aboriginal people surveyed in 1989 reporting that they had been removed from their parents in childhood. The writers of the report are more circumspect, judging that 'nationally we can conclude with confidence that between one in three and one in ten indigenous children were forcibly removed from their families and communities in the period from approximately 1910 until 1970'.

Then the history of each state's involvement with the stolen generation is told. It is, like this book, one of those stories which, by sheer weight of example, leaves the reader punch-drunk with despair and horror. Over and over again the same stories are told. Stories of solitary voices of humanitarians (in New South Wales a politician named McGarry insisted that stealing the children was an 'act of cruelty' designed 'to gain absolute control of the child and use him as a slave without paying wages') against boorish and insensitive bureaucrats and politicians who spend their time arguing about how 'quadroons and octroroons will be merged in the white population'. Of how the 'homes' became infamous amongst the Aboriginal community for their oppression, hardship and inhumanity. And of how Aboriginal people, like Fred Maynard in New South Wales, wrote to the Premier insisting 'that the family life of Aboriginal people shall be held sacred and free from invasion and interference and that the children shall be left in control of their parents'.

It is a story of Welfare Boards, of segregation, of so-called 'assimilation' policies which did not work, of assumptions about the benefits that would flow from such policies, of police forcibly removing children, of mothers fleeing into the bush with their babies, of the virtual slavery of the young girls who were sent out to rural properties to work as maids and nannies, of the children being treated like cattle ('We was bought like a market. We was all lined up in white dresses, and they'd come round and pick you out like you was for sale'), of well-meaning church groups with theological rigidity and missionary zeal using the laws to try and win converts, of sadists who beat and punished their young charges, of religious people who blindly refused to believe the stories they were told by their young charges, and, more than anything else, of a deep racism which, by the definition of the 1948 Convention on the Prevention and Punishment of the Crime of Genocide, was unambiguously genocidal.

All the time the warning signs about the damage being done were being telegraphed to the government and all the time the government was taking no notice. In 1938 Gladys Prosser, a Noongar mother, was interviewed by the Perth *Sunday Times* and declared:

> In many things the white people mean well, but they have so little understanding. My experience has convinced me that, psychologically, the Native Department is working on wrong lines . . . The same law that applies to the white race should apply to the native races in particular — Our Native mothers have all the natural feelings of mothers the world over, and to many of them the administration of the Native Department, by men only, is stark tragedy.

Twenty years later a Special Committee on Native Matters told the West Australian Government that 'the removal of a child from his mother at an early age can cause serious psychological and mental disturbances'.

In 1935 in New South Wales the Aboriginal Protection Board had to advise the manager of Kinchela Boys' Home 'to give up taking intoxicating liquor entirely' and 'that on no account must he tie a boy up to a fence or tree, or anything else of that nature, to inflict punishment on him, that such instruments as lengths of hosepipe or a stockwhip must not be used in chastising a boy, that no dietary punishments shall be inflicted on any inmate in the Home'.

Stories like this stand as the ultimate indictment of human frailty and cowardice.

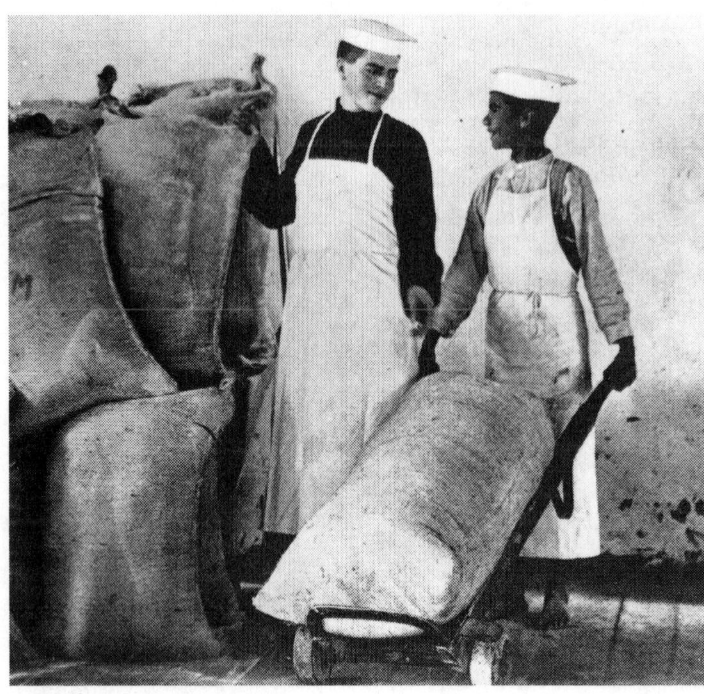

Brother Baker, a Benedictine monk at New Norcia in Western Australia, smiles benignly as his 'native assistant' wheels a bag of flour for breadmaking.

Where were the people of moral integrity? Why did they not stand up against this appalling behaviour? The answer is not to be found in the platitudes about 'good intentions', 'the values of the time' and 'thought they were doing the right thing'. It is to be found in the way that humans, knowing that to act is difficult and to do nothing is easy, will invariably take the easy option.

The consequences of such actions and inactions have been overwhelming. They stand, along with all the poisonings and killings, as acts of barbarism and inhumanity.

Try, just for a moment, to place yourself in the position of a South Australian woman, identified in the report as Fiona, who was taken from her mother in 1932:

> I guess the government didn't mean it as something bad, but our mothers weren't treated as people having feelings. Naturally a mother's got a heart for her children and for them to be taken away, no-one can ever know the heartache. She was grieving when I met her in 1968.
>
> When me and my little family stood there — my husband and me and my two little children — and all my family was there, there wasn't a word we could say to each other. All the years that you wanted to ask this and ask that, there was no way we could ever regain that. It was like somebody came and stabbed me with a knife. I couldn't communicate with my family because I had no way of

communicating with them any longer. Once that language was taken away, we lost a part of that very soul. It meant our culture was gone, our family was gone, everything that was dear to us was gone — and every sun, every morning as the sun came up the whole family would wail. They did that for 32 years until they saw me again. Who can imagine what a mother went through? But you have to learn to forgive.

CHAPTER 19

Racism — An Australian Tradition

It is popular mythology that white Australia is an egalitarian society. It is argued that if Australians occasionally stray from this egalitarianism it is always to support the underdog. The mythical 'little Aussie battler' is revered. Whatever the truth of these fanciful and self-congratulatory generalisations they have never been extended to Aboriginal Australians. For over two hundred years Aboriginal people have been underdogs and battlers yet not once has the white public consciousness been touched by their unhappy position.

The following incidents belong to no broad plan or design. They are like individual tiles: put them all together and they form a mosaic of bigotry and racism which is the burden of all Australians who really care about the so-called egalitarian and humanitarian values of our society.

First contact on the Nicholson River in Western Australia

As a child Robert Moses of the Djaru people used to listen to the old men of his tribe as they told of the early contact between whites and the Djaru. One story he remembered was of a time when the Djaru were catching fish in the Nicholson River. The method used was to build a trap and then for a number of fishermen to roll balls of spinifex through the water forcing the fish to swim towards the trap. As they were doing this a white man rode up to the riverbank and called out 'Get out of the water'. The instruction, shouted in English, was incomprehensible to the Djaru who stared in amazement.

Noting that the Djaru were not heeding his command, the rider raised his rifle and fired a shot into the water. The Djaru who had never seen or heard a gunshot, looked on in disbelief. Angered by the Djaru's apparent refusal to move, the man fired a second shot, closer this time, and called out 'Get away so I can give water to the cattle'.

The instruction was incomprehensible. The Djaru stared at the man. The man lost his temper and stormed down to the water's edge where he unfurled his long cattle whip and started cracking it just above the water. The Djaru leapt out of the reach of the whip and continued to stare. The man then rode his horse into the water and rounded up the fishermen. He told them, in a language they did not understand, 'Get out of the water. I am talking to you. I want to give water to my cattle.'

The Aboriginal people named this man Gurabalngana which in Djaru means 'open arse'.

From *This is what Happened: Historical Narratives by Aborigines*, a series of Aboriginal accounts of first contact edited by Luise Hercus and Peter Sutton

The Battle of Pinjarra — 1834

They might have called it the 'Battle of Pinjarra' but like all of the massacres of Aboriginal people it was more a case of wholesale slaughter than of some equally poised, European-style battle. It was the same story which had been enacted on every frontier: the same overreaction to 'black atrocities'; the same desire to 'teach the blacks a lesson'; the same random killing.

Ever since a small band of settlers had rowed up the Swan River looking for good pastoral land there had been 'trouble' with the local Aboriginal population. The local people had resisted the white advance. Cattle had been speared. The occasional white had been speared. Life on the frontier was fraught with dangers. The settlers developed a sense of antagonism and hatred. They were happy to attack and kill Aboriginal people whenever the opportunity arose. Two years before the Battle of Pinjarra a Swan River settler declared that he was prepared 'to watch and attack the natives, and kill, burn, blow up and otherwise destroy the enemy'.

It was in this kind of hostile environment that Captain James Stirling, Governor of the Colony of Western Australia, responded to continuing requests for military protection from a small group of settlers on the Murray River. The new settlement at Pinjarra lay some 80 kilometres south of the Swan River settlement. Stirling formed a party of about twenty-five whites. The group was a mixture of police, soldiers and a few settlers. Their plan was to 'punish' (that is, massacre) any Aboriginal people in the local area in order to drive home the message that white settlers and their cattle must not be attacked or speared. One account of the massacre explained the rationale for the attack as simply that 'the moment was considered propitiously favourable for punishing the perpetrators of such and other diabolical acts'.

The party came across a group of some seventy Aboriginal people. The Aboriginal people, sensing trouble, fled into the bush. Stirling divided the party and attempted to encircle the fleeing group. They caught them at a river crossing and when the Aboriginal people showed signs of retaliation, Stirling and his men opened fire.

No-one knows how many people were killed. Estimates vary from fourteen to thirty. Those who had not been shot cowered helplessly as the posse advanced. Then, with the scent of victory in his nostrils, Stirling called out for the bugle to be sounded and for his troops to cease firing. The Aboriginal people may not have seen the massacre as a 'battle' but Captain Stirling, who had seen action in the West Indies, South America and the American war, declared his forces victorious.

The remaining Aboriginal people were rounded up and taken prisoner but soon after this Stirling decided to set them free 'for the purpose of fully explaining to the rest of the tribe the cause of the chastisement, that had been inflicted'.

The 'battle' was regarded by both Stirling and the settlers as a success — it certainly did much to break the will of the local Aboriginal people.

Over the next twenty years the Aboriginal population around the Swan River was dispossessed and demoralised. Children were taken from their parents, a special prison for Aboriginal people was established on Rottnest Island, alcoholism became a major problem, and disease sent the death toll soaring. By the 1850s, as A O Neville wrote in his 1936 article 'Relations Between Settlers and Aborigines in Western Australia', 'ticket-of-leave men and parties of convicts in the bush mixed with the natives, supplied them with drink, and there were often hideous orgies. The dispossessed blacks had become paupers and mendicants and deterioration, already begun, proceeded apace.'

From Paul Hasluck's *Black Australians: A Survey of Native Policy in Western Australia*, 1829–1897, 1942, and other sources

A bizarre sense of humour

In Brisbane sometime before 1861 an Aboriginal man was employed by a man to cut some wood. The payment for the work was to be a loaf of bread. The Aboriginal man duly completed the work and was given a note to take to the local bakery. The Aboriginal man assumed the note told the baker to provide a loaf of bread. The order did not authorise payment, instead it suggested that the Aboriginal man 'be kicked about his business with very strong language'. The baker, obviously amused by the instruction, decided to comply with it.

From the evidence of R B Sheridan to the 1861 Queensland Select Committee

Ownership of the land

As recently as 27 April 1971 the Yirrkala of the Gove Peninsula in the Northern Territory had their claims for tribal land, which they had been living on for tens of thousands of years, thrown out of court on the grounds that after 1788 all land on the continent of Australia became the legal property of the British Crown.

Reported in L E Skinner's *Police on the Pastoral Frontier: Native Police 1849–59*

White response to sacred sites

In 1978 Aboriginal people on the New South Wales South Coast campaigned to stop the logging of Mumbulla Mountain. They argued that there was an important sacred site on the southern slope of the mountain. The leader, Guboo Ted Thomas, observed, 'We only talk about these things when we are forced to do so in order to protect our sacred places from ignorant white people to whom only the dollar is sacred.'

The whites in the area responded. Lionel Draper, a pulpwood contractor, defended his logging with the question, 'If they move to have the whole of Mumbulla Mountain declared a national park on the grounds that sacred sites are still meaningful to the present (almost white) Aborigines in the area, where will they stop?' The local newspaper reported the response of Lin Gordon, the New South Wales Labor Government's Minister for Conservation, 'Concerning the Mumbulla Mountain Aboriginal sacred sites, the Minister said that there would need to be more evidence than just someone "knocking two sticks together and chanting" to justify the claim.'

A local white landowner named McGregor argued that if his family didn't know about the site then it didn't exist:

> My family association in this area dates back to about 1845 and it's only in the last twelve months or so that I've heard any mention whatever of Aboriginal sacred sites. To be perfectly frank I think it's a figment of somebody's imagination. I don't think they ever existed because most certainly no member of my family had ever mentioned them to me and I would be positive that had they in fact existed that it would have been passed down by word of mouth.

From Denis Byrne's *The Mountains Call Me Back: A History of the Aborigines and the Forests of the Far South Coast of NSW*, an occasional paper issued by the New South Wales Ministry of Aboriginal Affairs in 1984

Warfare

It is common to assume that white occupation of Australia was met with little and ineffective Aboriginal resistance. This was never true. Aboriginal Australians resisted white encroachment with spears, boomerangs and clubs. The whites replied with guns, diseases and poison. It is difficult to measure the relative success of the two sides. The whites won but at what cost? The closest comparison available is the settlement of Moreton Bay. From 1824 to 1853, one hundred and seventy-four white men were killed by Aboriginal people. In reply, the early settlers killed at random and didn't keep count. Captain John Coley observed, 'the blacks were severely chastised on account of these murders. For want of police protection, the settlers had to protect themselves, and their retaliation, by shooting, was very severe.'

From *Report of Select Committee on the Native Police Force and the Condition of the Aborigines Generally*, Queensland, 1861

Mantraps

One of the most ingenious and sadistic products of the blacksmith's craft was the mantrap, which some graziers set outside the supply hut to catch any Aboriginal person who attempted to steal flour, tea or other foodstuffs. The trap, which was designed like a huge rabbit trap, was so carefully constructed that it needed the full weight of a grown man to hold the jaws open and the spring was so strong that when the jaws snapped shut no single individual could prise them apart.

The graziers became so confident of the efficiency of the mantrap that the sound of the jaws snapping shut upon an Aboriginal leg rarely caused the grazier to get out of bed. In the morning he would rise, go outside, and club the thief to death. Station hands would be expected to dispose of the body.

From a shearer's account of early settlement around Dubbo

Rationalising thrashing Aboriginal people

It was common practice on the frontier to employ Aboriginal people and to treat them like virtual slaves. If an Aboriginal person fled from their employer and was caught, he or she was likely to be lashed for disobedience. Lashings became so common that local magistrates were able to order them for Aboriginal people who had done nothing more serious than leave their place of employment.

One West Australian squatter claimed that a flogging with a cat-o-nine-tails didn't hurt Aboriginal people as much as it hurt white people because 'It should be remembered a native had a hide, and not an ordinary skin like ordinary human beings'.

Quoted in Michael Cannon's *Life in the Country: Australia in the Victorian Age*

A bizarre posed photograph in which a white settle is depicted in hand-to-hand combat with a 'savage'.

Poisoned payment

On the Clarence River in northern New South Wales there lived a particularly brutal squatter named Thomas Coutts. Coutts gained a reputation among both the local whites and Aboriginal people when, after the Aboriginal people had helped him with his harvest, he paid them with loaves of damper laced with arsenic. He was never brought to trial for the crime but over the next decade the local Aboriginal population killed over two thousand five hundred of his sheep and killed more than four of his shepherds.

Reported in Fergus Robinson and Barry York's *The Black Resistance: an introduction to the history of the Aborigines' struggle against British colonialism*

The *Bulletin* offers a solution

In its first year of publication the *Bulletin* suggested that the 'Aboriginal problem' could be solved as follows:

> The Australian aborigine is a doomed man . . . it is too late to talk of preserving the aboriginal race. It is and always was Utopian to try and Christianise it. Rum and European clothes have ruined the people who half a century ago were temperate and naked. The aboriginal race is moribund. All we can do now is to give an opiate to the dying man, and when he expires bury him respectably.

From the *Bulletin*, 1880

Exploitation of black workers

The 1850s gold rushes meant that just about every white labourer abandoned the land and went to the diggings. The settlers were forced to employ Aboriginal men as station hands. To their surprise the Aboriginal men quickly became consummate horsemen and skilled shepherds.

Treatment of the new Aboriginal workforce varied from benign paternalism to shameless exploitation. A settler at Warrego used to boast that he had run his small holding by using 'two men for the price of one'. He had employed a European and an Aboriginal person. The Aboriginal person had been given the cast-off clothes of the European. Even his tea came from the European's used tea leaves.

Other settlers took advantage of Aboriginal people's unfamiliarity with money to pay absurdly low wages. A traveller along the Macquarie River in the 1870s reported that settlers in the area believed that 'to give an ordinary blackfellow more than a shilling, on any occasion, or for any work from cutting a stick of wood to performing a journey of one hundred miles, is to throw away money'.

Perhaps the most inexcusable low payments of all were those given to the trackers who achieved feats requiring extraordinary bushcraft and skill. One tracker, who saved the life of a woman who had been lost for three days, was rewarded for his efforts with a single stick of tobacco.

From Bobbie Hardy's *Lament for the Barkindji: the vanished tribes of the Darling River region*

Keeping Aboriginal people at bay

From the 1830s to 1880s it was common for settlers to set traps for Aboriginal people to prevent stealing. A squatter named Peterson cut off an Aboriginal person's head and placed it in his storeroom to keep other potential thieves at bay. In Queensland a shepherd named Campbell killed and skinned an Aboriginal person, stuffed the corpse with grass and hung it outside his hut door to keep other Aboriginal people away. Another squatter cut off the heads of Aboriginal people he had killed and placed them on fence posts around his property as a warning to any Aboriginal people foolish enough to contemplate passing through 'his' land.

From *Life in the Country*

Name changes

Nothing is more symbolic of the ugliness of a conquering culture than its determination to demean the defeated people either by the use of joke names or diminutives.

In Australia derogatory terms such as 'nigger', 'piccaninny' and 'buck' were borrowed directly from the slave trade. The white inability, and lazy refusal, to pronounce Aboriginal names resulted in beautiful names being replaced by pedestrian or silly ones Marreeockoree, meaning 'leaping fish', was reduced to Peter: Wongoree Pilyarra, meaning 'the eaglehawk soaring for its prey' was inexplicably reduced to Mr McLean.

In Tasmania George Robinson delighted in renaming the Aboriginal people in his care with names taken from classical literature. Tunnerminnerwate became Napoleon, Truganini became Lalla Rookh, Wortabowigee became Fanny.

Various sources

Christianity in action

Life along the Darling River was hard and lonely for Europeans. It wasn't until 1873 that the Anglican church sent a clergyman to the parish. The clergyman was based at Wentworth where the Darling joins the Murray. From that base he was expected to travel up the Darling and into the surrounding areas ministering to his flock. It appears that he had little time for the local Aboriginal communities and rarely made an attempt to communicate the Gospel to them. In fact, it seems as though he had little respect for the Gospels himself. He employed an Aboriginal man to help him with his buggy. On cold nights when the Aboriginal man did not wake to rekindle the dying camp fire, the clergyman often roused him by shovelling burning coals on to his bare feet.

From *Lament for the Barkindji*

Another tale of Christian compassion

The missionary William Henry showed his 'humanity' and 'Christian compassion' when he wrote of Aboriginal people in 1799:

> They are truely the most writched and deplorable beings my eyes have ever yet beheld. I think the Greenlanders and Labradorians or the inhabitants of Terra da Fuega, can not be more sunk to a level of brute creation than they. O Jesu, when will thy kingdom come with power amongst them? When shall the rays of thine Eternal gospel penitrate the gross darkness of their minds (well represented by their faces) and illumine their benighted souls.

Quoted in James Miller's *Koori: A Will to Win*

Death by disease

Probably the greatest killer of Aboriginal people in the nineteenth century was influenza. Few Aboriginal groups remained unaffected. In the south-western corner of Western Australia there was a string of influenza epidemics in the 1850s and 1860s. The winters of 1851–54, 1860–63 and 1865 wreaked havoc on the local Aboriginal population. Between 1829 and 1901 an estimated 4500 Aboriginal people out of a total population of 6000 died, most as a result of imported diseases.

From Paul Hasluck's *Black Australians*

An expert's opinion on the success of the missions

F J Gillen, 'an expert on Aborigines', was asked during the 1899 Select Committee what he thought of the teaching of the Gospel to Aboriginal people. His reply was blunt, 'I think the missionary, in trying to make Christians of the blacks, destroyed all that was good in their organisation, and gave them nothing in return.'

From *Report of Select Committee of the Legislative Council on The Aborigines Bill, 1899* S.A.A.P. No. 77, 1899

How many Aboriginal people were killed?

It has been estimated that when the First Fleet arrived at Botany Bay there were at least 300 000 Aboriginal people living in Australia. Some experts have estimated that the figure was closer to one million. By 1901 the State censuses carried out in that year concluded that there were about 40 000 Aboriginal people and by the time of the first Commonwealth census in 1911 the figure had dropped to 20 000.

From *Life in the Country*

No concessions for dispossessed Aboriginal people

The Mardgany people of south-west Queensland were dispossessed by the large sheep and cattle stations which sprung up on their traditional lands. Those who could not find work on the stations were sent off to government reserves. The government at the time was unsympathetic and insensitive. Harold Meston toured the area and filed the following suggestions for the removal of Aboriginal people:

> To avoid any heavy expense it is necessary to exercise great caution in dealing in any comprehensive manner with so large a number of Aboriginals.
>
> For the present at least it is only necessary or desirable to consider those who are actually destitute, not employed on stations and not able to obtain sufficient food from the old source of natural supply . . . I would certainly not advise the feeding of any blacks who are to remain in their present surroundings. It is not only objected to on the score of expense but for the much more serious reason of unsatisfactory results.
>
> Blacks who remain in camp with gratuitous supplies of food and therefore lose all inducement and exertion, usually reach a lower stage of degradation than those who have to go hunting for a living, and the women are prostituted to obtain drink and opium . . .
>
> In advising the removal of destitute Western blacks to Durundun and Barambah I would deal first with those able to walk by easy stages to the nearest railway station, and so save the heavy coach fares of the West . . .
>
> To those whom it is absolutely necessary to feed I would give the option of walking to Cunnamulla on the way to the Coast Reserve or finding food for themselves if they wish to stay where they are.

From Hazel McKellar's *Matya-Mundu: A History of the Aboriginal People of South West Queensland*, edited by Thom Blake

A condition of sale

The colonisation commissioners who surveyed, carved up and sold large tracts of South Australia in the 1830s made it a condition of sale that twenty per cent of all land purchased by individuals must eventually be returned to Aboriginal people in a 'developed state'. This 'condition of sale' has been very conveniently forgotten.

From 'The Aborigines of South Australia: Their Background and Future Prospects'

The Mardgany people of south-west Queensland were dispossessed by the large sheep and cattle stations which sprung up on their traditional lands.

A very white solution

A O Neville, a West Australian Commissioner of Native Affairs, claimed in 1947 that he had a scientific solution to the 'Aboriginal problem'. Scientific research, he claimed, had revealed that skin pigmentation could be bred out of Aboriginal people in two or three generations. If he could only have the money and the legislative power to start a selective breeding programme he could, in a matter of sixty to seventy years, solve the 'Aboriginal problem' by breeding a race of white Aboriginal people.

From Michael Howard's *Aboriginal Politics in Southwestern Australia*

An instant judge and jury

In Maitland an Aboriginal man was captured and accused of a murder which had occurred 65 kilometres away. Seeing the complications of bringing the man to trial, the commanding officer decided on immediate execution. The suspect was tied between two saplings. Various soldiers used him as human target practice. The first soldier hit the Aboriginal man in the back of the neck. The second soldier's shot blew the man's jaw away. The third soldier put his gun against the man's face and blew half his head away. No-one ever determined whether the man was innocent or guilty.

From *Koori: A Will to Win*

Death by syphilis

It is impossible to measure the full extent of the impact of syphilis on Aboriginal Australians. Many authorities have attempted to estimate the number of Aboriginal people who died from the disease in the early years of settlement. It is clear that venereal disease was the single largest cause of death amongst Aboriginal people who came in contact with whites. In Victoria, for example, Captain Foster Fyans wrote to Governor La Trobe in the early 1850s claiming that 'two thirds of the natives of Port Phillip have died from this infection' and painting an image of whole families 'eaten up with venereal disease'. It has been estimated that probably 8000 Aboriginal people died around Port Phillip in the first thirty years of settlement as a result of venereal disease and tuberculosis — both imported by the new settlers.

From *Life in the Country*

The dog licence

It was a common strategy in the continuing government war on the 'Aboriginal problem' to enact legislation which either increased government handouts or increased government control. The Native Administration Act which became Western Australian law in 1936 was, by any measure, an appalling piece of racist legislation. Among its more extreme clauses were:

(a) no native, except adult half-caste males who do not live as aborigines, can move from one place to another without the permission of a protector and the giving of sureties.

(b) no native parent or other relative living has the guardianship of an aboriginal or half-caste child.

(c) Natives may be ordered into reserves or institutions and confined there.

(d) The property of all minors is automatically managed by the Chief Protector, while the management of the property of any native may be taken over by consent or if considered necessary to do so to provide for its due preservation.

(e) Natives may be ordered out of town or from prohibited areas.

(f) Subject to the right of appeal, the Commissioner of Native Affairs may object to the marriage of any native.

Looking at the legislation six years later, the historian and politician Paul Hasluck tartly observed that it gave Aboriginal people, 'a legal status that has more in common with that of a born idiot than any other class of British subject'.

The legislation was designed to control the lives of all West Australian Aboriginal people. The only escape from its Draconian provisions was a certificate of exemption which Aboriginal people, with ill-concealed distaste, nicknamed 'the dog licence'.

These 'licences' were issued to Aboriginal people who had 'integrated' into white society. Between 1937 and 1944, 276 certificates were issued of which 75 were revoked.

Various sources

The Christian values of the Bishop of Adelaide

During the 1860 Select Committee on Aborigines the Bishop of Adelaide was asked, 'Supposing that in endeavouring to Christianise them, you are in reality assisting to destroy them, do you not think that it would be inadvisable to injure their bodily health?' The bishop answered:

> In the first place, I do not think that it does injure their bodily health, more than allowing them to live in their wild state; and secondly, I do not think it inadvisable to Christianise them; for I would rather they died as Christians than drag out a miserable existence as heathens. I believe that the race will disappear either way . . .

How had Aboriginal Australians survived without Christianity for at least forty thousand years?

From *South Australian Parliamentary Papers*, 1860

The rights of New South Wales Aboriginal people one hundred and fifty years after white settlement

Attitudes and values change. In 1938 a New South Wales Public Service Report proudly recorded:

> It has been said from time to time that Aboriginals should be given full citizen rights. Briefly as far as can be seen at present, the majority of Aborigines, as defined by the Act have all citizen rights except the following:
> (a) They cannot exercise franchise at Federal elections.
> (b) They are prohibited from obtaining liquor.
> (c) If Aboriginal blood predominates they cannot receive maternity allowance or old-age or invalid pension from the Commonwealth Government. (Incidentally an Aboriginal, if resident on the stations, as already stated, is not eligible to receive the old-age or invalid pension).

(d) Residents on stations have been debarred from receiving relief work provided by the Government of this State.
(e) Family endowments payments are in general, made to Aborigines by means of orders for goods instead of cash.
(f) Certain restrictions may be imposed on Aboriginals in accordance with the provisions of the Act.

From *Report and Recommendations of the Public Service Board of New South Wales*, 13 July 1938

Edward John Eyre's assessment of Aboriginal people

The white explorers varied widely in their response to the Aboriginal people. One of the most compassionate was Edward John Eyre who observed:

> The character of the Australian native has been so constantly misrepresented and traduced, that by the world at large he is looked upon as the lowest and most degraded of the human species, and generally considered as ranking but little above the members of the brute creation. It is said, indeed, that the Australian is an irreclaimable, unteachable being; that he is cruel, bloodthirsty, revengeful and treacherous; and in support of such assertions, references are made to the total failure of all missionary and scholastic efforts hitherto made on his behalf, and to the many deeds of violence or aggression committed by him upon the settler . . .
>
> I believe were Europeans placed under the same circumstances, equally wronged, and equally shut off from redress, they would not exhibit half the moderation of forbearance that these poor untutored children of impulse have invariably shown . . .
>
> Without laying claim to this country by right of conquest, without pleading even the mockery of cession, or the cheatery of sale, we have unhesitatingly entered upon, occupied, and disposed of its lands, spreading forth a new population over its surface, and driving before us the original inhabitants.

From Edward John Eyre's *Journals of Expeditions into Central Australia*

Educating Aboriginal people

During the 1861 Royal Commission into the Native Police a series of questions were asked which gave a frightening insight into the bizarre approach to Aboriginal education which was being practised in Western Australia.

'Will you explain to the Committee what has been done?'

'In the first place, an attempt was made to collect the elderly natives together, and to teach them in schools, which was found to be altogether impracticable. Following upon this, an experiment was made to obtain and educate a number of young children; very young children were obtained; some of them were orphans, others were purchased from their parents; as many as possible were collected and brought in . . . But it was found that, when the children reached the age of thirteen or fourteen years, they began to die off, and at least fifty or sixty per cent were lost in this way, until it became apparent that the system could not be carried on any longer . . .'

'You are speaking of a kind of industrial school?'

'Yes. It was necessary to send the police continually after the children, as they were always running away, and the windows of the school-house had to be barred. When they were caught they were flogged, to teach them not to run away any more, and shut up again. In fact, had it not been for a good purpose, the system which was adopted was one which might be said to have belonged to the barbarous ages.'

From the *Report of the Royal Commission into the Native Police Force,* 1861

White travellers in the Outback

Talking to the South Australian Select Committee of the Legislative Council on the Aborigines Bill, Mounted Constable Thorpe accurately depicted the maltreatment of many Aboriginal people by stockmen:

> The so-called traveller, with four or five horses, styling himself a bona fide stockman, I would debar of being allowed to have a blackboy or gin at all, for these are the very worst individuals; they are invariably illiterate and cruel, and live under the impression that after the blackboy has walked miles for his horses the proper and orthodox thing then to do is to bring him down with a stirrup-iron, whether the poor boy deserves it or not . . . I have often passed these so-called stockmen (they are pure bush larrikins, and are the flashiest of the flash), on a bitterly cold morning, travelling over the plains on a cold winters' morning. They themselves are comfortably clothed

> and muffled, whereas their blackboys wear a mere bundle of dirty torn rags, a shivering pinched-up mortal in a black skin. 'Why don't you clothe your boy?,' I have often asked. 'Oh, he's only a bloody nigger,' is the reply.

From *South Australian Parliamentary Proceedings*, 1899

A strange cure for venereal disease

The spread of venereal disease, unknown in Australia until the arrival of the whites, had a devastating effect on the Aboriginal population. While some venereal disease was obviously transmitted in total ignorance, Mounted Constable Thorpe argued that there was a history of conscious transmittal by certain bushmen at the turn of the century.

A very silly yet general impression exists amongst some ignorant bushmen that when suffering from gonorrhoea all that they need do is to impart the disease to some female, then the severity of such disease upon themselves will be greatly modified, or perhaps totally cured . . . I have seen poor young gins, mere children between 11 and 14 years of age, suffering from syphilis in all its stages. The old blacks assured me that white men had run them down and ruined them.

From *South Australian Parliamentary Proceedings*, 1899

Racism on the labour front

In Western Australia in the early years of this century the community did everything possible to ensure that Aboriginal people did not enjoy equal opportunities. In 1912 the local Labor Party attempted to prevent all Aboriginal people from working, arguing that cheap Aboriginal labour was in direct competition with union labour. The Labor Party also advocated that all Aboriginal people be placed on reserves. This would ensure that they were kept out of the workforce.

From *Aboriginal Politics in Southwestern Australia*

The way we civilise

Not every person on the frontier was brutish and violent. There were some who saw what was going on and spoke out. An anonymous letter writer to the *Queenslander* observed:

> The white brutes who fancied the amusement have murdered, ravished, and robbed the blacks without let or hindrance. Not only

> have they been unchecked, but the Government of the colony has been always at hand to save them from the consequences of their crime. When the blacks, stung to retaliation by outrages committed on their tribe, or hearing the fate of their neighbours, have taken the initiative and shed white blood, or speared white men's stock, the native police have been sent to 'disperse' them. What disperse means is well enough known. The word has been adopted into bush slang as a convenient euphemism for wholesale massacre. Of this force we have already said that it is impossible to write about it with patience. It is enough to say of it that this body, organised and paid by us, is sent to do work which its officers are forbidden to report in detail, and that a true record of its proceedings would shame us before our fellow-countrymen in every part of the British Empire. When the police have entered on the scene, the race conflict goes on apace. It is a fitful war of extermination waged upon the blacks, something after the fashion in which other settlers wage war upon noxious wild beasts . . .

From the *Queenslander*

Have things really changed?

Well-known Queensland Aboriginal activist Mick Miller made a movie, called *Couldn't Be Fairer,* about the conditions of Aboriginal people in Queensland in the 1980s. In the movie one Aboriginal man recorded his experiences with the local police force:

> They threw me on the ground . . . had me by the neck and threw me on the ground . . . and while they had me on the ground they kicked me right there . . . that's when they busted my tongue. No whitefellers get locked up here . . . it's all blackfellers. We can be sitting around here sober or a bit pissed or something and they'll still lock us up. But the whitefeller can be drunk and even driving a car. Chook Henry he got a flogging from the coppers too. They gave him a hiding and when he was knocked on the ground they pissed on him. They were pissing on him . . . I'm not the first bloke to get a flogging from the coppers here.

From an interview used in Mick Miller's movie *Couldn't Be Fairer,* ABC-TV, 1987

An Aboriginal chain gang at Wyndham, Western Australia, in the early 1900s — an inevitable end for any 'station black' who left without notifying the authorities.

An expert's opinion on 'civilising' Aboriginal people

F J Gillen, 'an expert on Aborigines', was asked by the Hon. W Russell during the Select Committee of the Legislative Council on the Aborigines Bill in 1899, 'If a black and a white infant were brought before us would they not be on an equality in the matter of intelligence?' His reply was:

> Yes; at that period of life. If you take a black child from its mothers teat, sent to Europe and educate it — even were the black to be a graduate of a university — and he returned to his place of origin, he would revert to barbarism. I have seen an instance where a boy has been taken away from the interior and brought down here to civilization for six or seven years. He was pampered, fed well, educated and was always dressed well. On his return to the interior what happens? Off goes the clothing, and when I saw him he was smothered in red ochre and grease.

From *South Australian Parliamentary Proceedings*, 1899

Payment of Aboriginal workers on the cattle stations

Sandy McDonald was born in 1908 on Inverway station in the Northern Territory. He can remember a time in the 1920s when the pay for Aboriginal workers on the station was only food and supplies.

> In those days the fullblood Aboriginal never got wages, just a shirt, trousers, boots and hat, and a stick of tobacco. That was their payment. And tucker. And any bad boys, say a boy with a bit of intelligence who stuck up for his rights, they would flog him. See, that was going on a long time. The Aborigines got that way they could not open their mouths.

From Bruce Shaw and Sandy McDonald's 'They Did it Themselves: Reminiscences of Seventy Years'

The right to carry arms

It became accepted white folklore that a person wishing to protect him or herself on the frontier should be armed at all times. The fear Aboriginal people had generated was such that the simple operation of feeding the animals often required two or three men and a veritable arsenal.

A visitor to Wyndham in the far north of Western Australia in the 1910s was stunned to enter a pub and find that he was in a scene out of a Western novel. Most of the men were armed to the teeth with revolvers. He observed:

> It was strange to see men in rough moleskin pants and crimean shirts quietly playing billiards in an Australian hotel with a Colt or a Webley in a weather-beaten leather holster hanging on their hips. The right, openly to carry arms, did not extend to the local residents, but only to those men who came in from the back country where every man was armed as a safeguard against the Aborigines.

Quoted in Professor Henry Reynolds's *Frontier: Aborigines, Settlers and Land*

Land rights and Sir Joh Bjelke-Petersen

In recent times the issue of land rights has offered people a unique opportunity to express their concern about Aboriginal people. The former Premier of Queensland, Sir Joh Bjelke-Petersen, has been a vocal opponent of Aboriginal land rights. In 1983, after a confrontation with Aboriginal activist Charles Perkins, he observed:

> We've got Charlie Perkins buying a station in Queensland for $2 million. He's wasted $2 million. I would stop, immediately, land rights decisions in Australia.
>
> I'd stop it immediately. I've told Fraser [then Prime Minister of Australia] that half of the Northern Territory has been neutralised. You mark my word, they'll apply to the United Nations to form a nation within a nation. And Fraser will probably go along with it.
>
> It is a frightening situation because they are militant cows . . .

And in 1986 he was equally outspoken:

> More rights for Aboriginals? Well, I think everybody, not everybody but many people in high places, have gone mad. I always maintain that if an Aboriginal came and held his bare toe up, they'd lick it. And you can write that if you like.

Quoted in Thompson & Butel's *Joh: The First 10,000 Days*

How Aboriginal Australians were legally dispossessed

The Seaman Aboriginal Land Inquiry 1983–84 which was held in Western Australia offers the best explanation of how the British legally dispossessed Aboriginal Australians. Although it specifically relates to Western Australia, it applies to all of Australia.

> Relations between the first settlers and the Aboriginals were established, among other things, on the pretence that Western Australia was unoccupied. This led to the legal fiction that for the purposes of British law the colony was treated as being 'settled' rather than 'conquered'. 'Settlement' meant that statute law of England to the date of acquisition and the common law, which was deemed to be certain and unchanging, were to be applied throughout the State. Had it been treated as 'conquered' English law would have provided for the continuation of the indigenous people's laws with the reservation of the right of the Crown to override those existing laws and to introduce new laws. 'Settlement' envisaged the introduction of English laws and customs as if Western Australia was 'terra nullius', that is, nobody's land.

From *The Seaman Aboriginal Land Inquiry, 1983–84*

Sending skulls to England

During the massacres in the Bathurst region in the 1820s the police force caught a group of Aboriginal people in a swamp, surrounded them and wiped them out. The estimated death toll was somewhere between forty and fifty.

In his book *Australian Reminiscences and Papers* the English missionary L E Threlkeld recalled the gruesome aftermath to the massacre:

> Forty-five heads were collected and boiled down for the sake of the skulls. My informant, a Magistrate, saw the skulls packed for exportation in a case at Bathurst ready for shipment to accompany the commanding officer on his voyage shortly afterwards taken to England.

From L E Threlkeld's, *Australian Reminiscences and Papers*

An unhappy school experience

Leonie Simpson was born in 1956. Like so many Aboriginal people her experience of the State school system and the racism of her fellow students is not a happy one. It shows that the attitudes of white parents are inculcated into some white Australian children at a very early age.

'Oh, we used to get it at primary school,' she recalled in 1979, 'it was crazy. As infants we'd get our plaits pulled, and "boong" and stones pelted at us. White girls'd call us black so and so's, and when you'd get stuck into them, it was you that was stuck in the principal's office, not the white girls for calling you that.

'I got threatened. They were going to get the police up because I was forever fighting, swearing and everything, and I'd pelt stones at boys and hit them, and I'd be called out all the time. But they couldn't see that they were hurting me by just using "boong" and "coon". I don't like them names. They all knew me name, they should've called me by me name. I'm not a bit of dirt.'

From *Down there with me on the Cowra Mission: An oral history of Erambie Aboriginal Reserve, Cowra, New South Wales*, edited by Peter Read

Working for the manager

In 1909 the Aborigines Protection Act became law in New South Wales. One of its conditions was to establish a certain number of 'reserves' or 'stations' for Aboriginal people in the country which were run by white managers. These managers had enormous control over the Aboriginal residents on their 'reserves'. They inspected their houses for cleanliness, controlled the amount of alcohol coming into the reserve, and could send children away to be institutionalised if they felt that the parents were not capable of looking after them. The result was that few Aboriginal people wanted to live on managed reserves.

Apart from these regulations the managers also had the right to employ the Aboriginal people on the reserve and to withhold rations if the Aboriginal workers didn't do a 'reasonable amount of work'.

A regulation which appeared in 1915 gives an insight into the power which the Government gave the managers:

> Every able-bodied aborigine, half-caste or other person resident on one of the Board's stations shall do a reasonable amount of work, as directed by the manager; and whilst so engaged shall be remunerated at a rate to be arranged with the manager. Anyone persistently refusing to work when required to do so by the Manager, shall have all supplies for himself and his family withdrawn until he resumes work, and shall be liable to be removed from the station.

From the *New South Wales Government Gazette*, 9 June 1915

A deterrent for corn thieves

L E Threlkeld tells the story of the Aboriginal person who was shot while attempting to steal some corn. The farmer, in an attempt to dissuade other Aboriginal people from theft, hung the body from a branch of a nearby tree with a corn cob stuck in the lifeless mouth. It was a case of using a human as a scarecrow.

From *Australian Reminiscences and Papers*

The last testament before hanging

An Aboriginal man named Waaniltie was hanged in Port Lincoln in South Australia in 1856 for the murder of a white shepherd. Before he was executed he expressed his total bewilderment with British law which he saw as unfair and immoral.

> My dear Friends — Long time ago, when we were boys, the white-man first came to our hunting grounds. White-man then seemed plenty good, but soon white-fellow all gammon! We were then plenty strong, but now white-fellow stronger than us. White-fellow catch him kangaroo, oppossum, emu; catch fish in big net; shoot everything — nothing left for poor black-fellow. Then black-fellow

> feel plenty hungry, and ask white-fellow for tucker, but white-fellow plenty growl. Then me took white-fellow's sheep, and white-fellow got big knife open, and one big stick; then me threw spear at white-fellow, and he tumble down! Now they going to hang poor black-fellow.

Quoted in *Life in the Country*

Modern life in Wee Waa

It is easy to think that the frontier mentality of racism and bigotry is a thing of the past but all the evidence suggests that the average rural Australian is deeply prejudiced against Aboriginal people. This racism is still supported by the local law authorities as the young Aboriginal man, Richard Murray, explained in 1979:

> I was in Moree, where the blacks and the coppers are at loggerheads with one another all the time. Wee Waa, you can't walk down the street there. Or if you're asleep there, or something, on the bloody sidewalk, you're gone. Bloody big wagon pulls over and you're in it. When I worked in Wee Waa on the cotton up there, first day I walked into town, I had a place to stay, and money in me pocket, and I got vagged [arrested for vagrancy]. Got ten days out of it.

From *Down there with me on the Cowra Mission*

CHAPTER 20

Did These Massacres Really Occur?

In recent years — starting around 1996 and reaching something of a fever pitch in late 2000 when a series of articles appeared in *Quadrant* magazine — it has become fashionable for right wing commentators to challenge the accuracy, truth and scope of the stories of Aboriginal massacres and maltreatment.

Although *Blood on the Wattle* has now been continuously in print for fifteen years and was recently nominated as one of the twentieth century's ten most influential works of Australian non-fiction, both the book and the author have managed to avoid these attacks. In part this is undoubtedly due to the 'popular', rather than 'academic', nature of this text. Equally it is easier to attack the accuracy of specific massacres, where some of the facts of a particular incident may be a little shaky, than to attempt an assault on such a vast catalogue of depressing incidents.

Blood on the Wattle has only ever been (and only ever aspired to be) a record of all the massacres, murders and maltreatment available in books, magazines, newspapers and oral histories. It is not a piece of original historic research. As such it brings together, in a single volume, a vast number of shameful and horrific stories which are an integral part of this continent's history since European settlement. To attack the accuracy of these stories would be to argue that literally hundreds of reports — from court records relating to the Myall Creek and Coniston station massacres through the first person records of people like Blagden Chambers (*Black and White: The Story of a Massacre and its Aftermath*) to the meticulous local histories of both P.D. Gardner in *Our Founding Murdering Father* and Geoffrey Blomfield's *Baal Belbora* — are all wrong.

So, rather than seriously engaging with the issue of the massacres these critics and historical revisionists, like some cadre of unsuccessful guerillas, take pot shots from the sidelines hoping that they will occasionally pick off a small part of the total story. By doing this they hope to discredit all the other murderous accounts — by association.

The main critic has been Keith Windschuttle, a one-time left wing academic whose specialist fields tend more to media and sociology. In recent years Windschuttle, now in his fifties, has been happy to admit the error of his youthful left wing ways and embrace conservative views which, in one interview, he claimed as evidence that he now had a 'grown up' view of the world.

Windschuttle's major attack on the massacres spread across three issues of *Quadrant*. Under the general heading 'The Myths of Frontier Massacres in Australian History' he started with 'Part I: The Invention of Massacre Stories' (October 2000), followed it with 'Part II: The Fabrication of the Aboriginal Death Toll' (November 2000) and concluded with 'Part III: Massacre Stories and the Policy of Separatism' (December 2000).

It was meant to be a scalpel-like dissection, critique and persuasive rebuttal of what has become known as 'the black armband view of Australian history'. Its primary target seemed to be the writings of the influential historian Henry Reynolds.

So, what is Windschuttle's argument? Here is a summary of the arguments presented in the three articles.

Part I: The Invention of Massacre Stories

This article opens with a quote from the Australian-born, UK-based journalist Phillip Knightley. In his popular history *Australia: A Biography of a Nation*, published to coincide with the centenary of Federation, Knightley describes the events of the Forrest River massacre in Western Australia in 1926 and accuses Australia of 'a racist policy that included segregation and dispossession and bordered on slavery and genocide'.

Knightley then proceeds to quote from the *Bringing Them Home* report. He then goes on to describe, in detail, the Battle of Pinjarra in 1834, the massacre at Waterloo Creek in 1838, the Forrest Creek massacre in 1926 and the Coniston massacre in 1928.

Windschuttle uses Knightley's account of these four massacres as the basis of his attack. He asserts that Knightley has been duped. 'For it has now been established beyond reasonable doubt that there was no massacre at Forrest River of any kind. Moreover, the information Knightley relies upon for the murder of men, women and children at Waterloo Creek is mostly false. His account of the Battle of Pinjarra bears almost no resemblance to what happened there. Of the four incidents he describes, only that at Coniston deserves the label 'massacre'. The evidence for this last case is shocking enough in itself, but even here some historians have not been able to resist the temptation to embellish and exaggerate the story.'

So what is the evidence that Windschuttle uses to support his argument that 'Knightley has been duped'?

It is no accident that Windschuttle does not proceed through the massacres chronologically. He starts with the Forrest Creek massacre of 1926. He briefly describes the events which occurred in the Kimberley between May and July 1926. According to Windschuttle, after William Hay, the co-owner of Nulla Nulla station, was killed by an Aborigine named Lumbia on 23 May 1926 a party led by two policemen went into the Kimberley in search of the murderer. On 26 June Lumbia was arrested. He was returned to Wyndham on 12 July and subsequently was tried for murder and served ten years for the crime.

Windschuttle then argues that the Reverend Ernest Gribble, who was the head of the Forrest River Mission, 'recorded in his private journal and in the mission log rumours reported to him about the shooting of Aborigines by the police patrol' and subsequently brought these rumours to the attention of the Western Australian Aborigines Department. Subsequent investigations were contradictory with the Commissioner of Police in Western Australia insisting that 'there was no sustainable evidence that even a single individual had been murdered, let alone several.' A further Royal Commission disagreed with the commissioner. It concluded that eleven Aborigines had been murdered and subsequently two constables, St Jack and Regan, were sent to trial. Their case was dismissed because the magistrate found that 'no prima facie case had been made that even one individual had been murdered during the police patrols.'

Looked at objectively this evidence is, at best, ambiguous. A Royal Commission says eleven Aborigines have been killed. A magistrate says there is no case to answer. But, asserts Windschuttle, there's a book by Perth journalist, Rod Moran, titled *Massacre Myth* which argues that the massacre never happened.

Windschuttle writes of Moran's book:

> Here is a sample of the points he makes:
> - There were no eyewitnesses to any killings . . .
> - Apart from some teeth uncovered at one location, no human remains were found at any of the alleged murder sites . . .
> - No ballistic evidence was found of a massacre or even of more than one shot fired . . .
> - A substance thought to be blood on rocks . . . could not have been related to police patrols . . .

This would appear to be information worth considering but it ignores the time between the crimes and the investigation. While this would not be hugely significant in most parts of the world, in the Kimberley (and all you have to do is travel through the region in summertime to understand this point), the humidity, the rain and the harshness of the heat and sunshine would be enough to destroy evidence, particularly over a period of nearly twelve months.

Also Windschuttle fails to mention that Ron Brunton, an anthropologist currently working for the Institute of Public Affairs, a self-confessed conservative think tank based in Melbourne, and a person who, over the years, has become one of the country's most intelligent critics of the 'black armband' view of Aboriginal history, has conceded that Moran's book is open to serious academic challenge. Reviewing Moran's book in the Brisbane *Courier Mail* on 16 October 1999, Brunton wrote:

> Five years ago, Perth journalist Rod Moran wrote a lengthy article for *The West Australian* arguing that the 1926 Forrest River massacre of Aborigines in the Kimberley was simply a myth, despite its widespread portrayal as one Australia's worst crimes this century.
>
> The family of the late Constable James St Jack, who was supposedly a major participant in the murders, felt vindicated. They have long believed that St Jack was maliciously accused of an outrage that never actually occurred.
>
> Understandably, Kimberley Aborigines, whose forebears died in the disputed massacre, were deeply offended, saying that Moran was 'stealing their history'. Their sentiments were shared by many other people, both black and white.
>
> Unfazed by this anger, Moran continued his researches, and he has just published a book, *Massacre Myth* . . . Moran maintains that the massacre stories involved a fantastic distortion of much less egregious events — the slight wounding of a man during a raid on an Aboriginal camp, and Constable St Jack's shooting of the camp occupants' dogs.
>
> More sensationally, Moran maintains that the rumours that grew out of these incidents were promoted and embellished by Reverend Ernest Gribble, the head of the Forrest River Mission, as part of a devious plan to protect himself by discrediting Constable St Jack. Moran suggests that Gribble learnt the constable had obtained information that the reverend and his son were supposedly engaged in serious hanky-panky with Aboriginal women.
>
> The purported evidence comes from St Jack and his family, and includes reference to a long-destroyed personal diary, combined with some fanciful interpretations of scraps of other material. The slender grounds on which this allegation is based makes it hard to accept that Moran is the rigorous and sceptical researcher he would have us believe.
>
> The most comprehensive account of the killings has been presented by the Western Australian historian Dr Neville Green, in his 1995 book *The Forrest River Massacres*. Having worked with Green on another project, I have some confidence in his judgement and his respect for the facts.

The Forrest River Massacres makes no attempt to disguise the problems involved in uncovering the truth about the murders. Nor does Green shy away from revealing the extent of Reverend Gribble's many personal faults, which eventually led to his removal from the mission.

But unlike Moran, Green describes the massacre in the full context of four decades of bitter race relations in the Kimberley. Very few people felt impelled to seek justice for Aborigines who had suffered violence, particularly if the interests of respected local identities were threatened.

Green has no doubts that Aborigines were murdered by a police expedition led by Constable St Jack and Constable Dennis Regan. The party of fourteen, comprising Aboriginal assistants as well as whites, were trying to capture an Aborigine named Lumbia for the killing of a station owner who had raped his wife.

Although Lumbia himself was eventually found and brought in for trial, many innocent Aboriginal men, women and children were killed along the way, and their bodies were incinerated in an attempt to hide the evidence.

No-one knows the precise number. The Royal Commission concluded that at least eleven Aborigines were killed at three separate locations. Police Inspector William Douglas, who had been sent to investigate Gribble's allegations before the Royal Commission was established, reported that sixteen Aborigines were killed.

Reverend Gribble thought that the number was at least thirty. And in 1968 Charles Overheu, the brother of one of the participants in the massacre, told Neville Green that as many as three hundred Aborigines lost their lives, although Green believes this figure is far too high.

Commissioner Wood recommended that charges of murder be laid against Constable St Jack and Constable Regan. In May 1927, the two were arrested for the murder of just a single Aborigine, a man named Boondung. Fearing that public sympathy for the two constables in the Kimberley would preclude a fair trial, the committal hearing was held in Perth.

But, as the Royal Commissioner himself had been forced to admit, all the evidence for the massacre was circumstantial. It had not been possible to identify a single body of those who had been killed; and neither was it possible to state that any particular individual had been responsible for the deaths.

> Worse, at the committal hearing even Gribble could not state for certain that Boondung was dead. And the Government bacteriologist, who had examined the burnt and fractured skeletal remains collected at the massacre sites, testified that he did not think they were from humans. Green suggests that the material had been tampered with, because others who had examined it beforehand were convinced that it contained human remains.
>
> The presiding magistrate dismissed the case against the two constables, who were quickly reinstated into the police force. Gribble, whose determination had been almost solely responsible for bringing the case to public attention, was largely discredited.
>
> Gribble was clearly an extremely self-righteous, autocratic and intolerant man, which made it so easy for many to dismiss everything he said. But sometimes it requires a real ratbag to point us down the path towards truth. It would be most unfortunate if Rod Moran's writings lead people to believe that the Forrest River massacre is just another fabrication perpetuated by the Aboriginal industry.

It is hard to imagine that Windschuttle was not aware of this critique of Moran's book (particularly seeing as it is available to everyone on the Internet at http://www.ipa.org.au/Media/rbcm161099.html) and yet he insists that Moran's 'brilliant piece of detective work . . . has performed a valuable service for Australian historiography'. He goes on:

> Given that there are people who have been prepared to invent massacre stories, and given that these rumours can then take on a life of their own, historians should draw a firm line. They should ask hard questions about rumours, second-hand reports and similar evidence from those who were not at the scene of the crime.

There are, of course, a number of problems with this superficially reasonable approach to Aboriginal history. Firstly it does not allow for the value of oral history. Given that Aboriginal culture and communication is based on oral history, Windschuttle is basically shutting out any Aboriginal interpretation or recording of events.

Secondly it refuses to acknowledge the widely accepted problem of the silence of the frontier. There are vast amounts of evidence that after the perpetrators of the Myall Creek massacre were executed at Darlinghurst Gaol in Sydney on 18 December 1838 the frontier went silent. One Sydney newspaper even reported the following exchange in the wake of the decision on the Myall Creek murders:

> 'Have they hanged the men?' asked the countryman.
>
> 'Yes,' replied the city citizen.

> 'It's a damned shame,' went on the countryman. 'However, we have a safer technique in our part of the country.'
>
> 'Indeed,' said the citizen curiously. 'What is that?'
>
> 'Oh!' replied the countryman with sly enthusiasm, 'We poison them and have done so to a good many already. Serves them right, too.'

How does any historian deal with this code of silence? Suddenly the oblique reference in a journal or diary, the casual mention (often almost in code) of massacres in letters sent from peripatetic clergymen and, most importantly, the oral/folk memories of Aboriginal communities become vital in trying to unearth the truth. It does not help if some modern historian locked in his or her own cultural cage refuses to allow other methodologies or structures. In the case of Aboriginal history it is ultimately racist to argue that Aboriginal evidence is below some kind of acceptable Western standard. It is arguing that only the West has a monopoly on truth and accuracy. That is basically the game that Windschuttle is playing in order to ensure the true story of the massacres is not told.

In recent times the argument about oral evidence has raged with both the ex-Governor-General (Sir William Dean) and the ABC-TV *7.30 Report* being accused of accepting, without criticism, oral evidence of massacres in the Kimberley which have not been supported by written European evidence. This is a problem which needs to be resolved, without acrimony, by professional historians working in the field. Oral histories are used, and have been used, very effectively in American history. The U.S. Works Projects Administration (WPA) interviews done with ex-slaves in the 1930s have been used extensively but a sophisticated methodology has grown up around the evidence which instructs those using it about the pitfalls and problems of such evidence while justifying its usage on the grounds that customary evidence is unavailable for some topics. For example, attempts to reconstruct the world as it was viewed by African-Americans in pre-literacy days (ie the time of their slavery) and to recreate their consciousness and culture need to use, creatively, whatever evidence is available. In dealing with histories that were not documented at the time it is essential that historians be creative but clearly acknowledge the problems with such approaches.

It is easy to deal with Windschuttle's accusation about the Waterloo Creek massacre. Windschuttle accepts that the massacre occurred. All he is arguing about is the number of people killed by Major Nunn and his troops. Does it really matter whether ten or 300 were killed? The point remains that Major James Nunn and his mounted troopers — representatives of law and order in the colony at the time — shot and killed a substantial number of Aborigines at Snodgrass Lagoon which subsequently became known as Waterloo Creek. The point, and this is where Windschuttle seems to be more interested in the periphery and not the centre of the argument, is that there were many incidents (and this is a well chronicled one) where the so-called representatives of British law and order simply ignored their legal responsibilities and treated Aborigines in a way they would never have treated a similar group of Europeans.

The major historical work on Major Nunn's campaign is the huge *Waterloo Creek* by Roger Milliss. Windschuttle acknowledges its existence, accepts the fact that it won three literary awards but argues that the book suffers gravely from 'the sheer paucity of evidence Milliss offers'. There is no simple answer to this except to say that there are 155 pages of notes at the end of the book and the bibliography runs to 12 pages. Milliss was certainly thorough.

Windschuttle argues that Milliss engages in 'educated guesswork' about Major Nunn's route, and that Millis uses questionable local history sources. He is satisfied that some depositions for an inquiry taken from 'four officers and two pastoralists' are acceptable as an accurate historic record and he is forced to concede that at least five Aborigines (and possibly 'forty to fifty') were shot and killed at Waterloo Creek because, after being charged by Nunn and his party, the Aborigines who had camped at the creek had the audacity to fight back.

Windschuttle then turns his attention to the famous Battle of Pinjarra, which occurred near Mandurah south of Perth in 1834. Once again his argument is not with the accepted record (in this book my source is Sir Paul Hasluck's excellent *Black Australians: A Survey of Native Policy in Western Australia*) but with Philip Knightley's *Australia* and the *Oxford Companion to Australian History* — both popular, non-specialist texts.

And finally he comes to the massacre at Coniston station which occurred as recently as 1928. In this case, as has been recorded in this book, the evidence is overwhelming and consequently Windschuttle can do nothing more than acknowledge that probably more than fifty-two Aborigines were killed by Constable George Murray and his marauding parties around Coniston station in the Northern Territory in 1928. There is no reference (and this is surely the most frightening aspect of this last massacre) to the fact that the Coniston massacre was so recent that there are still many Australians who are alive today who lived in an Australian society where massacres of Aborigines could occur.

At the end of the first article it is hard to accept that Windschuttle has proved his case. The Forrest River massacre seems to be accepted as a reality by most experts (with a problem about the scale of the massacre) with the only voices of disagreement coming from a magistrate who was applying the strict rule of law to an event which had occurred nearly twelve months earlier and a Perth journalist who was building a case to help the family of Constable James St Jack come to grips with the fact that their relative had been a murderer. In the case of the other three massacres Windschuttle agrees that killings occurred and only argues with the scale of the killings and some details of the events as recounted in popular histories of Australia.

Part II: The Fabrication of the Aboriginal Death Toll

Everyone who has an interest in pre-colonised Australia will, sooner or later, try and establish how many Aborigines were living on the continent prior to 1788 and how many have been killed by Europeans since the arrival of the First Fleet. These figures range from pure guesswork (having read all of the literature on massacres and completed the first edition of this book I felt as though every hectare of this country had been stained by Aboriginal blood) to very careful calculations.

In the second article about 'The Myths of Frontier Massacres in Australian History' Keith Windschuttle focuses on the complex issue of how many Aborigines were actually killed. There is no way of knowing, with any accuracy, how many Aborigines were killed — either by gun, poisoning, being hunted over the edge of cliffs, or clubbed to death. What is absolutely certain is that anyone trying to estimate the numbers has to add a huge 'unknown' component because so many killings and small massacres were never reported.

Windschuttle starts this article by setting up a very easy target. He asserts that there have been three serious attempts to measure the numbers of Aborigines 'killed by Europeans in frontier conflict since 1788' — Henry Reynolds in *The Other Side of the Frontier*, Richard Broome in *The Struggle for Australia: Aboriginal-European Warfare 1770-1930* and Robert Murray in *What Really Happened to the Kooris?* — and, surprisingly, they all arrive at the figure of 20 000 killed, mainly by gunshot.

He then proceeds to shoot each of the estimates down. Reynolds, he claims, arrived at the figure of 20 000 by dubious guesswork. 'Reynolds simply cannot fill in the figures any way he likes,' he declares. He then turns to Richard Broome, claims that Broome reached his figure of 20 000 by guesswork and then asserts that, as there were many cases of individual killing 'To discuss all frontier conflict under the name of "massacres" is to falsify and wilfully exaggerate the down side of Australian history.'

This is not a new problem. When the first edition of this book was being written I came across dozens of minor skirmishes (for want of a better term) where one, two or three Aborigines had been killed. In part that is why this book has the subheading 'Massacres and Maltreatment'. I knew the problem. I didn't have the language to solve it with any accuracy. In fairness, English does not have a precise word to describe the situations which occurred with accuracy. What is the definition of a massacre? When does multiple murder become a massacre? When two are killed? Or three? Or four? Or ten or twenty?

It is quite impossible to find a definition of 'massacre' which actually proffers a number. The *Macquarie Dictionary* defines a 'massacre' as 'the unnecessary, indiscriminate killing of a number of human beings, as in barbarous warfare or persecution' which suggests that the killing of two or three people can reasonably be seen as a 'massacre' if the circumstances are 'unnecessary', 'indiscriminate' and 'as in barbarous warfare'. In other words when Windschuttle writes: 'According to regional studies, however, the majority of deaths on both sides resulted from individual conflicts. The phenomenon of mass killings was rare and isolated' he is being very selective in the way he would like the word 'massacre' to be defined. It would seem that deaths resulting 'from individual conflicts' if they involve two or three people and if they are 'unnecessary' and 'indiscriminate' can fairly be described as massacres. Therefore those forays into Aboriginal camps by squatters and their labourers which saw the Aborigines running for the bushes and a few unlucky ones being killed constitute 'a massacre' by any fair definition of the term.

Windschuttle continues his attack on Robert Murray whose figure of 20 000 killed agrees with both Reynolds' and Broome's. Windschuttle lightly brushes off 'rumours and urban myths about the murder of Aborigines through handouts of poisoned flour.' Yet there are plenty of stories, many cross-referenced to local communities, of squatters using poisoned flour to kill 'tiresome' local Aborigines. This was particularly common on the Queensland frontier and was reported by Ludwig Leichhardt — see the chapter titled The Massacre at Kilcoy — who witnessed the symbolic death by poisoning of a number of Aborigines at the annual Bunya Festival behind the Sunshine Coast.

At the end of the article the reader, hoping to find that some of 'The Myths of Frontier Massacres in Australian History' have been exposed, is left with the unremarkable discovery that a group of academics, knowing that all they can ever do is guess at the scale of massacres in Australia, has reached some kind of loose agreement that probably about 20 000 Aborigines were killed. This is not terribly useful or accurate. What we do know, if we read *Blood on the Wattle* and trust the sources it is derived from, is that during the nineteenth century, on the frontiers, as squatters and explorers pushed further and further into the continent, a vast number of innocent Aboriginal people were killed. This is not surprising. It has been the story of every contact between hunter-gatherer societies and expansionist societies since human beings first began to explore and conquer the world beyond their boundaries.

Part III: Massacre Stories and the Policy of Separatism

In the final article in the series, Keith Windschuttle argues that some of the people who feature prominently in Henry Reynolds' book *The Whispering in Our Hearts* were, in reality, rogues and scoundrels.

Let me explain: in 1998 Henry Reynolds published *The Whispering in Our Hearts*, a fascinating account of those rare people who, against the prevailing mores of the frontier, were prepared to stand up and criticise the maltreatment of Australia's indigenous communities, particularly in the nineteenth century. The people Reynolds focused on included George Augustus Robinson, Lancelot Threlkeld, Louis Guistiniani, Robert Lyon, John Gribble, David Carley, Ernest Gribble and Mary Bennett.

Windschuttle argues that these people were not entirely honest. They had vested interests and were prepared to 'invent and exaggerate' massacre stories 'to justify the policy of separating Aboriginal people from the European population'. He then proceeds to look at the careers of four of the people mentioned: Lancelot Threlkeld, John Gribble, David Carley and Ernest Gribble.

In the case of Threlkeld, Windschuttle asserts that his 'semi-annual reports to the London Missionary Society' were gross exaggerations (without offering any hard evidence to refute this claim) and that Threlkeld was treated with scepticism and disdain by many of his contemporaries. This is hardly surprising. He was reporting massacres along the frontiers. The majority of the colony's conservative elite would not have wanted to hear this information. Of course they would have tried to discredit the man. It is perhaps a near-perfect case of 'killing the messenger'. Once again Windschuttle falls back on very legalistic interpretations of 'truth' arguing that because Threlkeld had only a single source for certain stories that, therefore, those stories cannot be taken seriously.

It is possible that Threlkeld was exaggerating his stories. He was not a professional historian. He was a preacher and missionary outraged by what he heard and saw. As such his versions of events need to be looked at with great care but they cannot simply be discarded as being without any worth whatsoever just because Threlkeld appears to be prone to exaggeration.

Windschuttle's argument that these exaggerations were part of a broader plan by Threlkeld to establish havens for Aborigines where they could live removed from the sheer awfulness of contemporary colonial society may well be true. It is not surprising. There is an extraordinary amount of evidence that, when contact was made between Aborigines and European society, the results — including prostitution, alcoholism, violence and self-destruction — were devastating for the Aborigines. It was reasonable at the time to believe that separation was the solution although, as George Robinson was to demonstrate with the Tasmanian Aborigines, it simply did not work. European society was like a poisonous Pandora's box which, once opened, could never again be closed.

Windschuttle then moves on to John Gribble, a Methodist minister who grew up in Geelong and who ran a number of missions in Victoria, New South Wales and Western Australia. Gribble's notoriety rests largely on his actions in Western Australia where, after establishing a mission at Carnarvon on the Gascoyne River in 1885, he came to the conclusion that there was a 'native labour system' operating in Western Australia which wasn't hugely different to slavery. He recorded his findings in *Dark Deeds in Sunny Lands* and was duly pilloried by every establishment figure in Western Australia. The only question here is: was Gribble telling the truth or were those who attacked him fighting against Gribble's gross misrepresentation? Henry Reynolds believes Gribble was telling the truth. Windschuttle believes he was 'determined to unearth and elaborate any evidence he could to denounce assimilation' yet, when you read Windschuttle's description of Gribble's assertions it is hard not to feel that Gribble was doing nothing more than stating the obvious abuses of the time. Why? Because many of those abuses were still commonplace in the 1970s.

At one point Windschuttle writes:

> On the pastoral stations of the Gascoyne River, he [Gribble] had observed, the Aborigines were employed as shepherds, shearers and drovers. Despite the fact that the *Masters and Servants Act* said that a certificate of discharge must be given at the close of their term of engagement, the station owners ignored this, he claimed. The police had the power to return to his employer any native who absconded before his time had expired. However, the wife of 'a certain settler' had told him that the Aborigines could not read and so did not know when their period of employment had expired. So the natives were employed 'as long as their owners liked'.

Given that this kind of treatment was exposed during the famous Wave Hill protest in 1966 (when the local Aborigines led by Vincent Lingiari went on strike because of the appalling conditions on Wave Hill station), and it is self-evident that the Aborigines would have had no understanding of the *Masters and Servants Act*, it would seem that all Gribble did was expose an appalling travesty on one of the most isolated and lonely coastlines in the world.

Windschuttle concludes his section on Gribble by arguing that Gribble can be connected to the desire, common at the time, to separate Aborigines from Europeans and establish missions far removed from European influence. At this point Windschuttle also tries to discredit a man named David Carley who, in *Dark Deeds in Sunny Lands*, had offered a frightening description of the maltreatment of Aborigines by the pearling industry. This is a strange accusation for Windschuttle to make because the maltreatment of Aborigines all along the Western Australian pearling coast has been so widely recorded and reported that to criticise one account does not, in any way, invalidate the overwhelming evidence.

Windschuttle's fourth example is Ernest Gribble, the son of John Gribble. In the larger context of the article, and the broader context of the three articles, this is nothing more than an attack on Henry Reynolds and *This Whispering in Our Heart*, not the concept of 'the myths of frontier massacres'. All that Windschuttle does is try to discredit Ernest Gribble and expose him as a person who had sexual relationships (he does not even contemplate whether these relationships were loving or not) with Aborigines. Ernest Gribble had nothing to do with any massacres.

Windschuttle ends his series of essays by arguing that 'the mass killing of Aborigines was neither as widespread nor as common a feature of the expanding pastoral frontier in the nineteenth and early twentieth century as historians have claimed' and then adding that the exaggerations were the product of a group of people who were 'generating employment for themselves and furthering their careers' and therefore, he concludes, we should look at the policy of keeping Aborigines and Europeans separate with great scepticism.

So what do we learn from this debate? Sadly, not very much. Nothing that Windschuttle can muster can repudiate the overwhelming evidence of atrocities and massacres which are recorded in this book. It is a comment on the deepening conservatism of Australia in the first years of the twenty-first century that there are Australians who are prepared to argue, and to discredit, the 'massacres' by making points which seem designed to focus discussion on side issues rather than the tragic and unnecessary loss of Aboriginal life which accompanied the European settlement of this continent.

CHAPTER 21

A FEW QUESTIONS ANSWERED ...

Writing a book which attempts to chronicle a series of massacres is a strange, haunting experience. You search, often quite unconsciously, for explanations. You find truths in unlikely places. About halfway through the writing of this book I scribbled on a sheet of paper, 'It is dangerous to romanticise the past. The mind filters out the mundane. Those moments which are memorable coalesce into a perceived time which seems so much better.' I was trying to say, tentatively and without an overweening sense of cultural cringe, that I was fast coming to believe that pre-invasion Aboriginal life sounded like an earthly paradise. Then I read Graham Jenkins's *Conquest of the Ngarrindjeri* and noted that he was in no way tentative about such a conclusion. He writes:

> One thing that has impressed itself most forcefully on my mind during my study of Ngarrindjeri anthropology (as distinct from their history) is that Australians today have a great deal to learn from this small nation which once owned and occupied one of the finest corners of the continent. The most outstanding example of their genius lies in their ability to live so richly and harmoniously with each other and with their land.

He continues:

> They were a truly classless society and had reached the apogee as far as refined egalitarian socialism is concerned. Yet if they had to be placed in any European class scale, their mode of life could only be compared with that of the old aristocracy. Their dedication to cultural pursuits — the ballet, music, opera and art; their enjoyment of pomp and ceremony; their strong adherence to ancient codes of chivalry and etiquette; the pleasure they derived from sports and hunting; their great personal courage, pride and independence; their insistence on the right of an initiated man to bear arms and for

> honour to be honourably defended; their epicurean approach to food; their honest acceptance of human passions and lack of hypocrisy regarding them; these and other aspects of Ngarrindjeri life find distinct parallels in the outlook and way of life of the European aristocracy. The great difference lay in the fact that in Ngarrindjeri society everyone was an aristocrat. The Ngarrindjeri showed the world that it was possible for socialism and the aristocratic life-style to be married harmoniously, and for life to be a rich cultural and creative experience — without servants and without masters.

It is a conclusion not reached through some phoney, liberal, mixture of guilt and ethnophile passion. It is a considered and deeply held response which flows inevitably into anyone who reads about Aboriginal life and genuinely responds to it.

At another point in the writing my mind became fixated on the changes which 1788 had so unhappily wrought. It seemed so overwhelming and so sad. I wanted to find a way to convey that change so that every modern Australian could understand just what their forebears did to this country's original occupants. It seemed so easy to write about massacres, rapes, diseases, poisonings and casual killings. The words fell so easily from the pen. I feared they would be read with equal ease and nonchalance. The emotional scale of the invasion could never be captured by description or polemic. Another viewpoint, a more potent angle, was needed.

I wondered how modern-day whites would respond to an invasion of a similar scale. This wasn't like the Germans invading the Netherlands during World War II; that was conquest by a similar culture. This was more like the invasion in H G Wells's *The War of the Worlds*, more like an invasion from outer space. It was in response to this dilemma that I wrote the Introduction, hoping that a science fiction scenario would capture the sheer awfulness of those times when Aboriginal people first came in contact with whites.

In the course of writing the book, and in conversation with various colleagues and friends with whom I discussed the massacres, three questions kept recurring: (a) What was the legal status of Aboriginal people from first white settlement until Federation?; (b) How seriously did Aboriginal people attempt to repel the invasion? and (c) Is there any solution to the 'Aboriginal problem'?

The first question is made complex by the number of contradictions which it contains. The issue started in July 1768 when Captain Cook received his orders prior to his departure from Britain on the voyage which, in 1770, resulted in the discovery of the east coast of Australia. Cook's orders were unambiguous. He was 'with the consent of the Natives to take possession of convenient situations in the name of the King . . . or if you find the country uninhabited Take Possession for His Majesty'. Thus when Cook, on 23 August, made the following entry in his logbook:

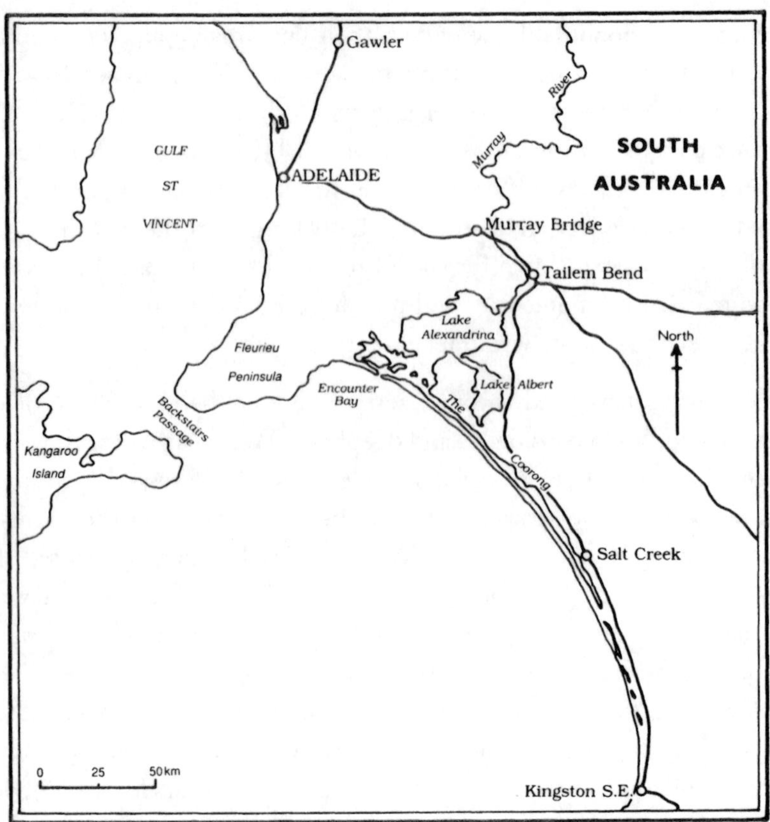

The Coorong, along the south-eastern coastline of South Australia.

> We could see no land so that we were in great hopes that we had at last found a Passage into the Indian Seas . . . in order to be better informed I landed on the island . . . I went upon the highest hill . . . but I could see from it no land between SW and WSW so that I did not doubt but what there was a passage . . . I now once more hoisted English Coulers and in the Name of His Majesty King George the Third took possession of the whole Eastern Coast . . . by the name of New South Wales.

There are only two conclusions to be drawn. Either Cook took possession of the 'whole Eastern Coast' under the delusion that the country was uninhabited or he was breaking his original order which was to only take occupied land with the explicit permission of 'the Natives'.

This sequence of events is what is often described as the notion of *terra nullius* — the idea that Australia was uninhabited before white settlement. It is now very obvious that not only was this nonsense but that the country had been settled some 40 000 to 50 000 years before and that, although sparsely populated by European standards, all of the country's land which was capable of bearing human habitation was, in fact, inhabited.

The next legal issue was raised with the arrival of the First Fleet. In his instructions, dated 23 April 1787, Governor Phillip was ordered quite explicitly:

> You are to endeavour by every possible means to open up an intercourse with the natives, and to conciliate their affections, enjoining all our subjects to live in amity and kindness with them. And if any of our subjects shall wantonly destroy them or give them any unnecessary interruption in the exercise of their several occupations, it is our will and pleasure that you do cause such offenders to be brought to punishment according to the degree of the offence . . .

Implicit in this instruction was the notion that Aboriginal people did definitely exist and that the moment Phillip arrived on Australian shores they became 'our subjects'. This was, at best, a wonderful rationalisation. At worst it was a neat piece of problem-solving. It instantly resolved the questions of treaties, land rights, and dispossession. How could any of these things occur to people who were already British subjects? This piece of neat hypocrisy served the early settlers well.

One of the best examples of this strangely contradictory attitude to Aboriginal legal rights occurred in 1837 when the then Colonial Secretary, Lord Glenelg, wrote to Governor Bourke in the following terms:

> . . . all the natives inhabiting these territories must be considered as subjects of the Queen and as within Her Majesty's allegiance. To regard them as aliens with whom a war can exist, and against whom Her Majesty's troops may exercise belligerent rights is to deny the protection to which they derive the highest possible claim from the sovereignty which has been assumed over the whole of their ancient possessions . . .

In his now classic analysis *The Destruction of Aboriginal Society*, C D Rowley sums up the problem succinctly when he writes:

> One assumption was that 'natives' in colonies would learn by precept and example to live in equality with the lower orders of the colonial society, with all the protections of the law. Powers vested in the Crown enabled the governors to act as the trustees of 'native' rights, actual and potential. From time to time, in the first years of settlement, instructions from the Secretary of State for Colonies reminded the governors of this duty, which extended in the line of

> tradition back to the time of Charles II. Instructions to Phillip had been in the tradition: he was to establish intercourse with the natives; 'our subjects' were to live in amity with them, and be punished for destroying them or for 'unnecessary interruption' of their occupations; the 'enforcement of due observance of religion' was enjoined upon the Governor. In all, the tradition could be interpreted as an injunction to Christianise the heathen. Governor Darling was to 'promote Religion and Education among the Native Inhabitants' while protecting their persons and the 'free enjoyment of their possessions' — somewhat difficult while at the same time establishing the settlers on their land. This royal command to protect Aboriginal British subjects follows an earlier instruction from Bathurst to Darling 'respecting the manner, in which the Native Inhabitants are to be treated when making hostile incursions for the purpose of Plunder . . . when such disturbances cannot be prevented or allayed by less vigorous measures . . . to oppose force by force, and . . . repel such Aggressions in the same manner, as if they proceeded from the subjects of an accredited State' . . . The only way in which Phillip could have avoided 'unnecessary interruption' of Aboriginal pursuits, or his successors have safeguarded the 'free enjoyment' of Aboriginal possessions, was to pack up the whole enterprise and return to England.

This, of course, was not going to happen. It is a comment on the British legal system that they wanted the 'rule of law' to operate. They wanted Aboriginal people to be equal in the sight of the law — a notion which resulted in the hanging of seven of the white murderers involved in the Myall Creek massacre — but they were loath to extend the full power of British law to people they regarded as primitive and ignorant. This lead to the bizarre situation of constant declarations of the rights of Aboriginal people as British subjects but the refusal of the law to recognise Aboriginal evidence (which was obviously vital in courts when cases against whites and involving Aboriginal people were being heard) because Aboriginal people were heathens and therefore could not swear on the Bible. It is contradictions like these which create moral minefields.

The question of the status of Aboriginal people was a continuing problem for the early settlers, particularly for those settlers who respected the British notion of the law. On 26 September 1831 a letter appeared in a Launceston newspaper which raised most of the questions which had bedevilled the more humanitarian settlers:

> Are these unhappy people, the subjects of our King, in a state of

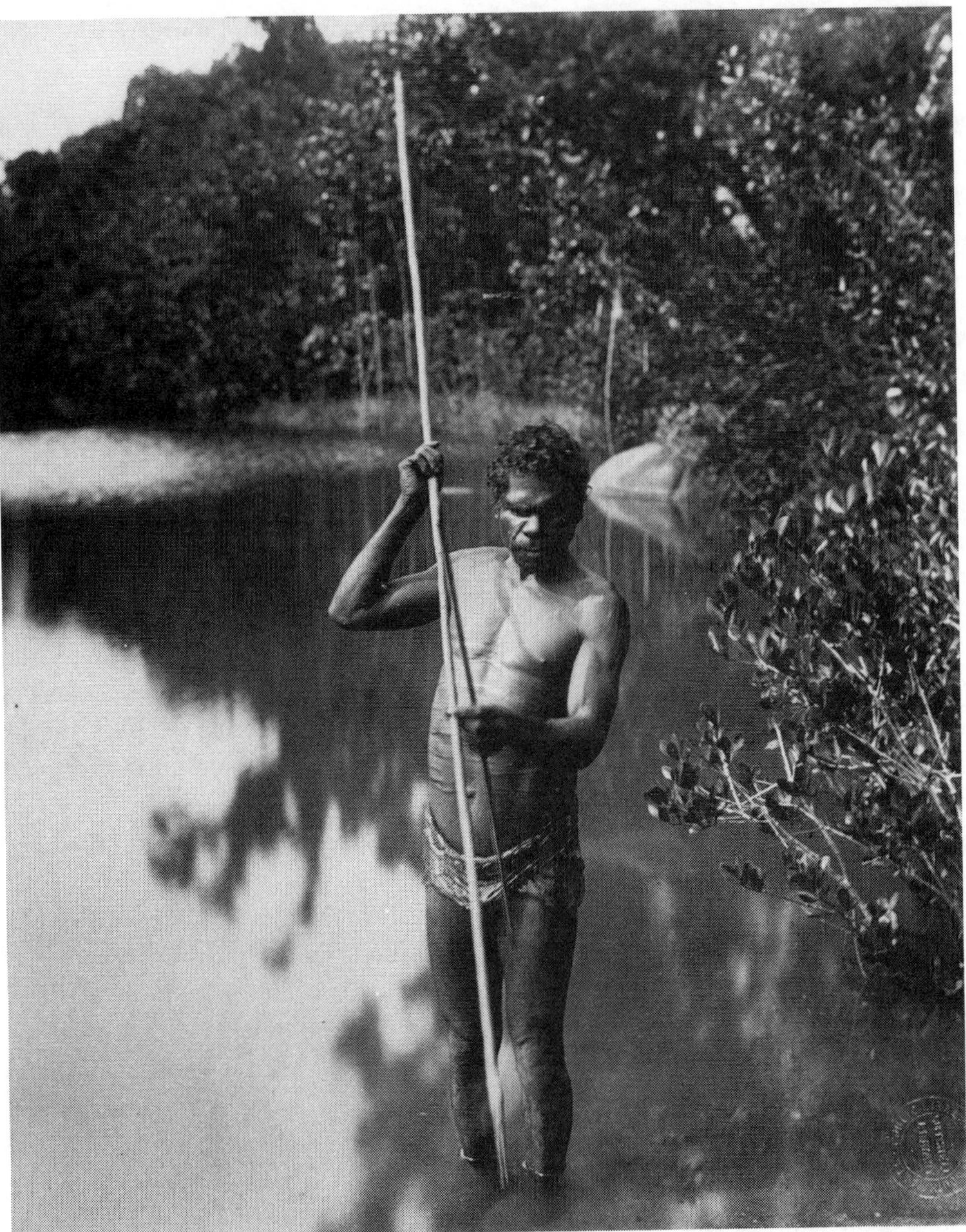

They were a truly classless society and had reached the apogee as far as refined egalitarian socialism is concerned.

rebellion or are they an injured people, whom we have invaded and with whom we are at war?

Are they within the reach of our laws; or are they to be judged by

> the law of nations? Are they to be viewed in the light of murderers, or as prisoners of war?
>
> Have they been guilty of any crime under the laws of nations which is punishable by death, or have they only been carrying on a war in their way?
>
> Are they British subjects at all, or a foreign enemy who has never yet been subdued and which resists our usurped authority and domination . . .
>
> We are at war with them: they look upon us as enemies — as invaders — as oppressors and persecutors — they resist our invasion. They have never been subdued, therefore they are not rebellious subjects, but an injured nation, defending in their own way, their rightful possessions, which have been torn from them by force.

There is probably no better example of the legal minefield which the British created for themselves than the case of the Coorong massacre. Sometime in early July 1840 a ship known as the *Maria*, travelling between Hobart and Adelaide, was wrecked on the Coorong, south of Adelaide. As far as can be determined, the passengers and crew successfully managed to reach the shore where they were met by members of the local Milmenruru or 'Big Murray' tribe. The tribe, recognising the plight of the shipwreck victims and acknowledging their desire to walk up the coast to the newly established settlement at Adelaide, showed the survivors the way. As the group travelled up the coast the Milmenruru helped to carry the children and fished and hunted so that the survivors would not go hungry.

After some days the party reached the northern border of Milmenruru land. Beyond it lay the territory of the Noongong whom the Milmenruru regarded as warlike and hostile. The Milmenruru, feeling that their duties to the whites had been completed and having no wish to trespass on Noongong land, informed the survivors that they were leaving and, according to tribal custom, sought payment for their services. They asked the whites for blankets and clothes. The whites refused to pay. Instead they promised payment upon their safe delivery to Adelaide. There was almost certainly a lack of understanding between the Milmenruru and the survivors. The Aboriginal law was unambiguous. Reciprocity was understood. It could not be broken. Payment was due. The survivors resisted, a fight broke out, and the Milmenruru killed the entire party.

A white search party arriving in the area on 30 July found a number of bodies which had been stripped of their clothing, 'dreadfully bruised about the face and the head', and buried in crude holes in the ground. In one hole they found the bodies of two teenage boys. In another hole were the bodies of two adult males, a ten-year-old girl and a young woman. On the ground nearby, unburied and picked clean by carrion eaters, were the skeletons of a woman and a female child.

On 14 August 1840, after he had received a report on the incident, Governor Gawler instructed Major O'Halloran, Commissioner of Police, 'to apprehend and bring to summary justice, the ring-leaders in the murder, or any of the murderers (not to exceed three)'. This was the first officially authorised punitive expedition. It was a very clear example of British law coming into direct conflict with Aboriginal law and it caused a very public legal argument which raged for over three months.

Gawler laid down a series of regulations by which O'Halloran and his forces were expected to operate. Many of the regulations were contradictory and ambiguous: (a) No killings were to occur and violence must be resisted but if O'Halloran had to use force, he would not be punished; (b) The inquiry into the murders was to be carried out 'on the principles of strictest judgement' but O'Halloran was to act on his own judgement. When he had reached his decision O'Halloran was expected to 'deliberately and formally cause sentence of death to be executed by shooting or hanging, upon the convicted murderers'. The 'strictest judgement' was to be achieved without a jury and (c) a maximum of three Aboriginal people were to be executed.

Gawler's instructions were bizarre. If put in a British context they were laughable. O'Halloran's response to his instructions was not surprising.

O'Halloran travelled to Lake Alexandrina where, on 23 August, his party captured a large group of Aboriginal people comprising about fifty women and children and thirteen men. Upon inspection of the living area, O'Halloran found evidence which implicated the Aboriginal people, either directly or indirectly, in the murder of the shipwreck survivors. Clothes stained with blood, a watch and some spoons were found. The men were taken prisoner. The women and children were set free.

The next day O'Halloran's party came across another group of Aboriginal people who were also wearing clothes stained with blood. The issue was now a question of who was really the guilty party. Both groups of Aboriginal people, eager to protect themselves, began to declare that the other group were the guilty party. While this debate was going on, one of O'Halloran's party noticed two Aboriginal people attempting to swim to freedom across the Coorong. A sailor's cap was noticed on the lake's edge so, contrary to Gawler's orders, O'Halloran opened fire. Both swimmers were hit but they managed to swim to the north-east shore of the Coorong and escape. The captive Aboriginal people immediately declared that the two swimmers were, indeed, the true murderers. A short time later the Aboriginal people, now clearly terrified by O'Halloran, changed their 'evidence' pointing one man out as the murderer of the entire crew of the *Maria* and another man as the murderer of a whaler named Roach who had disappeared two years earlier.

Given the contradictory nature of the evidence O'Halloran should have disregarded it. Instead he decided that the two men were guilty and sentenced them to death. The next day they were hanged for their 'crimes'.

O'Halloran returned to Adelaide where, on 12 September 1840, his account of his activities was reported in the *Register*. The *Register* was interested in the Coorong massacre and began a campaign which highlighted the fragility of the law with respect to the rights of Aboriginal people. On the day Major O'Halloran's report appeared the *Register* asked the critical question: What evidence did Major O'Halloran have which led him to execute the two natives? The report was adamant, in a very British legal sense, that O'Halloran must have had evidence which was conclusive and indisputable.

This was the beginning of a legal debate which twisted and turned until finally it was forced to recognise that British law was a totally inadequate tool with which to deal with circumstances like the Coorong massacre. The *Register* pointed out that as British subjects all Aboriginal people had an automatic right to trial by jury. It pointed out that execution by a legally unrecognised and unconstitutional tribunal — Major O'Halloran — was not good enough. The Acting Colonial Secretary, George Hall, argued that summary executions were a 'beneficial deterrent' to lawless Aboriginal people. It was pointed out that if O'Halloran had returned the two Aboriginal men to Adelaide for a formal trial, they would not have been able to give evidence. As heathens they were not permitted to offer sworn evidence because, so it was argued, they were morally and intellectually inferior to the British and consequently couldn't really understand the importance of the oath. If no Aboriginal person had been able to give evidence, there could have been no trial.

The *Southern Australian* came into the debate by arguing that although Aboriginal people were British citizens, by their actions in killing the survivors of the Maria they had forfeited their claim to protection and rejected their allegiance to the law. Was the *Southern Australian* seriously suggesting that everyone who was accused of murder automatically forfeited their rights to the benefits of British law?

By 19 September debate in the colony had reached such a pitch that Governor Gawler claimed that Major O'Halloran had not been operating under civil law. He had, instead, been operating under martial law. This was challenged as unconstitutional and illegal. In Britain a district could only be under martial law when the Habeas Corpus Act was officially waived. This had not been done in the Coorong.

The *Register*, warming to its task and revelling in the anomalies produced by the case, now declared, 'the natives have been condemned and executed, not merely by an unauthorised, illegal and unconstitutional tribunal, but upon evidence, which in a court of law either civil or military would not be sufficient to hang a dog'.

The Advocate General, Sir Richard Hanson, tried to defend the actions of Governor Gawler and Major O'Halloran by arguing that British law was selective and it didn't apply to 'a nation at enmity with Her Majesty's Subjects'. In other words 'good' Aboriginal people could enjoy the benefits of British law; 'bad' Aboriginal

A lithograph in George Angas's South Australia Illustrated, *1847 shows an Aboriginal woman similar to those who led the survivors of the Maria across the Coorong.*

people were outside the control of the law. The *Register* curtly replied to Hanson's argument by suggesting that if he was claiming that the Milmenruru were a separate nation, then maybe they could be allowed to exercise their own judicial control. This suggestion was, of course, ignored.

The truth of the Coorong massacre, the truth the British so hated to face, was that for all its claimed fairness and impartiality, British law was a very selective tool which could easily be used to support prevailing bigotries. The British could spout platitudes about Aboriginal people being British subjects and enjoying the impartiality of British law but at the bottom line they abused their own legal system and used it to further their mercantile ambitions. No treaty meant no acknowledgement of prior ownership. Citizenship meant easy dispossession. There have been few imperial powers in human history so devoid of morality and so greedy and arrogant as the nineteenth-century British at the height of their imperial might.

The answer to the question 'How seriously did Aboriginal people attempt to repel the invasion?' is simply 'To the limit of their limited abilities'. It has become popular in recent times to see Aboriginal resistance as some kind of coherent and concerted effort with individuals like Pemulwuy and Windradyne as Aboriginal guerrilla leaders — sort of antipodean versions of Che Guevara or Ho Chi Minh. This is an interpretation which does not tally with the facts. Aboriginal people resisted because whites were destroying their lifestyle. Their motive was simple: survival. If they didn't fight, they died.

A number of factors worked against any really successful Aboriginal resistance: (a) The structure of Aboriginal society made the formation of significant fighting forces almost impossible. Most Aboriginal groupings were small and semi-autonomous. They rarely exceeded sixty and more commonly numbered about twenty-five to thirty-five; (b) Aboriginal people were for the most part peaceful. Those dimensions of human behaviour which provoke aggressive responses (arguments over territory, ideology and rule by minorities) were simply not issues in Aboriginal society.

Consequently when confronted with the white invasion Aboriginal people were militarily inept. Perhaps the greatest military achievement of Aboriginal people in the nineteenth century was their realisation that it took a long time to reload a musket and that the interval was an ideal time to attack; and (c) The competition between the British and Aboriginal people was appallingly unequal. For all their skills with spears and boomerangs, Aboriginal people were no competition for whites with guns. For a long time they did not understand how guns worked. They did, however, understand that guns killed and consequently a single settler with a single gunshot could scatter a group of well-armed warriors.

The result was the saddest of all 'wars'. A war where the weakest, who were most commonly the innocent, were the victims. Aboriginal people fought for their land and their survival by rushing cattle, killing cattle and sheep, and attacking shepherds, boundary riders and lonely, isolated travellers. The frontier property owners and squatters replied by killing those Aboriginal people they could find who, most commonly, were the very old, the very young and the women. A peaceful society unused to war is no match when confronted with an aggressive, competitive military society.

'Is there any solution to "the Aboriginal problem"?' is a question that for all its earnestness smacks of a kind of paternalism. It's almost as though Aboriginal people are not a richly diverse collection of people but rather a single 'problem'. If the question is more carefully phrased, 'Is there a possibility that Aboriginal people can return to notions of their own worth and dignity after two hundred years of dispossession and degradation?' then the issue is as vexing and complex as that of Northern Ireland or Lebanon. History teaches us, over and over again, the ineluctable wisdom of Omar Khayyam's quatrain:

> The Moving Finger writes; and, having writ,
> Moves on: nor all thy Piety nor Wit
> Shall lure it back to cancel half a Line,
> Nor all thy Tears wash out a Word of it.

History cannot be rewritten. Time cannot be recaptured. All the willpower on earth cannot un-invent the nuclear bomb. All the goodwill and shame cannot return Australia to the idyllic paradise of 1787. The naivety which is implicit in sentiments like those expressed by the rock group Midnight Oil when they sing 'Let's give it back' is a nonsense. It is not a solution which has any viability or any contact with reality.

All that is left is for Aboriginal people to pick up the shards of their broken culture and slowly re-assert the power and potency of their remarkable heritage.

If Australians, black and white alike, are to come to terms with the past and live together in harmony in the future there are three points which we need to embrace both intellectually and emotionally. Firstly, without condition or qualification, Aboriginal culture is one of the world's most ancient and impressive cultures. Aboriginal cave art predates the famous cave paintings of bulls, horses and deer at Lascaux in the French Dordogne by nearly twenty thousand years. Evidence suggests that Aboriginal people developed religious beliefs and burial practices more than ten thousand years before similar ideas began to emerge along the Nile and in the Tigris-Euphrates delta. The boomerang is a masterpiece of aerodynamics not matched by European culture until recent times.

Secondly Aboriginal history is an integral part of Australian history. Until white Australia accepts this notion Aboriginal history and culture will be seen as little more than a footnote to a European history of Australia which is essentially a study in racial bigotry, explorations notable only for their ineptness, and a white mentality which sees Australia as a huge Butlin's holiday camp — everyone clinging to the coast uninterested in innovation or 'culture' and patting each other on their suntanned backs because they have created a mythical egalitarian and proletarian utopia.

Finally the problems of alcoholism, unemployment and high mortality rates are not, as white society has argued for nearly two hundred years, endemic to Aboriginal people as a race. They are problems which are a result of a universal human response to dispossession and despair. The vast majority of human beings, be they black or white or rich or poor, are driven by a simple 'reason to exist'. This is rarely stated explicitly. It is implicit in every culture. It is what makes a culture work and it is frequently the lowest common denominator answer to the vexing question of life's meaning. For example, in white Australian society, most people accept a 'reason to exist' which maps out our lives as follows: (a) stay at home and play until the age of five; (b) attend school from age five to sixteen, or perhaps eighteen; (c) leave school to either enter the workforce or continue studying at a tertiary level; (d) spend the bulk of our adult life working five days a week or raising children and (e) retire from the workforce at the age of sixty and live on a pension or accumulated earnings until we die. This may not sound like a very good 'reason to exist' but it is what most people do and few people challenge the value and merit of it. It is the rudder which gives direction to our otherwise pointless lives. If one part of that 'reason to exist' is taken away from us, we become rudderless and despairing. The man who is sacked or made redundant is more likely to turn to alcohol than he is to clap his hands with glee and head for the beach. His 'reason to exist' has been removed and replaced by despair.

In the case of Aboriginal Australians, their 'reason to exist', both as individuals and as an entire race, has been systematically leached away by two hundred years of dispossession. The intimate love of the land, the subtle ecological balance which recognised that there was a time to pick bush fruits and kill animals and a time to refrain from picking and killing, the careful response to the seasons, the powerful acknowledgement of the land's spirituality, the careful cycle of ritual and initiation which was at the centre of every life, the clear definitions of tribal land, these were all part of an elaborate and beautiful part of every Aboriginal Australian's 'reason to exist'.

We, the invaders, took all that away. We destroyed it. We took the land as if it was our own. We destroyed the native fruit-bearing trees to create pastures for cattle and sheep. We killed native wildlife so that it would not compete for the pastures. We replaced ecology with aggressive nineteenth-century exploitative capitalism. We built roads over sacred sites. We denied the land its spirituality. We killed off Aboriginal people with guns and poison and disease. We refused, through ignorance and arrogance, to see any tribal differentiation in those Aboriginal people who survived our insidious, long-term holocaust. Those Aboriginal people who survived were herded into reserves or 'allowed' to live in humpies on the fringes of towns. We took away their reason to exist and when, in their despair, they took to the bottle or simply threw up their hands in hopelessness and gave up life, we had the arrogance to accuse them of drunkenness and laziness.

The blood of tens of thousands of Aboriginal people killed since 1788, and the sense of despair and hopelessness which informs so much modern-day Aboriginal society, is a moral responsibility all white Australians share. Our wealth and lifestyle is a direct consequence of Aboriginal dispossession. We should bow our heads in shame.

FURTHER READING

Atkinson, Alan and Aveling, Marian, *Australians — 1838*, Fairfax, Syme & Weldon Associates, Sydney, 1987

Berndt, Ronald M and Catherine H, *Aborigines of the West — Their Past and Their Present*, University of Western Australia Press, Perth, 1980

Biskup, Peter, *Not Slaves, Not Citizens: The Aboriginal Problem in Western Australia 1898–1954*, University of Queensland Press, St Lucia, 1973

Blomfield, Geoffrey, *Baal Belbora: the end of the dancing*, The Alternative Publishing Co-operative Ltd, Sydney, 1981

Bridges, Barry, 'Pemulwoy: A "Noble Savage"', newsletter of the Royal Australian Historical Society, pp. 3–5, January 1970

Broome, R, *Aboriginal Australians: Black Response to White Dominance 1788–1980*, George Allen & Unwin, Sydney, 1982

Byrne, Denis, *The Mountains Call Me Back: A History of the Aborigines and the Forests of the Far South Coast of NSW*, NSW Ministry of Aboriginal Affairs, 1984

Cannon, Michael, *Life in the Country: Australia in the Victorian Age*, Currey O'Neil Ross Pty Ltd, Melbourne, 1983

Chambers, Blagden, *Black and White: the story of a massacre and its aftermath*, Methuen Australia, Melbourne, 1988

Cole, Keith, *The Aborigines of Western Australia*, Keith Cole Publications, Bendigo, 1985

Cribbin, John, *The Killing Times*, Fontana/Collins, Sydney, 1984

Davies, David, *The Last of the Tasmanians*, Shakespeare Head Press, Sydney, 1973

Ellis, Vivienne Rae, *Trucanini: queen or traitor?*, Australian Institute of Aboriginal Studies, Canberra, 1981

Evans, Raymond, Saunders, K and Cronin K, *Exclusion, exploitation and extermination: Race relations in Colonial Queensland*, Australia & New Zealand Book Company, Sydney, 1975

Flood, Josephine, *Archaeology of the Dreamtime*, William Collins, Sydney, 1983

Gardner, Peter, 'The Warrigal Creek Massacre', *Journal of the Royal Australian Historical Society*, pp. 47–51, June 1980

Gardner, P D, *Our Founding Murdering Father*, Ngarak Press, Ensay, 1990

Gill, Andrew, 'Aborigines, Settlers and Police in the Kimberleys 1887–1905', *Studies in Western Australian History*, Perth, pp. 1–28, June 1977

Gordon, Harry, *An Eyewitness History of Australia*, Currey O'Neil, Melbourne, 1976

Hamann, Judy, 'The Coorong Massacre: A Study in Early Race Relations in South Australia', *Flinders Journal of History and Politics*, Vol.III, pp. 1–9, 1973

Hardy, Bobbie, *Lament for the Barkindji: the vanished tribes of the Darling River region*, Rigby Ltd, Adelaide, 1976

Hasluck, Paul, *Black Australians: A Survey of Native Policy in Western Australia, 1829–1897*, Melbourne University Press, Melbourne, 1942

Hercus, Luise, 'Tales of Nadu-Dagali (Rib-Bone Billy)', *Aboriginal History*, Vol. 1, No. 1, pp. 53–62, 1977

Hercus, Luise and Sutton, Peter (ed.), *This is what Happened: Historical Narratives by Aborigines*, Australian Institute of Aboriginal Studies, Canberra, 1986

Hill, Marji and Barlow, Alex, *Black Australia: An Annotated Bibliography and teacher's guide to resources on Aborigines and Torres Strait Islanders*, Australian Institute of Aboriginal Studies, Canberra, 1978

Howard, Michael C, *Aboriginal Politics in Southwestern Australia*, University of Western Australia Press, Perth, 1984

Jenkin, Graham, *Conquest of the Ngarrindjeri*, Rigby Ltd, Adelaide, 1979

Jones, Stephen, *A Submerged History: Baroon, Aborigines and White Invasion*, Cairncross Press, Maleny, 1990

Kelly, Roma and Evans, Nicholas, 'The McKenzie Massacre on Bentinck Island', *Aboriginal History*, Vol. 9, No. 1, pp. 44–52, 1985

Loos, Noel, *Invasion and Resistance: Aboriginal-European relations on the North Queensland frontier, 1861–1897*, Australian National University Press, Canberra, 1982

McBride, Isabel (ed.) *Records of times past: Ethnohistorical essays on the culture and ecology of the New England tribes*, Australian Institute of Aboriginal Studies, Canberra, 1978

McKellar, Hazel, *Matya-Mundu: A History of the Aboriginal People of South West Queensland*, Cunnamulla Australian Native Welfare Association, Cunnamulla, undated

Miller, James, *Koori: A Will to Win*, Sydney, Angus & Robertson, 1985

Organ, Michael (ed.), *A Documentary History of the Illawarra & South Coast Aborigines 1770–1850*, Aboriginal Education Unit, Wollongong University, 1990

Pearson, Michael, 'Bathurst Plains and Beyond: European Colonisation and Aboriginal Resistance', *Aboriginal History*, Vol. 8, No. 1, pp. 63–79, 1984

Pepper, Phillip and de Araugo, Tess, *The Kurnai of Gippsland*, Hyland House, Melbourne, 1985

Read, Peter, *The Stolen Generations: The Removal of Aboriginal Children in NSW 1883 to 1969*, NSW Ministry of Aboriginal Affairs, undated

Read, Peter (ed.), *Down there with me on the Cowra Mission: An oral history of Erambie Aboriginal Reserve, Cowra, New South Wales*, Pergamon Press, Sydney, 1984

Reid, Gordon, *A Nest of Hornets: The Massacre of the Fraser Family at Hornet Bank*

Station, Central Queensland, 1857, and Related Events, Oxford University Press, Melbourne, 1982

Reynolds, Henry, *The Other Side of the Frontier*, Penguin, Melbourne, 1982

Reynolds, Henry, *Frontier: Aborigines, Settlers and Land*, George Allen & Unwin, Sydney, 1987

Robinson, Fergus and York, Barry, *The Black Resistance: an introduction to the history of the Aborigines' struggle against British colonialism*, Widescope International, Camberwell, 1977

Rowley, C D, *The Destruction of Aboriginal Society*, Penguin, Melbourne, 1972

Salisbury, T and Gresser, P J, *Windradyne of the Wiradjuri: Martial Law at Bathurst in 1824*, Wentworth Books Pty Ltd, Sydney, 1971

Shaw, Bruce, *My Country of the Pelican Dreaming: The life of an Australian Aborigine of the Gadjerong, Grant Ngabidj, 1904–1977*, Australian Institute of Aboriginal Studies, Canberra. 1981

Shaw, Bruce, Banggaiyerri: *The Story of Jack Sullivan*, Australian Institute of Aboriginal Studies, Canberra, 1983

Shaw, Bruce and McDonald, Sandy, 'They did it Themselves: Reminiscences of Seventy Years', *Aboriginal History*, Vol. 2, No. 2, pp. 123–39, 1978

Skinner, L E, *Police of the Pastoral Frontier: Native Police 1849–59*, University of Queensland Press, St Lucia, 1975

Stone, Sharman N (ed.), *Aborigines in white Australia: A documentary history of the attitudes affecting official policy and the Australian Aborigine, 1697–1973*, Heinemann, Melbourne, 1974

Stow, Randolph, *To the Islands*, (revised 1982), Picador, Sydney, 1983

Threlkeld, L E, *Australian Reminiscences and Papers* (edited by N Gunson), Australian Institute of Aboriginal Studies, Canberra, 1974

Turnbull, Clive, *Black War: The Extermination of the Tasmanian Aborigines*, Sun Books, Melbourne, 1974

Wannan, Bill, *Early Colonial Scandals: the turbulent times of Samuel Marsden*, Lansdowne, Melbourne, 1972

Willey, Keith, *When the Sky Fell Down: The Destruction of the Tribes of the Sydney Region 1788–1850*, William Collins Pty Ltd, Sydney, 1979

Willmot, Eric, *Pemulwuy: The Rainbow Warrior*, Weldons Pty Ltd, Sydney, 1987

Bringing them home — Report on the National Inquiry into the Separation of Aboriginal and Torres Strait Islander Children from Their Families, Human Rights and Equal Opportunity Commision, Sydney, 1997

First Report from the Select Committee of the Legislative Assembly upon Aborigines. Part 1 — Report and Minutes of Proceedings, NSW Government Printer. 1980

Second Report from the Select Committee of the Legislative Assembly upon Aborigines, NSW Government Printer, 1981

Aboriginal Land Rights and Sacred and Significant Sites — First Report from the Select Committee of the Legislative Assembly upon Aborigines, NSW Government Printer, 1980

The Seaman Aboriginal Land Inquiry, 1983–84, WAPP, 1984

Report of Select Committee of the Legislative Council on The Aborigines Bill, 1899, South Australian Parliamentary Proceedings No. 77, 1899

Report of Select Committee on the Native Police Force and the Condition of the Aborigines Generally, Report, Q V & P, 1861

Van Diemen's Land — Copies of all Correspondence between Lieutenant-Governor Arthur and His Majesty's Secretary of State for the Colonies, on the subject of the Military operations lately carried on against the Aboriginal inhabitants of Van Diemen's Land, Tasmanian Historical Research Association. Hobart, 1971

Of all these books the two that prove invaluable to the researcher are Marji Hill's and Alex Barlow's excellent bibliography and Henry Reynolds's *Frontier* which includes a detailed and comprehensive bibliography of recent journal articles and a wide range of contemporary sources. Without them my task would have been much more difficult.

INDEX

About the Author

Bruce Elder was born in the Sydney suburb of Mosman in 1944 and grew up on the edge of the Snowy Mountains in Tumut New South Wales. At school, on the sportsfield, and in the everyday social interaction of an Australian country town in the 1950s, he witnessed the racism and daily maltreatment of the local Wiradjuri people who lived in the village of Brungle between Tumut and Gundagai. He believes that his response to the sight of an unconscious Wiradjuri man being dragged by his feet for an entire block of the town's main street by a local policeman was the original inspiration for this book.

Blood on the Wattle was written in 1988. Much of the difficult research had already been done and published in Marji Hill and Alex Barlow's excellent *Black Australia: An annotated bibliography* (1978). This bibliography helped the author to access most of the sources of the stories about the major massacres. In 1999 and 2003 Elder added additional chapters as new research came to light and it became clear that the original publication had some major omissions.

Blood on the Wattle has now been continuously in print for fifteen years. In 1999, a 'Spectrum Poll of the Century' numbering 4657 readers of the *Sydney Morning Herald* and *The Age* and ninety prominent Australians, placed it at number ten in the Australian division of the category 'Most Influential Works of Non-Fiction of the Twentieth Century'.

Bruce Elder currently is a senior journalist with the *Sydney Morning Herald* specialising in popular culture, mass media and travel. As a mass media critic he won the Geraldine Pascall Prize for Critical Writing in 1996. He appears regularly on ABC's Tony Delroy NightLife program, which is broadcast around Australia, and on Sally Loane's ABC morning program, which is broadcast around New South Wales. He has also written over fifty books, is the writer and editor of the two million word-long Internet travel guide Walkabout (www.walkabout.com.au) and is also the editor of *Trivial Pursuit* in Australia. He is on the board of Lifeline South Coast and, for the past six years, has been an Australia Day Ambassador.